Spirits
of the
Deep

Seth and Ruth Leacock

Spirits
of the
Deep

A Study of an Afro-Brazilian Cult

ANCHOR BOOKS
Anchor Press/Doubleday
Garden City, New York
1975

SPIRITS OF THE DEEP was originally published for The American Museum of Natural History by the Natural History Press, a division of Doubleday & Company, Inc. in 1972.

Anchor Books Edition: 1975
ISBN: 0-385-06880-8
Copyright © 1972 by Seth Leacock and Ruth Leacock
All rights reserved
Printed in the United States of America
Photographs by the authors

Contents

Preface

This book is intended to be a comprehensive description of the Batuque, a contemporary non-Christian religious sect found in Belém, Brazil. The Batuque is one of a large number of closely related religious groups, all stressing spirit possession, that are flourishing today in every urban center in Brazil and in many parts of the interior. Usually referred to as "Afro-Brazilian," and sometimes studied as survivals of a religion brought from Africa, these religious sects have in fact become well adapted to contemporary Brazilian culture. This book is consequently not about some exotic religion of the past but is concerned with a viable and prominent aspect of modern Brazilian religious life.

For the authors, respectively an anthropologist and a historian, the understanding of any religion requires some consideration of its historical, sociological, and psychological dimensions. This very broad approach has led us first to explore the origins of Batuque rituals and beliefs, to the extent that this is possible, and to speculate about some of the processes involved in their development. But we have also tried to identify the members of this religion in terms of class affiliation, economic status, and other social characteristics. And finally, where our book differs most from earlier studies is in the emphasis we have placed on the individual, his motivation in joining the sect, and especially the benefits that he derives from participation.

The book is based on research undertaken in Belém during seven months in 1962–63 and two months in 1965. Traditional anthropological techniques of collecting data were employed. We attended thirty-seven major public ceremonies, ten minor events, and ten curing sessions. We attended ceremonies in thirteen different cult centers, but we knew the personnel of only four centers fairly well. Observations of ceremonies contributed to our understanding of ritual and trance, facilitated contacts with rank-and-file members, and provided material for follow-up interviews. We gave a short questionnaire to eighty-seven members and obtained some kinds of information for about 150 members altogether. By far the greatest amount of data was collected during intensive, open-ended interviews with known informants. All interviews were carried out in the native language, Portuguese.

The research situation was in most respects ideal. The people of Belém are noted nationally for their hospitality and friendliness. Most of the leaders of the Batuque were literate, they were aware that a number of books had been written about the Afro-Brazilian sects in other cities, and they were extremely interested in co-operating in the production of a book about their own sect. Both they and their followers were eager to have photographs of themselves in trance, and the several hundred photographs we took served both as documentation of ceremonial activity and as entry into the good graces of the participants. We also gave our informants periodic presents of money, but never in a context suggesting that we were paying for information. During our first stay in Belém we rented a house where we were sometimes visited by our informants, but during the second trip we lived in a hotel and could only interview in our informants' homes.

We saw our first Batuque ceremony in 1956 as guests of George Colman, then American Consul in Belém. We were passing through the city on the way to study Indians in the interior, and Mr. Colman, who is still remembered with fondness and respect because of his interest in the local culture, made a point of inviting visiting Americans to attend Batuque ceremonies. Recognizing our interest, Colman was our guide on two later occasions. Our first debt, then, to those who helped make this book possible, is to George Colman.

Our second debt is to the National Science Foundation, which furnished the funds for both trips to study the Batuque (Grants G24065 and GS801). We are also indebted to the University of Chicago for making it possible for the senior author to remain in Brazil an extra three months in 1963. The Research Foundation of the University of Connecticut awarded the senior author a grant to aid in paying publication costs and also provided for the typing of the manuscript. We would like to thank Mrs. Selma Wollman for doing the typing, Sol Wollman of the University of Connecticut Photo Lab for printing our photographs, and Raymond Blanchette for drawing the map.

The initial phases of our study were greatly facilitated by several members of the staff of the Museu Paraense Emílio Goeldi in Belém. Eduardo Galvão, head of the Division of Anthropology and at the time acting director of the museum, placed a number of the facilities of the museum at our disposal, introduced us to a key informant, and throughout our research was a constant source of support. Other members of the staff shared their knowledge of Afro-Brazilian religions with us, especially Edson Diniz and Protásio Frikel. We had many helpful discussions with Professor Arthur Napoleão Figueiredo of the University of Pará, who has since carried out his own study of the Batuque.

We owe the greatest debt of all to the Batuque members who welcomed us so hospitably, treated us always with consideration, and spent so many hours answering our questions. Among the many who contributed to our understanding of their religion, we would like especially to thank Maria de Aguiar, Raimunda Moreira Cardoso, Manoel Colaço, Conrada Ribeiro Coutinho, José Ferreira, Apolônia Leonicio, Leontina Santos, Maria José Paixão Santos, and Miguel Silva. We are aware that they will all be keenly disappointed that we have not used their real names in the text, but for obvious reasons we have used pseudonyms throughout, except in a few cases of historical interest.

The city of Belém has changed considerably in the decade since 1962, as we discovered during a recent visit. There are many new buildings, many more cars in the streets, more television sets in more homes, more stores stocked with a greater variety of goods, and there are a great many more people. But from all indications, the Batuque continues much as we have described it. A few *terreiros* have closed, but many new ones have opened. Without exception, our informants agreed that the Batuque is flourishing.

SETH LEACOCK
RUTH LEACOCK

Manaus, Amazonas, Brazil
April, 1971

Spirits of the Deep

Chapter I

A Batuque

When the peoples of Africa were torn from their homes and brought to the New World to serve as slaves, most of their cultural heritage was left behind them. But in some parts of the New World, especially in Latin America, the Africans managed to salvage their religious beliefs from the wreckage of their old way of life and, clinging tenaciously to their gods, found them a source of solace in a difficult, alien environment. Although the slaves came from many parts of Africa and brought with them a variety of religious beliefs, it was those religions that stressed possession by supernatural beings that found most favor in the New World. It came to be an article of faith that when the drums spoke and the proper songs were sung, the gods in Africa could hear their children across the sea and came swiftly to possess them and participate in their ceremonies. To prevent officious interference by their masters, the slaves quickly provided their gods with "white masks" by identifying them with Catholic saints.[1] Since the white man rationalized his treatment of human beings as chattel on the grounds that the slaves were being made fit to enter the Christian heaven, he had to be at least nominally concerned with the religion practiced by the slaves. But as long as the saints were venerated, the masters did not inquire too carefully into the details of the rituals by which this was done.

Today, more than a hundred years since the last slave was brought directly from Africa, in thousands of cult centers throughout the West Indies and Brazil, drums still sound and the faithful dance and sing and wait for the deities to possess them. In a few instances the gods invoked are still African gods, and the songs are still, at least ostensibly, in African languages. But in most parts of the New World the original African religions have been greatly modified. The basic idea, that supernatural beings come to earth and possess people, remains the central belief, but conceptions of who these supernaturals are, what their nature is, and what they can be expected to do once they have taken possession of a human body have changed drastically. In part, these changes can be attributed to the direct borrowing of ideas from the Christian and indigenous Indian religions with which the slaves came in contact. But the development of these Afro-American religions has gone far beyond the mere borrowing stage, and in each local area a coherent, integrated system of belief has developed that is in some ways distinctive.

In the city of Belém, Brazil, port of entry to the vast Amazon river basin, such an African-derived religion is flourishing. Almost every week, somewhere in the city, devotees gather to invite their spirits to possess them. These ceremonies, locally called *batuques,* are open to the public and are usually well attended. The number of ceremonies held, the number of active participants, and the number of spectators who stay far into the night to watch the proceedings all indicate that the cult in Belém represents a thriving religion.

Spectators at a *batuque* need not, however, actually be believers in the religion. Their role at a ceremony is entirely passive. No attitude or act of worship is demanded of them and most members of the audience attend simply to be entertained. Above all, a *batuque* is a spectacle. There is music, dancing, color, excitement, and mystery. The mediums who court possession by supernatural beings appear to be engaged in dramatic and perhaps dangerous activities, dancing on the edge of the unknown, entering mental states that seem only slightly removed from madness. Even to the skeptic the wild, uncontrolled behavior of some mediums while in trance provides compelling evidence that there is, indeed, some direct participation by the supernatural in the proceedings.

Drums and *cheque-cheques* (the elongated metal cylinders) provide the rhythm for dancing during ceremonies.

It is only a short step, once the presence of spirits is accepted, to seeking out one of the mediums in trance and asking the supernatural being to solve some pressing personal problem. Those who come to the *batuque* to witness a spectacle often return as clients and some eventually become participants. It is not surprising that enterprising leaders try to make the ceremony as dramatic as possible.

Since the ceremonies are public, any visitor to Belém can attend a *batuque* and, in fact, will usually receive a warm welcome. Americans in particular have a reputation for being fascinated by the ceremonies. A stranger to the city who wishes to attend a ceremony may have some difficulty, however, in locating a *terreiro*, as the cult centers are called, since most *terreiros* are located on back streets in the poorer, outlying neighborhoods, where it is difficult to find one's way at night. The back streets of Belém have neither street lights nor signposts and are not only unpaved, but sometimes also peter out completely in a tangle of overgrown weeds and tall grass that is impassable to all but foot traffic. In some cases the "street" is actually a sluggish creek or a marsh and even foot traffic is difficult. The houses lining these watery thoroughfares are perched on stilts and can be reached only by way of a narrow elevated board walk, not always in perfect repair, that runs the length of the street.

If one has mastered the difficulties of locating a *terreiro,* it is wise to arrive a half hour or so before the scheduled beginning of the ceremony. By the time the ceremony begins, usually around 9:00 P.M., the pavilion where the *batuque* is held is likely to be solidly ringed with spectators and visibility limited.

The pavilion (which is the *terreiro* proper) is usually an open building without walls on three sides. The roof is palm thatch or tile, and the floor is beaten earth or cement, depending on the resources of the cult leader. There is usually a railing around the perimeter of the ceremonial area that separates the participants in the ceremony from most of the audience. In most *terreiros* there are benches and chairs placed inside the railing for special guests. The area inside the railing is sacred and spectators seated there may not smoke, cross either arms or legs, or engage in any kind of disrespectful behavior. What goes on among the audience on the other side of the railing is rarely of concern, as long as the ceremony is not disrupted.

Towards the back of the *terreiro* on the walled side of the building are the drums, usually three in number, arranged on a raised platform. Behind the drums is an enclosed room, or occasionally simply a curtained alcove, that serves as a chapel. The chapel may be decorated with a variety of ritual objects and sacred symbols and may include several small altars, but its main altar invariably dominates the room. Here, arranged on step tiers, stand images of Catholic saints. No longer simply the "white masks" used by the slaves to disguise their deities, these images now have a double meaning. In one sense they stand for the saints they represent; the slaves accepted Catholic beliefs at a very early date, and the saints have been venerated ever since. But in addition, the images of the saints represent the non-Christian supernatural beings that are thought to come to earth and possess people. On most altars there is one image larger than the others or situated in a prominent position— this image symbolizes at one and the same time the patron saint, so to speak, of the *terreiro* and the most important non-Christian spirit that the leader of the *terreiro* "receives."

In addition to the images of saints, the altar also contains a few figurines of American Indians, usually crudely modeled and garishly painted. It does not take much imagination to guess that these figurines represent spirits of the New World, another addition to the original African pantheon.

A glance under the altar, once the ornate altar cloth has been pushed aside, reveals a row of bowls containing stones of varying sizes in liquids such as rum, wine, beer, or the oil of the *dendê* palm. Other bowls contain only beverages, oil, or food mixtures without the stones. The stones serve as the "seats" of the principal spirits received in the *terreiro,* and the beverages and foods represent "obligations," or offerings, to the same deities.

If the upper part of the altar—the tiers of images with lighted candles placed in front—has a very Catholic appearance, the lower part—the stones and offerings—suggests an African tribal religion. As will become clear later, neither of these impressions is completely correct. Although the altar is no longer deliberately designed to mask the real beliefs of the participants in this religion, it is still true that scrutiny of the symbols of the deities gives a quite erroneous notion of the nature of the modern pantheon.

As a survey of the altar indicates, many fundamental changes have taken place in the religion that the slaves once practiced. A visitor to a modern *batuque* should be prepared to witness a ceremony which has very little to do with the slaves or with Africa. The cult, of which the *batuque* is the central ceremony, has become a Brazilian religion, practiced by Brazilians, and dedicated to a group of supernatural beings most of whom have Brazilian names and speak only Portuguese.

If a visitor were to attend a *batuque* at the *terreiro* of An- tônio,[2] a well-known cult leader in the Pedreira section of the city, there would be little difficulty in finding the center, which is located on a street that is passable to motor vehicle traffic. Cult members attribute the fact that this unpaved street is kept in fair condition to their leader's "fame" and his influence with the political powers that be in the city.

Ceremonies at Antônio's rarely begin on time. At 9:00 P.M., the scheduled hour, only the members of the audience are ready, crowded around the pavilion. But shortly thereafter the preliminary activities to the main ceremony get under way. A young woman enters the pavilion swinging a small charcoal brazier by its long wire handle. Incense is scattered over the smoldering charcoal, yielding a thick fragrant smoke. It is believed that this smoke has cleansing or purifying properties and, as the brazier is carried around the *terreiro,* some members of the audience stand up and lean over to get a puff of the smoke on their bodies, crisscrossing their extended arms over the brazier as they do so. After the chapel is also given a smoke purification, the brazier is carried back into the leader's house, which is located in front of the *terreiro.*

Three men who will serve as drummers seat themselves at the drummers' bench and test the sound of the drums, tuning them by tightening the clamps that hold down the leather heads. The drums, made of wood and often brightly painted, are beaten with the hands.

The mediums who will participate in the ceremony begin to appear in the *terreiro.* In contrast to the drummers and the spectators the mediums are splendidly costumed. Antônio has designated blue and white as the colors to be worn for this *batuque.* The female participants, who greatly outumber the men, wear white blouses with puffed short sleeves and full, light-blue skirts that reach to mid-calf. Most of the mediums have obviously purchased their skirt material from the same shop, from the same bolt of cloth; it is a heavy satinlike material that shimmers in the light. The few men who take part have the colors reversed—white trousers and short-sleeved shirts made of the same light-blue material as the women's skirts. All participants wear open-heeled sandals; in a few cases the sandals have been made to order of a blue leather to match the skirts. Some of the mediums carry folded *espadas,* long scarves made of expensive material, often embroidered. The colors of these *espadas* vary according to the spirit that the individual is expected to receive. The only other ornament worn by some of the mediums is one or two long strands of beads, with a crucifix, medallion, or *figa* (a good luck amulet) attached.

The over-all effect of the costumes is one of unexpected opulence, considering the location of the *terreiro* and the clothing of the members of the audience. After one gets to know some of the participants, one discovers at what price they are able to outfit themselves in such colorful fashion.

About 9:30 Antônio appears in the *terreiro*. Although he is the *pai de santo* (the title given male leaders), he is dressed just as any other male participant except that he wears four long strands of beads, two over each shoulder, crossed to the opposite hip. On the whole Antônio has the harassed air of a leader saddled with incompetent followers who insist on doing things incorrectly as he rounds up the mediums and leads them into the chapel. At Antônio's *terreiro* the first public act of a *batuque* is a short Catholic prayer. The purpose of this prayer is not to ask the blessings of the Christian supernaturals on the ceremony to follow, since what follows is concerned exclusively with non-Christian spirits, but is intended to petition the saints for blessings *in addition to* those received from the non-Christian spirits. This is a good example of the way in which Christian and non-Christian elements tend to be combined into a unified system but are never actually merged.

At the conclusion of the prayer, the *pai de santo* begins an introductory song. As soon as he completes the first stanza, the drums begin to sound, to continue with only brief pauses for six or eight hours. Continuing to sing, the *pai de santo* backs out of the chapel and moves in front of the drums, bending down and touching the floor in front of each drum in a kind of salute. His actions are imitated by each of the mediums in turn. There are thirteen women and two men, in addition to the *pai de santo,* participating in the opening phase of this *batuque*. When all of them have completed this part of the ritual, the important business of the evening can begin— the calling of the spirits. The drums pause. The *pai de santo* sings:

Averekete da Caluna é rei do mar,	*Averekete of Caluna is king of the sea,*
Averekete da Indá é rei do mar.	*Averekete of Indá is king of the sea.*

At the conclusion of the two-line stanza, the drums begin again and the mediums sing the same lines as a chorus. All singing takes this form, with one individual leading and the others singing as a chorus, often repeating the same one- or two-line stanza sung by the leader.

In addition to the drums, the singing is accompanied by two other instruments, both shaken by hand—a gourd rattle (*maracá*) and an elongated metal cylinder, partially filled with lead shot, called a *ganzá* or *cheque-cheque*. Especially at the beginning of the *batuque,* when the drummers and *ganzá* shaker are fresh, the combined effect of all these percussion instruments is almost overwhelming. This is particularly true if the visitor is occupying a seat of honor, which is always placed close to the drums. It is often impossible to distinguish the words as the singing continues:

Averekete, nossa guia, é rei do mar,	*Averekete, our guide, is king of the sea,*
Averekete da Indá é rei do mar.	*Averekete of Indá is king of the sea.*

Together with the earlier lines, this comprises a complete song, or "doctrine" (*doutrina*), to the spirit Averekete. Each doctrine is usually sung for about two minutes (occasionally much longer), and three doctrines are sung for each spirit. Whatever the wording, the song, in effect, invites the spirit to possess one of the participants. If no one is possessed, attention is turned to another deity. It is a fairly closely followed tradition that no doctrine is ever repeated during the same *batuque* (repetition weakens the doctrine, it is believed), and if the ceremony lasts six or eight hours, obviously a very large number of different songs are sung before the night is through.

After completing three doctrines to Averekete, Antônio leads three to another spirit named Rainha Barba. At most *terreiros* in the city these two spirits, Averekete and Rainha Barba, are the first to be called. After they have been invited to descend, a variety of other spirits will be called, in no particular order, depending on the whim or momentary inspiration of the cult leader or whoever is leading the singing.

While each doctrine is being sung to the accompaniment of the drums, the mediums dance in a dignified, somewhat sedate

A typical *batuque* dance formation. Participants move in a counterclock-wise circle.

fashion. They are either grouped in rough lines facing the drums and dancing forwards and then back or grouped in a circle and moving in a counterclockwise direction. The dance formation depends either upon the doctrine being sung or upon the explicit direction of the song leader.

Singing chorus after chorus, the mediums shuffle from one dance into the next. On the dance floor the heat is suffocating. The closely packed bodies of the spectators ringing the pavilion

A less common formation, in which two lines of participants dance facing one another. The boy seated between the drummers shakes gourd rattles. The wall is decorated with paintings of spirits.

shut off the evening breezes that normally bring relief from the heat of the afternoon. Before half an hour has elapsed perspiration is trickling down the faces and necks of the participants; the women's crisply starched blouses begin to wilt. The trapped tropical night air, heavy with humidity, seems to inhibit the normal outward ripple of the sound waves. The monotonous boom of the drums, the rustle of the gourd rattle, the metallic chatter of the *cheque-cheque,* all seem held in oppressive suspension directly over the *terreiro.* Spectators and mediums alike begin to acquire a glazed look. Two young children seated on the benches within the *terreiro* railing doze off. Nothing, it seems, is at all likely to happen, when the *pai de santo* suddenly goes into trance.

Antônio, who senses some alteration of consciousness, stops singing, spins around to face the drums, closes his eyes tightly, grimaces, and then pitches convulsively backwards. He is caught

A large white shawl called a *toalha* is placed around the shoulders of a medium possessed by a high-ranking spirit.

by two mediums who have noted the signs of imminent trance and moved directly behind the *pai de santo*. After a final jerk backwards, Antônio lunges forward and begins to dance in a very animated manner, bending low with much knee action, then straightening up and whirling gracefully.

Or the *toalha* may be fastened around the waist of the medium in trance.

After a minute or so of animated dancing Antônio stops the drums, by waving vaguely towards the drummers, and sings:

Cidade bonita de Taculumi,	*Beautiful city of Taculumi,*
Estrada de prata por onde andei,	*Street of silver that I strolled along,*
Chegou Dona Rosalina,	*Dona Rosalina has arrived,*
Cobra Grande da Lagoa.	*Giant Snake of the Lake.*

This song identifies the spirit who is now thought to be possessing Antônio: Dona Rosalina. She has not actually been called but has arrived anyway and must be made welcome. One medium hurries into the chapel to get a large white embroidered shawl called a *toalha,* which is reserved for spirits of high rank. The *toalha* is fastened around Antônio's waist as he continues to sing the lead to the "Cidade bonita" doctrine.

There is then a brief pause in the singing and dancing as participants line up to greet the spirit Dona Rosalina. The ceremony of greeting a spirit is quite stylized and fairly intricate. Bowing or kneeling as he approaches the *pai de santo,* each medium crosses his extended arms and touches the floor in front of the *pai de santo*'s feet. Antônio bends down, clasps hands with the kneeling medium, and raises him to a standing position. The medium kisses the back of the right hand of Antônio, and, in the final act of the greeting ritual, the medium and Antônio, still clasping hands, embrace by touching first their right shoulders together and then their left shoulders.

Before all participants have greeted the spirit, the *pai de santo* starts a new song, and dancing resumes while the ceremony of greeting continues. When this is completed, Antônio joins in the dancing briefly, then, ordering someone else to "call Dom João," he walks off the floor, leaving the *terreiro* for his house to attend to some unfinished preparations for the evening.

Dom João does not need a prolonged invitation. As the first song to this spirit is being sung, an elderly woman goes into trance. There is another pause, because Dom João needs not only a *toalha* but also requires that the head of the medium he has possessed be tied up with a white kerchief. But after all of the preparations, Dom João does not stay very long. His medium dances briefly, greets a few fellow participants, then retires to the chapel, where she comes out of trance. After a few minutes'

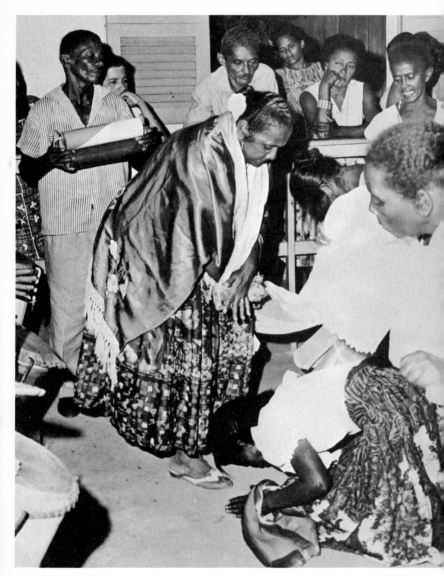

High-ranking spirits are granted the courtesy of a formal greeting. The salutation begins with the greeter kneeling before the medium in trance.

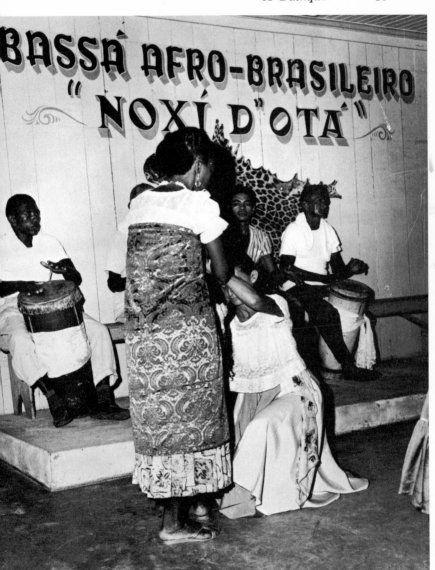

The medium in trance grasps the crossed hands of the greeter and helps her to her feet.

rest, the woman returns to the floor, looking refreshed and quite pleased with herself.

The *pai de santo* rejoins the dancing after a ten-minute interval, singing the responses with the other participants. As soon as there is a lull, he takes over the lead again. While leading, he abruptly reels backwards as the first supernatural who possessed him leaves. But instead of returning to a "pure" state, he enters a second trance. He jerks and struggles in the arms of the mediums who hold him; then, yelling incoherently, pulls himself free, whirls and dances wildly, eyes closed, in the center of the circle of dancers. When he pauses to allow a medium to drape a new strand of beads around his neck, his body is trembling violently, and when he leads a new song, his voice appears to have been altered by the new possession; it is gruffer and has a strained quality.

Cheguei, cheguei,	*I've come, I've come,*
Cheguei da beira do mar.	*I've come from the edge of the sea.*
Para vodunsi-ê,	*For mediums-ê,*
Para vodunsi-á.	*For mediums-á.*

All of the mediums have been watching this new possession very impassively, giving every indication of having witnessed it all many times before. Although the doctrine sung by the new spirit mentions no proper names, participants know as soon as they hear it that the spirit Legua Bogi has descended; Legua always sings this song first when possessing Antônio. Again the ceremony of greeting the spirit is carried out, and this time some members of the audience also go up to perform the ritual of salutation. Actually, although Legua Bogi appears to be of lower rank than the first two spirits to descend—Dona Rosalina and Dom João—and does not rate a *toalha,* he is a more important spirit for this *terreiro* because he is one of the major "chiefs" of Antônio and is believed to be a very powerful spirit who does impressive "work" while possessing the *pai de santo.*

After leading a few more songs and again ordering someone else to lead, Antônio leaves the *terreiro* a second time. He will change his shirt, which is soaked with sweat, have a drink, and then grant brief consultations to participants and to members of

Other participants continue singing and dancing as the salutation ritual proceeds.

the audience who wish to speak to the spirit supposedly possessing him.

It is now after 10:30, and the drummers begin to take rest breaks. As a new drummer appears to take over, one of those who has been beating goes to the house to have a cigarette and a drink of *cachaça* (rum). A few drinks and the camaraderie of participation are the only payment drummers ordinarily receive for their services.

Thus far the *pai de santo* has been the center of attention, with other participants playing a supporting role. But once he has disappeared, the mediums seem much less inhibited. One young woman suddenly cries out, throws up her arms, and falls backward hard on the floor before anyone can catch her. Helped to her feet, she kicks off her sandals, pitches forward and begins a frenzied dance in front of the drums, her arms pumping up and down, her hands making tearing motions at her hair. An older woman catches her arms and holds her while another medium removes the bobby pins from the young woman's hair. Released again, the possessed woman again moves in front of the drums and dances wildly, flopping her hair in front of her face. Her head bobs up and down very rapidly in an obviously involuntary movement, giving the impression that she is being held by the shoulders and shaken violently. After tossing her head in this frenzied way for approximately twenty-five seconds, the medium appears calmer. The *espada* she has dropped is thrown around her neck and the drums stop. All wait briefly to see if the newly arrived spirit wants to sing, but when the young woman simply staggers about looking foggy, an older woman starts another song.

Several other mediums go into trance in rapid succession in the next few minutes. A male participant stumbles and then pirouettes as a spirit seizes him. No one pays much attention to him, but when a stout, middle-aged woman is possessed, most of the participants and some members of the audience go up to greet her spirit. She evidently has more prestige than most of the other participants and, although in theory it is the spirit and not the medium who is granted the courtesy of a formal salutation, in practice cult members ration their demonstrations of respect in accordance with the status of the medium.

A rather violent possession. The man standing behind the medium in trance is preparing to place a ritual scarf over her shoulders.

One reason why the middle-aged woman has more prestige than other participants soon becomes obvious. She has what cult members admiringly speak of as "force," i.e., the magnetic ability to induce other mediums to enter trance states. A number of mediums who come forward to greet the woman's spirit reel off into trance states as she embraces them. Another medium, simply waiting in line to salute the spirit, crashes into a bench of onlookers as his spirit suddenly descends. A pregnant woman sitting in the audience is possessed and is helped to the middle of the floor by her neighbors. Although she goes in for a bounding, whirling style of dance and eventually falls down very hard on the cement floor when her spirit unexpectedly abandons her, no one appears worried that she might injure herself.

Not all spirits leave in so precipitous a fashion. Often they clearly announce their intentions of departure. A medium possessed by a spirit about to depart takes a position in front of the drums and leads one of various farewell songs:

Adeus, terreiro,	*Good-by, terreiro,*
Eu já me vou.	*I'm leaving now.*
Adeus, terreiro,	*Good-by, terreiro,*
Eu já me vou.	*I'm leaving now,*
Vocês são Mina,	*All of you are Mina,*
Eu sou Nagô.	*I am Nagô.*

After singing the song through a few times, the medium stops dancing and begins to revolve her torso from the waist. Finally she falls backward into the waiting arms of other participants.

There is great variation in the behavior of mediums while in the trance state. Some dance with greater vigor and self-assurance while in trance, but others only stagger about. Some move with smooth grace and expertise, others more stiffly and awkwardly. Some mediums appear unconscious, oblivious to everything around them except the beat of the drums. Others, after a brief initial period of what appear to be involuntary movements, seem perfectly "normal," interacting readily and cheerfully with their fellow participants and with spectators. Some mediums in trance insist on taking over the lead in the singing for long periods, others are mute throughout their trance.

To a certain extent, some differences in behavior may be dictated by the rank or status of the spirit believed to be in possession of the medium. For example, when mediums in trance leave the pavilion for a rest break, those possessed by the higher status spirits usually go into the chapel. Here they kneel before the altar and pray briefly and are then seated in chairs provided for them. A woman who serves as the chapel attendant brings them refreshments—a drink of water, beer, wine, or rum, depending on the available supply and the preference of the spirit. Mediums possessed by lower ranking spirits may also enter the chapel to make obeisance before the altar, but when this is completed they go into the *pai de santo*'s house for their rest

The woman in the foreground sings a farewell song, signaling the imminent end of her trance. Two mediums move into position to catch her.

Three mediums in trance retire to the *terreiro*'s chapel for a rest and a smoke. The woman seated at left, not in trance, is serving as chapel attendant.

and refreshments. A medium who takes a rest break while "pure," i.e., not in trance, drinks nothing stronger than coffee.

Shortly before midnight the *pai de santo* rejoins the ceremony, ties a scarf around his head, closes the door to the chapel, and turns off the two main lights in the *terreiro*. Only a small bulb over the chapel door still burns. All of the mediums also tie scarves around their heads, and everyone who has been sitting down, with the exception of the drummers, gets to his feet. Midnight is the hour of the Exus, the demons, and they are about to be invited to descend and dance. The audience buzzes with uneasy excitement, and those standing outside the pavilion strain to get a better view of the dance floor.

The mediums form two lines facing one another. The *pai de santo,* pacing back and forth between the two lines, starts a song to Exu Tranca Rua.

Seu Tranca Rua disse	*Mr. Tranca Rua said*
Que a sua banda é maior,	*That his band is larger,*
E nós dizemos	*And we say*
Que sua banda é de fé.	*That his band is one of faith.*
Seu Tranca Rua	*Mr. Tranca Rua*
Com sua banda girando,	*Whirling with his band,*
Oi, viva Pembá, oi, viva fé	*Oi, long live Pembá, oi, long live faith*
Em Guiné.	*In Guinea.*

Mediums and some spectators supplement the drums by clapping rhythmically. But nothing happens, no Exu descends, and the *pai de santo* switches to a "stronger" song:

Exu, que tem duas cabeças,	*Exu, who has two heads,*
Êle faz sua gira com fé,	*Does his turning in faith,*
Uma é Satanaz ao inferno,	*One is Satan from hell,*
Outra é de Jesus Nazaré.	*The other is of Jesus Nazareth.*

As this song is sung the second time the Exus descend. A teen-age girl in the audience cries out hoarsely and catapults into the mediums standing in front of her. One of the mediums guides her to the center of the pavilion where she begins to dance in a contorted position. Her body is bent forward from the waist, her arms held rigidly straight out behind her, but her head is tipped upward and her eyes are wide open, staring blankly. A young man standing outside the *terreiro* is also "seized" by an Exu. He falls to the ground and rolls in the mud before he can be brought into the pavilion. As he dances, he barks like a dog. The hand clapping, drumming, and singing increase in tempo. Then, as everyone appeared to anticipate, one of the drummers who has been taking a rest break stumbles forward and begins to dance stiffly, barely bending his knees. Another song to Tranca Rua is sung. When it is concluded, the *pai de santo* steps up to the drummer, pours some gunpowder into the palm

A cult leader begins a midnight ceremony by receiving Rompe Mato, a spirit who is believed to control Exu demons.

of the drummer's left hand, then ignites it with the burning tip of a cigar. The drummer's hand will show no powder burns later.

The Exu ceremony is concluded when the drummer is seated in a chair placed at the entrance to the pavilion. More gunpowder is placed near his feet and then ignited. When the powder flares

The *pai de santo* ignites the gunpower held in the bare hand of a medium possessed by a demon.

this time, everyone claps loudly, and all of the Exus present take their departure. The lights are turned on again and the *batuque* resumes its normal course.

There is something of a let-down in the proceedings after the Exu drama. Spectators yawn and begin to go home. Mediums who have not already done so go off on long rest breaks to change their costumes. No definite color was prescribed for the second costume, and now, though the array of bright colors is more profuse, the over-all effect is less striking. Only two of the three drums are being beaten by men; the other has been taken over by a young boy who is obviously learning. Another small boy shakes the *maracá* and a girl picks up the *ganzá* when no adult spectators appear interested in operating these instruments.

The *pai de santo* leads a song that is evidently merely a "filler":

Terra de Mina-Nagô.   Land of Mina-Nagô.

This one-line song is repeated over and over again. Then, whirling

The medium, still in trance, waves lighted candles . . .

smoothly, Antônio is possessed by a new spirit and immediately, without the customary pause, switches to a new song:

Ha muito tempo que eu andava,	*I've been traveling for a long time,*
Agora que vim chegando.	*I just got here now.*
É Toi Joãozinho,	*It's Toi Joãozinho,*
Venho do mar oceano.	*I come from the ocean sea.*

Joãozinho is a gay, lighthearted spirit, whom everyone greets with smiles. Apparently bursting with energy, he reanimates the *batuque* by introducing a new dance form. He has the mediums line up in two lines facing each other from opposite ends of the dance area. Following Antônio's lead, each line crosses to the other end, the mediums taking long gliding steps

and slowly passes the flame along the underside of his arms and under his chin.

instead of the short dance steps usually taken. They miss steps, laugh and giggle, and bump into each other as they cross the floor in the unfamiliar routine. When the drums stop, João-zinho-Antônio cheerfully shouts, *"Boa noite, minha gente"* (Good evening, folks), to the audience and waltzes off to the house to have a drink and joke with bystanders.

One of the older women starts a song and is also possessed by a lighthearted spirit. After enthusiastically leading the songs that identify her spirit, she also goes off into the house for a drink. From this time until the end of the *batuque,* few solemn spirits descend. The spirits that do put in an appearance are a happy, playful lot, but since these gay spirits seem to be thirstier than the dignified ones and spend considerable time in the *pai de santo*'s house, the dancing activity in the pavilion often drags and nearly falters. At one point only four mediums remain ready to dance and none of them is prepared to lead. They argue mildly over who should sing. One of the two remaining drummers finally leads. But there are spurts of animated dancing and singing as mediums possessed by the playful spirits return periodically to join in the dancing. One woman returns wearing two large hats, one on top of the other. She joins sedately in the dancing, but when the drums stop she does a series of vigorous bumps and grinds to the great amusement of both participants and spectators. Antônio returns, the exuberant spirits of Joãozinho still undimmed, borrows an umbrella from a specta-tor, and improvises a short dance using the umbrella as a cane.

A slight diversion is created by a man in the audience who has been leaning against the wall near the drums, evidently in a drunken stupor. After suddenly swaying forward and then back against the wall and then forward again, the force of gravity asserts itself and he crashes forward on his face. Members of the audience titter uncertainly, not sure whether the man has been seized by a spirit or laid low by alcohol. The mediums ignore the drunk for a while, dancing around his prone body, but, at a word from the *pai de santo,* two male participants pick up the drunk, carry him outside the *terreiro* and uncere-moniously dump him on the ground. The drunk sits up, rubs his battered face thoughtfully, then slowly staggers off into the darkness.

Two mediums, possessed by carouser spirits, dance with their arms around each other—a departure from the customary dance style.

By four o'clock in the morning the mediums are yawning and complaining that they are tired. Two have already left for their homes. Antônio decides to close the *batuque* and persuades all of the remaining mediums to return to the dance floor. Four mediums, still possessed by spirits, link arms, kneel down in front of the drums, and sing a farewell song. At precisely the same time, at some imperceptible signal, all four keel over backward as their spirits leave them.

All participants again tie scarves around their heads and begin a circular dance as the *pai de santo* leads the closing songs. Bringing a long embroidered white scarf from the chapel,

Antônio then dances alone directly in front of the drums. As the final chorus of a final doctrine is being sung, he drapes the scarf over the drums; the drumming, the rattle of the *cheque-cheque,* the singing all stop abruptly. The penetrating predawn chill of the tropics settles down on the *terreiro* as the spectators and mediums depart for a few hours of sleep, and the spirits, saints, and demons either soar swiftly and silently into outer space or sink noiselessly beneath the earth.

FOOTNOTES

1. See Bastide (1960, p. 225).
2. All names used for cult members are pseudonyms except in a few cases of historical interest.

Chapter II

The Setting

Although all of the African-derived cults now flourishing in Brazil share some fundamental ideas and practices,[1] the differences among the cults practiced in different parts of the country are so great that a cult member from one section would have some difficulty participating in a ceremony at a *terreiro* in another section. The spirits that are invoked, the songs, and the rituals all differ from one region to another.

To a minor extent these regional differences may reflect differences in the provenance of African slaves brought to different parts of Brazil; it is possible, for example, that more slaves from Dahomey were sent to the state of Maranhão than were sold in the area around Rio de Janeiro. But in the long run, in view of the mixture of slaves from many tribes in all sections of Brazil and in view of the rapid modification of the African religions once transplanted to the New World, the provenance of the slaves is probably less important in explaining differences among these cults than are the differences between regions of Brazil. In other words, it is Brazilian history, rather than African, that helps explain the regional diversity of the cults today.

It should be pointed out that even today Brazil has nothing like a nationwide road, railroad, radio, or telephone system or network, and, until the development of short-wave radio as a method of communication and the popularization of the airplane as a mode of transportation, vast stretches of Brazil were only tenuously connected with other parts of the country by foot trail, canoe, and ship. Under such conditions of geographic isolation considerable cultural diversity is to be expected.

Isolation from the rest of the country has been a predominant characteristic of life in the north of Brazil, the heavily forested, sparsely populated Amazon Basin. The city of Belém, the largest city of the north, was the locale of our study. As a seaport and as the capital of the state of Pará (a vast state, considerably larger than Texas), Belém was never as cut off from national influences as were the cities, towns, and villages of the interior, but until recent decades even Belém was remote from the other urban centers of Brazil. The relative isolation of the city helps explain the failure of any African-derived religion to develop there until the comparatively recent past. Until the Batuque was introduced in the late nineteenth or early twentieth century, Belém, as opposed to other urban centers of Brazil, probably had no religious movement with any substantial African element.

From the start of its history as a Portuguese colony, the Amazon Basin was recognized as an area that was quite distinct from, and somewhat marginal to, the colonial settlements in the areas now known as Brazil's Northeast, Center, and South. For the first century after the discovery of Brazil, Amazonia was more or less ignored, but when it appeared that the French, Dutch, and/ or English might establish control over parts of the basin, the Portuguese (at the time subjects of the King of Spain) moved to establish permanent settlements in the area. French forces were driven from the Maranhão coast in 1615 and in December of that year three ships were dispatched from São Luís, the principal settlement in Maranhão, with orders to secure Portuguese control of the lower Amazon.

The force of 150 men sent out from São Luís never reached the Amazon River proper, but entered instead the complex of waterways that converges to the south of the mouth of the Amazon. Hugging the coastline, on the lookout for hostile vessels, the three ships entered first the Bay of Marajó and then the narrower Bay of Guajará. These bays are actually merely continuations of the Pará River, into which flow the Tocantins and a number of smaller rivers. The large land mass of the island of

BRAZIL

Marajó separates these waterways from the mainstream of the Amazon River.

On January 12, 1616, when the relatively high ground where the Guamá River empties into the Bay of Guajará had been reached, the commander, Francisco Caldeira de Castelo Branco, decided that the party had gone far enough and that the location was favorable for the establishment of a permanent military outpost that might serve as a base for further penetration of the Amazon area. A fort and a chapel were soon constructed and all of the land around the fort, then inhabited by still friendly Tupinambá Indians, was placed under the protection of Nossa Senhora de Belém (Our Lady of Bethlehem) (Varnhagen 1948, II, pp. 166–69, 196–98).

The frontier military post grew very slowly and somewhat fitfully, with an extraordinary amount of internal dissension, into a colonial village and then into a small city. By 1716, or a century after its founding, the city had so far surpassed its mother city, São Luís, in population, wealth, and activity, that the Portuguese governors of the colony began to spend more time there than in the official capital of São Luís.

The distinction of outstripping São Luís, of course, was only an honor in a narrowly local sense, since both cities, if compared to colonial cities to the south such as Recife, Salvador, or Rio de Janeiro, were impoverished way stations where metal currency was lacking and rolls of cloth and cocoa beans were the established mediums of exchange (Calmon 1959–61, IV, pp. 1287–88). To the south, in Minas Gerais, a gold rush was well underway by 1716, but this had little effect on the colonial settlements in the Amazon area. In fact, the colony of Maranhão (later called Maranhão e Grão Pará) was not administratively a part of the colony of Brazil at all. Since adverse winds and ocean currents made it more difficult for a ship to sail from São Luís to Salvador, then the capital of Brazil, than to sail to Portugal across the Atlantic, the Amazon colony was administered directly by the court at Lisbon rather than through the viceroy of Brazil.

Today, with a population of over 400,000,[2] Belém is the seventh largest city in Brazil, but any judgment as to its significance as a city still depends on the vantage point from which it is viewed. Brazilians from the urban centers of the south, temporarily exiled to Belém due to the exigencies of employment or business, complain bitterly that the city is not only hopelessly backward but also extremely dull. But viewed from the vantage point of the small Amazon river towns, Belém looks impressively up-to-date. It has air-conditioned cinemas, several skyscrapers, television and radio stations, imposing churches, paved streets, and public utilities—telephone, water, electricity—that are usually functioning. Judged by the living standards of Amazonia, Belém is a splendid modern metropolis.

It would be fairest, perhaps, to judge the city from the viewpoint of the Amazonian interior, for the development of the city has from the start been closely linked to the development of the whole river basin, and the river basin forms an economic world set apart from the rest of Brazil. For three and a half centuries the relative positions of the city and its vast hinterland have remained unchanged. Belém has always, on the one hand, served as the seat of the regional administrative bureaucracy. The regional headquarters of various federal agencies as well as the principal organs of the state government are located in the city. On the other hand, Belém has always served as the commercial center—the banker, exporter, importer—for Amazonia. It is the place where products collected in the jungle are exchanged for manufactured goods and food from the south of Brazil or from other countries. The construction, in the late 1950s, of a highway linking Belém with the national capital, Brasília, over 1300 miles away, tremendously enhanced the importance of Belém as commercial center and gateway to Amazonia. The direct land route is much shorter than the sea route around the bulge of Brazil and less expensive than air transport.

Like other urban areas of Latin America, Belém has, in recent decades, attracted large numbers of rural migrants. The population has doubled in the last twenty years and continues to grow rapidly. In an era when the prices of manufactured goods are rising much more rapidly than the prices of raw materials, the economic position of the producers or collectors of raw materials obviously worsens. Every year hundreds of people who have been eking out a meager subsistence in the interior collecting rubber, nuts, rosewood, resin, cocoa beans, cloves, or lumber give up the unequal struggle and make their way to Belém, or, if they cannot escape their debts, at least manage to send some of their surplus children to the city.

Belém is hard pressed to absorb the impoverished, unskilled, and functionally illiterate rural migrants. Even those Brazilian cities with an expanding industrial base have difficulty providing employment opportunities for their mushrooming populations, and Belém lacks an expanding industrial base. In spite of the influx of raw materials into the city, no substantial regional industry ever developed. The existing light consumer industries (primarily food processing, furniture, leather goods, tobacco products), the service industries, and the commercial outlets provide few new jobs. Government agencies, city, state, and federal, are large employers, but bureaucracy cannot be expanded indefinitely to provide jobs for all. In fact, the state and city governments often have great difficulty providing money for the jobs already in existence, and the salaries of the police, the public school teachers, the street sweepers, and the garbage collectors are frequently months in arrears.

At the time this study of the Batuque was undertaken, the one sector of the local economy that did demonstrate vitality was the smuggling trade. Belém was, in fact, the acknowledged smuggling capital of Brazil. American automobiles, appliances, and cigarettes, Japanese radios and rubber sandals, Scotch whisky, and French perfumes were the leading items smuggled into Belém in exchange for cash or for Brazilian products, especially coffee. Various factors made the city a natural smuggling center. The combination of a complex of waterways with dense jungle foliage made it easy to move smuggled goods into the area and to conceal them. The high tariffs imposed on legally imported foreign goods allowed a wide margin for profits even after necessary bribes were paid or occasional lots of contraband confiscated. The fact that local police officials were not merely poorly paid, but irregularly paid, increased their vulnerability to bribes.

Since 1964, however, Belém's contraband enterprise has apparently suffered a drastic decline. The military *coup d'état* of that year was ostensibly directed against corruption as well as against Communism and resulted in the removal of both the governor of the state and the mayor of the city and the installation of a new state and local administration that was reputed to be less "comradely" to smugglers. An even more serious blow to smuggling was the granting in 1968 of free-port status to Manaus, the capital city of the state of Amazonas, upriver from Belém. If the transshipment of contraband to southern Brazil continues to be profitable, Manaus rather than Belém will probably benefit.

Besides its questionable reputation as former contraband capital, Belém has other distinctive features that set it apart from other Brazilian cities.[3] The oldest part of the city, Cidade Velha, has the narrow streets and cheek-by-jowl buildings of a medieval European town. Portuguese architectural styles predominate and residents claim that the Cidade Velha is more like Lisbon than is any other Brazilian city. Most of Belém's larger retail stores, business offices, wholesale outlets, and warehouses are concentrated in one section of the Cidade Velha. Adjacent to this commercial section, along the Bay of Guajará, is the city's largest and most colorful open air market, Ver-o-pêso. This market has a national reputation as a picturesque and "unspoiled" reminder of an earlier Brazil when sailboat, canoe, oxcart, and the heads of porters and vendors were used to transport goods to market and where, over a portable box stall, buyer and seller confronted each other directly in an atmosphere highly charged with the pungent animal-vegetable-fish aroma of a tropical market.

Outside of the Cidade Velha the streets of Belém are considerably wider. During the late nineteenth and early twentieth centuries shade trees were planted along some of the principal thoroughfares, an unusual practice in Brazilian cities. A variety of European architectural influences can be seen in the buildings dating back to the nineteenth century. A French vogue, for example, prevailed during the height of the rubber boom, at the turn of the century, when the Grande Hotel and a number of private mansions were constructed. A highly visible reminder of this French "period" is the Caixa d'Agua, three water tanks built upon an elaborate iron scaffolding. The structure was not only supposed to meet the water needs of the city, but was also to serve as Belém's "Eiffel Tower," i.e., it would be a wrought-iron work of art and a distinctive landmark that would tower over the urban landscape. The Caixa d'Agua was completed in 1904, but due to serious engineering defects, was only intermittently and briefly used to dispense the city's water. By 1930 all attempts to correct the defects had been abandoned. Today the structure, overshadowed by the new skyscrapers, rusts away serenely in the constantly high relative humidity.

After World War I the architecture of Belém became more definitely Brazilian as buildings in Rio de Janeiro began to furnish the models for the newer high-rise apartment buildings and the single family homes of the upper and middle classes. The aesthetic appeal of the skyscrapers may be debatable, but the private homes are generally attractive concrete, brick, and tile structures, equipped with modern conveniences, set back somewhat from the street behind a small walled-in patio or flower garden.

As in every large city throughout the world, in Belém there is a sharp contrast between the neighborhoods of the well-to-do and middle-class citizens and those of the working class and indigent poor. The spatial distribution of these neighborhoods is,

There is a sharp contrast between streets in the upper-class areas and those in the working-class districts.

however, different from that found in the United States. In Belém
it is the middle-class and upper-class neighborhoods that occupy
the central part of the city and line the main arteries of traffic
leading outward, while the neighborhoods of the poor sprawl out
around the central city, fill in the interstices between paved
streets, and spill into suburbs located outside the city limits. The
reasons for this particular spatial distribution are fairly obvious.
The land on which Belém is built is naturally low and swampy,
dissected by numerous creeks, with a limited amount of higher
ground that does not flood. The Cidade Velha and the roads
leading outward were constructed on the high and dry land and
the homes of the poor filled in the undesirable but inexpensive
semiflooded spaces. Some of the original marshes near the central
city have been drained and dikes constructed to keep the Guamá
River from overflowing, but Belém has grown into other flooded
areas. The combination of large areas of stagnant or sluggish
water with a large human carrier population has so far made it
impossible for federal health officials to eradicate the two main
mosquito-borne diseases, malaria and filariasis. The incidence of
these diseases is especially high in the lower-class neighborhoods
of the city.

The homes of the lower-class citizens have remained unaffected
by the fluctuations in architectural style. Today, as in centuries
past, the poor man's house is the *barraca,* a simple building with
mud walls, a roof of palm leaf thatch, and a floor either of
earth or rough planks. The windows of a *barraca,* uncomplicated
by either glass or screens, can be closed by means of heavy
board shutters. If the kitchen is an integral part of the house
rather than an open shed in the back, the kitchen walls stop
short of the roof, leaving an open space to facilitate the dispersal
of smoke from the open charcoal fire used for cooking. The
more pretentious *barraca* may have some or all walls of unpainted
boards, smooth wooden flooring, a tile roof, a butane-burning cook
stove, perhaps even a refrigerator. Most *barracas* have electricity
but lack plumbing. If there is no well in the backyard, all water
must be carried from the nearest public faucet.

In some respects the lower-class neighborhoods seem to be a
century or so behind the wealthier sections of the city. They
differ from the small towns of the interior only in that there

The two-year-old son of a medium plays happily on the earthen floor of his home. This one-room *barraca* is somewhat more dilapidated than the houses of most mediums.

is less living space and the inhabitants worry more about thieves and about being accosted on the streets at night by rowdies high on hashish. As in any small Amazon town, pigs and chickens wander freely in the streets and vacant lots, picking over the trash piles, competing with the indigenous scavengers, the vultures, for the choicer refuse. An occasional goat, ox, or horse can also be seen, but these animals are usually tethered. Women spread out clothes on the grass and weeds to dry. Naked infants and small children, tended by slightly larger small girls, scream and play in the streets. Small boys trudge along carrying wooden

The exterior of one of the larger and more prosperous *terreiros* in Belém. Prosperity is attested by the tile roof.

trays of fruit or sweets on their heads, on their way to busier streets to hawk their wares. Teen-age girls, carrying water from the nearest public faucet or supplies from the nearest outdoor market, pause to rest and giggle with friends before continuing home. Everywhere people stop to stare at strangers with the frank curiosity of isolated country folk unused to novelties. The most striking evidence of the mid-twentieth century in these back streets are the radios blaring away in many of the houses. Towards evening the radios may be drowned out by a loud-speaker from some corner bar that broadcasts shouting commercials interspersed with brief blasts of music.

But, in spite of the somnolent small-town atmosphere, the lower-class neighborhoods are dynamic in the sense that they are the most rapidly growing sections of the city. Only thirty years ago, for example, the two large working-class districts known as Pedreira and Guamá were still primarily cut over forest with only a few houses scattered along the principal roads. Today the forest is a long way off, there are few vacant lots, and *barracas* line even the creeks and marshes that are honored with street names.

It is from districts such as Pedreira and Guamá that the Batuque derives most of its active membership. The cult predates the current urban population explosion but does not, apparently, date very far back in the history of the city. Cult members insist that the first *terreiro* in Belém was founded only some sixty or seventy years ago by the *mãe de santo* (female cult leader), Dona Doca, who moved to Belém from Maranhão, bringing her spirits with her. Before Dona Doca arrived, the older cult members state, Belém had only *pajelança,* the healing ceremonies that are based primarily on Indian shamanism and are still held today, both within and outside the Batuque cult. While it is true that Dona Doca's personal success may have overshadowed earlier, shorter-lived *terreiros,* there seems to be no specific reference to the cult in the historical literature of the city.[4]

Elsewhere in Brazil similar African-derived religions developed wherever a large Negro slave population was concentrated, and well-organized cult centers were in operation in the larger cities by the late eighteenth and early nineteenth centuries (Bastide 1960, p. 65). In Belém the institution of slavery dates back to the founding of the city, but until the mid-eighteenth century practically all of the slaves were Indians, not Africans. The same was true for the entire Amazon region, from Maranhão in the east to the settlements on the Rio Negro and Madeira in the west. The Jesuit missionaries attempted but largely failed to check the practice of enslaving Indians. The Portuguese crown backed up the Jesuits' efforts by officially outlawing Indian slavery, but in the face of the bitter protests and open rebellion of the colonists so many exceptions to the rule were allowed that the law prohibiting enslavement of Indians was meaningless.

The alternative of importing African slaves to do the work, successful elsewhere in Brazil, failed in seventeenth-century Maranhão and Pará, for the simple reason that the colonists of Amazonia were too poor to pay for African slaves. Indian slaves might be less hardy and have less immunity to European diseases, but they were much cheaper. African slave traders preferred to take their cargoes to other ports in Brazil where higher prices could be realized. By April 1, 1680, the Portuguese crown had decided to subsidize the transportation of African slaves to the Amazon territory (Biblioteca Nacional 1948, 1ª Parte, p. 52), but the program never really got underway. When a private company was given a twenty-year monopoly of Maranhão trade in exchange for a commitment to bring in five hundred black slaves per year, a revolt promptly occurred in São Luís because of the increase in the prices of imported goods and the high-handed methods of the company (Calmon 1959–61, vol. 3, pp. 845–49). The private company was dissolved and the crown resorted to direct subsidies of some shipments of slaves from the Guinea coast of Africa, but the results were not encouraging. The colonists complained continually that the price of the slaves was too high and quarreled among themselves over the division of the slave cargoes. Half of each shipment was supposed to be put up for sale in Belém, but the slave ships from Africa usually stopped first in São Luís and disposed of most of their cargo there. Only a few hundred African slaves reached Belém before 1750 (Biblioteca Nacional 1948, 1ª Parte, pp. 146, 149–50, 155–56, 167, 170, 227; Bibliotheca e Archivo Publico do Pará 1902, vol. 3, p. 209).

In 1755, when the Marquis of Pombal took control of the administration of Portugal as minister to the new king, José I, the economy of Maranhão was transformed. Portuguese encouragement of cotton and rice production combined with the subsidized importation of African slaves on a large scale ended that state's participation in the extractive-subsistence economy that characterized the rest of the Amazon territory. But in Pará only a small area around and to the east of the city of Belém was successfully converted to a settled commercial agriculture that was based in large part on African slave labor. The rest of Pará and Amazonia continued as before to rely on the collection of forest products as the primary souce of income, and on the forced labor of Indians (Wagley 1953, pp. 37–38).

There are no incontrovertible figures on the number of African slaves brought to the state of Pará, but the total number was certainly less than 50,000 and probably not much over 30,000. The number, by any calculation, is small in comparison with the estimated numbers of slaves introduced to other Brazilian states: Maranhão, 133,000; Rio de Janeiro, 146,000; Bahia, 147,000; Minas Gerais, 168,000 (Reis 1942, p. 74; Ramos 1939, pp. 7–8). Most of the black slaves brought to Pará were employed on the coffee and cocoa plantations near Belém and in domestic service in the city itself. Even though concentrated in a relatively small corner of the state, the slaves were probably too scattered to maintain African religious rituals. In addition, the African slaves undoubtedly worked alongside the bondsmen of Indian origin, intermarried with them, and were soon influenced by what survived of Indian culture. There is no record of any deep hostility between the black and Indian slaves in Pará, unlike the situation in some other Brazilian states. Certainly during the Cabanagem, an uprising against the white ruling class that began in Belém in 1835, black slaves promptly made common cause with the Indians and lower-class mestiços involved. The rebellion, similar to a medieval peasant revolt in its haphazard violence and lack of clear-cut objectives, spread deep into the interior of Amazonia before it subsided in 1840 (Reis 1942, pp. 60–67; Smith 1879, pp. 69–75; Ramos 1939, p. 39), and by the time it was over many slaveowners discovered that their slaves had disappeared into the interior.

In Pará by 1900 the ex-slaves, the freedmen, and their descendants had probably been completely absorbed in the local lower-class culture that included Indian religious ideas as well as much of Indian material culture. It is unlikely that any religious cult that emphasized exclusively African traditions could have succeeded in Belém. But the cult, as it was introduced from Maranhão, was one in which Indian beliefs and Brazilian folk Catholicism had already been incorporated.[5]

Today there are more than 140 cult centers registered with the authorities and functioning in Belém. A few of these centers were organized by individuals trained by Dona Doca, the first *mãe de santo* in the city, but the majority were established by other immigrants from Maranhão or by natives of Pará who either experienced some special "call" to become cult leaders or who successfully made a transition from simple *pajelança* (shamanism) to Batuque.

Basically, there are two types of cult centers in the Batuque:

At a *seara* (a cult center that has no musical instruments) mediums stand in two lines and mark the beat by clapping hands. Only mediums in trance dance.

the *terreiro* and the *seara* (also called *tenda*). Variations in ritual differentiate the two types, but the chief difference is whether or not musical instruments are used in ceremonies. In a *terreiro,* as indicated in Chapter I, two to four drums provide the basic rhythm for dancing, supplemented by one or two *ganzás* (metal cannisters filled with lead shot) and a large gourd rattle (*maracá*). In a *seara* no musical instruments are used. Rhythm is marked by hand clapping, and dancing is limited. At a *seara* ceremony, the participants, all clapping their hands, are likely to move in a sedate circle while awaiting possession or to mark time while standing in two rows facing each other; only those mediums who are in a trance engage in more vigorous dancing.

Cost appears to be one factor in a cult leader's decision to open a *seara* rather than a *terreiro*. In the case of a *seara,* not only are there no musical instruments to purchase, but no separate building need be constructed; any fair-sized room in a private home can be used for the ritual in view of the limited dancing. A number of existing *terreiros* began as *searas,* with the cult leader adding the musical instruments and a pavilion as he gained fame and fortune as a leader.

However, some *searas* are located in well-maintained, specially constructed buildings with elaborate chapels and built-in seating arrangements for an audience. Expense is clearly not the only factor influencing the decision to open a *seara.* Some cult leaders insist that they do not want drums because of all the "confusion" a full-fledged *batuque* causes. The drumming and more exuberant dancing performances in a *terreiro* are much more likely to attract bored idlers and potential troublemakers from miles around. Because of the resulting fights as well as because of the noise, neighbors are more likely to protest to authorities and to petition for the closing of the center. A special police permit is in fact needed for every evening ceremony if drums are used, but no special permit, other than the annual license, is necessary for ceremonies at a *seara.*

Some cult leaders object to the *terreiros* and the use of drums on doctrinal grounds and insist that their *seara* represents an entirely different religious sect than that of the *terreiros.* They call their sect "Umbanda" and contrast it with the Mina or Mina-Nagô that is practiced at the *terreiros.* In the Belém cult group, these terms, "Umbanda," "Mina," and "Nagô," are supposed to refer to distinct Afro-Brazilian sects, but all three terms are somewhat ambiguous. Actually, before being used to designate religions, both "Mina" and "Nagô" were used to designate the tribal origin of African slaves. Slaves brought from the Guinea coast of Africa were called "Minas" by the Portuguese colonists, a term also used more specifically to designate the Gold Coast, which is one section of the Guinea coast. Since a number of African tribes furnished the slaves shipped from the ports of the Guinea coast, the slaves were often further identified as Minas-Gêges, Minas-Nagôs, Minas-Mahys, Minas-Cavallos, and Minas-Fulupas (Eduardo 1948, pp. 7–16; Bastide 1960, pp. 59–65).

Of these tribes, the Minas-Gêges, today identified as Dahomeans, and, to a lesser extent, the Minas-Nagôs, today identified as Yorubans, were especially important in the development of the Afro-Brazilian sects of Maranhão. Although the actual number of Dahomeans and Yorubans brought to that state represented only a small percentage of the slave population, their highly organized religious traditions were preserved, while those of other tribes faded into oblivion (Eduardo 1948, pp. 104–5). In São Luís, the capital city of Maranhão, slaves and freedmen of Dahomean and Yoruban origin probably practiced their religious ceremonies, somewhat modified by Catholicism, from the time African slaves were introduced to Maranhão in significant numbers, i.e., the last half of the eighteenth century. The existing prestigious Gêge religious center in São Luís, the Casa das Minas, may have been founded as early as 1796 (Bastide 1960, p. 65). A less celebrated Nagô center dates back to the mid-nineteenth century (Eduardo 1948, p. 47).

In terms of gaining proselytes, however, the most successful Afro-Brazilian sect of Maranhão is neither the traditional Casa das Minas nor the old Nagô center, but the sect that Eduardo, the foremost student of the Afro-Brazilian religion in Maranhão, has termed "Yoruban-derived" (1948, pp. 48, 82–83). The Yoruban-derived sect is characterized by a combination of both Yoruban and Dahomean beliefs with a large admixture of Indian shamanism, folk Catholicism, and local folklore. It was this highly syncretized Yoruban-derived cult that Dona Doca introduced to Belém some seventy years ago. Although some cult leaders assert that their religion is "pure Nagô," most cult members associated with *terreiros* use the terms "Mina" and "Nagô" interchangeably as names for the sect, with "Mina" perhaps used more frequently.

A majority of the cult members associated with *searas,* on the other hand, call their religion "Umbanda" instead of "Mina." Umbanda is a fairly recent religious import to Belém. The *mãe de santo* Dona Maria de Aguiar is generally credited with first introducing Umbanda to the city. At some point in the mid-1930s, Dona Maria, already established as a leader of a Mina-Nagô *terreiro,* visited several centers of Umbanda in Rio de Janeiro, and on her return to Belém, "crossed" the "line" of Umbanda with that of Mina-Nagô. In July 1938, when a research team was sent to Belém by the Brazilian Department of Culture to record folklore and the music of the cults, the *pai de santo* who was interviewed by the team, named Satiro, briefly mentioned Umbanda but apparently did not consider it established as a distinct sect in Belém (Alvarenga 1950a, p. 21). Today, thirty years later, every cult leader in the city is acutely aware of the local strength of Umbanda and usually has strong feelings, pro or con, about it.

Umbanda first appeared in Rio de Janeiro after World War I. It is the product of the combination of certain beliefs of the Brazilian spiritualist movement (Kardecismo) with the basic ritual and concepts of *macumba,* the Afro-Brazilian cult dominant in Rio at the time. The spiritualist strain in Umbanda is evident in various ways: an emphasis on reincarnation and on the idea that mediums might receive the spirits of the dead; a stress on doing good or "practicing charity" rather than stressing the utilization of supernatural contacts for one's own ends; a general tendency to develop a sophisticated cosmology and a rationalistic theology, as evidenced in the production of the extensive literature devoted to explaining Umbanda. However, in spite of the strength of spiritualist ideas, Afro-Brazilian religious elements are still apparent in the ritual, the organization of cult centers, the preoccupation with undoing sorcery, and the exaltation of African (Yoruban) deities and Indian spirits (Bastide 1960, pp. 435–75; Camargo 1961; Kloppenburg 1961).

The Batuque in Belém today involves a synthesis of the older "Yoruban-derived" cult with certain ideas and practices of Umbanda. The "crossing" attempted by Dona Maria de Aguiar was eminently successful and widely imitated. In spite of claims to the contrary by some cult leaders, no cult center we visited was pure Mina-Nagô; all reflected some Umbanda influence, although the degree of influence varied from center to center. On the other hand, there are reportedly some cult centers in the city that are modeled entirely on the Umbanda of Rio de Janeiro to the total exclusion of local Mina-Nagô elements. We did not determine the number of such centers nor include them in our study.

Although we have called the Afro-Brazilian cult in Belém the "Batuque," it should be noted that this is not the usual term that cult members use as a name for their religion. Strictly speaking, as the word is used by cult members, *batuque* is synonymous with *tambor* (the term used in Maranhão) and both mean the public ceremony when the spirits are invited to descend and possess their devotees.

Fashions in names change. Thirty years ago when the Department of Culture made its brief investigation of the cult in Belém, the researchers reported that outsiders called the cult "Babassuê," a name derived from one of the most important spirits in the cult Barba Sueira, or St. Barbara (Alvarenga 1950a, p. 21). Today this name is never used, and only one informant mentioned that the cult used to be called that when she was a child. Today outsiders may occasionally call the cult "Batuque" but more frequently use the name "Macumba," adopting the term used in Rio de Janeiro for the Afro-Brazilian sects there. In Belém, the term "Macumba" has a somewhat derogatory connotation, perhaps the equivalent of "voodoo" in English, and cult members only employ the term when joking about themselves. When speaking more seriously, adherents call their religion either "Mina" or "Nagô" or "Umbanda." In view of the actual mixture of these elements, however, the use of a more neutral and more general name, such as "Batuque," seems desirable.

FOOTNOTES

1. Cf. Carneiro (1961, pp. 11–34).

2. The population was 402,170 in the 1960 census (Instituto Brasileiro de Geografia e Estatística, 1969).

3. See Tocantins (1963).

4. Cf. Figueiredo and Silva (1967, p. 102); Silva (1968).

5. A synthesis of African, Catholic, and Indian beliefs had been achieved in the Catimbó cult of the Northeast as well as in Maranhão. It is perhaps significant that approximately 500,000 Northeasterners migrated to Amazonia between 1890 and 1913, many of them eventually settling in Belém after the rubber boom collapsed (Furtado 1963, pp. 143–44). Already familiar with similar cults, the Northeasterners may have been important early supporters of the Batuque in Belém.

Chapter III

The Belief System

The people who participate in the Batuque are for the most part extremely poor and live difficult, sometimes desperate lives. Yet the economic privations that they endure and the health problems that they constantly face do not make them apathetic or even fatalistic. Most of them struggle mightily with their problems, sustained in large part by their religion. Batuque theology is extremely supportive, with great stress on the idea that the supernatural takes an active part in everyday life, aiding the members of the religion in a variety of ways.

A great deal of the behavior of Batuque members is directed in one way or another toward acquiring and maintaining the support of the spirit world. In Chapter I the public ceremony was described, in which individuals go into trance and are "possessed" by the spirits. Taking part in these ceremonies and "receiving" the spirits is the most important obligation that the Batuque member has. It is believed that the spirit enjoys occupying the medium's body and participating in the ceremony, and that the spirit must be given the opportunity to do so on a regular basis. Although the public ceremony does have some group aspects, it is basically individualistic, in that each medium is primarily concerned with fulfilling an obligation to a particular spirit. As will be indicated later, there are other obligations that a Batuque member has in addition to serving as a medium. But the central feature of the Batuque religion is a kind of contract between a human being and a spirit—the human receives the spirit and allows it to participate in ceremonies, and in return the spirit looks out for the welfare of the human being.

But what is the nature of these spirits that are thought to possess people? In the first place, Batuque spirits are seen as being quite distinct from the Christian deities, but as belonging to the same supernatural universe. Batuque members accept Catholic teachings on most matters, and they certainly believe that, in some remote and probably beautiful place called heaven, God, Our Lady, and Jesus live with the saints and angels. But they also believe that much closer to man, both physically and spiritually, there are many thousands of other spirits. Some of these are souls of the dead, drifting in space between heaven and earth. Even closer to man, living under the earth or in the seas and rivers, are another group of spirits, highly diverse in origin and nature, that form the core of the Batuque pantheon. These are the spirits that are thought to like to possess people.

A variety of terms are used by cult members to designate this special class of supernatural beings. In many of the songs sung during ceremonies, the terms *vodun* and *orixá* appear. These are African (Dahomean and Yoruban, respectively) terms for "deity," and are sometimes used in non-ceremonial contexts. Other terms that frequently occur in everyday conversation are *guia* (guide), *santo* (literally, saint), and *invisivel* (invisible one). But perhaps the most common term is "encantado."[1] Literally, this term can be translated as "enchanted one," but since the term in English suggests creatures held in some sort of temporary magic spell that might be broken, the translation is inappropriate. While it is true that some encantados are conceived of as former men and women, it is believed that their natural destiny was somehow permanently altered and that under no circumstances will they ever revert to the human condition. Besides, many encantados were born as such and never lived on earth as mortals, and the origin of still others is quite unknown. The encantados, cult members point out, are a mystery that humans cannot understand, just as the Virgin Birth or the Holy Trinity are mysteries incomprehensible to man.

The encantados are thought to live below the surface of the

earth or seas in their own special dwelling places called *encantarias*. The nature and location of the *encantaria* varies with the type of encantado. American Indian encantados live in villages in the depths of virgin forests; water spirits have their *encantarias* under water in rivers, lakes, or the sea; while still other encantados live in elaborate cities that may be directly under human cities. While they remain in their *encantarias,* the encantados are thought to have bodies, but when they rise above the earth they rise as spirits, invisible to man, and it is thus that they enter human bodies.

According to cult beliefs, all of the supernatural beings in the cosmos—as well as certain inanimate objects such as the stars, sun, and moon—have power and influence over the lives of men. God is conceived of as the supreme arbiter and governor of the universe. "No one is greater than God," Batuque members are fond of remarking. "No one gives orders to Jesus." Nevertheless, God's interest in man is thought to be somewhat limited. God is terribly remote, high up in his majestic heaven, and since he is preoccupied with the problems of supervising the universe, he has little time for all the petty troubles of individual men and women. The saints, who once lived on earth and who still derive nourishment from men's prayers, are much more inclined to notice man's problems and to hear his voice crying for help. Informants cited numerous examples of how saints had helped them through personal crises such as childbirth or illness. But though the saints can be petitioned for help, their response is by no means certain, for saints are so pure and "elevated" that they are more attuned to the celestial sphere than to the terrestrial. Although much closer to man than is God or the Virgin, the saints are never as accessible as the encantados. Rather than appeal directly to their favorite saint for assistance, Batuque members often ask the saint to assist their encantado in producing whatever result they desire.

Not only are the encantados considered to be much more accessible than the saints, but their nature is considered to be much closer to human nature. While the saints are seen as virtuous, elevated, and pure, the encantados are considered to have most of the characteristics, good and bad, of people. Some informants insisted that there was hardly any difference at all:

Images of saints, some nearly hidden by flowers, occupy the *terreiro*'s main altar. The image of the saint being feted (in this case, St. Benedict) is placed at top center.

Drinking and smoking are contrary to Jesus. I've drunk and smoked —it's contrary to Jesus. But the encantados also smoke and drink and they have children. The saints don't do anything contrary to God. They have no children. The nourishment of the saints is just the prayers we pray to them and the light from the candles we light to them. But the encantados eat and drink.

Other Batuque members felt that their own encantados were more charitable and prone to do good than most humans might be, but that there were other encantados who were given to drinking too much, and some who were downright immoral. Even the most prestigious and honored encantados were admittedly fond of wearing fancy costumes and dancing—vain and frivolous behavior that would never be expected of a saint.

As the foregoing discussion indicates, the members of the Batuque distinguish clearly between saint and encantado; the two supernatural beings are not equated or syncretized as may occur in some other African-derived religions.[2] Although the term "santo" is sometimes used as a synonym for encantado, it can more properly be translated as "spirit" or "guardian spirit" in such a context, rather than "saint." *"Encantado é do fundo, mas santo é do céu"* (Encantados are of the deep, but saints are of heaven) is a common way in which cult members explain the distinction. Another basic difference is that saints are not expected to possess people, except in a few exceptional cases.

Although evincing human predilections and failings, the encantados are believed to possess a wide range of superhuman powers. They can travel in the wind or catch a ride on an airplane if they so choose, reaching any place on earth quickly. They can hear humans calling them regardless of where they may be, and, if so inclined, come at once from great distances. Regardless of their location, they are able to observe what is going on among their followers, and they are thus able to keep a constant lookout for the best interests of their devotees. The encantados also know what is going to happen in the future, and their ability to predict is one of their most valued attributes.

Of even greater importance is the supposed ability of the spirits to actively cause strangers to behave in ways that benefit their devotees. Encantados are believed to induce rich people to make contributions to *terreiros,* to cause employers to offer jobs to the faithful, to force philandering husbands to return to their families —in all cases, of course, without the coerced person recognizing that he is being manipulated. Several of our informants stated quite explicitly that the reason we had come to them to find out about the Batuque, and in the process had provided them with financial assistance of various kinds, was because their encantados had brought us, all unknowing, to help them out in a time of need. In general, almost any behavior of other people

At this *terreiro* a separate altar holds the sacred stones of the encantados.

vis-à-vis a Batuque member may be attributed to the intervention of an encantado.

The encantados are also thought to be able to produce calamities of various kinds, usually as a form of punishment for the humans involved, but sometimes simply as a demonstration of power. They can hurt or even kill people by causing them to fall in front of automobiles, by turning over their canoes, or by causing many other types of accidents. They can close down a factory or store causing general unemployment or force an individual to lose his job through illness or some other cause. Some encantados, but not all, can aid humans in working sorcery against their fellows, as will be discussed in a later chapter. By simply withdrawing their shield of protection, encantados can expose those who have lost their favor to dissension, sorcery, and disease.

Another kind of power is demonstrated when the encantados descend and take possession of a person's body. It is believed that the individual's own spirit is forced outside his body by the encantado; it remains nearby, ready to re-enter when the encantado leaves. Once in full possession of a human body, the encantado may be expected to engage in a myriad of activities of the type described earlier. He may dance, sing, drink, smoke, joke with bystanders, give advice to those with problems, etc. In general, however, the encantado is expected to perform all of these acts more gracefully and with greater gusto than the person would be capable of doing when in a "pure" or unpossessed state. Some encantados are thought to be able to perform feats that would cause damage to the body of an unpossessed person. They may burn gunpowder in the palm of the hand, slowly pass the flames of candles along the skin of the arms and face, walk on live coals, or wash the hands in boiling oil.

Some contact between man and these powerful supernatural beings is thought to be inevitable, since both must share the same environment—the earth. It is the immortal encantados who are thought of as the real owners of the earth, while men are only transitory residents. It is believed that everything in nature belongs to the encantados: all bodies of water, the forests, the animals of the jungle, the birds of the air. Even certain man-made structures are pre-empted by these spirits. Vacant houses, for example, are immediately claimed by the spirit owners of the real estate on which the house was built. All streets, roads, paths, and trails, though made and maintained by human communities, really belong to the demon encantados, the Exus.

The omnipresence of so many spirits in the immediate environment of course complicates human life. Unless properly handled and mollified, the spirit owners of a house, piece of land, wooded area, creek, or well cause all manner of disturbances. They steal and hide human possessions, open and slam doors or windows, rap loudly on house walls, whisper among themselves in the dead of night, or, to properly frighten the unflappable, appear visibly as animal or human phantoms that melt into nothingness as one approaches. But if the presence of so many spirits makes life more complicated, the reverse is also true: the burden of human existence is considerably lightened by the possibility of enlisting supernatural aid in solving day-to-day problems. Since man can provide things that the supernatural is thought to want, it is possible for a mutually satisfactory arrangement to be worked out whereby a human and an encantado provide one another with certain kinds of services.

The relationship between a human and an encantado is in some ways similar to the relationship between an individual and a saint. Foster (1961; 1963) has suggested that a useful way of describing the man-saint relationship in Latin America is in terms of a "dyadic contract." The basic idea underlying this conception is that there are only two parties involved (thus the relationship is dyadic), and there is an informal agreement between the parties to exchange services. The human partner performs certain ritual acts, and in return the saint is expected to grant supernatural assistance of various kinds. Foster developed this model from a study of a Mexican village, but it applies equally well to the Catholics of Belém, including those who are also Batuque members. Each person has a particular saint, or several saints, whom he is said to "adore." In return for prayers, candles, and respect, each of these saints is expected to provide long-term and continuous surveillance over the well-being of his devotee. When a crisis arises, the devotee often makes a *promessa* (vow); he promises to carry out some special act of devotion if the saint grants his petition. Sometimes the vow is made to one of the saints with whom the person has a long-term relationship, but more commonly an appeal is made to a saint with a reputation for solving special kinds of problems and of working miracles. In Belém the most prominent *santo milagroso* is Nossa Senhora de Nazaré (Our Lady of Nazareth), whose annual festival is the religious event of the year. Thousands of people accompany the image of this saint through the streets, many walking barefoot, most of them having promised to walk in the procession in return for being cured of illness.

There are two special characteristics of this relationship between people and saints that should be stressed. In the first place, the relationship is indeed dyadic, it is conceived of as pertaining to two specific partners only. No one else—priest, relative, or other supernatural—is thought to be involved. And secondly, there is almost complete freedom of choice on the part of the human partner. If a person appeals to a particular saint and gets no response, he may and usually does direct his petition to a different saint the next time a similar occasion arises. The basic attitude is one of trial and error, and there is no stigma attached to shifts of allegiance.

The relationship that is expected to obtain between a medium and an encantado is like the human-saint relationship in that it is also dyadic. Ideally the contract is simple and direct: the human makes his body available periodically to the encantado so that the spirit may come to earth and take part in ceremonies, and in return the spirit provides various kinds of assistance. But unlike the human-saint compact, there is very little choice on the part of a man as to which encantado he will serve. According to Batuque doctrine, it is the encantado who initiates the relationship and not the human being. The medium is "seized" by the spirit, usually suddenly, and it is only by means of this experience that the contract is brought into being. No matter how much an individual may feel drawn to a particular encantado, or how much he may want to be possessed by it, there is no way in which this may come about except through the volition of the supernatural. If a person has been told by a *pai de santo* that an encantado wants to possess him, he can try to expedite matters by joining in the public ceremony and fulfilling other obligations. But the belief is that there is no way to guarantee success. Every living human is thought to be a potential medium, and it is possible through divination to discover which encantado is the potential possessor of each person. But why some encantados insist on seizing the body of their mediums even when resisted, and others refuse to appear even when urged to do so, is considered to be another mystery that man cannot hope to understand.

As will be discussed in the next chapter, there are many people who never become mediums, but who believe in the encantados and seek their assistance. In some cases the attitude toward the encantados exactly parallels the attitude toward the saints described earlier and is clearly the same approach applied to a different supernatural. *Promessas* may be made, for example, in which the petitioner promises to engage in some behavior pleasing to the encantado if some request is granted. In most cases, however, the petitioner approaches the encantado while it is incorporated in a medium and asks it what kind of actions it would find pleasing. Under the circumstances, it is not surprising that what is pleasing to the spirit is also pleasing to the medium who delivers the message. The petitioner is usually given elaborate instructions about herb baths to take, candles to light, and other ritual activities to perform. He is also usually urged to contribute money, cloth, or other valuable items to the medium, or in the case of a Batuque leader, to the cult center. The contract between the petitioner and the spirit in these cases is not really dyadic, since the medium almost always is involved in one way or another.

For men and women who become mediums, the relationship with the encantados is seen as extremely intimate, especially with one spirit that is considered to be the person's *chefe* (chief). Terminologically, the relationship is equated with the parent-child relationship, and the medium refers to the encantado as *pai* (father) or *mãe* (mother), and to himself as the *filho* (son) or *filha* (daughter) of the spirit. The medium thus becomes the earthly child of the encantado, and the spirit is expected to keep as close a watch over his devotee as a good human parent does over his offspring, as long as the devotee keeps his part of the contract and fulfills his ritual obligations.

The obligations that a medium must assume, in addition to receiving the encantado, are not standardized, since in most cases the encantado specifies what the obligations are to be, and a wide

range of ritual actions are appropriate. If a person is just beginning as a medium, the *pai de santo* often explains what the
proper obligations are for the encantado involved. There are only
a few ritual regulations that are binding on all mediums. The
individual must make his body fit for possession by having his
head "washed" by a cult leader, i.e., he must be baptized or initiated into the cult. He must also take ritual baths of purification
and observe the dietary and sexual restrictions that are in force
before each public ceremony. One dietary restriction that is
stressed is the prohibition of alcoholic beverages on the day of
the ceremony. Sexual relations are prohibited for three days
preceding a *batuque*. Individuals who fail to observe these ritual
prescriptions, or female mediums who are menstruating, have
corpos sujos (unclean bodies) and may expect supernatural retribution for their audacity if they invite possession in such a
condition.

The most expensive obligation that the medium has is to provide
himself with a number of ceremonial costumes, as well as ac-
cessory regalia such as *espadas* (ritual scarves), beads, and sandals. The purchase of the costumes represents a very large outlay
of funds for most mediums. Cloth, like most manufactured goods,
is expensive in Brazil, and the fabric used for the ceremonial
skirts and shirts is of the more costly drapery quality. In some
other Afro-Brazilian sects a devotee need only provide one costume for his deity, since each deity has a specific costume of a
certain color and design. In the Batuque, however, although the
encantados are thought of as owning the costumes, the costumes
have no necessary relationship to any specific encantado. The
design and color of the costume is specified by the cult leader,
and for any given ceremony all mediums dress as much alike as
possible. A medium who plans to participate in a ceremony must
wear the designated colors, and if she does not already own a
skirt of the appropriate color, she is expected to purchase a new
one. Occasionally a cult leader may purchase cloth for a few
mediums who have contributed a great deal of work to the
terreiro, but most mediums must provide their own costumes,
and it is a standing complaint of rank-and-file members that
leaders call for new costumes too often. Any medium who has
been active in the cult for any length of time has a trunk full of

A medium poses before the private altar she maintains in her home. The emblem on top of the altar—Solomon's seal with a cross—is a Catholic religious symbol used throughout Brazil.

ceremonial costumes that can be used for no other purpose. When a medium dies, his ceremonial clothes and other regalia are supposed to be thrown into some body of water.

Another obligation that most mediums have is the maintenance of a shrine to their encantados in their homes. The shrine may be a simple shelf below a saint's picture or a glass-enclosed case with shelves. In other words, the shrine may be no different than that which any Brazilian might provide for his favorite saints. On the other hand, the shrine may be a small replica of the altar found in *terreiros,* with saints placed on the shelves above and with stones in earthenware bowls underneath the altar. At this private shrine, at various intervals, the medium must furnish offerings of his encantado's preferred beverage (rum, wine, beer, or water) and light candles to the encantado and to the encantado's saint. On the anniversary of the encantado's first possession of the medium, or perhaps on the encantado's saint's day, the medium may have to prepare special offerings of food and drink.

All of these obligations in the home are extremely variable; the nature and extent of the private rituals are determined by every individual's own encantados and privately revealed to him. The same encantado will require different things of different mediums. For example, as the *chefe* of Zuzu, the encantado Tapinaré might demand a glass of rum every Monday and an anniversary feast once a year, but as the *chefe* of Lourdes might ask only for an offering of wine once a month, and as Guillerme's *chefe* only require regular contributions to the upkeep of a *terreiro.* Some mediums have separate obligations for several of the encantados they receive, others have obligations only to their chief encantado. But most cult members must furnish some regular private offerings to their spirits, and for most members these offerings represent a financial burden.

By becoming the devotee of an encantado the average individual assumes duties that require a considerable outlay of cash and an investment of time that cannot easily be spared from gainful occupations or from the unpaid and unending duties of a housewife with small children. In addition, belonging to an encantado sometimes complicates family life, since spouses or young children occasionally demonstrate jealousy of the encantados who monopolize so much of the time of one's mate or parent. In spite of these disadvantages, however, the majority of mediums feel their status as mediums is definitely worthwhile. They are proud to be the chosen instruments of powerful supernatural beings and, as such, to be sought out by their neighbors for advice and assistance. Moreover, the devotee of an encantado is assured a direct and continuing supernatural interest in his personal life, no matter how humble that life may be. No non-medium can have the same certainty of supernatural protection.

Cult members readily cite examples of how their encantados look after and guide them. In general it is the encantados that are credited with maintaining the economic well-being of the household in the face of frequent financial crises. Clara, a washerwoman whose husband died recently, is the head of a household that includes a somewhat promiscuous unwed daughter with her four small children, three adolescent children who are frequently out of work, two young foster children, and an old friend who has a steady job as a cleaning woman in a public school but whose salary is often in arrears due to the vagaries of city finance. Clara sometimes wakes up in the morning to the realization that the family has nothing to eat, the neighborhood grocer has already refused further credit until something is paid on the bill, and the family valuables (gold chains worn around the neck with a saint's medal or good luck charm) are already in the pawnshop. She then comments to her encantado, "Look, Seu Japetequara, I don't have a cent in the house today. Why don't you help me?" Then lighting a candle to the image of Japetequara's saint, the Sacred Heart of Jesus, she prays to it to give Japetequara sufficient force to arrange something for her. He has never failed to turn up something, although this is often only the idea that Clara should go to her "patron," one of the women for whom she does washing, and request another advance on her salary. In such a situation the encantado is expected to cause the patron to advance the money, even though Clara has already borrowed her next two months' salary.

Another way in which encantados provide their mediums with financial assistance is by performing services for clients who then contribute money to the medium. The practices of giving "passes" (withdrawing evil influences), prescribing medicinal or good luck baths, herbal teas, and cleansing fumigations are not restricted to cult leaders or full-time Batuque curers. Probably most of the "developed" or experienced mediums supplement their incomes by occasionally engaging in similar activities. When relatives, neighbors, or acquaintances of a medium have a problem, they may first turn for help to the medium they know personally before trying the higher-priced services of a cult leader or curer. Inês, for example, primarily supports herself, her daughter, and her foster son by operating a small boardinghouse. Despite irregular child-support payments from her husband, from whom she is separated, Inês finds it difficult to make ends meet, especially since she is determined that her daughter should receive a secondary school education. She credits her chief encantado, Tabajara, with frequently coming to her aid by causing clients to appear and then solving their problems. Inês herself makes no attempt to attract clients, since she does not consider herself a curer, but she is willing to ask her encantado to help those who do appear. A teen-age boy in the neighborhood looked for work for months without success. His mother came to Inês for help. Inês placed offerings of rum and beer on her altar for Tabajara and lit a candle for him. He then "descended" and prescribed nine baths, of specific herbal ingredients, to be taken by the young man on nine successive days. Inês prepared the infusions and gave them to her neighbor. As soon as he had completed the last in the series of baths, the boy found a good job; his mother gave Inês 5000 cruzeiros (then approximately $7.00). Another recent client was referred to Inês by the proprietor of the neighborhood grocery. The woman's husband was leaving her and had started to remove his personal possessions from the house. Inês instructed the woman to bring her a pair of the man's socks. After making an offering to Tabajara, Inês recited a secret formula over the socks. When the husband returned to his wife a few days later, Inês received 2000 cruzeiros from the grateful woman. The sums of money thus gained were small in absolute terms, but they represented very significant additions to Inês' income.

Devotees also credit their encantados with maintaining them and their families in reasonably good health. Of course it is not expected that perfect health can be maintained forever, since pains, colds, fevers, and liver complaints are the natural lot of humanity.

But if an encantado is unable to prevent illness, he should show special solicitude in caring for his devotee when ill. Justina, for example, had a serious accident during a period when she was recuperating from a major operation. Returning home from the *terreiro* one dark night, she lost her footing, fell into a ditch, and tore open the operation. Infection at once set in, and Justina was believed to be again near death. At this jucture Justina's chief encantado, Dona Rosalina, descended, and while possessing the bedridden Justina left the message that Justina was to take two strong purgatives to clean out the infection. Justina followed these instructions and was soon up and about again.

In addition to providing for the material and medical needs of their devotees, encantados also meet the psychic need for relaxation and recreation. *"Cada vodunsa tem um farrista"* (Each medium has one carouser), one informant stated, as though it were a law of nature. We met several mediums who had never received any *farrista* encantado and some who received more than one, but, as a general rule, every "developed" medium had at least one serious encantado, who served as the devotee's chief, and one more lighthearted hedonist. The happy carouser is thought to leave most of the problems of providing for the medium's welfare to the chief encantado and dedicates himself primarily to having a good time while possessing the devotee.

In their pursuit of pleasure, the carousers may engage in behavior that the medium himself does not engage in when in a pure, or unpossessed, state. Few of the women cult members are habitual smokers, but when possessed by a carouser they all smoke cigarettes or cigars. Few of the women drink anything stronger than soft drinks, at least not publicly, but all of the carousers are unabashed tipplers, often consuming astonishing amounts of alcoholic beverages. Most women maintain a measure of decorum in their speech, especially in public, but even the most proper of them may gaily shout ribald vulgarities when possessed by her carouser.

A few of the *farristas* turn surly and mean as they pass a certain point in their drinking and may insult or pick fights with bystanders or engage in other types of destructive or anti-social behavior. The carouser of one *pai de santo,* for example, was inclined, when extremely drunk, to lock the doors and windows and then smash furniture and dishes and slash the clothes of the *pai de santo* into

A medium possessed by a carouser spirit named Mariana insists on having her picture taken. Bystanders appreciate Mariana's wit.

ribbons. As a general rule, however, carouser encantados are genial, gregarious spirits who want to keep the party going rather than to break it up.

According to cult theory, the medium is completely unconscious and devoid of sensation while in trance and therefore could not personally be enjoying himself while his carouser encantado is in possession of his body and enjoying itself. It is quite clear, however, that mediums derive considerable recreational benefit from the symbiotic relationship with their carousers. Far from being completely unconscious during the trance, most mediums can recollect in fond detail the amusing antics of their *farristas*. In addition, although the encantado may engage in behavior that might be considered improper in other contexts, there is no reason for the medium to feel any guilt afterward, since he is not responsible for what the spirit does. In fact, in terms of cult belief, the medium may actually be rewarded later for enjoying himself during the ceremony. Since the *farrista* is gratified by having a human body

Mediums possessed by child spirits may demand a soft drink and suck their thumbs like children.

available in which it can carry out its high jinks, the spirit can be expected to reciprocate by assisting its medium in time of need. The Batuque is one of the few religions in which individuals are believed to derive supernatural blessings from enjoying hedonistic pleasures.

The *farristas* sometimes possess their devotees for hedonistic purposes entirely outside any cult-connected ceremonial. For example, on one local holiday, Clara encountered a group of cult members, two of whom were possessed by their carousers, drinking beer in a café. Clara joined the group, but refused, despite the urging of the others, to join in the drinking. She had scarcely made her refusal clear to her companions when her own *farrista* possessed her and drank up everything in sight.

The alcoholic proclivities and generally loud and immodest behavior of carouser encantados may exacerbate family tensions. Although outsiders may find the spectacle entertaining, spouses and children may react with embarrassment and hostility to the uninhibited behavior of the medium possessed by a carouser. Justina's daughter, a prim and proper eleven-year-old, confided that she hated it when Bombeiro (her mother's *farrista*) "comes and says dirty words." Clara reported that her husband had detested her *farrista,* the encantado Mariana, but had always enjoyed conversing with her serious encantado, Japetequara.

Considering the type of relationship that is thought to exist between a medium and the encantado, it is inevitable that the supernatural will come to play a very important and intimate role in the family of a medium. An experienced medium may enter trance at any hour of the day or night and may receive any of his encantados. Obviously it is impossible for the other members of the household to ignore the presence of supernatural beings, and some accommodation has to be made. A family crisis of any kind may lead to the prompt appearance of an encantado, who is expected to resolve the difficulty. As an example of the kind of complexities that can arise when several mediums become involved in a family crisis, the following domestic drama may be related.

We arrived at the home of Clara one afternoon to discover two other guests already present. The visitors were young cult members whom we had never met before, named Zita and Nair, both girls in their early twenties. A short time after our arrival, Nazaré, the

Or, in the case of the twin child spirits, Cosme and Damião, they may drink rum and act more like tipsy adults.

mother of Nair, also appeared, greeted us and Clara, but refused to speak to or look at her daughter or her daughter's friend. As it developed, Nair, after numerous battles with her parents, had just left home against their wishes and was now living with Zita. After another ten minutes of strained conversation, Zita and Nair (complaining *sotto voce* that her mother followed her everywhere) prepared to depart. Their exit was forestalled when Zita, in the process of crossing the room on the way to the front door, stopped, looked sick, stumbled, threw up her arms, and pitched backward. She had, with no apparent stimulus, fallen into trance and received her chief encantado, Rompe Mato. Announcing that he had come to try to resolve the family conflict, Rompe Mato invited everyone into the adjoining room where the altar was located to discuss the situation. Nazaré had refused to speak to Zita but had no objection to speaking to Rompe Mato. She and her daughter were soon locked in indirect battle, not speaking to each other, but detailing their mutual grievances to Rompe Mato and all other adults present. As it became clear that Rompe Mato would be unable to restore harmony between mother and daughter or even to end the on-going combat, a second encantado arrived. The hostess, Clara, had been seated near the altar, putting in a word now and then, trying to moderate the dispute. Then she fell silent, began to grimace, closed her eyes tightly, trembled, and went into trance. She sang the first two lines of one of Japetequara's doctrines to make it clear which of her spirits had descended. Her daughter at once brought a candle, placed it on the altar, and lit it. Japetequara was not only of higher rank than Rompe Mato, but he was also regarded as the "owner" of the house, since he was Clara's chief encantado. Japetequara at once took charge of the situation. He offered words of consolation to Nazaré (who burst into tears when Japetequara greeted her) but also urged her to accept the situation and let her daughter "follow her own road." The daughter, Nair, and her friend, Zita (whose encantado, Rompe Mato, left her a short time after Clara went into trance), were given short lectures by Japetequara, urged to conduct themselves beyond reproach, and then sent on their way. The American visitors were also dismissed, and thus peace was restored to Clara's house.

Cult members believe that their chief encantados are always concerned about maintaining harmony within their families and, if other tactics fail, may lose patience and kill a disruptive family member. Clara believes that it was Japetequara who killed her husband, Nonato, who was always "half-unbelieving" about the cult. Nonato never did anything for the encantados, never purchasing as much as a handkerchief for any of them, and he quarreled continually with Clara over her participation in the activities of the *terreiros*. It is Clara's opinion that Japetequara tried for thirty years to educate Nonato and reconcile him to the cult, but, finally recognizing the futility of further effort, killed Nonato suddenly while he was enjoying himself at a party.

Sometimes the medium herself may petition her encantado to take drastic action with a troublesome member of the family. Ione, the thirty-year-old daughter of the *mãe de santo* Marina, has long been a source of embarrassment, pain, and disgust to her mother. Ione has many faults, but the most serious is her habit of going off on drunken sprees. Marina's anger with her daughter's misconduct reached the breaking point at the time of a *festa* for St. John the Baptist. Since St. John is the favorite saint of Marina's chief encantado, Dom João, this festival is the largest and most important of the year for Marina. Throughout the morning of the saint's day Marina was busy supervising the decoration of the *terreiro,* the cooking of the food to be served to participants and selected guests, and other last-minute preparations. About noon Ione was carried in, drunk, covered with mud, and wearing shorts (felt to be extremely immodest apparel for a mature woman). Marina was so angry that she went into the chapel, lit a candle, and prayed to Dom João and to all the encantados to take her daughter from her. Within one year, she prayed, she wanted to be crying over her daughter's corpse. If Dom João and the other encantados were unwilling to take her daughter, she requested that they take her, since she could not bear to live any longer with such a burden.

Not only are the encantados expected to be dominant figures in the kind of dramatic situation we have been describing, but they are also expected to be involved in mundane, day-to-day decisions. Ordinarily a medium does not take a trip, make any important purchase, sponsor a ceremony, have the house repaired, or do anything else of significance, without first consulting an encantado. Since the medium is supposedly unconscious while the spirit is possessing his body, direct communication between the medium and the encantado during possession is precluded. But there are several indirect ways of getting the supernatural's views on a given question. Most commonly, perhaps, the medium lights a candle at his shrine or altar, then outlines the problem and asks the encantado to send a response. The answer sometimes comes in a dream, or the encantado may possess the medium and leave a message with some member of the medium's household. Children, especially daughters, are the most likely intermediaries in such cases, and they dutifully wait until their mothers have come out of trance and then repeat the message the encantado has just given them. Another related technique is to provide the child with a query ahead of time, so that when the mother becomes possessed the child is ready to present the question to the encantado.

There is a more direct way of communicating with an encantado. Although it has perhaps not been made explicit, more than one individual may receive the same encantado. Not at the same time, of course, since the encantados are conceived of as being non-divisible, but on different occasions. It is consequently feasible for a devotee of the encantado Mariana, for example, to seek out another medium who receives this spirit, and after the medium has become possessed by Mariana, to speak to the encantado directly. Although it might seem that this would be the simplest way of contacting one's encantado, in fact this approach is not popular. It seems to be used only when the two mediums are good friends, or at least trust one another, and this rarely occurs. As will be pointed out later, there is often a great deal of jealousy and suspicion manifested between mediums who receive the same encantado, to the point that one medium may even attempt to cast doubt on the authenticity of the possession of the other. Where such hostility occurs, messages from the supernatural via one medium would not be given much credence by the other.

A consideration of the ways in which the encantados are believed to intervene in the daily lives of their devotees would be incomplete without a discussion of supernatural punishment. As has been indicated, Batuque members interpret many of the fortunate things that happen to them as being due to the solicitous care of their supernatural guardians. The logical obverse of such a belief is the idea that many of the unfortunate things that happen to them are punishment inflicted by the same supernatural beings. When adversity strikes, cult members are inclined to first consider the possibility that they have in some way offended their encantados and are consequently being punished.

The actions that the encantados are thought to punish are primarily connected with obligations or the failure to follow the law of the cult. Except in unusual circumstances, the Batuque spirits are expected to be indifferent to infractions of the moral code of the larger society. Robbery, theft, murder, assault, and incest are regarded as major crimes that merit imprisonment or other retribution by civil authorities, and that will also be punished by the Christian supernaturals. Malicious falsehood, dishonesty, quarrelsomeness, disrespect to parents, neglect of children, friendship with bad companions, excessive consumption of alcohol—all are regarded as serious personal shortcomings and are generally condemned. However, none of these activities is thought to bring punishment by the encantados. In the case of the second list, this is quite reasonable, since many of the encantados are believed to have one or more of these same shortcomings.

The attitudes of Batuque members toward sexual behavior are typical of lower-class Brazilians. Chastity in women until marriage is highly regarded, but the loss of virginity is usually accepted rather philosophically. One cult member calmly explained that she would very much like to have a photograph of her thirteen-year-old daughter in her confirmation dress as a "bride" since by the time the girl did marry she would probably no longer be entitled to dress in white. Unwed mothers face little social disapproval unless their pregnancy is the result of numerous casual affairs rather than one fairly long-term one. Similarly adultery is condemned as such only if the relationship is a casual one. If a man and woman live together monogamously for any length of time, their relationship is regarded as thoroughly respectable, though unsanctioned by law or church. If the relationship between the individuals concerned is fairly stable, even bigamy is accepted, although it is regarded as inherently ridiculous. One case of bigamy involving cult members, where the husband did not maintain a separate household for the second wife, but all lived together, was regarded as both hilarious and in poor taste, but not as particularly sinful.

Deviant sexual behavior such as homosexuality is deplored and generally ridiculed, but is not regarded as a crime that merits societal intervention. "I don't know if it is a sin or a sickness," commented one informant. In general the feeling in the cult seemed to be that homosexuality, like alcoholism, contained within itself its own chastisement. Nor is prostitution regarded by cult members as either a crime or clearly sinful; rather it is viewed for the most part as a particularly unpleasant and difficult method of earning a living. As will be indicated in the next chapter, both homosexuals and prostitutes are active cult members, recognized as the chosen instruments of important encantados. Homosexuals are always subject to an undercurrent of ridicule, but no particular hostility is expressed toward prostitutes if they obey the rules of the sect. Owners of brothels are rather admired as self-made, successful business women; they and smugglers figure prominently among the more prosperous supporters of *terreiros*.

Although encantados are generally believed to be interested only in the ritual behavior of their mediums, not all Batuque members are willing to accept this idea, and even those who do sometimes show a certain amount of ambivalence. In one of the numerous interviews we had with women who were in trance, we asked our informant Justina if the spirits would punish a medium who was immoral. Justina, speaking as the encantado Dona Rosalina, ansered, "The private lives of the mediums do not interest us." But when we asked if she would accept a thief as a *filho,* Dona Rosalina said she would not, because it would reflect on her reputation. When pressed, most members of the Batuque will agree, as did Justina. that the encantados do disapprove of major human delicts and will probably manifest their displeasure in some way. To the degree that cult centers are influenced by ideas from Umbanda, there is an increasing emphasis on the close association of encantados and Christian morality. Some cult leaders, for example, may interrupt ceremonies to deliver long exhortations in which the Christian ideals of faith, hope, and charity are stressed. But when formal statements of beliefs and inspirational generalizations are ignored, and one considers the stories that mediums tell to illustrate supernatural retribution, the connection between the Batuque spirits and morals appears to be very tenuous.

In these stories the encantados seem to ignore infractions of the moral code of society but are swift to punish violations of the law of the Batuque. This law is neither learned nor taught as a coherent body of regulations but is always presented piecemeal as the moral of specific stories. Each developed medium seems to have his own stories, some based on personal experiences, others derived from the accounts of others. Whenever questions of doctrine arise, the stories that have bearing on the issue are recalled and told, usually at length—many of our informants could go on for hours. In the examples that appear below, it should be pointed out that it is highly unlikely that any of the events recounted happened in exactly the way they are described. All of these stories have been adapted to illustrate a point of doctrine, and the facts have undoubtedly often suffered in the process.

The methods used by encantados to punish cult members are varied. The simplest and most straightforward is corporal punishment. The disciplining encantado possesses the offending medium and forces him to kneel and repeatedly beat his hands on the special punishment stone that some *terreiros* have for this purpose or, lacking a stone, on the floor of the *terreiro* near the drums. When forced to punish themselves in this fashion, mediums do not simply go through the motions of smacking the floor; Justina showed us a crooked finger that she had broken years before while hitting the punishment stone. This form of punishment may also take place in the home. Clara reported that she was often forced to kneel and beat the floor by the encantado José Tupinambá, who often took it upon himself to keep her in line.

Another form of corporal punishment attributed to the encantados is the *jogada* (literally, thrown, here the act of being thrown down). When entering or leaving trance, mediums often fall down. This is interpreted as a deliberate act on the part of the encantado, who "throws" the medium down. There are two kinds of *jogadas*. In the less serious type, the encantado throws the medium on the floor or against hard objects, often with such violence that the medium is bruised. In the more serious type of *jogada*, the encantado not only throws his devotee down but leaves him in a coma. In other words, in cult theory, the medium's own spirit, for some reason, does not re-enter his body nor does any other encantado take possession, and the body is left without a spirit.

The first type of *jogada* may sometimes be attributed to the fact that the spirit did not "get a good hold" on the medium's body.

The spirits sometimes "throw" their mediums when taking leave. Here a woman, possessed by the mermaid spirit Jamaína, dances serenely one moment . . .
and a few seconds later falls flat on her face on the cement floor as Jamaína departs.

This might be due to a lack of development on the medium's part or perhaps a failure to complete some ritual obligation. In addition, certain spirits are considered to be by nature temperamental and malicious and simply enjoy throwing down their mediums.

But the medium might also be thrown down as a form of punishment. Clara, for example, one year violated the very strict cult rule against participation in *carnaval* (the three-day festivities prior to Lent) while wearing a mask. Cult members may join in the dancing of impromptu street groups or may dance as members of organized samba groups, providing their encantados do not object. But at no time may the medium wear a mask. Clara reported that one year she ignored this rule and went out dancing in the streets, wearing a mask with a large nose. A few days later, while participating in a *festa* honoring St. Lazarus and the encantado Akossi-Sapata, her own encantado, Japetequara, seized her and threw her down so hard that she was knocked unconscious. Her head had struck a drum, and when she came to Clara discovered that she had a large bump on her forehead. Other participants said the bump looked like a chicken's beak, but Clara realized that Japetequara had duplicated the false nose she had worn during *carnaval* as a sign of his displeasure. The *pai de santo* Antônio was fond of relating how his encantado Joãozinho threw him down a well head first. The encantado was offended because the day before Antônio had stacked several cases of beer destined for a secular dance on the floor of the *terreiro,* thus violating the rule that only alcoholic beverages intended for ceremonial use should be brought into the *terreiro.* A medium may also suddenly be thrown down by his encantado outside a ceremonial setting. After a bitter quarrel with her husband over her participation in the cult, Joana announced she would burn her encantado's clothes and finish with the Batuque, once and for all. She had barely gathered together the costumes of her encantado, Averekete, when he seized her and threw her across the room with such force that she cracked her head against the wall.

The other type of *jogada,* when the medium is left lying in a coma, is usually ascribed to a fit of explosive rage on the part of the encantado involved. Some encantados are thought to be dangerously temperamental and may have a temper tantrum simply because the other participants in a ceremony fail to sing the responses correctly or fail to show proper deference to the encantado. It may not be the medium who is at fault at all. However, encantados can also be provoked into one of their fits by a medium's misconduct. Isolda, for example, began to neglect her obligations to her chief encantado, Goiabeira, when she became interested in cultivating the good will of another encantado, Tranca Rua. As punishment for the neglect, Goiabeira caused Isolda's husband to desert her, and he himself withdrew, refusing to possess her. Very much upset, Isolda asked the help of another devotee of Goiabeira, who, on behalf of Isolda, petitioned Goiabeira to return, possess Isolda, and explain what must be done to make amends. The petition was granted and Goiabeira descended to possess Isolda. While in possession he ranted and raved about how he had been neglected, but finally promised to bring the wandering husband back home. In a final burst of peevishness and resentment, Goiabeira then threw Isolda down, leaving her in a coma. It was very difficult to rouse her, but she was restored to her senses shortly before her husband returned. Goiabeira had kept his promise.

Some encantados are hypersensitive about their dignity and might deem simple corporal punishment insufficient chastisement for mediums who have personally insulted them in some way. The misfortunes of Tito illustrate the somewhat indirect but drastic punitive measures that an offended encantado might resort to. Tito was first prepared in Belém years ago, but then went to Rio de Janeiro, where he had all of his Belém encantados "taken out of his head" and replaced by other encantados from southern Brazil. When he finally returned to Belém, Tito spoke scornfully of the local encantados, in particular stating that his former *chefe,* Jarina, had the face of a monkey. Jarina soon took revenge by possessing Tito and going on a three-day drinking spree, during which time she did not allow Tito to sleep or to eat and forced him to visit the homes of female cult members, remove his clothes, and parade around nude. At the end of the third day, Jarina, still possessing Tito, "borrowed" a radio from the home of an acquaintance. The theft landed Tito in jail.

Instead of directly administering the punishment while possessing the offending medium, as in the above examples, encantados can, it is believed, cause other things to happen that will make the medium suffer. An encantado might move someone else to beat up his devotee instead of forcing the medium to beat the punishment stone. Rosa, a prostitute, was badly beaten up by one of her customers after she committed the error of dancing in a *Boi-bumbá festa* (a regional folk festival) without first getting the permission of her encantado, Ubirajara. Edna decided to stop dancing in *batuques* when she began living with a man who opposed her participation. Ever since she stopped fulfilling her obligations, her life has been miserable. She is sick half the time, and the man she lives with frequently beats her up.

Edna's offense, cult members feel, is perhaps the most serious a medium can commit—the refusal to continue working as a medium or the refusal to develop as one after receiving some clear sign from the supernatural sphere that one has been chosen by an encantado. Unemployment, sickness, insomnia, desertion by family members or lovers, accidents, even sudden death may be arranged by encantados as retribution for a medium's decision to "close his body." Almost every cult member could cite several examples, drawn from his own circle of relatives and acquaintances, of sudden disaster striking someone who refused to continue as a medium, or who was, for some reason, unable to develop his mediumistic gifts. Thus Mimi recalls that when she was a child, her older brother, then fifteen, was one day dramatically possessed by an encantado. Her parents, who were "very Catholic," refused to allow him to go to a *terreiro* to be prepared. A short time later, though he had not been ill, he suddenly died; it was assumed that the encantados had carried away his spirit. In a parallel case, Conceição's younger sister was stricken with incurable blindness when, as an adolescent, she was possessed by an encantado but was not allowed to develop as a medium by their mother. When Justina was nine years old her mother, an experienced medium, announced that she was through with the cult. Two days later, she dropped dead at the age of twenty-nine. Justina reports that she herself suffered a great deal when she was young and rebellious and made repeated attempts to stop receiving her spirits. On one occasion, in a gesture of defiance, Justina burned all of the ceremonial clothes belonging to her chief, Dona Rosalina. Within a short time she lost her job in a factory, was deserted by her lover, had to sell or pawn all of her possessions, and was left with nothing more than the clothes on her back. Rosalina is not an encantado to be trifled with.

It is striking with what enthusiasm and satisfaction these stories are told by cult members. They clearly consider the stories proofs of the great power, living presence, and ready intervention of encantados in the affairs of man. No informant scored the unfairness of the spirits, even when punishment fell on some innocent person rather than on the offending individual. It would appear that fairness and loving kindness are simply not attributes to be expected of the encantados.

But irascible and arbitrary as the encantados may be, they are still conceived of as open to argument. One can reason with them, attempt to dissuade them from following a certain course of action, or persuade them to follow an alternate course. The medium who wishes to stop receiving his spirits without suffering supernatural punishment can often personally negotiate permission to stop or can go to a cult leader for help. The cult leader will perform a ceremony to withdraw the spirits. The encantados involved may not always consent to withdraw, in which case the medium will suffer if he ignores his obligations to the spirits. The encantados may at first consent to withdraw but later change their minds and return. This happened to Lourdes, whose father is a curer in a country village near Belém. Lourdes began receiving spirits at the age of five or six and worked with her father at his curing sessions. As she grew older, Lourdes became dissatisfied and unhappy with her role at curing sessions, primarily because "boys don't like mediums." When she was sixteen she petitioned her encantados for permission to stop receiving them, and her father performed a ritual to facilitate the withdrawal of the spirits. All went well for the next six years (except that Lourdes did not find a husband). At age twenty-two she suddenly lost her good health and had one ailment after another. Her father and other curers in the area diagnosed her difficulty as disturbance by the encantados who had changed their minds and wanted Lourdes to serve as a medium again. Since participation in curing sessions did not seem to help Lourdes, her father decided her spirits wanted her to work in a *terreiro* and brought Lourdes to Belém to be treated by a Batuque cult leader.

Instead of refusing to receive his encantados entirely, a medium may wish to limit the trances to certain times and places. Bargains are sometimes made between encantado and devotee providing for possession only within the privacy of the home. Mediums may also find it necessary to regulate the behavior of their carouser encantados if these spirits drink excessively or behave in an exceptionally boisterous or improper manner. In such a case the medium may negotiate with his chief encantado for advice and help in controlling the carouser, or he may accept the advice of a cult leader that the carouser be "baptized" and thus tamed. Carousers subjected to these pressures may obligingly moderate their drinking (except for occasional backsliding), or they may refuse to possess the medium again.

One type of bargain that is frequently negotiated between cult members and encantados involves minor children. As a general rule, most parents do not want their children to become active mediums until they are adult or close to adulthood, since working with the encantados is time-consuming and interferes with the child's education. In addition, child mediums are often difficult for parents to manage, since the child belongs to a supernatural being whose desires must take precedence over parental wishes, and the encantado's commands are revealed by the possessed child himself. If children show signs of unusual sensitivity to the call of the drums, parents may try to keep them from attending ceremonies. Should an encantado "seize" a child in spite of precautions, the parents can still petition the encantado for a respite. The spirit will be asked to let the child alone for a specific period of time, perhaps five or ten years, to allow the child to grow up. In exchange, the parents promise to themselves furnish the necessary offerings of food, drink, and candles. If the encantado agrees to such a contract, the child is expected to show no further evidence of close affinity with the spirit world until the contract term has expired.

Although most of their religious life is directed toward the encantados rather than toward the Christian supernaturals, the great majority of cult members in Belém consider themselves to be Roman Catholics. Most realize, of course, that the beliefs of the Batuque do not coincide exactly with Catholic theology, but few cult members see any basic or irreconcilable contradictions. They know that the priests do not accept their beliefs about the encantados, but they are convinced that in this respect the priests are simply mistaken. For most, the theology of the Batuque represents an additional set of beliefs superimposed on basic Christian truths; it does not replace or negate those truths.

Only a few cult members believe that the Batuque represents a

Very few children are mediums. This eleven-year-old girl, possessed by Pena Verde, is an exception.

religion that is quite distinct from Catholicism. One of these is João, the president of the newly organized Federation of Afro-Brazilian Cults, who chided fellow cult leader Marina for ordering a mass for St. Benedict when she was going to fête the encantado Averekete. "You should not be ordering masses," João told her. "We are not Catholics." Marina, whose attitude is more typical, reported that she was deeply shocked and replied that João and the rest of the federation could do as they liked, but she would continue in the way she was brought up. "The saints help us and deserve masses and *ladainhas*," Marina observed. "The encantados take care of us, and they have their *batuques*."

The extent of actual participation by cult members in the established ritual of the Catholic Church varies greatly. A few stated they attended mass at least once a week, more claimed to go once a month, others reported they went only once or twice a year, and some observed that they never went inside a church except for baptisms and funerals. Nor are all of the children of cult members given formal religious instruction in the Catholic faith, since most are enrolled in the state public schools rather than in parochial schools, and parents do not always insist on the learning of the catechism. The girls in a family, however, usually are formally confirmed in the church, and in preparation for confirmation learn some of the catechism, but boys often omit this sacrament.

The only Catholic sacrament that cult members appear to regard as necessary is the sacrament of baptism. All infants are taken at some time during their first year to a church to be baptized by a priest. Sometimes babies are taken to a *terreiro* for a second baptism with a cult leader officiating and with encantados incarnate in cult members serving as the godparents. Occasionally a cult member who is possessed by an encantado accompanies the mother and child to a church to serve as godparent. In these cases the priest who performs the ceremony is not informed that one of the participants is in trance.

We witnessed one baptism in church in which the encantado Japetequara served as godfather to the infant son of Lucia. Japetequara possessed his medium, Clara, before the party started for the church. Certain complications had been foreseen and provided for. Clara herself, in her pure state, was to serve as the baby's godmother. The priest could not be expected to understand how one person could be both godfather and godmother at the same time, nor, of course, would he be likely to accept a disembodied spirit as godparent anyway. To avoid conflict, a neighbor man was asked to stand in as godfather. The ceremony went smoothly. Eleven other babies were being baptized at the same time, and the young priest officiating never noticed the broad grins of Lucia and her guests or the fierce scowls of Clara (Japetequara said several times that he did not like churches). The neighbor's name was entered on the baptismal certificate as godfather, but as far as he, Lucia, and Clara were concerned, the real godfather was Japetequara. If the baby survives the dysentery from which it was suffering as as well as other hazards of infancy, it will grow up with an encantado as godfather.

Though never heard criticizing Catholic doctrine, cult members occasionally do express some hostility to the clergy as officials of the Church. "I don't like priests" was usually the only explanation given for infrequent attendance at mass. The Brazilian motion picture *Pagador de Promessas* (released in the United States under the title *The Given Word*), which portrays a priest who is unsympathetic to the Afro-Brazilian cults, was cited by cult members as evidence of how some priests "fight" the Batuque. One informant insisted that neither St. Barbara nor St. George were recognized as saints by the priests (this was some years before the Vatican pronouncement questioning these and other saints). "St. Barbara and St. George are *ours*," she stated with much the same kind of pride with which Brazilians announce that the country's petroleum resources belong to them rather than to foreign exploiters. Other cult members reported that priests sometimes ask whether the images of saints they have been asked to bless are going to be used in *macumba*, implying that they could not be blessed for use in the cult. Those mediums who did take their own or the *terreiro*'s images to a church for a priest's blessing regarded such clerical suspicion as amusing and apparently invariably gave noncommittal or evasive replies; no one reported any difficulty in obtaining the desired blessing. Not all cult members felt that such a priestly blessing was at all necessary, since they believed that some of the more "elevated" encantados were capable of bestowing a blessing on the images that was as good as that of a priest.

The Catholicism of Batuque members is a folk Catholicism that is largely independent of the official Church. As far as Batuque members are concerned, the Christian supernaturals are honored in the *terreiros*, and the believer need not have recourse to churches to fulfill most of his obligations as a Christian. The official clergy are not really necessary for Catholic devotions. The lengthy prayers that precede the major *festas* in a *terreiro* are occasionally led by the cult leader, but more frequently by some neighborhood woman who has a local reputation for knowledge of the prayers and skill in leading them. Fairly elaborate processions through the streets of the neighborhood in honor of a saint are organized by cult leaders without clerical assistance or prior consent.

Mediums must, as individuals, honor the saint who is adored by their chief encantado, and, as indicated above, usually place an image or picture of this saint on the private shrines in their homes. However, they are also free to venerate any other saints that they particularly like, to pray to them, and to enter into contracts with them. Thus, when Mauvina's husband was jailed after being involved in a fight, she prayed for aid to St. Sebastian, a saint she has always been fond of, rather than to St. George, the saint favored by her encantado, Rompe Mato. Mauvina asked St. Sebastian to

A medium's twelve-year-old daughter, who has just received first communion in a Catholic church, poses in front of the religious shrine that is actually much more important in her life—her mother's altar. The door in the woodwork below provides access to the bowls containing the sacred stones of the encantados.

get her husband out of jail, vowing to hold a *ladainha* for him on his day, January 20, if he would do so. St. Sebastian soon heeded her request, her husband was freed, and she has kept her vow every year since that date. This has involved considerable expense, since everyone who attends the service in her home must be served refreshments after the prayers are concluded. In a similar case, when Zuzu was having a difficult time in childbirth, she turned to St. Benedict for help rather than to Our Lady of Conception, the saint preferred by her chief female encantado, Navéroaim. Zuzu became convinced, as her labor became more and more prolonged, that both she and the unborn baby would die. She asked the midwife attending her to place St. Benedict's image on her abdomen, and she prayed to him to help her, vowing that the baby would be named after the saint and be taught to adore him. A few minutes after her prayer, her son was born.

The Catholic saints, as these stories demonstrate, are expected to respond to direct petitions of the laity without any clerical intercession. They are also expected to grant assistance without regard to the individual's participation or non-participation in the rites and sacraments of the Church.

The indifference shown by cult members to the sacraments of the Church is undoubtedly connected with a lack of interest within the cult in what has been the central concern of Christianity—the salvation of souls from eternal damnation. As a religion, the Batuque, like the other Afro-Brazilian cults, is not notably otherworldly. It is primarily concerned with coping with the problems that beset the living; the possible trials and tribulations of the dead excite little speculation.

There is no consensus of opinion among cult members about the afterlife. All agree that the souls of the dead can harass the living and that the souls of deceased infants and very young children go to be with the angels, but beyond these two beliefs there is little agreement about what precisely happens to the soul after death. Three different views on the subject were discernible in discussions with individual cult members.

The cult members who have been most influenced by the doctrines of Umbanda are inclined to accept what might be called the spiritualist conception of eternity. In their view, hell does not exist and access to heaven is virtually impossible. After death all souls rise into space for an indefinite period, pending reassignment. Only a tiny fraction of the most elevated and saintly souls win access to heaven to live with God and the angels. Those souls (in greater number but still a small minority) who have, on the whole, lived good lives while on earth, practicing charity and showing love for their fellow men, are awarded the privilege of accompanying the hosts of "guides" and encantados in their travels about the universe as they fight the forces of evil in this world and on other planets. These are the "spirits of light" who descend at spiritualist séances to give treatments, information, and comfort to the living. But by far the great majority of souls do not qualify for this honor. Instead they must remain drifting in space, often suffering pain, cold, loneliness, until they are reincarnated, i.e., assigned to a newborn infant and thus born again into the world to again face the hazards and opportunities that are the lot of mortal flesh. The process of reincarnation is repeated over and over until the soul finally attains eligibility to be a spirit of light.

This belief in reincarnation was explicity rejected by those cult members, probably a majority, who were inclined to a more basically Christian view of the afterlife. Insisting that newborn infants are given a completely new soul by God, never an old one, the cult members who accept the Christian interpretation point out that children never volunteer any information about any previous life. The ordinary destiny of the soul after death, according to this second school of thought, is assignment to either heaven or hell. "We all have a body which is material and a soul which is a spirit," explained Zuzu. "When a person dies, the soul leaves the body here and goes into space. There St. Michael weighs the soul. Everything the person has done on earth has been noted down in heaven. Jesus takes a note of everything done—every single little thing! St. Michael weighs the soul to see if the good the person has done weighs more than the bad." If a soul's good works outweigh its evil, it is admitted to heaven; if the reverse is true, it is sent to hell. Should the good and evil balance, the soul must stay in space indefinitely. It is these souls from space that come down at spiritualist séances. The souls in hell and in heaven never return.

According to this viewpoint, the encantados have no power at all over human beings once they have died. They cannot intercede to save their mediums from hell or get them admitted to heaven;

they have no influence with St. Michael or with Jesus. Nor can they rescue a medium's soul from space and take it with them to an *encantaria*. The only humans ever admitted to an *encantaria* are those who are taken there while still alive, "body and all." This is thought to happen sometimes. A person suddenly vanishes and though a search is made for years, no trace of him is ever discovered. He has been carried off to an *encantaria* and after living there for seven years will be able to appear on earth as an encantado, but under a new name. However, if the body of the person who disappeared is ever found, one can be sure that he simply died and was not carried off, for the encantados, as living beings who have never died, will have nothing to do with dead souls.

The third opinion about the afterworld insists on the continued close association of encantados and their human devotees after death. According to cult members who subscribed to this view, the souls of deceased mediums are taken by their encantado owners to the *encantarias* beneath the surface of the earth and sea. Here they must remain for a minimum of five years, after which they might be permitted to rise and return to earth as encantados under new names. During the period in the *encantaria,* the medium's soul is punished for the sins it committed as a person on earth. If the medium's life was very sinful, he might never be allowed to leave the *encantaria.* Little is known about the forms of punishment used in the *encantaria,* for the encantados never tell and very few mediums who are taken to see an *encantaria* ever return. But a few mediums claim to have had this experience. Isabel, for example, was taken by Rompe Mato in a dream to visit the *encantaria* of Japetequara. There she saw Joana Pipiri, a recently deceased medium, taking care of the many small children of the encantados; the task was apparently her punishment. Isabel also observed Laurinho, the son of a former cult leader, sitting quite still in a chair. He reported that he had not stirred out of that chair since he had died four years previously. The unpleasant immobility was his punishment for his unfortunately numerous sins.

Only the souls of mediums, however, go to *encantarias.* "Catholics do not go there," said Clara, "nor do Protestants. Only those who have an encantado to carry them can get there." The destiny of all the souls of non-mediums is uncertain. Perhaps some might reach heaven, though few have the power to get that far. Perhaps some go to hell, if there is a hell. "I don't think hell exists," commented Clara. "I think hell is here in this world, because when a person does evil, he pays here. They say that hell is the place of the Exus, but I don't believe it because hell is here and the Exus are there down below."

Though in disagreement about reincarnation, the existence of hell, and the power of encantados over the dead, the three schools of thought do agree on the difficulty of attaining heaven. No one felt that membership in the cult or the achievement of the status of a developed medium was any guarantee of reaching heaven or eternal bliss. But no one felt that the established Christian Churches could provide any certain passport to heaven either. Fulfillment of all of the good works prescribed by the Church might fail to prepare a soul for heaven. Pedro Costa told of his aunt who was "very Catholic" during her lifetime; she went to mass every day and she devoted all the time and money she could spare to church-sponsored charities and to the maintenance of the church itself. But some months after she died, her spirit descended at a spiritualist séance that Pedro was attending, possessing another medium at the table as a "suffering soul" that moaned and sobbed a great deal. To make certain that it was actually the spirit of his aunt, Pedro first questioned the spirit about family details. Then he asked why she, who had led such an exemplary Christian life, should be suffering so after death. "Ah," sighed the spirit of his aunt, "everything I did was for show; it was not from the heart."

At the bottom of the supernatural ladder, so to speak, are the souls of the dead. Batuque members accept the idea that the souls of the dead can contact the living, but since the souls are thought to have little or no power, they are not considered to be very important. The proper place for the souls of the dead to make their appearance is at a *mesa de espiritismo* (spiritualist séance). In some *terreiros* a séance is held every week, the idea being that if the souls have a chance to express themselves periodically, they will not harass the living or try to possess mediums at other ceremonies. A few men and women are equally at home receiving encantados or souls of the dead and may participate in both *batuques* and *mesas de espiritismo,* but most mediums do either one or the other. Those who dance in *batuques,* in fact, often have a deep aversion to the souls of the dead and consider possession by them to be highly undesirable. On the other hand, it is taken as a matter of course that some encantados will appear at séances, apparently not sharing the aversion to association with the dead that some of their mediums evince.

Some of the souls who appear at séances are those of people who have recently died and who wish to leave messages of comfort and reassurance to the friends and relatives they have left behind. But the greatest number of spirits that appear belong to the category called the "suffering souls," the unhappy ghosts that drift through space pending reincarnation or some other final disposition. If one of these suffering souls takes possession of a living person outside of a séance, it is thought to create all manner of difficulties, but when they descend in séances, the suffering souls are simply a nuisance. They usually sob uncontrollably instead of answering questions put to them by the president of the séance and have to be ordered repeatedly to go in peace to outer space before they heed the command.

At some *terreiros,* especially those where ideas from Umbanda have caught on, more stress is placed on receiving benefits from the souls of the dead. The souls called the "spirits of light" are encouraged to appear. As indicated above, these spirits are thought to be the souls of saintly individuals who during their lifetime were dedicated to the service of suffering humanity. Some of them were physicians, teachers, religious or political leaders, or old servants or slaves who were learned in folk medicine. The high point of the séance occurs after a number of these spirits have arrived and possessed their mediums. The mediums then give *passes* to members of the audience, i.e., mediums make wiping motions, which are thought to withdraw evil influences.

However, spectators who attend séances to obtain *passes* often show greater desire to receive them from the encantados that have descended than from the spirits of light. Informants stated that the encantados who appeared at spiritualist séances were "working in the star current" (*corrente astral*), an area of operation quite distinct from that of *batuques* and curing sessions, and one which all encantados did not find congenial.

Asked to explain the difference between the souls of the dead and the encantados, Zuzu appeared struck by the inanity of the question. "The encantados are not *dead*," she exclaimed. "They are *living!*" The distinction is a crucial one. In the conceptual scheme of the Batuque there is an immediacy about the encantados that is not shared by any of the other supernatural beings. As living creatures with a sensory apparatus that registers pain, pleasure, boredom, rage, disgust, pride, and all the other sensations that humans have, the encantados have a far more intimate understanding of human nature than the saints or other supernaturals could possibly have. Their support is all the more to be valued.

FOOTNOTES

1. This term is also used for the deities in Candomblés de Caboclo of Bahia and in the Catimbó cults of the Northeast (Carneiro 1937, 1961; Bastide 1960, pp. 241–54).

2. Herskovits (1948, pp. 553–54) took the position that in all of the Afro-American religions the African deities were "identified" with the Christian saints. The exact nature of this identification, however, is rarely spelled out in the literature. See Bastide (1960, pp. 362–87) for a discussion of some of the issues involved.

Chapter IV

The Believers

Most studies of the African-derived religions in the New World lack specific detail about the ordinary believers who support, rather than direct, the religious centers. For several reasons investigators have spent most research time with cult leaders. The leaders are not only more knowledgeable about doctrine and ritual, but also much more approachable, since they are accustomed to dealing with strangers. Followers tend to be more reserved, if not excessively timid, and, even after some of the social barriers are breached, often prove to be rather inarticulate about their religious beliefs.

The leaders of the Batuque, however, were not in all respects ideal informants, since they were occupationally given to magnifying their personal role in ritual activities and grossly exaggerating both the numbers and the submissiveness of their followers. In addition, the leaders were likely to have read books about African-derived religions elsewhere in Brazil and were strongly inclined to substitute the ideal for the reality when explaining the Batuque to literate outside investigators. From the beginning of our study, therefore, we made an effort to get to know rank-and-file members of the Batuque and to check what the leaders said about doctrine against what the followers appeared to actually believe, just as we checked what leaders said about ritual by repeated observation of ceremonies.

One idea that leaders and followers consistently agreed upon was that the Batuque in Belém had expanded considerably in recent years and daily gained new adherents. It is very difficult, however, to verify such an impression and to determine just how many individuals do belong to the Batuque. If we define "belonging" in terms of active participation in ceremonies and more or less regular trance experiences, the number of members is relatively small. If, on the other hand, we include as members all those who share beliefs in the encantados, the number of believers in the city is considerable.

There are no public documents that contain membership records or even estimates of membership. The Afro-Brazilian cults are not recognized as comprising a separate denomination by census authorities, and all members are listed in census data as Catholics (Willems 1966, p. 207). Since the overwhelming majority of Batuque believers do, in fact, consider themselves to be good Catholics, the classification practices of census officials are not unwarranted.

It is possible that eventually there will be a record of active cult members. A local Federation of Afro-Brazilian Cults (described in more detail in Chapter VII) was organized in August 1964 and undertook the task of registering every active member of the Batuque in the city. One year after its foundation, when we revisited Belém, not all of the curers and cult leaders in the municipal district had as yet paid their dues and completed their registrations, and relatively few rank-and-file members had registered. However, if the federation expands the legal and social services offered its membership, it is possible that its rolls will eventually include a higher proportion of the active cult members in the city.

In the absence of any official data one can only estimate the numbers of believers through actual observation of cult centers. The most readily identifiable cult members are, of course, those who wear costumes, dance, and enter trance states; an estimate of their number is given below. In addition to such visibly committed believers, the Batuque is sustained by an indeterminate number of more passive believers who demonstrate their faith in the existence of the encantados without themselves ever experiencing a trance.

One method of supporting the religion is to attend the public ceremonies regularly. Cult leaders definitely welcome an audience and for major festivals may even send out printed invitations or advertise the ceremony on the radio, in the newspapers, or over the loudspeaker at the nearest bar or shopping area. Participating mediums are invariably appreciative of a large turnout of spectators, and one way of ridiculing a rival cult center is to suggest that few spectators attend its ceremonies. A *batuque* is primarily designed to enable mediums to receive their spirits, but it is also definitely a public performance. The descent of immortal spirits into the world would lose poignancy if no ordinary mortal witnessed the event.

Although their physical presence at a ceremony may contribute something to sustaining the cult, not all spectators are believers. Undoubtedly at every ceremony there are some spectators who have come simply to see a free show, to watch the dancing and the gyrations of mediums as they fall into trance states. Other spectators come to ceremonies primarily for social reasons, to exchange greetings and gossip with acquaintances, or, in the case of the young, to flirt with the opposite sex.

But irrespective of possible social and recreational inducements for attendance, the majority of spectators clearly share most of the beliefs of the dancers, watch possessions with apparent interest, comment knowledgeably on procedures, and obey the rules for spectators without admonition. These rules are simple. Smoking is prohibited inside the pavilion but permissible in the chapel or outside the side railing of the pavilion. Everyone in the audience who has a seat must stand during the opening and closing ceremonies and during the Exu ceremony at midnight. All spectators, whether seated or standing, must carefully refrain from crossing either legs or arms throughout the ceremony.

Nothing else is ever asked of members of the audience; they are never exhorted to make any declaration of faith or to participate in any communal ritual. Occasionally, if the supply is plentiful, select members of the audience are invited to partake in ritual "obligations," when sacred foods or beverages are communally consumed by cult members. All spectators are welcome to join in the religious processions for the saints and the *ladainhas* (a prayer and hymn service to a saint) that are sometimes held before a *batuque* begins. Participation in the prayers or processions is entirely voluntary; the audience is never exhorted to join in. Occasionally a medium in trance will be inspired to take up a general collection, and spectators may donate small sums of money toward the expenses of the center (or of the medium), but at most centers the audience is not ordinarily solicited for funds.

A more active way of participating in the Batuque is to consult one of the encantados about some personal problem. The number of people in Belém who have taken their problems to the encantados probably cannot compare with those who have taken their problems to the saints, but the number must still be considerable. At every ceremony there are clients about, either consulting the cult leader or searching out individuals who receive encantados from whom they have received help before. The clients' role in the Batuque is obviously important, since their financial contributions or payments for services are the principal source of income for most cult leaders. A client may come to the *terreiro* as a spectator and consult the encantados after they have arrived during the ceremony, or he may visit the center at any other time to consult the leader more privately or to purchase his prepared medicinal baths and teas.

The extent to which the Batuque's paying customers are believers in the cult doctrines varies. Many of the clients are themselves mediums or the close relatives of mediums and, as such, convinced believers. Other clients may have faith only in certain aspects of cult doctrine, in two or three encantados, or in the sorcery powers of certain cult leaders. Some customers may be generally skeptical, but are trying cult remedies simply because other tactics have failed. The encantado, for these skeptics, is the last resort; personal effort, patent medicines, relatives, doctors, and the saints have failed, and, without much confidence in the probable outcome, the skeptic decides to try *macumba*. If the encantado consulted gives advice leading to the amelioration of a chronic illness, or the return of an errant husband, or the procurement of employment, the skeptic may become a confirmed believer.

The third way in which one might demonstrate faith in the Batuque without personally being possessed by the spirits is by serving as a drummer or other musician or by acting as general factotum around the *terreiro* during ceremonies. Drumming requires some skill or natural aptitude, but little musical ability is needed to shake the *maracá* or the *ganzá*. In addition, there are many other small chores to be done during a ceremony. Coffee and other refreshments must be prepared and served, dishes washed, ritual paraphernalia brought out at the proper moment, and someone is needed in the chapel to assist mediums who enter there while in trance for the purpose of resting or giving consultations. Every *terreiro* seems to have a number of hangers-on who are ready to assist in any way necessary under the direction of the *mãe* or *pai de santo*. The musicians and other hangers-on usually appear to be quite informed about cult matters, occasionally lead the singing, and are clearly believers in cult doctrine. They receive no compensation for their labors except a few drinks, and they do not necessarily expect benefits in the form of the special protection of the encantados.

Spectators, clients, musicians, hangers-on, all are believers and contribute something to maintaining the Batuque. However, the most important members of the sect are those individuals who are believed to receive the spirits. In Belém those who enter trance states are called *filha de santo* (daughter of the saint) if female, and *filho de santo* (son of the saint) if male. These are general terms referring to persons who receive any supernatural being. More specifically the individual may be referred to as the devotee of a particular spirit, as *filha da Jurema,* for example. Occasionally the Dahomean term *vodunsa* is used as a synonym for *filha de santo* by older cult members, but this is rare. The term *médium,* obviously borrowed from spiritualism, is much more frequently used as a synonym. In Bahia and in other sections of Brazil, the term *cavalo* (horse) is commonly used to designate a medium. This designation is rarely employed in Belém, but a similar equestrian concept is evidently present, since a devotee is often spoken of as "carrying" an encantado, e.g., *"Ela carrega Dom João"* (She carries, or receives, Dom João). In Belém in indirect address the cult member is more likely to be referred to as the *aparelha* (apparatus) used by the spirits rather than as their horse. "Apparatus" as a synonym for "medium" is also borrowed from spiritualism.

Although there is no accurate record of the number of mediums in Belém, it is possible to make a rough estimate of their numbers. In 1965, according to the records of the Federation of Afro-Brazilian Cults, there were twenty-nine *terreiros* in operation in the city and its near suburbs. The four *terreiros* that we studied had about thirty mediums each. Assuming that this number is approximately the same in the other *terreiros* in the city, there would be 870 mediums in Belém affiliated with some *terreiro*. *Searas* (the cult centers that do not use musical instruments) are much more numerous. In 1965 there were at least 110 in operation. Assuming a membership of about fifteen mediums for each (the average membership of the six we visited), the total mediums in *searas* would be 1650. An additional sixty-six mediums were registered with the federation as practitioners of Jurema or healers. Since curing is prohibited by law, the euphemism "working in the *linha de Jurema*" is used to describe curing practices.

According to these estimates, there were, in 1965, approximately 2600 men and women in Belém who considered themselves to be mediums—that is, they more or less regularly entered trance states which were interpreted as possession by the supernatural beings recognized by the Batuque religion. It should be stressed that this is a minimal figure. All of the centers in the city are not registered with the federation. As indicated in Chapter II, an undetermined number of *searas* in the city consider their doctrine and ritual to be pure Umbanda with no crossing, or mixture, with Mina-Nagô and therefore shun affiliation with the Mina-Nagô dominated federation.[1] It must also be stressed that the estimate of 2600 represents the religious elite and not all of the active participants in the Batuque. If the number of hangers-on, regular spectators, and steady clients were added to that of the mediums, the total number of convinced and committed believers in the Batuque in Belém in 1965 would certainly be greater than 10,000.

As has been found to be the case in other African-derived religions in the New World, the great majority of the active members of the Batuque come from the lower socioeconomic ranks. Information was secured about the occupational status of 120 members—87 women and 33 men.

Nine of the women were heads of *terreiros* or *searas.* Seven of these *mães de santo* supported themselves and their dependents by their religious activities, with minor financial aid from husbands or other family members. One *mãe de santo* earned very little from the cult and was supported by her son. The other who did not make a living from the Batuque was financially independent with income from inherited property. This financially independent *mãe de santo* owned her own automobile, a home in a fashionable section of the city, as well as the *terreiro* property and another house in the working class Pedreira neighborhood. Her social position was so clearly exceptional that she appeared to puzzle our informants, who frequently commented on her generosity and wealth and generally refrained from criticizing her religious techniques and personal life, a restraint definitely not exercised in the case of other *mães de santo.* She was, in short, treated with the polite deference shown to upper-class patrons. Four additional women made their living from the cult, although they were not leaders. Three of these four were *ogans,* or caretakers of *terreiros,* and one supported herself by fortunetelling and preparing medicinal baths.

Twenty-four of the women stated that they were housewives with no other employment and were supported by their husbands or their children. In twenty-two of the twenty-four cases the principal wage earner in the family was employed in a low-paying and low-status job such as laborer, cabdriver, street vendor, sales clerk, butcher, painter, or carpenter. The two exceptions were an accountant and a high-salaried mechanic in the Brazilian Air Force.

Nineteen of the eighty-seven women took in washing. Eleven of the nineteen were self-supporting or the principal wage earners in their families, while the other eight washed clothes as a method of supplementing family income.

The occupations of the remaining thirty-one women were:

    7 schoolgirls, living with parents
    4 domestic servants (housemaids)
    3 dressmakers
    3 factory workers (Brazil-nut packaging plant)
    3 prostitutes
    2 food vendors

- 2 office clerks
- 1 manicurist
- 1 cleaning woman in a public school
- 1 operator of small boardinghouse
- 1 bus owner (operated by sons)
- 3 unemployed, one of whom, over seventy years old, was supported by a daughter, another, age nineteen, lived with her parents, and the third, age forty-one, was supported by her siblings and was unemployable because of alcoholism

Of the thirty-three male cult members for whom occupational data were secured, eleven were *pais de santo*. Six of the eleven supported themselves and their dependents by their religious activities. Five had other sources of income besides the Batuque: one was head of a post office department, one a sanitary inspector at the public markets, one a technician in an optical company, one an office clerk, and one lived on income from a fish market that he owned. The former occupations of the six full-time *pais de santo* were:

- 1 elementary school teacher
- 1 street vendor
- 2 laborers
- 2 cooks (in houses of prostitution)

Four additional men earned their living from the cult, two as *ogans* and two as curers.

The occupations of the other eighteen men were:

- 3 office clerks
- 3 factory workers
- 2 stevedores
- 1 department head of an import firm
- 1 mechanic in Brazilian Air Force
- 1 carpenter
- 1 truck driver
- 1 hairdresser
- 1 nurse
- 1 waiter
- 1 bus conductor
- 1 street vendor
- 1 porter (in a house of prostitution)

From the standpoint of occupational status and income, perhaps eleven of the men and six of the women listed above could be ranked above lower class. It is possible, however, that if a different selection of cult centers to be studied intensively had been made, the proportion of middle-class mediums might have been somewhat higher. A few *searas* were criticized by some of our informants as being "for rich people only." Very likely, at these centers for the "rich," middle-class mediums are in the majority. Another informant, himself lower-middle-class, was fond of observing that "the Batuque used to be all lower-class [*classe média para baixo*] but now upper-class people [*gente da primeira*] are in it."

Although the middle-class component of the active membership might be somewhat higher than our data indicate, at present the overwhelming majority of active participants are from the lower class. Upper- and middle-class believers in the cult are more likely to take part as the clients and patrons of important cult leaders. It should not be assumed, however, that the ideology of the Batuque is such that better educated, more sophisticated individuals are automatically repelled by it. Our contacts with middle- and upper-class Brazilians were relatively limited, but we did encounter a number of individuals from middle-class backgrounds who were willing to accept many of the basic ideas of this religion. For example, at the home of Milton, a lower-middle-class medium, we once encountered a high official of the Conselho Nacional de Pesquisas (National Research Council). The official had come to Belém on business, had heard of the elaborate private shrines to the encantados maintained by Milton, and was paying a visit to see them. After telling us something about the Afro-Brazilian cults in Rio de Janeiro, the official began relating some of his personal experiences with spiritualism. He reported that his sister-in-law was a medium, and it became quite clear that he was personally convinced that the dead communicate with the living at spiritualist sessions. On another occasion we met an ex-doctor turned cattle rancher who was a convinced believer in the reality of the encantados and their ability to possess mediums. He had traveled widely throughout Brazil and professed to be deeply impressed by the fact that, though the same spirit descended in different sections of Brazil under different names, it always sang the same song; this was impressive, he felt, because most mediums were lower-class illiterates who neither traveled nor read books. The rancher had received his M.D. in Rio de Janeiro and had practiced medicine for a number of years, yet told us, with enthusiasm, several stories of untrained mediums successfully performing complex surgery while in trance.

We compiled data on the age or approximate age of 180 active Batuque members, the 120 mentioned above and 60 additional members (see Table 1). As in most religious sects, the

TABLE 1. Age of Active Batuque Members

Age	Female	Male
10–19	11	0
20–29	22	14
30–39	33	18
40–49	41	9
50–59	18	4
60–69	7	1
70 and over	2	0
Totals	134	46

majority of the active membership is adult, over the age of thirty. Five of the eleven girls under age twenty had not as yet had a trance experience at the time of our study, but they danced regularly because their parents wanted them to be prepared to receive the spirits, either to maintain a family tradition or because it was felt that the girls were born mediums and their eventual possession by encantados would take place more smoothly if the girls were prepared. One of these girls, Carolina, aged ten, was revealed as a *filha* of the encantado Joãozinho at the age of two. Carolina was very ill and appeared to be "drying up." Doctors could do nothing for her, and her parents finally took her to a cult healer. The healer diagnosed the illness as a sign that Joãozinho had chosen her as his future medium. The healer gave the baby *passes* and told her parents they would have to prepare Carolina to receive Joãozinho when she reached the proper age. Carolina had not been possessed again by Joãozinho, but her "owner" revealed his proprietorship in her behavior. Instead of playing quietly with other little girls, Carolina was a tomboy, preferring to run around the streets with boys, and she was especially prone to fight with her older brother. Puzzled as to how to cope with her,

her parents decided to start her in a *terreiro,* although they felt she was still rather young.

There were two other very young girls in this group, one aged ten, the other eleven, but both were already developed mediums. One, the daughter of a *mãe de santo,* is said to have been first possessed by Pena Verde at the age of six. The other, her close friend and the granddaughter of the *ogan* of the *terreiro,* was "seized" by the encantado Zezinho a year later, when she also was six. As noted earlier, other Batuque members are somewhat critical of the practice of allowing such young children to participate regularly in ceremonies; ordinarily, parents ask the encantados to postpone possession until the children are at least teen-agers and "know what they are doing." Nevertheless, age seven is the traditional or ideal age for the first manifestation that a person is a medium. Many cult members insist that they were first possessed at age seven, but then their "owner" did not return again until they were teen-agers.

The two *filhas* over age seventy rarely dance anymore. Lasting as it does from nine in the evening until dawn the next morning, a *batuque* is strenuous physical activity, and it strikes the observer as remarkable that elderly women in their sixties can dance for hours without showing signs of fatigue. During the three- or four-day celebrations that are sometimes held for the patron encantado of a *terreiro,* very few of the age group over fifty will appear every night as do the younger mediums.

Table 1 also indicates that in Belém there are three times as many women participants as men. This same predominance of women has been noted in Maranhão and Bahia. In her survey, "World Distribution and Patterns of Possession States," Bourguignon (1968, p. 20) found that a predominance of women was characteristic of possession religions in many parts of Africa. To a certain extent, then, this predominance in Brazilian cults may represent the survival of a tradition. Various other hypotheses to explain the imbalance have been advanced. Herskovits (1955, pp. 512–13) suggested that there is a simple economic explanation: the men, who are the principal breadwinners for their families, cannot as easily spare the time for the lengthy initiations. Pierson (1967, p. 285), on the other hand, suggested that men in Bahia have wider social contacts than women do and therefore are more "Europeanized" than are Bahian women, who cling more closely to African traditions. Neither explanation will do for Belém, since there is no lengthy initiation in the Batuque and there are no African traditions to speak of. Carneiro (1940, pp. 272–73) explained the predominance of women by pointing out that most of the duties associated with maintaining a *terreiro*—cooking sacred foods, taking care of altars, cleaning and decorating the pavilion—are women's work. In Belém, however, most of these routine tasks are performed by the cult leader's own family or by the *ogan* with the assistance of hangers-on—that is, by individuals who are not necessarily mediums and might be of either sex.

One factor that does clearly inhibit the participation of men in ceremonies is the widespread belief, both within and outside the Batuque religion, that men who wear ritual costumes and dance in public ceremonies are either effeminate or, in most cases, active homosexuals. In part, this belief is based on fact—some of the men are indeed homosexuals. Although this topic was not one that could be readily discussed with the men involved, there was often unanimity among our informants, both male and female, that some male mediums lived with other men with whom they had sexual relations. It proved impossible, however, to determine exactly how many men were homosexual. Some of our female informants were quite cavalier in assuring us that all of the men in the religion were homosexual. Closer questioning, however, led to the conclusion that the evidence seemed indisputable in only fourteen cases out of the forty-six men listed in Table 1. Of these fourteen homosexuals, several were *pais de santo.* As far as the other thirty-two men were concerned, several were married and seemed to be exclusively heterosexual, whereas several others, including one *pai de santo,* were often criticized for their amatory conquests among the female mediums. For most of this group, however, the evidence was simply inconclusive.

To some extent, then, the belief that male mediums are homosexual is based on fact. But the belief is firmly held by many who do not know the facts and who are influenced in part by a consideration of the way some male mediums behave during ceremonies. There is, for example, a certain amount of female impersonation. A man who supposedly is possessed by a female spirit may carry a fan or wear earrings and may attempt to appear feminine in facial expressions and certain gestures. One *pai de santo* would go on for hours as the female encantado Jarina, wearing a turban and mincing about the floor. His behavior was so extreme that it often provoked derisive comments from the audience. On the other hand, in most cases a man in trance does not act very feminine, and it is usually impossible to tell if a man is supposed to be possessed by a male or a female encantado. It would appear that the immoderate behavior of the few makes a stronger impression on spectators than the unexceptional conduct of the majority.

In part, the mere fact of participation in the public ceremony calls a man's masculinity into question. In Brazil, the *macho* (ideal male) is supposed to be virile, dashing, and oversexed. A man who takes part in a *batuque,* wearing a costume, dancing sedately with a group of women, and waiting for a spirit to possess him, is clearly not conforming to the masculine ideal. The situation is somewhat different with the *pai de santo,* who in his position of leadership is clearly manifesting part of the masculine role and who, if he is dynamic and forceful enough, can largely avoid the ridicule that ordinary male mediums are subjected to.

The argument most frequently advanced by our female informants against male participation was simply that it looked "ugly" for large numbers of men to take part in ceremonies. They also stressed that their husbands did not like it when men participated in ceremonies, not because of jealousy, but because the husbands assumed that all male mediums were homosexuals and did not want their wives associating with such immoral types. In spite of these objections, often made with considerable vehemence, in actual ceremonies women usually accepted male mediums as full participants, interacted with them freely, and showed concern over their behavior only when it became too blatantly effeminate.

It is clear that the attitude toward male participation is ambivalent. On the one hand, male mediums are held up to ridicule as *safado* (immoral) or *efeminado* (effeminate), and there is always concern that the *terreiro* will become a recognized gathering place for homosexuals and thus liable to public opprobrium and persecution by the police. All of the leaders whom we interviewed, both male and female, were defensive about the number of men associated with their *terreiros* and invariably asserted that there were at most only one or two *filhos* who took part in ceremonies. On the other hand, some of the most forceful leaders are men, and many women prefer a *pai de santo* to a *mãe de santo* as head of a *terreiro*. In addition, since it is believed that mediums are chosen by the supernatural, it is unthinkable that a man who has been selected by an encantado to serve as its "apparatus" should be prohibited from receiving that spirit during ceremonies.

One way in which this conflict is resolved is by making a distinction between those men who take part in ceremonies from the beginning and those who participate only after they have entered a trance state. According to this widely accepted compromise, a man must fulfill his mission if the spirits desire to possess him, and there is consequently no stigma attached to possession itself. A "real" man, however, does not wear a costume or dance in front of the drums. He simply sits in the audience, or serves as drummer or other functionary, until the spirit manifests itself. After he has entered trance he is given an *espada,* leads the appropriate songs and may dance briefly, but he spends relatively little time in public view. Of the forty-six men listed in Table 1, eleven more or less conformed to this ideal pattern. For those men who wear costumes and dance, and who are either alleged or actual homosexuals, the doctrine accepted by most Batuque leaders is that as long as they carry out their obligations and show respect during ceremonies, their sex life should be of no concern either to their fellow members or to anyone else.

The problem of male participation seems to have been solved more simply in some of the *searas* where Umbanda ideas predominate. According to Umbanda beliefs, no stigma should be attached to a male medium, and any ridicule expressed by the larger community is simply ignored. Quite often husbands and wives participate together in Umbanda ceremonies, which greatly reduces the possibility of accusations of sexual deviance. In addition, the *macho* ideal can be more easily reconciled to the ceremonial activities in an Umbanda oriented *seara,* where costumes are less colorful, men and women line up on opposite sides of the room, and there is little dancing by anyone before the trance state has been achieved.

In one *terreiro* in Belém no men at all were allowed to participate as mediums. This was an unusual *terreiro,* however, in that the policies were not set by the *mãe de santo* but by her son, who supported her and financed the *terreiro.* The son was not a medium himself and felt very strongly that only women should be mediums. Not only were men not allowed to dance in this *terreiro,* but if a man became possessed while in the audience, he was forthwith ejected from the premises. On one occasion a young man associated with another *terreiro* was watching a ceremony when he suddenly went into trance, presumably possessed by the spirit Mariana. He was immediately seized by another son of the *mãe de santo* and brought out of trance by being struck on the forehead with what was obviously more than the necessary force. This episode created a minor scandal, since even those of our women informants who spoke most disapprovingly of male participation in ceremonies were in agreement that the treatment of the young medium had been unduly drastic. On the other hand, this *terreiro* was often referred to with respect because of its policy of prohibiting male participation.

All other *terreiros* in Belém had several male mediums, although the number varied considerably. At the *terreiro* of Dona Ana, the number of men who lined up in front of the drums at the beginning of ceremonies often equaled the number of women, a situation often commented upon unfavorably in Batuque circles. In most other *terreiros,* men made up a small minority of the participants, at least during the initial phases of the ceremony.

It will be noted in Table 1 that the number of active women mediums increases with age, reaching a peak after forty. For men, however, the situation is quite different. It would seem that of the young men who are attracted by the Batuque, only a few continue active into middle age, and most of these become *pais de santo* or curers. Considering the pressures against male participation, this is not surprising. The *pai de santo* receives respect from his followers and is shown at least some deference by his clients, approbation that sustains him in the face of other criticisms. Men without the status of the *pai de santo* either abandon the religion altogether as they grow older or, more commonly, support their wives or female relatives and do not themselves actively seek possession in public.

Women outnumber men as cult leaders as well as in rank-and-file membership, but the disproportion is not as great. Of the 139 cult centers registered with the federation in the summer of 1965, ninety-two were headed by women, forty-seven by men. Women thus had roughly a two-to-one margin over men. In the *linha de Jurema,* or curing, the proportion was three-to-one; fifty women and sixteen men were registered as practitioners of Jurema.

It has been traditional among American, European, and Brazilian students of African-derived religions to consider the study of these religions as synonymous with the study of the "Negro." In the past this approach might have been appropriate, since these religions were brought to the New World by Africans and were first practiced exclusively by slaves and then the descendants of slaves. In Belém today, however, and in many other parts of Brazil, the African-derived religions draw their membership generally from the lower classes, regardless of race. In Belém, where most of the population is the result of intermarriage between peoples from Europe and Africa, with a substantial contribution from the indigenous American Indians as well, the members of the Batuque are also largely of mixed origin. Just as the cult is a much broadened and elaborated version of an originally African religion, the membership is also much expanded and includes individuals of a variety of racial backgrounds. It is therefore quite unjustified to consider the study of the Batuque as a study of the "Negro" in Belém.

In discussing the racial affiliation of Batuque members, it is more reasonable to use Brazilian categories than to impose North American or European usage.[2] To North Americans and Europeans there are two basic kinds of people in the world, white and colored. Usually any "colored" individual with known or visible African ancestry is classified as "Negro"; that is, the category includes all individuals of mixed European-African ancestry, regardless of the proportion of the two racial stocks involved. This system of classification has the advantage of neatness and simplicity, but it does considerable violence to the facts of biology.

In Brazil the classification of racial types differs somewhat in different regions, but what all of the classifications have in common is a greater respect for biological realities than is found in the North American system. There are always at least three categories: *branco* (white), *preto* (black), and the mixed segment of the population that is designated by a variety of terms. The official census designation for this segment is *pardo* (brown), but this term is never used in conversation. In Belém individuals of mixed ancestry are usually referred to as *moreno* (brunette) and may be further distinguished as *moreno escuro* (dark brunette) or *moreno claro* (light brunette). These terms are applied to all individuals of visibly mixed parentage, regardless of whether they are descended from African-European, Indian-European, or African-Indian crosses. Since intermarriage between members of these three racial stocks has been going on for at least three hundred years, it is not surprising that most individuals have long since lost track of their racial backgrounds. There is no interest in tracing exact ancestry, and people are classified simply according to their physical appearance. Someone who is very dark is classified as *preto*. A person who has a medium dark complexion is called *moreno*. A very light individual is a *branco*. Hair form and facial features may also play a part in assigning individuals to particular categories, but skin color is by far the most important criterion. Since the inheritance of skin color is quite complex, it often happens that children are lighter than one or both of their parents, and when this happens parent and child may be classified as belonging to different categories. Even brothers and sisters may end up in different categories. It is obvious that in such a situation a racial classification is not going to be very meaningful, and in fact will be as much an exercise in arbitrary decisions as anything else.

According to the official census, the majority of the population of Belém falls into the *moreno* category (see Table 2). The figures given in Table 2 must be accepted as only rough approximations, however, for the reasons discussed above. There is one other consideration that sometimes influences racial classification and that is social status. A wealthy person is much more likely to be classified as *branco* than a poor man with the same physical characteristics. Since practically all cult members were relatively poor, this source of distortion would not be significant for our study.

Accepting the fact that no attempt to classify the people of

TABLE 2. 1950 Census of Município (County) of Belém

Color	Number	Percentage
Pardo (brown)	132,941	52.2
Branco (white)	109,721	43.1
Preto (black)	11,652	4.6
Amarelo (yellow)	201	0.1
Totals	254,515	100.0

Source: Instituto Brasileiro de Geografia e Estatística, *Enciclopédia dos municípios brasileiros,* vol. 14, p. 302. Total population in the *município* was 254,949; 434 individuals were evidently not classified as to color. Of the total population all but 29,000 lived within the city itself.

Belém will be completely satisfactory, it is still of some significance to know whether the members of the Batuque are primarily *pretos, morenos,* or *brancos.* In an attempt to answer this question, however crudely, we classified the 180 members described in Table I in terms of three characteristics: skin color, hair form, and facial features. Our judgments were made on the basis of visual observation. Our results are given in Tables 3 and 4, Table 3 dealing with skin color and hair form, Table 4

TABLE 3. Physical Characteristics—Hair Form

Hair form	Skin Color						Totals
	1	2	3	4	5	6	
Kinky–very curly	1	6	13	26	24	15	85
Curly–wavy–straight	33	31	20	9	2	0	95
Totals	34	37	33	35	26	15	180

TABLE 4. Physical Characteristics—Facial Features

Facial features	Skin color						Totals
	1	2	3	4	5	6	
African	0	2	12	16	18	14	62
European	34	35	21	19	8	1	118
Totals	34	37	33	35	26	15	180

with skin color and facial features. A range of six shades of skin pigmentation was set up, from a very light "1" to a very dark "6." In Table 3 two hair-form categories were used: kinky–very curly as one category and curly–wavy–straight as the other. In Table 4 an individual was classified as having "African" features if (1) the nose was relatively broad and flat, and/or (2) the lips were especially prominent. The most salient American Indian facial feature, the epicanthic eye fold, is also found in the Belém cult group, but was ignored in this classification.

It is our contention that a Brazilian census taker would probably classify about thirty-three of the individuals listed in the tables as *preto*—those with shade 6 skin color (fifteen) and those with shade 5 skin color and African features (eighteen). About sixty-five would be classified as *branco*—those with shade 1 skin (thirty-four) and those with shade 2 skin and curly–wavy–straight hair (thirty-one). The remaining eighty-two would be classified as *pardo* (*moreno*). In terms of percentages, *moreno* 46 per cent, *branco* 36 per cent, and *preto* 18 per cent.

If these figures are compared with the census figures given in Table 2, it will be seen that the percentage of *pretos* is considerably higher in the Batuque than in the general population. In part this is due to the fact that the Batuque members are primarily from the lower class, and in Belém most individuals with dark skins are in the lower socioeconomic brackets. In any case, our general point is made: the members of the Batuque are mixed in racial composition and there are, in fact, twice as many *brancos* as *pretos*. There is clearly no reason to consider the Batuque as a religion of "Negroes."

Nor does leadership in the cult seem to be obviously related to skin color. Twenty-seven of the 180 cult members described above were cult leaders. Of these, three were *preto,* twelve were *moreno,* and twelve were *branco.* The color distribution of the cult leadership appears to be roughly proportional to that of the membership as a whole.

In his comprehensive study, *Les religions africaines au Brésil,* Roger Bastide (1960, pp. 519–58) has suggested that increased racial discrimination and exploitation, related to the stresses of industrialization, are the important underlying factors in the recent proliferation of the non-traditional African-derived sects in Brazil. Bastide terms the rapidly growing cults such as Umbanda "sects of imitation" and considers them to be basically religions of, and for, a colored proletarian class, even though the sects might have mulatto or white leadership. These "sects of imitation" serve simultaneously, he argues, as outlets for "the racial protest of blacks and *caboclos* [Indians or uneducated backwoodsmen of mixed ancestry] against a society dominated culturally by white models" (p. 525), and as vehicles for the assimilation of blacks (who have clung tenaciously to African traditions) into modern Brazilian multiracial society.

Such an analysis has little relevance for the Batuque, in which, as demonstrated above, the membership is not predominantly black. Even if individuals with dark skin pigmentation were predominate in the religion, it would not be meaningful to consider them a distinct group with interests, attitudes, or traditions significantly different from those of their lighter-complexioned fellow cult members. Dark-skinned individuals do not represent a separate racial caste in Belém. Their dialect, their homes, their food and dress, their entire culture, in fact, are identical to that of their lighter-skinned neighbors. They are neither spatially nor culturally segregated.

The really significant social grouping in Belém is class, not race. The identity that the average cult member is most aware of is that he is one of the large class of the poor, not that he is "colored," "black," or "white." The class of the poor includes individuals of all possible skin shades, hair textures, and facial features, and racial discrimination is not one of its collective complaints. Unemployment, high prices, disease, food shortages, inadequate housing—these are the problems that engross the attention of the poor. Compared to the magnitude of these problems, the slight discrimination that exists against the very dark-skinned is a minor irritation. Only two cult members mentioned racial prejudice as affecting their lives. One young *mãe de santo* complained that when she was an adolescent her religious development had been seriously hampered when a white *mãe de santo* strung her along, taking her money but refusing to baptize her "because of my color." In the other case, Clara, whose life history is given in Appendix B, related that her husband's relatives had opposed his marriage to her because she was much darker than he was. In both cases the women were young and poor, and their social inferiority was probably at least as important as their skin color in inspiring their "superiors" to treat them shabbily. Racial discrimination is simply not a burning social issue in northern Brazil.

The active members of the Batuque are recruited primarily from the ranks of the poor, but only a small minority of the poor become active in the religion. For every person who becomes a convinced believer, for every woman who becomes a medium, there are other individuals, similarly situated on the socioeconomic scale, with similar needs and aspirations, who remain indifferent or antagonistic toward the cult. Why do only certain individuals become active Batuque members? Are there any individual experiences that believers had in common before they became believers?

It has been suggested that migration from rural to urban areas may be an important factor in the increase in membership in religions such as the Batuque. Migration from country to city increased in tempo after World War II, roughly the same time that marked the take-off point in the rapid expansion of the African-derived and other possession religions in Brazil. Camargo (1961, pp. xii–xiii, 65–69, 96–97) and Willems (1966, pp. 224–25) argue that mediumistic religions have spread so rapidly in Brazil because they are particularly suited to helping the individual adjust to the urban environment. Rural migrants would presumably be more in need of the type of direct supernatural support offered by mediumistic religions than would native-born residents who had been conditioned from birth to cope with the pressures and insecurity of urban life. In addition, lost in the impersonal city, migrants could perhaps find in the religious group a substitute for the rural primary groups that had always ordered their lives.

Judging from our data, however, rural–urban migration does not appear to be a major factor in inducing individuals to join the Batuque. Admittedly, Belém is not as impersonalized or urbanized as are the southern Brazilian cities, and an individual moving to the city from the rural interior would not have as difficult an adjustment problem as the rural migrant to São Paulo or Rio de Janeiro. However, economic hardship and health problems are as great in Belém as in any of the southern cities. Mediumistic religions (spiritualism and Pentecostalism as well as the Batuque) are rapidly growing in Belém as in the south. Such religious movements may represent responses to the stresses of rapid social change, but our data suggest that the possession religions attract the native-born, lower-class urban population more than recent rural migrants. A majority of the members of the Batuque whose origins we investigated were natives of Belém. Of one hundred mediums, sixty-two were born and brought up in the city. The origins of the thirty-eight migrants are summarized in Table 5.

TABLE 5. Batuque Members of Non-local Origin

Came to Belém before age 10		Came to Belém after age 10	
Origin	*Number*	*Origin*	*Number*
Interior of Pará	8	Interior of Pará	4
Rural areas of other states	6	Rural areas of other states	5
Others cities (e.g., São Luís, Fortaleza, Manaus)	1	Other cities (e.g., São Luís, Fortaleza, Manaus)	14
Total	15	Total	23

The fifteen cult members who were brought to Belém as young children, before age ten, should probably not be considered rural migrants. They were undoubtedly gradually conditioned to urban life since they completed their maturation in the city. Fourteen of the twenty-three individuals moving to Belém after age ten came from other cities and therefore do not represent rural migrants either. Ten of the fourteen moved from São Luís, which is a considerably smaller city than Belém, but all ten were already members of the very similar Mina-Nagô sect in São Luís before they moved; they did not join the Batuque in response to problems of adjusting to a larger city. One migrant came from Manaus, also smaller than Belém, but he had moved for the express purpose of seeking out treatment by Batuque curers. Two of the remaining nine adolescent-adult migrants from rural areas were also mediums and, in a sense, cult members before their arrival in the city. Both had developed as mediums in the *pajelança* (shamanism) found throughout rural Amazonia. For only seven out of the hundred members, then, was the experience of moving from a stable rural environment into a depersonalized, insecure urban environment a possible factor in the decision to become an active participant in the Batuque.

In this inquiry into some of the characteristics of cult members, there is another question to be answered. Are the elect of the Batuque, the mediums, primarily converts or were most born into the religion, following the example of their mothers or other close relatives and developing as mediums as a matter of course? Several factors complicate the question and make a simple answer impossible. In the first place, exposure to the Batuque from infancy does not mean that an individual will automatically become a medium. There is some feeling that a daughter, or at least one of the daughters, should follow her mother into the cult, and often a daughter in time comes to receive the same spirits that her mother received. To a certain extent it is believed that the ability to be possessed can be inherited, and those mediums whose parents were active in the Batuque often speak proudly of their own talents as being "brought from the cradle." On the other hand, it is also believed that mediums are divinely selected without regard to family traditions or laws of heredity. Consequently no medium expects all of his or her children to be equally interested in the cult. A few cases were encountered where several brothers and sisters were active participants, but, more commonly, among several children, only one was an active member. In distinguishing members who are "born" into the Batuque, then, the intent is to indicate those individuals who from birth have intimate contact with someone who is an active medium; it is not being suggested that membership is in any real sense considered hereditary.

A convert, on the other hand, is someone who has no close relative in the Batuque, and who, according to his own testimony, had little contact with the religion as a child. Considering how widespread the knowledge of cult ideology is, however, it is probable that few if any of the converts were completely unaware of Batuque doctrine or ceremonies before they became actively interested in the religion. Many of them reported that their families did not approve of the Batuque, but with the exception of a few converts from Protestant families, there seem to have been few cases when contact with cult members and ceremonies was actually prohibited. The individuals classified as converts in Table 6, then, had less contact with the Batuque than those listed as being born into the religion, but this obviously was a matter of degree.

Table 6 indicates that there are significant differences between

TABLE 6. Comparison of Converts and Born Cult Members

BORN INTO CULT

Age when became active member	Number	Number reporting personal problem at time of joining
Before age 20	32	4
20–29	5	1
30–39	1	0
40–49	2	2
50 and over	1	1
Totals	41	8

CONVERTS

Age when became active member	Number	Number reporting personal problem at time of joining
Before age 20	12	4
20–29	14	9
30–39	14	10
40–49	6	4
50 and over	1	0
Totals	47	27

the born member and the convert with respect to (1) the age at which the individual became an active participant and (2) the awareness of being personally "troubled" (*perturbado*) at the time of the first trance experience. About 78 per cent of those born into the cult had their first trance experience and became active members before the age of twenty. In the convert group only about 26 per cent became mediums before age twenty. Those individuals born into the Batuque are also less likely than are the converts to report that they were suffering from mysterious ailments or had other serious personal problems at the time they first were "seized" by a spirit. Fewer than 20 per cent of the born group recalled such difficulties, but 57 per cent of the converts insisted that they were much "persecuted" by the spirits shortly before their first trance or before their decision to prepare to be mediums.

The likelihood that the daughter or son of a medium will also become a medium appears to decline sharply after age twenty-five. All five of the individuals in the twenty to twenty-nine born member age group were in their early twenties at the time of their first trance. But occasionally the first trance experience comes much later in life, as in the case of Arnaldo. Both of Arnaldo's maternal grandparents, his mother, an uncle, an aunt, and his wife were all mediums. Arnaldo was familiar with cult ideology and ritual from infancy on but was never much interested in it. He attended many Batuque ceremonies but never "felt" anything. After he grew up, spiritualism interested him more than Batuque, and he attended more spiritualist sessions than Batuque ceremonies. However, he occasionally accompanied his wife to the *terreiro* with which she was affiliated. At age thirty-four, while sitting placidly in the audience one evening, Arnaldo was suddenly possessed, without any type of advance warning at all. His "time" had simply arrived, according to cult members.

Zélia's case was similar, though her time arrived considerably later in life. Her father had been a Batuque curer, but Zélia had never been much interested in the encantados. Like Arnaldo, she found "pure" spiritualism more interesting than Batuque. However, when she became seriously ill at age fifty-six, the spiritualist leaders were unable to help her. A curing ceremony run by a young *pai de santo* in the neighborhood did seem to help, and Zélia began to attend all of the ceremonies at his *terreiro*. While watching a *batuque* there, the encantado Averekete "seized" her. Her health improved markedly as Zélia learned to dance and sing to the encantados.

Mediums who were born into the religion may, as in Zélia's case, recall that their health was bad or their peace of mind troubled immediately before achieving their new status as the chosen apparatus of an encantado, but, more typically the born member recalls no particular personal difficulties prior to his first trance. For many the first trance experience comes almost as an extension of childhood play. For example, Mauvina as a child played *batuque* with other neighborhood children in the pavilion of the *terreiro* to which her aunt belonged. Like the other children, she not only danced and sang, but pretended that she was possessed. Later, at age sixteen or seventeen, because she enjoyed singing, dancing, and dressing up, Mauvina began dancing as a *filha de terreiro,* wearing the proper costumes and following all of the ritual prescriptions of a medium. At age nineteen, during a *batuque,* she "really fell," i.e., went into trance for the first time, when she was whirled by another medium who was also in trance. Another example of gradual entry into the cult is the case of Carlito. At age twelve he began filling in occasionally as a drummer at a *terreiro,* when the adult drummers were taking a break. Both Carlito's mother and father were *filhos* of the *terreiro* where he began his informal apprenticeship as drummer. By the time he was fourteen, Carlito was accepted as one of the regular musicians of the center. A few weeks after his fourteenth birthday, during a *batuque,* the encantado Jarina (possessing the *pai de santo*) came over to the musicians' bench and told the boy he would have a surprise that day. Carlito interpreted the remark to mean that someone was going to give him a present. He understood Jarina's true meaning when she possessed him a short time later in the ceremony.

Perhaps most of the children of mediums have childhood play experiences similar to those of Mauvina, but, it must be stressed again, by no means do all turn out to be mediums, nor do cult members expect this to happen. Children are watched for early signs of mediumistic gifts, and, as discussed in the preceding chapter, if such signs appear, special "contracts" regulating the child's religious development may be worked out between the parent and the child's spirits. Only in rare cases is the child of a medium considered a "born" medium before he gives any indication of having such talents. Edson, for example, was dedicated to the encantados even before he was conceived. Dona Irene, Edson's mother, grew up in Soares, a small town near Belém. At age seventeen, while being treated by her uncle, the local *pajé* (curer), for some ailment, Irene fell into a trance. Since she definitely did not want to follow through and develop her spiritual powers, Irene begged her uncle to try to remove the spirits who claimed her. The *pajé* succeeded in persuading them to withdraw, but the encantados did so on the condition that Irene would dedicate her first male child to them. Irene kept her vow. When Edson was one year old he was formally dedicated to the encantados, and a rededication was held on each succeeding birthday. Edson finally "fell" after his fifteenth birthday and developed very rapidly as a medium. At age nineteen he opened his own center.

The first trance experience was apparently often a very dramatic event in the lives of the converts, who did not have the kind of contact with the cult that the children of mediums had. Some converts stated that their first contact with *terreiros* was when they visited one in search of a solution to a personal problem such as a stubborn ailment that doctors were unable to cure. Mundane ailments such as liver trouble, skin diseases, and chills and fever were occasionally mentioned as the problems bringing the outsider to a cult center, but more frequently the illnesses mentioned were of a "nervous" nature with symptoms such as persistent headaches, insomnia, nausea, loss of appetite, generalized anxiety, an inability to stop crying, and difficulty in grasping anything with the hands. Sometimes the catalogue of symptoms suggests some severe mental illness. Chica, for example, began to be very disturbed when she was about thirty-two years old, just after the birth of her third child. Although she became very anxious and fearful when left alone, she could not get along with other people. According to her *pai de santo,* Chica nearly murdered her husband in one of her rages. She could not sit still or stay in the house. "I felt like getting out in the street and just running, running," she recalls. She would take a bus to go downtown to shop, but could not bear to stay on the bus for more than a few minutes; she would have to get off and walk. Nothing the doctors prescribed had any effect. "My house resembled a pharmacy, there were so many medicines." Finally Chica went to a cult leader in her neighborhood. He told her she was a medium, persecuted by spirits who wanted to possess her, and persuaded her to develop in his center. She was soon possessed by the encantado Barão de Goré and now, ten years later, receives four additional encantados. Her health rapidly improved and her extreme nervousness diminished. However, her bellicosity has not been entirely irradicated. Chica soon quarreled with her first *pai de santo* and then joined the center of his greatest rival in the neighborhood. After a little more than a year she fought with the second leader and returned to the first. She has been repeating switches of this type at almost regular intervals ever since. Each of the two cult leaders involved naturally blames the other for the incomplete nature of Chica's cure.

Mental illness of any type is felt by the local population to be particularly within the competence of the *macumbeiros,* since mental derangements are seen as mysterious and thus perhaps of supernatural origin. All cult leaders are proud of the number of *loucos* (crazy people) they have cured, some of whom remain as *filhos de terreiro.* One cult leader had himself been a patient in a mental hospital and enjoyed relating his experiences there. Since insanity is regarded as a form of extreme persecution by evil spirits, for which the individual bears no personal responsibility, no particular stigma is attached to the condition, and informants talked freely of their bouts of *loucura* (insanity).

Maria José's breakdown started about seven years ago when she was twenty-one years old. It began with a terrible headache that nothing would relieve. For over a year she tried doctor after doctor to no avail. Then, as she began to lose contact with reality for periods of time, she was admitted to a mental hospital and given shock treatments. The treatments seemed to help, her headache disappeared, and she felt normal for a time. But she became convinced that the treatments ruined her teeth. She requested permission to leave the hospital to have her teeth taken care of. All went well for some months, but then her headache began again, and her nervousness, insomnia, and inability to eat returned. Three years ago she "went out of her mind" a second time. There is a two-year period of which she remembers nothing except the pain in her head. During this time her family brought her to a *terreiro* for treatment instead of taking her back to the hospital. Under the treatment of the *pai de santo,* Maria José began receiving Rompe Mato in trance and reports that she no longer has headaches. She believes that her guardian, Rompe Mato, has driven back the evil spirits persecuting her.

Illness, physical or mental, is not the only type of personal problem that brings outsiders to *terreiros* as clients and leads to their active participation as mediums. Marital difficulties, especially desertion and philandering spouses, are often interpreted as due to supernatural causes. The ministrations of a *mãe de santo* may not lead to the return of the wandering husband, but if they lead to a new life as the chosen medium of powerful supernaturals, the pain of the desertion is likely to be forgotten. Long-term unemployment is another type of personal problem that induces outsiders to try the services of Batuque leaders. Manoel, who had an ailing wife and four young children to support, was unemployed for two years. He states that the only thing that prevented him from committing suicide was the fact that his sister helped him out with a little money from time to time. Finally, Manoel and his wife went to consult a cult leader. She gave them a charm to be left at a crossroads. The next week Manoel found a steady job. He is now a believer and his wife is a medium. In a similar case, Cláudio, well-educated by Belém standards, was unable to find any white-collar employment and finally went to consult Dona Ana. In a trance as the encantado Jarina, the *mãe de santo* assured Cláudio that she would help him find a job. Within a week not only was Cláudio employed by a bank, but his sister also found a good clerical position at the American consulate. Grateful for the encantado's assistance, Cláudio financed a *batuque,* then was baptized, and is now a *filho de terreiro.*

Many other stories such as those of Chica, Maria José, Manoel, and Cláudio could be related. By concentrating on such recollections of past tribulations, one could develop the impression that the Batuque attracts primarily the mentally deranged, the neurotic, or the economically defeated. It would not be at all surprising if this were the case, since the Batuque in some ways seems almost tailor-made for people in trouble. But there is plenty of evidence to suggest that not all mediums are "sick" or even faced with serious problems at the time they join the religion. One kind of evidence comes from their own accounts. Over 40 per cent of the convert group, as well as 80 per cent of the born member group, insisted that they were not "disturbed" in any way when they first began receiving spirits.

A variety of explanations for joining the Batuque were offered by non-disturbed converts. Three women reported they had first joined as *filhas* of cult centers simply because they thought the ceremonies were very beautiful. Two men stated that they became active because they became convinced of the truth of cult doctrines and wanted to share in the good work done by the mediums. Most of the others appear to have become active participants after experiencing a trance. In some cases the trance occurred far from a cult center, completely apart from any ceremony. Benedita, for example, was in good health and good spirits when she fell down unconscious on a street corner. Since she was unable to explain such an attack, she was ready to accept a friend's suggestion that it must have been possession by an encantado. Dico's experience was even more unusual. He is a truck driver by occupation and one day blacked out while driving down one of the city's main thoroughfares. He regained his senses as he was driving into the factory gate on the opposite side of town. Feeling that his loss of consciousness was possession by a spirit and that possession while driving a truck could be extremely dangerous, he decided to be prepared properly as a medium.

Most of the unexpected trances occurred while the informant was watching a Batuque ceremony, and in most cases the individual had come to the ceremony primarily for recreational reasons, to watch a free show. Suddenly, without warning, he lost his spectator's detachment and became a part of the spectacle. Members of the audience who fall into trance are usually allowed to dance after their shoes have been removed. Often, however, the person in a trance state for the first or second time does not have enough muscular control to dance or even to stand up, but simply staggers about. In these cases, or if for some reason the cult leader does not choose to allow unknown outsiders to dance, the individual is led into the chapel, seated, and brought out of trance. As soon as it can be seen that consciousness is returning, the outsider is promptly abandoned by those who were assisting him. The person usually sits for a while looking extremely bewildered and confused, then shakily gets up and leaves the *terreiro*. No one corners him to attempt to persuade him that he must now become a member of the cult. The outsider may decide at once that this is the proper course of action, but more characteristically goes home to think it over and does not decide to become an active participant until he has been possessed a second time or has had some other unmistakable warning from the world of the supernatural (such as unemployment or illness) that it is dangerous to refuse to work with the encantados.

Possession, or entering the trance state, appears to be the clinching argument in any internal debate between credulity and disbelief that may have been going on within an individual. The experience of actually having been possessed by a spirit appears to be such an overwhelming one that any reservations the individual may have had about the reality of the encantados, or the desirability of being a medium, are swept away.

To summarize, we find that Batuque mediums tend to be poor, over thirty, female, of varied physical characteristics, and native to the city. About half were born into the religion and half were converts. However, no combination of such sociological specifications will automatically produce a Batuque member. There are many lower-class women of mixed ancestry, Belém-born and -bred, whose mothers are mediums, who never join the Batuque despite health, employment, or marital problems. In a religion where the individual must perform in trance—a kind of activity that is not equally congenial to all persons—it is impossible to discuss membership strictly in terms of sociological variables. The psychological factors which must also be taken into account are discussed in Chapter VI.

FOOTNOTES

1. There is, in addition, another large group of mediums affiliated with the spiritualist centers that specialize in receiving souls of the dead. Although some Batuque centers regularly hold spiritualist séances (*mesas de espiritismo*) and have won over some mediums from the spiritualist centers, spiritualism (which excludes encantados from the supernatural pantheon) is not identified as an Afro-Brazilian religion and the established spiritualist centers belong to a separate federation.

2. For extended discussions of Brazilian racial categories, see Wagley (1965) and the introduction to Pierson (1967).

Chapter V

The Spirits

Considering the nature of the Batuque, it is not surprising that the supernatural beings that make up its pantheon should be exceedingly numerous and of highly diverse origins. In a religion in which individuals in a trance state identify the spirit supposedly possessing them, the possibilities for the creation of new and exotic supernaturals would seem to be almost limitless. Indeed, to the uninitiated, the first impression of the Batuque pantheon is one of boundless confusion. Almost any member of the religion can offer a list of forty or fifty encantados, but none of the lists are exactly alike. Moreover, it soon becomes apparent that the same spirit may have several names and may, it is believed, possess people under different guises.

Patient inquiry reveals, however, that there are some underlying principles of organization with respect to the pantheon. Most of the encantados are grouped either into "families" or into "lines." Moreoever there is a definite consensus about what the general families and lines of spirits are, and although the identity or family assignment of some encantados may be disputed, the position of most of them is generally accepted by cult members. One discovers also that the number of spirits is not infinite, and that the number is relatively constant. Although new spirits are introduced from time to time, older ones lose their popularity and are forgotten. The creation of new spirits is restricted by a number of factors to be discussed below.

The origin of many of the spirits seems clear enough, and the eclecticism displayed is little short of amazing. Supernatural beings from African religions, from American Indian religions, and from Catholicism have been combined with figures from Portuguese and Brazilian history and folklore into a large but fairly homogeneous pantheon. Some of the complexities involved in this wholesale borrowing will be spelled out in detail as the description of the pantheon proceeds.

As we noted in Chapter III, the encantados are conceived of as being part of the same supernatural universe as God and the saints but as occupying a considerably lower status. Ordinarily a sharp distinction is made between a Catholic saint and an encantado: the saints live in heaven with God and the angels and never descend to earth to take possession of human beings as the encantados do.

There is, however, a close connection between each encantado and a particular saint, this relationship being modeled after the relationship between people and saints. As has already been pointed out, in Belém, as in Latin America generally, Catholics usually have favorites among the saints to whom they direct most of their petitions and from whom they expect the greatest assistance. The relationship is expressed as "adoring" a particular saint. As far as the encantados are concerned, each encantado is also said to "adore" a particular saint. The devotee of the encantado is expected to adore the same saint and to manifest this adoration by maintaining a small altar where candles can be lighted to the saint's image and by observing the saint's day with special prayers, fasting, or some other ritual. The image of the saint comes to represent both the saint itself and the encantado (who otherwise is represented only by a more or less nondescript stone), and ceremonies honoring the encantado are often held on the day of the saint it adores. It is not surprising, then, considering this close association, that there is at times a certain ambiguity as to the distinctive traits of saint and encantado in the minds of some of the less sophisticated believers. But, as far as we were able to determine, in only three cases were the separate identities of saint and encantado generally confused or blurred: the cases of St. Barbara, St. Sebastian, and the twins saints Cosmas and Damian.

Of these saints, St. Barbara is the most important. She is a very popular saint in Brazilian folk Catholicism and is considered by many cult members in both Belém and Maranhão to be the special patron saint of the Afro-Brazilian cults. In one song St. Barbara is definitely urged to come to earth, presumably to possess someone.

Solo:

Minha divina Santa Barbara,	*My divine St. Barbara,*
Venha ver seu mundo.	*Come see your world.*

Chorus:

Ai—ai, céu!	*Ai—ai, heaven!*
Venha ver seu mundo.	*Come see your world.*

Solo:

Venha, venha na carreira,	*Come, come down the trail,*
Venha ver seu mundo.	*Come see your world.*

Chorus:

Ai—ai, céu!	*Ai—ai, heaven!*
Venha ver seu mundo.	*Come see your world.*

Solo:

Pecador adora santo,	*Sinners adore saints,*
E santo adora Deus.	*And saints adore God.*

Chorus:

Ai—ai, céu!	*Ai—ai, heaven!*
Venha ver seu mundo.	*Come see your world.*

Solo:

Maria Barba, vinha vendo?	*Maria Barba, did you come to see?*
Jesus Cristo perguntou.	*Jesus Christ asked.*

Chorus:

Ai—ai, céu!	*Ai—ai, heaven!*
Venha ver seu mundo.	*Come see your world.*

Solo:

Onde vai a Barba Virgem?	*Where is Virgin Barba going?*
Vai no mundo dos pecadores.	*Into the world of sinners.*

Chorus:

Ai—ai, céu!	*Ai—ai, heaven!*
Venha ver seu mundo.	*Come see your world.*

Solo:

Venha, venha, venha, Mãe,	*Come, come, come, Mother,*
Venha olhar seu mundo.	*Come watch your world.*

Chorus:

Ai—ai, céu!	*Ai—ai, heaven!*
Venha ver seu mundo.	*Come see your world.*

If one of St. Barbara's devotees falls into a trance after the singing of this doctrine, the less sophisticated participants are likely to say that St. Barbara came down and possessed her medium. If pressed, however, most Batuque members will agree that it is really the encantado Rainha Barba, who is also called Barba Sueira and known as Inhaçan in Umbanda, who possesses people and not the actual saint.

St. Sebastian is another very popular saint in Brazil. Because his image features arrows (according to martyr legends, he was sentenced to be shot to death with arrows), St. Sebastian has a special appeal in a religion such as the Batuque that has a strong Indian bow-and-arrow motif. It is not surprising that he should be considered to be more personally involved in cult ceremonies than other saints. A few cult members confused the saint with his encantado namesake, Rei Sebastião (who is discussed below), while others equated him with Oxossi, an Umbanda encantado only recently added to the Batuque pantheon.

The twin saints Cosmas and Damian are generally confused with two encantados who bear the same names. According to Catholic hagiography, Cosmas and Damian were both physicians, famous for their charitable work, who were martyred in the Near East. According to Batuque leaders, the encantados Cosme and Damião were, as infants, thrown into the waters of Bahia by their earthly mother, but were saved from death by the encantado queen, Rainha Oyá, who raised them as her foster sons in her *encantaria* beneath the sea. These two identifications have become merged in the minds of many cult members, and Cosme and Damião are believed to descend regularly in Batuque ceremonies as gay, playful, child encantados (with an unchildlike thirst for rum), but at the same time, like the saints, they are believed to be experienced physicians and master healers.

With the exception of these three instances, the distinction between saint and encantado is usually made with considerable emphasis and without ambiguity.

Just as the encantado associated with St. Barbara has three or four alternate names—Rainha Barba, Maria Barba, Barba Sueira, Inhaçan—so do many other encantados. The multiplicity of names is due in part to the merging of the various traditions —Catholic, Mina-Nagô, Umbanda—but it is also due to an inordinate fondness for nomenclature on the part of cult members. Names are regarded as extremely important; to acquire a knowledge of all of the names of a spirit is to acquire a certain intimacy or familiarity with the supernatural and, in that sense, a certain power over that supernatural force. To properly mystify the uninitiated, it is believed that encantados are likely to adopt nicknames or even to change their names completely, especially when "working" in curing sessions.

A plurality of names for the same spirit, then, is accepted philosophically by cult members, but it does contribute yet another element of confusion to the pantheon, since a name change announced by one medium in trance may not be accepted by other devotees of the spirit. Confusion about who the spirits are and how to deal with them would be much greater if the practice of grouping spirits into families and lines had not developed. The participant in a ceremony may not recognize the personal name announced by a fellow medium in trance, but if the family connection is made clear, he knows how to treat the spirit who has descended. Considering the number of the encantados and their multiple names, the amount of agreement about the major spirit families is really quite striking. The genealogies given below might not be completely acceptable to every cult member in Belém, but objections would be restricted to details and the placing of relatively unimportant encantados.

It seems likely that the grouping of the encantados into families is traceable ultimately to an African tradition and is derived directly from the Casa das Minas in Maranhão (Eduardo 1948, pp. 76–80). The Batuque's debt to the Casa das Minas is obvious in the case of the small but prestigious encantado family of Averekete:

Averekete=(wife unknown)
|
Avereketino
Princesa d'Alva (foster daughter)

Averekete is identified in Belém as the "saint of the night" or as the "owner of the night." He adores St. Benedict, a black saint, one of the most popular Catholic saints in the Amazon area. In most *terreiros, batuques* begin by calling first Averekete, then Rainha Barba. According to Eduardo (1948, p. 84), in Maranhão it is believed that St. Barbara founded all *terreiros de Mina* and installed Averekete as her delegate to guide the ceremonies. This idea of Averekete's position was never suggested by anyone in Belém, and in fact, cult leaders were unable to explain why they called Averekete first.

Averekete is one of the few encantados who is clearly of African origin. He is the Dahomean deity Averekete or Verekete, youngest member of the Kevioso (Badé) family (Eduardo 1948, p. 79). In the Batuque, however, Averekete does not appear as a young, fun-loving trickster, as does the youngest member of each family in the traditional Dahomean pantheon. In Belém, Averekete invariably appears as an old, dignified *senhor*.

With a few exceptions, such as that of Averekete, the membership of most of the encantado families is no longer African, nor are any other features of an African tradition in any way prominent. The largest family of encantados in the Batuque is that of Rei Turquia (King Turkey), more commonly called Seu Turquia (*Seu* is an abbreviated form of *senhor,* Mr.). The members of this family are all called *turcos* (Turks), a term that is used in Brazil to apply to anyone from the Middle East and was formerly used as a synonym for "Moor." The family of Seu Turquia is said to have two hundred members, the most important of which are shown in Table 1. The family is typical of encantado families in that the father is known but not the mother and in that the names are highly diverse, some being Portuguese names, some being names from Indian languages, and some being the names of things (e.g., *goiabeira* is the guava tree).

According to a Batuque tradition, the members of Seu Turquia's family are all great warriors and have defeated the encantados of many other nations. Once defeated, some of these foreign encantados joined the Turquia family as foster children or were given to Seu Turquia by their own parents as peace pledges. Thus, after Goiabeira and his Italian relatives were defeated by Seu Turquia, Goiabeira and his wife gave up their own kinfolk and became Turks. The Brazilian encantado Dom Pedro Angaço and his family were also defeated in battle by Seu Turquia. Dom Pedro was then placed in the forest of

TABLE 1. Family of Rei Turquia

Rei Turquia = (various wives)

Sons

Flecheiro (twins)
Laurencino (twins)
Mariano (twins)
Caboquinho
Guapindaia
Guerreiro
Guido
Jatórana
João Fama = ?
  | Nilo Fama
Joaquimzinho
Mensageiro da Roma (Armin)
Mirian
Pindá
Pindaié (Tata)
Rondado
Sentinella
Tabajara
Tapinaré
  | Ita (foster daughter)
Ubirajara
Ubiratan
Zizué

Foster sons

Caboclo Nobre (son of Pedro Angaço)
Goiabeira (Mosê do Sangue), Principe d'Italia

Daughters

Flecheira
Laurencina
Mariana
Ana Joaquima = ?
  | Siriaki
Ciganina
Menina Daleira
Princesa Dora
Princesa Flora
Jaguarema
Juracema
Noxinina (Bela Cigana)

Floripe = ? (sister)
  | Flor do céu
  Flor do ouro
  Flor dos nuvems
  Flor do mar
  Flor do vinho

(brother) = ?
  | Jandira

Codó in Maranhão to govern over the spirits there as the lieutenant of the King of the Turks. One of Dom Pedro's sons, Caboclo Nobre, was handed over to Seu Turquia at this time. It is said that there is also a defeated North American encantado enrolled as a foster son of Seu Turquia, but as yet this Yankee spirit has not possessed anyone in Belém, or at least has not identified himself.

There is no general agreement about the physical appearance of the encantados. Judging from the paintings of encantados that have been made to order for some members, some devotees picture their *turcos* as North American Indians. One doctrine, which can be sung by any of the Turks, makes such an identification explicit, or at least it seems to equate the *turcos* and some kind of Indian:

Solo:
Eu sou mouro, eu sou mouro!   *I'm a Moor, I'm a Moor!*

Chorus:
Indio é,   *He's an Indian,*

Solo:
Eu sou turco, turco eu sou!   *I'm a Turk, a Turk I am!*

Chorus:
Indio é.   *He's an Indian.*

Other songs to the Turks include references to bows, arrows, feathers, and other paraphernalia of Indian culture. But when asked specifically whether the *turco* encantados were Indians, most informants insisted that they were *brancos* (whites) from Turkey, not Indians from the forest. As invisible spirits capable of assuming various guises, it is believed that the encantados can reveal themselves in different ways to different devotees. Within very wide limits, it is possible for each Batuque member to decide for himself what the appearance of his encantado is, depending upon his private revelations.

The origin of the *turcos* in the Batuque can undoubtedly be traced to the *mouriscas* that once were a popular part of religious festivals in both Portugal and Brazil.[1] The *mouriscas* were mock battles which commemorated the medieval crusades of Christians against the Moors in the Iberian peninsula. In Brazil the Moors in these staged battles were often called *turcos* rather than *mouros*

(Cascudo 1956, p. 297; Alvarenga 1950b, pp. 50–54). The Turquia family of encantados is probably based on the Moorish contingent of the *mouriscas*. This interpretation is strengthened by the presence of a Muslim princess named Floripes in one of the traditional Portuguese *mouriscas* (Cascudo 1962, p. 251). It will be noted in the genealogy given in Table 1 that this is the name of Seu Turquia's sister.

An important difference between the *turcos* of the Batuque cult and those of the *mouriscas*, however, is that in the cult the *turcos* are conceptualized as conquering warriors, not as defeated spirits. In the dramas of the *mouriscas*, the Moors were invariably defeated and then baptized. It has been suggested that the Portuguese adaptation of the *Song of Roland*, titled *Carlos Magno e os doze pares de França*, is the ultimate source of the Moorish theme in Brazilian folklore (Alvarenga 1948, pp. 5–6). It is true that in this medieval epic the Moors defeat and massacre the outnumbered Christian rear-guard forces, but the Moors are essentially portrayed in an unsympathetic fashion even in their victory, and in the finale Charlemagne exacts vengeance. Only by a creative reinterpretation of some kind could the Moors be transformed into the heroes of the drama. A possible explanation is that the African slaves and freedmen in Brazil, who usually participated in these dramas, secretly identified with the Moors, the opponents of their European masters. In the publicly staged dramas, the European Christians won, but in the privacy of cult ceremonies the victorious Moors were honored.

Although some of these "Turkish" encantados appear to have become good Christians, others are regarded as unbaptized pagans. One informant insisted that the entire family of Seu Turquia is still pagan and worships a golden lion. (*"O leão de ouro é o santo dêles."*) Other cult members, however, rejected this version and insisted that their own *turcos* were baptized Christians who adored the saints.

In Belém the most popular member of the Turquia family is Mariana, who is definitely a Christian, dedicated to Nossa Senhora de Batalha (Our Lady of Battle). Mariana is not only the most popular of the *turcos*, she is, in fact, the most popular of all the encantados known in Belém of any family. An unusually complex set of attributes has been attached to this encantado, undoubtedly due to her popularity and the many individuals who, as her devotees, have had the opportunity to contribute to the lore about this spirit. In several of the songs directed to her, Mariana is identified as the special protector of sailors and of the Brazilian Navy, and she is thought to spend much of her time with the fleet at sea. At the same time she is considered to be a skilled midwife, who guides both mother and child through the birth crisis. She is also a nurse, attending and soothing the sick. In addition she is very good at helping people find employment, and is also something of a Cupid, adept at arranging lovers. Because of this latter attribute, many prostitutes regard Mariana as their special protector.

The informant who remarked that "Mariana is so cherished because she does so much good" might have had any of the foregoing attributes in mind, but was probably thinking of Mariana's role in curing disease. Mariana often figures prominently in curing ceremonies, during which she is identified, as the following doctrine indicates, as "the queen of the curers." Such an identification somewhat exaggerates the role and importance of Mariana in Batuque curing, but she does have a reputation among believers as a great curer.

Chegou, arara cantadeira,	*She's here, the arara songstress,*
Chegou, arara cantadeira,	*She's here, the arara songstress,*
Chegou, a rainha das curandeiras.	*She's here, the queen of curers.*
Ela é arara, é arara, a—ê,	*She is the arara, is the arara, a—ê,*
Ela é arara, é arara, a—ê.	*She is the arara, is the arara, a—ê.*

It will be noted that in this doctrine Mariana is equated with the *arara* (the macaw, a bird of the parrot family). This is a clear instance of the incorporation into the Batuque of ideas derived from the Amazonian shamanistic tradition. In the first place, in *pajelança* (shamanism) the spirits are often animals or birds. Secondly, the *arara* has a special significance in shamanistic curing in that a bundle of the long red tail feathers of this bird is manipulated by the shaman as part of the curing rite. We thus have in Mariana a Turkish princess who is at the same time an animal spirit and the guardian spirit of sailors. At one ceremony we attended, a *pai de santo* who received Mariana wore a sailor suit and carried an *arara* perched on his arm.

Since these two associations are clearly the most prominent of Mariana's various attributes, there does not seem to be any very obvious reason why she should be included in the Turquia family. In fact, this point can be made with reference to all of the families—they serve as a means of organizing the spirits, but the specific encantados included in each family often seem fortuitous.

Mariana's twin brother, Mariano, is not identified with an animal spirit and is not particularly popular in Belém, although he is said to be more prominent in Maranhão. The second most popular member of the Turquia family is Tapinaré, a male encantado identified with the *onça pintada* (jaguar), another important spirit in Amazonian shamanism.

Guapindaia, who ranks third in popularity in the Turquia family, is not clearly identified with any animal spirit. Like his brother Tapinaré and his sister Mariana, Guapindaia is considered to be a powerful healer who works in curing sessions as well as in *batuques*. According to some informants, Guapindaia sometimes gives his own name in curing sessions but usually calls himself "Tango do Pará." Other informants, however, seemed unaware of any identification of Tango do Pará with Guapindaia and thought of the two as distinct personalities. To complicate matters, when he descends in curing sessions, Tango do Pará sings a song in which he says that his "real" name is Mestre Belamino. Whether or not he can be equated with Guapindaia, Tango do Pará is another very prominent and popular figure in Batuque curing. It seems probable that the *tangaru-pará,* a songbird that figures in several Amazonian Indian legends (Oliveira 1951, pp. 169–72; Cascudo 1962, p. 726), was the prototype of Tango do Pará, although our informants never explicitly made such an identification.[2]

According to Batuque legends, Seu Turquia did not bring up all of his children. Some were adopted by other families and now usually appear in ceremonies when their foster parents are being called rather than when Seu Turquia or their own brothers and sisters are called. For example, the Princesa d'Alva listed above as a foster daughter of Averekete[3] usually "descends" early in ceremonies when the doctrines to Averekete are sung, but she is actually, our informants pointed out, one of Seu Turquia's daughters. Basilio Bom (who uses the name "Guillerme" in curing ceremonies) was also brought up by foster parents rather than by his father, Seu Turquia. Basilio was adopted by another highly respected encantado, Dom João Sueira.

Dom João Sueira═Fina Joia
│
Menino Agudui
Conceição Sueira
João de Ouro
Joãozinho Sueira
Leovergio Sueira
Basilio Bom (foster son)

Dom João is said to be the "noble who tamed the Exus" and is sometimes identified as the Yoruban god of war, Ogun, as illustrated in the following song:

Rei Dom João,	*King Dom João,*
Êle é rei maior.	*He is the greatest king.*
Êle é rei de cada mi-a,	*He is king of every [mine?],*
Êle é Ogun maior.	*He is the greatest Ogun.*
Ogun mada-zê-bê,	*Ogun mada-zê-bê,*
Olha, rei de cada mi-a!	*Look, king of every [mine]!*
Ogun-ô,	*Ogun-ô,*
Olha, rei de cada mi-a!	*Look, king of every [mine]!*
Ogun-ô.	*Ogun-ô.*

It seems likely that in Dom João Sueira we have an encantado whose name derives from a relatively obscure figure in Brazilian history. The term *"sueira"* is colloquial for *"suleira"* (southerner), and in fact Dom João's name is occasionally pronounced "Suleira" (Alvarenga 1948, p. 35). Another song identifies the part of southern Brazil that Dom João hails from:

Dom João, Dom João
É de Mina.
Dom João, Dom João
É mineiro.

Cult members stated that the second line means that Dom João is a member of the cult of Mina, but the fourth line means that he comes from the state of Minas Gerais.

Around 1725 an area rich in diamonds was discovered around the city of Tijuco in the province of Minas Gerais. In order to limit production and thus maintain prices, and in order to insure the collection of the royal "fifths," the area was closed to free-lance miners in 1734. All mining rights were turned over to a single contractor. The contractor holding the monopoly from 1759 to 1771 (when the contract system was abandoned) was João Fernandes de Oliveira. João was the son and heir of the previous contractor, and he greatly increased the family wealth by his efficient exploitation of the concession. He had over 3600 slaves, and his mistress, Chica da Silva, was a former slave. João maintained Chica and her children in ostentatious luxury; her house in Tijuco was celebrated as the most splendid in Minas Gerais (Calmon 1959–61, vol. III, pp. 1032–33; Boxer 1962, pp. 219–23).

It is possible that João Fernandes de Oliveira and Chica da Silva are the historical antecedents for Dom João and Fina Joia (the name "Fina Joia" means "precious jewel"). Batuque members today seem quite unaware of this episode in Brazilian history, but the story of Chica da Silva is still popular in other sections of Brazil, as is shown by its adoption as a theme by a samba group in Rio de Janeiro in the 1963 *carnaval*. It should be stressed that this reconstruction of the origin of Dom João is a hypothesis which can obviously never be completely verified. It is presented as an example of how some of the encantados may have acquired names. Most new encantados are named by cult leaders, either while in a trance state or while interpreting the trance behavior of others. The leaders have not simply given the first name that occurred to them, but have usually chosen a name from a limited number of sources. In many cases the names have been chosen from the pantheon of other religions, but sometimes the source has been folklore, and in a number of cases the names refer to real persons prominent in history.

The case of the encantado Rei Sebastião illustrates the adoption of a historical figure into the Batuque spirit pantheon by way of folklore. Rei Sebastião (who, as mentioned above, is equated with St. Sebastian by many cult members) heads a small, prestigious spirit family:

Rei Sebastião (Xapanan) = (wife unknown)

Sebastino
Jarina

He is given the alternate name of Xapanan, which is the name of the deity of smallpox and skin diseases in some other African-derived cults in Brazil. In Belém and Maranhão, however, another encantado, Akossi-Sapata, is associated with skin diseases and Rei Sebastião has nothing to do with such ailments. He is a warrior king as the following two doctrines indicate:

Rei Sebastião, guerreiro militar,	*King Sebastian, military warrior,*
Rei Sebastião, guerreiro militar,	*King Sebastian, military warrior,*
O Xapanan.	*O Xapanan,*
Êle é pai de terreiro.	*He is father of the terreiro.*
Êle é guerreiro	*He is a warrior*
Nesta guerra imperial.	*In this imperial war.*
Rei, Rei, Rei guerreador!	*King, King, warrior King!*
Rei, Rei, Rei guerreador!	*King, King, warrior King!*
Êle vem tirando esmola,	*He comes collecting alms,*
Mas não é por carecêr.	*But not because of need.*
Êle vem tirando esmola,	*He comes collecting alms,*
Mas não é por carecêr.	*But not because of need.*

Rei Sebastião's historical origin is clear-cut and entirely European. He is the Portuguese King Sebastian who died at the age of twenty-four in the battle of Alcazar-Kebir in Morocco on August 4, 1578. King Sebastian's intervention in Moroccan civil strife was regarded as a holy crusade against the infidel by his subjects. Many of them could not believe that their gallant young king had actually been killed and felt that he must still be alive and would reappear at some opportune moment to rescue Portugal from Spanish rule. As time went on, the legend developed that King Sebastian and his army had all been enchanted somewhere and could only reappear when the spell was broken. According to Batuque cult members, the king's family and his warriors are all enchanted on Lençol Beach in Maranhão. If one walks on this enchanted beach on a dark night one can hear the enchanted children crying and enchanted roosters crowing. King Sebastian himself walks along this beach on nights when there is no moonlight. He takes the form of a large black bull and looks for a woman who will have the courage to approach and give him a good kick instead of fleeing. Once he meets such a woman the king will free all of the encantados still held on the beach. At this moment all of the encantados will rise to the sur-

The carouser spirit named Jarina is quite popular in the Batuque. A medium in trance as Jarina leads a lively song.

face of the earth and all of the humans in São Luís and its vicinity will sink into the lower depths of the *encantaria*.[4]

At present only Rei Sebastião, his son Sebastino, and his daughter Jarina have the same freedom of movement as other encantados. Jarina is the most popular of the three in Belém. She appears in Batuque ceremonies as a very gay, playful spirit who is usually a heavy drinker. Her name suggests an animistic origin—the *jarina* is the ivory palm tree. According to legend, Jarina was imprisoned in a stone wall at Lençol Beach by her father, the king, and it was Mariana of the Turquia family who landed at the beach with a squadron of the Brazilian Navy and "disenchanted," or liberated, Jarina.

Another encantado who may be based on a historical personage is Dom Pedro Angaço, but we were unable to discover any clues as to his origin. As far as Batuque members are concerned, Dom Pedro is the lieutenant of Seu Turquia, governing the forest of Codó in Maranhão for the king. Cult members who have come to Belém from Maranhão tend to regard Dom Pedro's spirit family as native to Maranhão and as their special property. This possessive attitude has led to a certain amount of resentment on the part of mediums who are native to Pará and who feel that they are as fully qualified to receive Dom Pedro's family as anyone else. The family is quite popular in Belém (see Table 2).

Legua Bogi da Trinidade (called "Seu Legua" for short) is the most popular member of the family and the most puzzling. His name suggests that he is a combination of two Dahomean deities from the Casa das Minas—Legba and Podi-Bogi—as well as being associated in some way with the Christian Trinity. Legba is the Dahomean trickster deity, the equivalent of the Yoruban Exu. Podi-Bogi in the Casa das Minas is a son of Akosa-Sapata of the Dã or Danbira family (Eduardo 1948, p. 78). In Belém, Legua Bogi does not appear to have the character traits that might mark him as a trickster; he appears as a serious spirit, although he is inclined to drink a lot. However, his brother Bombeiro and all of his sons are conceived of as playful, mischievous encantados, which may represent some carry-over of the African tradition. None of Legua Bogi's family display any saintly characteristics that might explain their association with

TABLE 2. Family of Dom Pedro Angaço

Dom Pedro Angaço = Rainha Rosa
|
Esmeralda Edite
Moça da Guia
Angacino
Bombeiro
Floriano
Pedro Estrelo
Legua Bogi da Trinidade = (wife unknown)
|
Codóensa Boa da Trinidade
Folha Seca
Joãozinho Boa da Trinidade
Joaquimzinho Boa da Trinidade
José Raimundo Boa da Trinidade
Manoelzinho Boa da Trinidade
Miguelzinho Boa da Trinidade

the Trinity. In addition, the saints they adore are not the Santissima Trinidade (Holy Trinity—locally thought of as one distinct saint since it is represented by one image) but vary with the encantado. Legua Bogi adores St. Expeditus, Joãozinho adores St. John, Miguelzinho adores St. Michael, while Manoelzinho has never revealed that he adores any particular saint.

All of the encantados mentioned thus far are believed to come from areas outside the state of Pará and thus distant from Belém. There are spirits, however, that are regarded as having a local origin. One such group is the family or tribe of Japetequara:

Japetequara = (wife unknown)
|
Dona Rosalina
Cabocla Tartaruga da Amazonas
Caboclo Pemba
Curupira (Surupira)
Curupira-airara
Curupira Chica Baiana
Curupira Piriri
Guerreiro
Itapaquara
Itaquara
Itaquari
Jacitaria

Japetequara, also called "Caboclo Velho," is identified by his devotees as an Indian king living in an *encantaria* in the forest of Ararí on the island of Marajó. In addition to being a "pure" Indian, he is also identified as the *jacaré* (alligator). Very serious and dignified, as befits a king, Japetequara's arrival at a *batuque* invariably is the signal for a number of possessions of mediums by his own children or subjects, by other Indian encantados, and often by encantados of the Turquia family. Prominent in these mass possessions are the Curupiras, easily recognized by their manner of dancing, which is unusually wild and abandoned, and their tendency to yelp or bark while dancing.

The Curupiras (pronounced Surupira by some cult members) are believed to be untamed, black-skinned children of Japetequara who live in dense forest in thorn trees or in the *sacupema,* the great elevated root masses of various trees of the tropical rain forest. It is stated that anyone possessed by a Curupira can climb thorn trees without feeling pain. Curupiras are inclined to be mischievous and to play tricks on anyone venturing into the forest without their consent. They particularly enjoy causing people to lose their way in the forest by assuming human form, pointing out short cuts, and luring the traveler away from the established trails. However, Curupiras are not thought to be truly malicious spirits; they are simply mischievous. It is easy to win their good will by leaving them gifts of rum, tobacco, and honey. Some cult members picture their Curupiras as resembling African Pygmies, but the Curupiras' origin is ultimately Indian—they came into Brazilian folklore from some of the Tupí-speaking tribes. They are still quite prominent in Amazonian folk beliefs (Galvão 1955, pp. 99–102).

After Japetequara himself, the highest ranking member of this family is Dona Rosalina, who is identified as the Cobra Grande da Lagoa (Giant Snake of the Lake). Giant snakes, like the Curupiras, constitute an ancient, well-established theme in Amazonian folklore (Galvão 1955, pp. 98–99; Moraes 1960, pp. 75–80). These legendary snakes are monster-sized anacondas thought to inhabit the Amazon River and its tributary rivers and lakes. Since they ordinarily emerge from the watery depths only in the dead of night, they are rarely seen by man, but occasionally they leave unmistakable traces of their presence. It is widely be-

A group of mediums possessed by Curupira spirits dance with hair loosened, heads down.

lieved in Belém that the Giant Snake that lives in Lake Utinga (the lake supplying the drinking water for the city) decided one night to cross over to the Guamá River. The next morning a wide trail was discovered through the forest that separates the two bodies of water; the Giant Snake had snapped off the enormous trees as easily as if they were toothpicks. There are many other stories in the same vein that attest to the immense size and often voracious appetite of the Cobra Grande.

Despite the frightening image of the Giant Snake in local legend, the encantado associated with the monster, Dona Rosalina, appears in cult ceremonies as a dignified, refined lady. She smokes a pipe if it is available and will accept a cup of tea, but she rejects all alcoholic beverages. This is another illustration of the highly selective manner in which only some connotations are carried over when a figure is transferred from one tradition to another. There seems to be no general principle which will

account for the connotations chosen—this seems to depend ultimately on the individuals who first made the associations and
on subsequent mediums who received the same spirit and gradually modified the original conception.

Another group of encantados thought of as native to Pará is
the *Falange de Bôtos* (Phalanx of Dolphins).

```
                Bôto Araçu
                Bôto Branco
                Bôto Castanho
                Bôto Preto
                Bôto Tucuxí
                Bôto Vermelho
                Dona Dada = ?
                          |
                     Belo Encanto
                     Dur Encanto
                Dona Ina
                João da Lima
                Parazito
```

This dolphin group is not organized as one family as in the
other cases we have been considering. It is believed that each
dolphin encantado has an encantado father and mother and
probably children of its own, but with the exception of Dona
Dada and her two sons, informants were unable to give details
about dolphin families. All of the dolphin encantados are native
to Pará. The Bôto Tucuxí, the most popular dolphin spirit, is
thought to live in the Guamá River, which forms one of the city
limits of Belém. At one of the beaches of Mosqueiro, a large
island near Belém, the Bóto Branco makes its home. Almost any
river, lake, or creek is thought to have either a dolphin, mermaid,
or snake encantado "taking charge" of it.

The fresh-water dolphins, which are common in the larger
rivers and lakes of the Amazon Basin, have always impressed
the human inhabitants of the region as being imbued with supernatural power, most of it of an evil nature. The Brazilians
have elaborated on the original Indian conceptions and have
come to fear the dolphin more than any other animal. Dolphins
are dreaded and avoided because of their alleged habits of
seducing young girls, overturning canoes, and casting malignant
spells over those humans who attract their displeasure (Galvão

1955, pp. 91–97). It is thus again somewhat surprising that in Batuque ceremonies the dolphins appear as relatively tame and gentle spirits. One informant who received both *turcos* and *bôtos* stated that, compared to the *turcos,* the *bôtos* are "almost saints." Mediums who are possessed by dolphins usually dance barefoot, hop about a great deal, and lead songs about their origin:

Eu sou paraense,	*I am paraense,*
Eu sou do Pará.	*I'm from Pará.*
Eu sou do Pará,	*I'm from Pará,*
Eu não sou de Mina.	*I'm not from Mina.*
Meu pai se chama	*My father's name is*
O mestre João da Lima.	*Master João da Lima.*

There are a number of small families of encantados, which may be considered together.

Dom José (Rei Floriano) = (wife unknown)
|
Zezinho

Rainha Eowa = (husband unknown)
|
Toia Navéroaim

Principe de Espanha = (wife unknown)
|
Pequenino

Barão de Goré = (wife unknown)
|
Gorézinho

João da Mata (Rei da Bandeira) = (wife unknown)
|
Dorina
Tanbacê

The first three families of this group are considered to have royal rank. Of these three, Dom José and his son Zezinho at present have the most devotees in Belém. None of our informants could offer any explanation as to the significance or origin of Dom José's alternate name of King Floriano. Rainha Eowa adores St. Ann, the mother of the Virgin Mary, and may have once been identified as St. Ann. At present, however, an encantado named Nana Burocô is more frequently spoken of as being associated with *a Velha* (the Old Lady), as St. Ann is referred to. Neither Rainha Eowa nor her daughter Navéroaim have many devotees at present in Belém; both were apparently much more popular a generation ago. Pequenino, the son of the Prince of Spain, appears in *batuques* as a somewhat irresponsible, fun-loving *farrista,* or, at least, has several devotees at present who receive him in this guise.

Informants stated that neither Barão de Goré nor João da Mata (Rei da Bandeira) are actually "nobles" in spite of their titles of "baron" and "king of the banner." According to two informants, the Barão de Goré is actually a shark, *tubarão* in Portuguese, who slyly shortened his name in order to pass himself off as a noble and to mystify the uninitiated. João da Mata was once an ordinary human being, a carefree vagabond minstrel who traveled from place to place with his guitar, singing and playing for his keep. He had been named João da Mata because he was born on February 8, the day of St. John of Matha.[5] Somehow João was transformed from human into encantado. His basic personality was little altered by the transformation. He is still a happy carouser who likes to drink and dance and affects outsized hats as a part of his costume. But, notwithstanding their lowly origins and boisterous natures, both the Barão de Goré and João da Mata are considered powerful curers and important encantados.

In addition to the above mentioned families of encantados, four different "lines" of spirits are frequently mentioned in Belém: the lines of Jurema, Ogun, Oxossi, and the Exus (Table 3). The line method of classification reflects the influence of the Umbanda sects of Rio de Janeiro and São Paulo, where the vast pantheon of "guides" are organized into seven lines. Each line is more like an army than like a family. Each has a supreme commander, a defined area of operation, and each is subdivided into a number of legions headed by subordinate officers.

As yet, little of the schematic detail of the line classification has caught on in Belém. The most popular line is that of Jurema, but not all of the encantados ascribed to this line are from Rio de Janeiro's Umbanda. Part of the group appears to have come to Belém from the Catimbó cult of northeastern Brazil. According to our informants, Jurema herself (as well as her husband, Seu Jurema) is from Ceará, and her *encantaria* is located in the neighboring waters. There is a biological family of Juremas at

TABLE 3. Encantados Grouped into "Lines"

The Exus	Jurema	Ogun	Oxossi
Biranan	Seu Jurema	Ogun	Oxossi
Exu-Caveiro	Jurema Velha	Ogun Beira-Mar	Dora da Mata
Exu-mirim	Jureminha	Ogun de Ronda	(Pena Verde)
Cibiru	Mirací	Ogun-iara	(Sete Flechas)
Inambé	Dom Carlos	Ogun-megê	
Pomba Gira	Cabocla Roxa	Ogun Sete Ondas	
Sete Encruzilhados	Capingueiro	(Rompe Mata)	
Tiriri	da Jurema		
Tranca Rua	Flecheiro		
	Juçara		
	Junqueira		
	Juremé		
	Juremeia		
	Juruwa		
	Paraguaçu		
	(Pena Verde)		
	(Rompe Mata)		
	(Sete Flechas)		

the head of this line. Jurema Velha and Seu Jurema are the mother and father, and there are at least five children in the family. Their real names are not "Jurema" at all, but most members of the family have not revealed their real names. Only one of the daughters, Jureminha, and one of the sons, Mirací, have given their true names. The others are simply addressed as "Dona" or "Seu" Jurema.

All are called Jurema because the family and the entire line regard the jurema tree (*Pithecolobium diversifolium Bent.*) as a sacred tree. When soaked in water, the roots and bark of the jurema apparently yield a vision-inducing narcotic that was aboriginally used in religious ceremonies by various Tupí tribes. It was later adopted in the Catimbó cult of the Northeast and in the Candomblé de caboclo of Bahia as a method of encouraging possession (Cascudo 1962, p. 408; 1956, pp. 512–14; Bastide 1960, pp. 243–54). In the Batuque the leaves of the jurema are used in ritual baths and burned in some of the ritual fumigations. Some cult leaders make a tea of the flowers, leaves, and bark of the jurema and leave it in a bowl underneath the altar to be drunk by the encantados, either in their invisible, disembodied state or after they have possessed a medium. Few of the encantados, however, are thought to drink the jurema infusion. The narcotic properties of the tree are unknown in Belém. Informants ascribed any "kick" the beverage might have to the fact that rum rather than water might be used in preparing the tea. Only extremely disreputable *terreiros* (shunned, of course, by our informants) would use such a "medicine" to induce trance in the mediums.

In addition to the biological family of Jurema, many other encantados have become affiliated with the Jurema line. One of the best known is Dom Carlos. Like João da Mata, Dom Carlos was once just an ordinary human being, distinguished only as a heavy drinker. One day he fell into a drunken stupor under a jurema tree. He slept there for three days and three nights, and when he woke up he was an encantado, ready to practice curing. A song gives his history:

Carlos Velho é bom mestre,	*Old Carlos is an excellent curer,*
Aprendeu sem se ensinar.	*He learned without any teaching.*
Tres dias amanhece, caido	*After three days he woke up, lying*
Em baixo de uma jurema.	*Underneath a jurema tree.*

Another song suggests that Carlos' weakness for alcohol has persisted:

Amigo, me da um gole,	*Friend, give me a swig,*
Eu também sou bebedor.	*I'm a drinker too.*
A garrafinha que eu trazia	*The little flask I was carrying*
Caiu na pedra e quebrou.	*Fell on a stone and broke.*

A slightly different version of Dom Carlos' doctrines was collected in Belém in 1938 (Alvarenga 1950a, p. 129). Dom Carlos is definitely not a newcomer to the Batuque, but other encantados in the line, such as Capingueiro, Juremeia, and Flecheiro, are recent arrivals in the city.

In the Umbanda cult of southern Brazil, Jurema is merely one of seven subchieftains in the line of Oxossi, the African god of hunting and of the forest (Camargo 1961, p. 38; Fontenelle 1953, p. 136). In Belém, Oxossi is considered a newcomer and as yet is not very popular. There are already a number of other hunting and forest spirits, and Oxossi is not likely to be accepted as the superior of Japetequara. Since cult members are already

A separate shrine to Pena Verde was set up at one *terreiro*, with a life-sized image of the spirit. The headdress and skirt on the image feature feathers of the blue macaw, the bird the spirit is identified with. The *mãe de santo* who had this image made to order visualized Pena Verde as having straight blond hair.

familiar with Jurema, the tendency is to put her at the head of all of the new forest encantados coming to Belém from Umbanda. Some cult members even consider Oxossi to be Jurema's subordinate, and only a few realize that he is an African deity.

There is no agreement as to the "line" assignment of the popular spirit Pena Verde. Some cult members insist that he is the son of Rei Pena Real, and thus a member of a separate family with no affiliations with either the Jurema or the Oxossi group. Pena Verde is identified with the blue macaw (which for some reason is often called the *arara verde,* or green macaw, in the Amazon region) and probably originated in local shamanism rather than in Umbanda.

The Umbanda line of Ogun is not very popular in Belém as a group, but one of its members, Rompe Mato, appears to be second only to Mariana in popularity among cult members, i.e., only Mariana has more mediums who claim to receive her. Older informants reported that Rompe Mato was "brought from Rio" only twenty-five or thirty years ago. Actually, Rompe Mato's identification as an Ogun is somewhat uncertain in Belém. He adores St. George, the saint of most of the Umbanda Oguns, but for most cult members in Belém, Rompe Mato is the chief hunter of Jurema and appears in her line, not in that of Ogun. It is believed that he is the son of an Exu, but since he was adopted and brought up by Jurema as her foster son, Rompe Mato lost the demonic qualities of the Exus.

The part of Umbanda that seems to be the most acceptable in Belém is the emphasis on the demon spirits, the Exus.[6] Some cult members deplore this development and state that in the old days no one ever sought possession by an *homem da rua* (man of the street) as an Exu is called. The Exus were respected but regarded as much too dangerous to cultivate. Before every ceremony they were "dispatched," of course, as they still are, by being given an offering of rum, gunpowder, and a candle. Then their permission to hold the ceremony was formally requested in a series of introductory songs (see Appendix A). At midnight, the hour reserved for the devil, the ceremony stopped and a special doctrine was sung to *salvar o terreiro* (salute the *terreiro*):

A medium possessed by Ogun-iara emits a war whoop.

Lá vem meu pai, Badé,
E, lá vem mãe, Navé.
A-ba-lô-a-ê
A-ba-lô-a-ê, Nagô.

There comes my father, Badé,
And there comes mother, Navé.
A-ba-lô-a-ê
A-ba-lô-a-ê, Nagô.

After singing this song all mediums left the floor for refreshments and rest. Dancing did not resume until one o'clock.

At present this hour break is rarely observed, and at most *terreiros* a *gira dos Exus* (turn of the Exus) is observed instead, as described in Chapter I. At midnight the lights are turned off, all spectators stand up, the mediums cover their heads with

At some *terreiros* the demon Exus are never invited to possess mediums. Midnight is marked by kneeling and singing a special song.

scarves, and the Exus are called. The demon spirits may possess members of the audience as well as the participating mediums. People possessed by Exus usually dance very wildly, grunting, yelling, yelping, and often holding their eyes wide open in an unfocused vacant stare. After gunpowder is burned and the lights turned back on, all of the Exus are expected to leave, and any individual still possessed is brought out of trance as quickly as possible. Most cult members say it is necessary to hold the Exu ceremony not only as a mark of respect for these powerful spirits, but also to *descarregar o terreiro* (decontaminate the *terreiro*) and remove any ill feeling stirred up by the Exus that might otherwise lead to fights. The *gira dos Exus* appears to be quite popular with the regular spectators of *batuques* as well as

At most centers the Exus are invited to descend at midnight. Here a medium in trance as Exu Tranca Rua ignites the gunpowder he holds in his bare hand.

with most mediums, and this new feature of the ritual will probably be continued.

Although the Exus are identified as demons, their devotees insist that if they are handled properly the Exus can do good as well as evil. Tranca Rua, the Exu with the most devotees in Belém, is regarded as more "elevated" and tractable than others in the line.

Some Batuque leaders consider St. Anthony the patron saint of the Exus. They place a small image of this saint in the Exu shrine (which is usually located in a small shed near the pavilion) and hold ceremonies to honor the Exus on St. Anthony's day, June 13. It is hard to account for the connection of St. Anthony and the Exus. St. Anthony is one of the most esteemed saints of

Mediums possessed by other Exus typically dance with their eyes open in an unfocused stare.

both Portugal and Brazil, an amiable, comradely saint who is adept at finding lost articles and at arranging marriages. His connection with devils must be very indirect. In his study *Os três santos de junho no folclore brasílico,* Bettencourt (1947, pp. 68–71) reports that in some of the early Afro-Brazilian cults St. Anthony was identified with Ogun, the Yoruban war god. Bettencourt suggests this association was made because St. Anthony was the favorite saint of the soldiers in the colonial armies.

Ogun is believed to have some authority over the Exus, and it may have been in this indirect way that St. Anthony came to be the patron saint of the demon spirits.

In the Umbanda-oriented centers another category, or fifth line, of spirits is frequently mentioned: the line of the Pretos Velhos (Old Blacks). The Pretos Velhos are supposedly gifted curers, but the group as a whole is not very popular in Belém, and only a few Preto Velho spirits actually put in an appearance at Umbanda curing sessions: Pai Benedito, Pai Tomas (identified as the Uncle Tom of Harriet Beecher Stowe's *Uncle Tom's*

As soon as the midnight ceremony is concluded, all mediums possessed by Exus are forced out of trance by others pressing their heads and, if necessary, blowing into their ears.

Cabin), Pai Jeronimo, and Senhora Ana. All of the Pretos Velhos are conceptualized as very old, humble spirits who once lived and suffered a great deal as slaves on this earth. All the hatred and resentment they felt against their masters and their fate was purged from their souls in the course of their difficult existence. They learned to turn the other cheek and now represent "pure charity." Such goodness must be formally praised, but Batuque cult members show a decided preference for more militant spirits.

Although most of the encantados in the Batuque are considered to be members of some specific family or associated with a definite group, there are a number of solitary spirits who, in the words of informants, "live alone without relatives" (see Table 4). These unaffiliated encantados can be divided into two groups according to their social standing. Those considered to be of high status are called interchangeably *senhores, brancos,* or *orixás.* The lower-status encantados, who do not have noble rank or who seem more interested in having a good time than in working, are called *caboclos.*

For most cult members, Oxalá, who heads the roster of unaffiliated *senhores,* is a very remote supreme spirit-deity, the "father" of everyone, whose position in the spirit world approximates that of God in the sphere of the saints and angels. He is powerful, a lawgiver, and morally incorruptible, but he is very distant from man and from the ordinary press of encantados. Nana Burocô is his female equivalent, a powerful but remote "mother" of everyone, but she is not considered to have any family relationship with Oxalá. Both Oxalá and Nana Burocô have devotees who maintain "obligations" to them, but it is believed that they rarely descend to possess anyone. Some cult members in fact insist that these two very "elevated" spirits never descend to earth at all, but others feel that under special circumstances they might descend briefly to possess certain carefully chosen mediums. Both spirits are of Yoruban derivation and are more emphasized in the cult centers that stress Umbanda.

Xangô is the Yoruban name for the deity of thunder and lightning; Badé is the Dahomean name for the same spirit. Both names are used in the Batuque, with Badé more frequently

Table 4. Unaffiliated Encantados

SENHORES

Male	Female
Oxalá	Nana Burocô
Xangô (Badé)	Rainha Barba (Inhaçan)
José Tupinambá	Imanjá
Dom Luiz	Jamaína
Rei Toi Aduçu	Oxun
Akossi-Sapata	Princesa Sinha Bê
Ben Boçu da Cana Verde	
Rei de Nagô	
Rei Noé	
Rei Salomão	
Rei Taculumi	
Urubatan Jesus	

CABOCLOS

Male	Female
Antonio Luiz Corre-Beirado	Herondina
Boiadeiro da Visaura	Indaiê
Caboclo Brabo	Iracema
Caboclo Luar	Maria Mineira da Luz
Caboclo de Olha Dagua	Preta da Mina
Cidalino	
Constantino (Bahiano Grande)	
Seu Gavião	
Juruparí	
Marabá	
Marinheiro	
Mestre Marajó	
Pombo do Ar	
Ricardino	
Seu Risca	
Tubian	

used in the older Mina-Nagô doctrines and Xangô in the newer Umbanda songs. Xangô-Badé is believed to be an austere, dominating spirit who rarely condescends to possess anyone. He is important to the cult, however, because he is thought to be the provider of the stones that serve as the "seats" of the spirits. Whenever possible, the stone used as the seat of an encantado is a prehistoric stone axhead. These axheads, which were made by the Indians and are found near former Indian settlements, are fairly common throughout the Amazon Basin. Ignoring their true origin, the inhabitants of the area often consider the axheads to be "lightning stones," formed when a bolt of lightning struck the ground and penetrated to a depth of seven meters. Over a period of seven years the stone slowly works its way to the surface. The members of the Batuque have adopted these basically folk-European ideas and have added the belief that it is Xangô who sends the lightning bolt. It should be noted, however, that since there are not enough prehistoric axheads to go around, most cult members settle for any kind of unusual stone found under conditions that suggest supernatural intervention.

Rainha Barba-Inhaçan (St. Barbara) is also believed to have power over thunder and lightning. According to Catholic hagiography, St. Barbara's pagan father was struck dead by lightning after he murdered his Christian daughter. Those cult leaders most influenced by Umbanda argue that Inhaçan is one of the wives of Xangô, but many cult members reject this theory. For them Rainha Barba is a solitary virgin queen with no family ties, who rules over and sends the encantados to dance in the *terreiros*. She is much more approachable than Xangô-Badé, Nana Burocô, or Oxalá, and frequently descends to possess her devotees.

Compared to African-derived cults in other parts of Brazil, in the Batuque there is relatively little emphasis on the mermaids and the "mothers" of waters. Only three mermaids have songs more or less regularly sung to them and a few devotees in the city: Imanjá, Jamaína, and Oxun. Jamaína is the most popular of the three. She is considered a mermaid of salt water. Both Imanjá and Oxun are African deities of Yoruban derivation. Oxun appears to be a fairly new arrival in Belém, and many cult members do not know just what she is the "mother" of. Some suggest that she is the mother of fresh water as Jamaína is of salt water, while others, because of the similarity of names, have confused Oxun with the Exus and consider her a female Exu. Imanjá is considered the mother of water in general and is thought to be the highest ranking water spirit. Most *terreiros* have a special shrine to Imanjá, sometimes with running water. But the elaborate ceremonies of feting and taking presents to Imanjá that are so popular in Bahia and Rio de Janeiro do not take place in Belém. One obvious explanation may be that Belém is not on the ocean, and transportation to the nearest beach on the island of Mosqueiro is somewhat difficult. But, probably of greater importance, in Belém attention is focused on the rivers as the major bodies of water, and the rivers are already full of supernatural beings—dolphins, the Cobra Grande, other snakes, giant turtles, and certain fish. At least at present there is not much interest in an additional encantado associated with water.

José Tupinambá has more devotees in Belém than any other encantado in the unaffiliated group. His name, Tupinambá, is the name given by the early Portuguese to a large number of Indian tribes, most of them cannibalistic, who inhabited the Brazilian coast from Belém to Rio de Janeiro. José is conceptualized as an Indian and is believed to reside in his ancestral home at the beach of São José Ribamar in São Luís. He shows none of the ferocity of his namesakes, and in ceremonies he usually appears as a dignified old gentleman who is often inclined to deliver moralistic exhortations.

Dom Luiz is identified as King Louis XVI of France, the king executed during the French Revolution. Louis XVI would seem a most unlikely candidate for metamorphosis into an Amazonian supernatural. Unlike the other historical figures who have been turned into encantados, Louis is neither Portuguese nor Brazilian, and although São Luís in Maranhão was founded by the French, there was no lasting imprint of French culture. In addition, the character and life story of Louis do not exactly make him the stuff out of which folk heroes are molded. In this case, however, we do not have to guess about the origin of Dom Luiz; the facts are known. He was introduced into the Batuque by Dona Maria de Aguiar, the *mãe de santo* who is credited with first "crossing" Umbanda and Mina-Nagô. Dona Maria states that she first began to receive Dom Luiz some thirty-five years ago while visiting the city of São Luís. When she returned to Belém, Dom Luiz became her chief "guide" and the protector of her *terreiro*. Since Dona Maria believes that in a previous incarnation her soul inhabited the body of Queen Marie Antoinette, she was not particularly surprised to receive the spirit of the queen's husband while visiting a city dedicated to Louis IX

A medium, possessed by the *senhor* Rei Toi Aduçu, insisted on wearing an elaborate brocade shawl instead of a *toalha*. Rei Toi Aduçu is thought of as a very old spirit who moves very slowly; as a result, dancing has almost come to a standstill.

(St. Louis), the ancestor of Louis XVI. Not all cult members share Dona Maria's belief in reincarnation, but her reputation as a cult leader is such that Dom Luiz has been generally accepted as an important encantado, although no one else has as yet received him. Since he is now widely known, it is probably only a matter of time until some other medium will claim to have been possessed by him. If those who receive him tend to prosper, there is no reason why Dom Luiz should not become a permanent member of the Batuque pantheon. It would appear, then, that at least in the case of prominent cult leaders, it is possible to range somewhat further afield in search of likely figures to convert into new encantados. If the cult leader's reputation is great enough, his identification will tend to be accepted.

Akossi-Sapata, Rei Toi Aduçu, Rei Noé, and Ben Boçu da Cana Verde were undoubtedly all borrowed from the Dahomean-oriented Casa das Minas in São Luís (Eduardo 1948, pp. 76–79; Pereira 1947, pp. 33–34). Akossi-Sapata is the deity of skin diseases and therefore a dangerous encantado to receive, since it is believed that the medium who receives him must be handled correctly or he will fall ill with some serious skin disorder. Akossi-Sapata is feted and invited to descend only once a year, during the festival for the saint he adores, St. Lazarus, on February 11. At present only one *terreiro* in the city holds a festival for St. Lazarus. Informants stated that the saint and Akossi-Sapata were much more popular in the *terreiros* of Maranhão than in Belém.

The festival for St. Lazarus in the Batuque is patterned on an Amazonian traditional celebration that antedates any Afro-Brazilian sect (Monteiro 1961). A unique feature of the St. Lazarus festival, whether in the Batuque or outside the cult, is a feast for dogs, during which at least eleven dogs are seated around a table and hand-fed various delicacies. Although the official St. Lazarus is the brother of Mary and Martha whom Jesus raised from the dead, in one of the parables of Jesus there is a story of a beggar named Lazarus, whose body was covered with sores and who was befriended by dogs that came and licked his sores (Luke 16:19–31). The two men named Lazarus are fused as one saint in folk religion and representatives of the canine species are appropriately honored at his feast.

There is very little that can be said as far as identifying the unaffiliated *caboclos* is concerned. Two of them, Boiadeiro da Visaura (Cowboy of Visaura) and Constantino, also called Chapeu de Couro (Leather Hat), are identified as natives of the state of Bahia. One cult leader suggested that both might be sons of Lampião, a famous outlaw leader who terrorized the back country of the Northeast, from Ceará to Bahia, in the period 1920–38 (Cascudo 1962, pp. 416–18). Perhaps this identification represents a new myth in the making. Herondina, the most popular female spirit of these unaffiliated *caboclos,* probably came to Belém with the Jurema group of spirits. A Rei Heron is a prominent figure in the pantheon of the Catimbó cult (Cascudo 1951, p. 155; Andrade 1963, pp. 58, 82–83). In Belém today, however, Herondina's family connections have been forgotten. All of the unaffiliated *caboclos* "work" in curing sessions, but two of them, Antonio Luiz Corre-Beirado and Mestre Marajó descend exclusively in *cura* and never appear in the public ceremonies.

The above list of unaffiliated *caboclos* could be greatly expanded by listing the names of the legion of spirits who descend very briefly or "make a passage" in curing sessions. Such transient spirits, however, have little fame or supernatural power and are rarely sought out by Batuque clients anxious to have services performed by the encantados.

As has been noted in the course of this chapter, in the Batuque there are two methods of organizing the encantados: by membership in a family, tribal group, or line, and by classification into the two categories of *senhores* or *caboclos.* The emphasis on the family organization of encantados probably reflects the influence of the Dahomean Casa das Minas of São Luís, where all *voduns* are members of some family. While there are various family relationships in the roster of Yoruban deities in Bahia, the family pattern is not as emphasized.

Although the basis of organization may be a holdover of African tradition, the families of encantados are modeled directly on Brazilian society, and especially on the family patterns of Amazonia. The patriarchal family is definitely the ideal; all of the spirit families, with the exception of that of Rainha Eowa, are headed by male encantados. The fact that some cult members are themselves born out of wedlock, are brought up primarily by their mothers, and never know their fathers in no way diminishes the patriarchal ideal. The Amazonian custom of both freely giving away and readily adopting children is reflected in the various foster child-foster parent relationships in these encantado families. While the real parents of the foster son or daughter are carefully stipulated, the adopted encantado is expected to have more

A *mãe de santo* whirls enthusiastically as she receives her *cabocla* carouser, Herondina.

in common with his foster family than with his real family. These conceptions are faithfully reproduced from the human relationships of the Amazon region (Wagley 1953, pp. 179–84).

The other principle of organization, that of classifying the encantados as *senhores* or as *caboclos,* is also derived from the Brazilian social system, and clearly reflects the division of the society into two basic classes—the wealthy, prestigious, upper-class *senhores* and the poor, humble, lower-class *caboclos*. As far as the classes of encantados are concerned, the members of the upper-status group are referred to as *brancos* or *orixás* as well as *senhores*. *Branco* (white) in this context is a social rather than a racial term and is a synonym for *senhor*. *Orixá*, used much less commonly, is simply the Yoruban word for "deity" and has no relation to the class situation. Another term that is sometimes used for the prestigious encantados, *gente fina*, is again a term that is used by members of the lower classes to refer to members of the upper crust (Figueiredo and Silva 1967, p. 118).

The classification of encantados as *senhores* or *caboclos* cuts across family lines, with most heads of families included in the *senhor* category and many of their children classified as *caboclos*. All of the encantados with titles like "Rei" (king), "Rainha" (queen), or "Dom" (a titled noble) are included in the *senhor* category, but many of those without titles are also included. José Tupinambá, Japetequara, and Dona Rosalina are all *senhores*, as well as Rei Turquia and Dom João. There do not seem to be any common characteristics shared by all of the upper-status encantados, and their designation as such seems to be quite arbitrary. In addition, certain encantados are believed capable of descending as either a *caboclo* or as a *senhor*. The *pai de santo* Carlos, for example, received Mariana of the Turquia family as a *senhora*, but the same spirit was Clara's *caboclo* carouser. The encantado Guapindaia, of the same family, was received by Ernesto as a hard-drinking *caboclo*, but Guapindaia was Sara's *senhor* and *chefe*.

In other Afro-Brazilian religions, *caboclo* seems most commonly to mean "Indian." In the Batuque the term has two meanings. Sometimes it does mean "Indian," as when Japetequara, conceptualized as an Indian chief living in the forest, is called "Caboclo Velho" (Old Man Indian). However, the term is also used to mean any lower-status encantado, and when used in this way *caboclo* does not necessarily refer to any ethnic or racial characteristics. The dolphins are called *caboclos*, as are the "Turkish" children of Seu Turquia. In this second sense of the term, Japetequara is not a *caboclo*, but a *senhor*—a high-status encantado.

This usage of *caboclo* to refer to the lower-status encantados is based on the general usage of the term in the Amazon Basin. A *caboclo* is a backwoodsman, or someone whose immediate forebears came from the backwoods, an individual, usually of mixed Indian and European ancestry, who is rough, uneducated, and lacking in sophistication and good manners. His tastes are simple and rather crudely physical rather than refined or cultivated. As used by middle- and upper-class Brazilians, the term has definite perjorative connotations—the *caboclo* is considered lazy, lacking in ambition, content to live like an animal rather than to exert himself (Wagley 1953, pp. 140–41). As the term is used by cult members to apply to encantados, the connotations of laziness and shiftlessness are absent. In other respects the image is the same, except that the qualities ascribed to the *caboclo* are, to a certain extent, admired rather than consistently denigrated. The *caboclo*'s lack of polish and elegance is compensated for by his forthright vigor, frankness, and intuitive understanding of nature.

As far as cult members are concerned, the encantados who assume the guise of the rough-and-ready backwoodsman do not merit the deference shown to spirits who come as ladies and gentlemen—they deserve to be relegated to a lower status. Nevertheless, it is believed that the *caboclo* encantados are likely to enjoy themselves more than are the *senhores*. Some of the *caboclos* are *farristas* and obviously motivated by a search for pleasure. Others are more serious and dedicated to working, but even the serious *caboclos* are inclined to drink and smoke, to enjoy vigorous dancing, and to speak bluntly, brusquely, and perhaps too loudly. In fact, *caboclo* encantados probably behave a great deal like the mediums themselves might behave at home, when not putting on their company manners. Assuming the role of a *caboclo* supernatural is probably less of a strain on the medium than assuming the role of a dignified *senhor,* and cult members' impressions that *caboclos* have a better time are undoubtedly justified.

The lists of spirits given above cannot of course be considered either closed or complete. Almost forgotten encantados might reappear in Belém, gain new devotees and become more popular. Entirely new spirits might appear at any moment and have to be added to one category or another. All cult members acknowledge that any family of encantados might have many more children living in the *encantaria* beneath the earth or sea than are at present known. Human beings can know nothing about them until they decide to first rise as invisible spirits and then descend to possess some human "apparatus" and "speak," i.e., sing some song that identifies the family connections and the name of the "invisible."

Actually, though new encantados can in theory be added *ad infinitum* to the existing roster, all indications are that the creation of new spirits occurs at a slow rate. Only mediums of long standing who already have won the respect of their fellow cult members are likely to successfully introduce new encantados to the Batuque, but since they are already respected for the spirits they receive, they do not have much incentive to introduce novelties. People becoming possessed for the first time invariably are *told* by some cult leader what spirit is possessing them, and the leader usually picks some fairly well-known and therefore "easy" encantado. Inexperienced mediums or young people are regarded too critically by older mediums to feel encouraged to be creative. A successful *mãe de santo* such as Dona Maria de Aguiar was able to introduce King Louis XVI of France to the Batuque, but in one episode that we witnessed, when the relatively inexperienced Ione claimed to be receiving Oxalá, she was informed that her encantado was really a Curupira or an Exu giving a false name. The other participants in the ceremony refused to sing the responses to the Oxalá doctrines that Ione attempted to lead and generally refused to believe that her possession was genuine.

Most of the new encantados that appear in the Batuque are not actually new but are merely transplanted—brought from some other part of Brazil to Belém by some specific medium. In the recent past the neighboring state of Maranhão has been the principal source of new religious ideas for the cult in Belém. According to our informants, most of the encantados now honored in the *terreiros* were brought to Pará from Maranhão. The majority of cult members in Belém still speak of Maranhão as a kind of "Holy Land," the home of so many *voduns,* the source of true Mina-Nagô doctrine, where all *terreiros* are much better organized than in Belém. Cult leaders from Maranhão who have moved to Belém to open *terreiros* stress their origin as a proof of doctrinal superiority. Leaders native to Pará often claim to have been initiated into the cult and prepared for leadership by some ancient *mãe* or *pai de santo* from Maranhão who died some time ago.

However, in spite of the influence of Maranhão on the Batuque, mediums from Maranhão newly resident in Belém complain that the local mediums are singing the doctrines wrong and are singing strange new doctrines taken from phonograph records and books instead of the old unwritten, unrecorded, true doctrines. In addition, the Maranhão migrants express dislike of the midnight Exu ceremony and disapproval of the new encantados from Umbanda. These criticisms indicate that the *batuques* of Belém are no longer as close to the *tambores* of Maranhão as once may have been the case, and that cult members of Belém have moved more rapidly than those of Maranhão to accept new ideas emanating from the urban centers of southern Brazil. In fact, for those cult members who identify themselves as "pure" Umbandistas, it is Rio de Janeiro that is the fount of religious authority, the place where things are done properly. This group, still a minority within the cult, tends to disparage Maranhão as a backward place where little of Umbanda is known and to rank it below Pará in religious development.

In reviewing the names and the identifying lore of the non-Christian Batuque spirits, it is fairly easy to isolate the three distinct traditions that have contributed to the Batuque: European or Luso-Brazilian, indigenous Amerindian, and African. The array of princes, nobles, and Turks, and some of the curer-carousers such as Dom Carlos and João da Mata, are all obviously derived from European or Brazilian folklore and history. Most of the Batuque's Indian encantados are of similar origin. Figures such as José Tupinambá, Flecheiro, or Sete Flechas represent Brazilian idealizations of the original inhabitants of the land; they neither represent survivals of Indian religions nor reflect the actual history of Amazonian Indian tribes. Cult members are dedicated to an Indian mystique, and many of them had some Indian ancestors, but they are poorly informed about the actual history and culture of Brazilian Indians. The Indian image in the Batuque appears to be drawn principally from U. S. "Western" movies and the Brazilian popular press.

There is, however, a genuine Indian contribution to the Batuque and that is the addition of animal spirits to the roster of anthropomorphic deities. The mysterious dolphins, the legendary Giant Snake, the alligator (Japetequara), the jaguar (Tapinaré), the hawk (Seu Gavião), the turtle (Tartaruga da Amazonas), the *tangaru-pará* songbird (Tango do Pará), the shark (Barão de Goré), and the two macaw encantados (Mariana and Pena Verde) are derived from local shamanism and probably originated in the religions of the Tupí tribes. The small black people of the forest, the Curupiras, are definitely an Amerindian contribution to the Batuque, and the tree spirits, Jarina, Jurema, and Goiabeira, may also have an Amerindian origin.

It should be noted that none of the mediums who received encantados that were identified as animal spirits imitated the animals their encantados represented when in trance. In the curing ceremonies of some Tupí tribes the shamans attempt to imitate the characteristic movements and sounds of their animal spirit helpers (Wagley and Galvão 1949, pp. 110–18). We never observed any attempt at imitation in Batuque ceremonies. In fact the identification of encantado with animal was always somewhat ambiguous since most devotees of animal spirits appeared to conceptualize their spirits exclusively in human form.

Most cult members in Belém are not very Africa-minded, i.e., they have little interest in that continent or its peoples. Nevertheless the Batuque obviously owes a fundamental debt to black Africa. Although the original African religious themes have been considerably diluted, identifiable African elements are evident, and a number of African deities have survived the influx of European, Brazilian, and Indian spirits. Dahomean deities stand out most prominently among the *voduns* imported from Maranhão: Aduçu, Akossi-Sapata, Averekete, Badé, Ben Boçu, Legua Bogi, Noé. An indirect effect of borrowing from the Umbanda of Rio de Janeiro has been the introduction or re-emphasis of Yoruban-derived *orixás* such as Ogun, Oxossi, Oxun, Inhaçan, Xangô, Imanjá, and Exu. Exu appears to be firmly established and Xangô seems to have replaced Badé, but it is still impossible to predict the ultimate fate of the other Yorubans.

FOOTNOTES

1. Although the ceremony is no longer staged in northern Brazil, *mouriscas* are still apparently occasionally held in other parts of the country. See Cascudo (1954, pp. 90–91, 256–57, 409; 1956, pp. 70–71, 92–93, 96–97); Araújo (1959); Willems (1952, p. 240).

2. The same spirit appears in the Catimbó cult under the names "Ritango do Pará" (Cascudo 1951, p. 155) and "Tangaru-pará" (Andrade 1963, p. 90).

3. Princesa d'Alva means "Princess of the Dawn." The poetic concept of the saint of the night adopting and raising the princess of the dawn might be noted.

4. For a slightly different version of this legend, see Cascudo (1962, p. 745).

5. In an earlier article (Leacock 1964b, p. 106), João da Mata was erroneously equated with John the Baptist.

6. Many cult members in Belém pronounce the name of the demon spirits "Exun" rather than "Exu," the pronunciation used in Rio de Janeiro. Similarly the Iemanjá of Rio is pronounced "Imanjá" and Iansan is given the local spelling and pronunciation "Inhaçan."

Chapter VI

Possession

Of the varied activities that take place in the Batuque, the most important are those that are interpreted as possession by supernatural beings. Since the whole belief system centers around the concept of possession, the act of receiving the encantados is the final validation of Batuque cosmology. For the individual, possession is the ultimate proof that the encantados really do exist.

To the outsider it is the trance that gives the Batuque its exotic aura, and for many, its fascination. This is what draws large crowds to the *terreiros* and inevitably attracts new adherents. At the same time, it is the sometimes uncontrolled behavior of the mediums—the wild gyrations, the flying hair, the staring eyes—that gives the uninformed skeptic grounds for suspecting the worst. Zealous members of other religious groups, whether Catholic or Protestant, are likely to view the phenomenon of possession with horror and to see in it the direct intervention of the Devil. Skeptics without strong religious convictions but with some knowledge of psychology may be inclined to pity the mediums as victims of hysteria or other psychological disorders. Either kind of critic is likely to suggest that in many cases the mediums are consummate actors who are putting on a show for the sake of money and attention.

It is not our intention to argue that all Batuque members are perfectly normal psychologically or that no medium ever pretends to be possessed. As was pointed out in Chapter IV, a few of our informants described what seemed to be psychotic episodes in their past, and it seems quite likely that mediums sometimes pretend to be possessed when they really do not believe that they are. What we will argue, however, is that it is not necessary for a man or woman to be abnormal psychologically in order to be a successful medium and that no medium pretends all of the time. Becoming a medium does require a certain aptitude, but this aptitude is probably not too different from that needed by a good hypnotic subject in American society. Before we can develop this argument further, however, it is necessary to look much more closely at the nature of the behavior we have been calling "possession."[1]

In the foregoing chapters many instances of possession have been described. These examples have demonstrated that possession occurs in many different contexts: in the public ceremony at *terreiros,* in the home, on the street, in a church, in a café. In each of these varied circumstances, it is hoped that one aspect of the behavior described has been made clear. That is, that when possessed, a medium usually acts in a relatively controlled manner and engages in very complex activities. This is not always the case, of course, and sometimes people do fall down or lose control in other ways. But ideally the behavior of a medium when possessed is not too different from his behavior when "pure," except that when possessed he acts as though he were an encantado.

It is necessary to stress this point because the misconception persists that possession is a state of frenzy or ecstasy and that it is typified by extreme and largely uncontrolled behavior. This may be the case in some religions, but it is not true in the Batuque and probably not true in any of the other Afro-Brazilian religions. Although in the early moments of the trance there may be some uncontrolled movements, the medium must quickly gain control if his or her activity is to be interpreted as representing possession by a supernatural being. It is certainly not enough to fall on the floor and thrash around, or stagger about, or make incoherent sounds, or give other evidence of having some kind of unusual psychological experience. The meaning of this kind of behavior is ambiguous in terms of Batuque beliefs. It may

When some mediums enter trance they are initially subject to a violent shaking of the torso.

mean that an encantado has "seized" the person, or it may mean that the person is drunk or insane. In order to prove that an encantado is really present, the medium must dance, sing the proper songs, and interact with the other participants in the ceremony in an acceptable manner. The behavior that is most admired in the accomplished medium is very often the behavior that appears the least frenzied and the most normal to the outside observer.

It must be admitted that it took us some time to accept this idea. We had naïvely supposed that the most violent and uncontrolled trance behavior would be the most convincing, since it would prove that the individual was really possessed. But Batuque members judge the validity of the presence of the encantado not by the gyrations that the medium goes through, but by what the encantado says and does. Since the encantados are conceived of as being very close to the human condition, their behavior is expected to be much like human behavior. The medium must act accordingly if his possession is to be accepted as genuine.

The members of the Batuque believe that the ability to control oneself during trance and to behave properly as an encantado is learned. The expression they use is "development." When a person is possessed for the first time, it is expected that he will fall on the floor, stagger about, and be unable to sing. As he "develops," however, the medium gains "control" and is able to dance, sing, and speak as the encantado. In order to facilitate this development, most mediums go through some kind of training program. In the larger and more traditional *terreiros,* the medium may have an opportunity to go into trance only during the public ceremonies held every few weeks. But in some *terreiros* and in many of the small *searas,* a regular session is held once or twice a week that has the explicit purpose of enabling the mediums to practice going into trance. All of the mediums, especially the novices, are urged to attend regularly and are encouraged by the leader to receive their encantados during the session. As the mediums have more and more trance experiences, their performance as the encantado is expected to improve steadily.

We are convinced that the Batuque members are right and that learning plays a very important part in the career of the medium. In analyzing the situation, it is useful to consider the roles that the mediums learn to take. As was indicated above, individuals must behave in appropriate ways in order to prove that they are possessed. These appropriate ways constitute a "role," i.e., a group of behaviors associated with a particular position in a social system. In this case the position is that of possessed medium, a person possessed by a supernatural being. A careful consideration of the behavior that occurs during trance states suggests that there are actually at least two roles involved, and that these roles vary in specificity. One role, the general role,

After early frenzied body movements, an experienced medium dances in a controlled manner. Here a medium in trance whirls expertly, her full skirt billowing, her *espada* flying.

consists of those behaviors expected of anyone who is possessed. There are also a number of subroles, however, that relate to particular encantados or categories of encantados. This distinction is important, because, as will be pointed out, some individuals can master the general role but are unable to go further and perform as specific encantados. Although it is desirable that the medium be proficient in a number of roles, he must at least be competent in the general role if he is to be accepted as a full-fledged medium.

By introducing the concept of role, we do not mean to imply that individuals who take the role of the encantado are only play-acting or that they consciously pretend to be a supernatural being. Informants occasionally hinted that sometimes other mediums feigned possession, which suggests that on occasion they may have had the experience themselves. But most of their comments indicated a calm certainty about the uniqueness of the trance experience and, moreover, a conviction that when they were possessed they behaved quite differently than when they were "pure." They not only maintained, but seemed to believe, that when possessed they could dance all night without feeling tired, drink heavily and have no hangover, undergo ordeals and feel no pain. They took it for granted that they sang and danced with much greater skill when in trance and also assumed that their appearance must change when an encantado was present, especially their facial expression. When shown photographs of themselves in trance, mediums invariably exclaimed that people in trance certainly looked different, although to the outside observer the difference might seem minimal.

Our data, then, suggest that Batuque mediums have unusual subjective experiences when in trance. Our basic assumption is that most of the behavior interpreted as possession occurs while the mediums are in trance. It is likely that their perception of the roles they are expected to take as encantados, and perhaps the actual process of learning the roles, are different when they are in trance than when they are not. This does not alter the fact that the roles do exist and that they are learned.[2]

The major components of the general role of "the possessed medium" were described in Chapter I and need be reviewed only briefly here. There is an appropriate way to enter and leave trance. In both cases the medium keels over backward but should never actually fall to the floor. If there is no one nearby to catch the medium as he falls, he should manage to regain his balance. Once in trance, the medium usually dances vigorously for a few minutes and should then lead a song that indicates which encantado has arrived. He accepts the embrace of the other mediums who come to greet the encantado. After a reasonable length of time, the medium leads a song indicating that the encantado is about to leave, falls over backward, again without hitting the floor, and returns to normal.

Very few individuals who are possessed for the first time can carry out even these simple actions. The neophyte often falls hard on the cold cement floor, thrashes wildly with arms and legs when being helped to his feet, stands mute when expected to sing. It is usually months and sometimes years before the general role can be adequately handled.

The most important subroles that a medium is expected to master are related to the different categories of encantados. As was noted in Chapter V, there are two basic kinds of encantados,

A medium suddenly arches over backwards as she is "seized" by a spirit. She will recover her balance.

the upper-status *senhores,* conceived of as serious and dignified, and the lower-status *caboclos,* many of whom are expected to be playful and ready for a good time. A medium receiving an encantado of either type should be able to act appropriately. Since most mediums receive at least one *senhor* and one carouser *caboclo,* the ability to take these two subroles is expected of almost every developed medium.

In most cases these two subroles are not defined very precisely. Almost any *senhor,* for example, is expected to act much the same, regardless of sex, origin, or associated characteristics. As was pointed out in the last chapter, Barba Sueira, Averekete, and Dom Pedro Angaço are three quite diverse encantados, yet an observer watching a medium possessed by one of them would ordinarily have no clue as to which one was supposed to be present. The sober, dignified demeanor of the medium would suggest only that one of the *senhores* had arrived, and unless the observer knew the medium well enough to know which *senhor* he was likely to receive, he would not recognize the personal touches that in fact might provide some indication of the encantado's identity.

In addition to the two basic subroles of *senhor* and carouser *caboclo,* there are others that are appropriate only for mediums who receive encantados of certain special categories. A medium who receives a dolphin encantado, for example, is expected to dance in a particular way—there is a great deal of hopping involved. A woman who receives a mermaid should let her hair grow long and swirl it about as she dances. Curupiras are expected to bark like dogs, while an Exu should dance in a frenzied manner with the medium's face contorted in a frozen, eyes-open stare. In a few cases individual encantados have certain characteristics that identify them. Mediums who receive Rompe Mato are expected to affect the open-eyed stare, apparently in keeping with this spirit's relationship with the Exus. João da Mata is thought to have a special penchant for hats, and the medium expecting him to descend should have a hat available for him to wear. For the great majority of encantados, however, there are no special actions or costumes that identify them. The individual has a considerable amount of leeway in developing the characteristic behavior of the encantado, as long as the gen-

Most of the mediums in this group are in trance. The woman (center) with her eyes open, her hand raised, is possessed by Rompe Mato, a spirit believed to often effect this particular stance while dancing.

At another center, another medium receives Rompe Mato in a similar manner.

eral role is performed properly and the basic distinction between *senhor* and carouser is maintained.

In a religion as individualistic as the Batuque, it would probably be impossible for the roles of the encantados to be defined very precisely. As it is, most developed mediums personalize each of their important encantados to a certain extent, adding behavior patterns and bits of costume until their characterization often becomes quite distinctive. In some cases this is carried to the point that an encantado ordinarily thought of as a *senhor* may become a carouser, or vice versa. Such a basic shift in role could probably only be instigated by a leader or a medium of considerable reputation, but it has apparently happened often enough in the past that today several encantados can be received either as serious or gay, largely at the discretion of the medium. Mariana is a good example, as noted in the last chapter. Most people receive Mariana as a hard-drinking *cabocla,* but for Carlos and several other mediums she is a *senhora.* In Batuque theology, this variation is explained as a choice by the encantado. It may choose to descend either as a *senhor* or as a *caboclo.* Although it has come to be accepted that any encantado may be received in either guise, in actual practice none of the most important *senhores* are ever received as carousers, and only a few of the notorious carousers ever turn up as someone's *senhor.*

It is expected that when an individual becomes a member of the Batuque, he or she will quickly learn the general role of possessed medium, and in time will learn the subroles pertaining to the specific encantados received. The ideal to which all mediums aspire is exemplified by the behavior of the leader, the *mãe* or *pai de santo.* Most leaders can enter trance at will, take any subrole with ease, and while in trance engage in a large number of complex activities without strain. During ceremonies the leader directs the dancing, leads the singing, conducts rituals, supervises the handling of individuals who have unusual trance experiences, and watches for and welcomes important guests. When an especially popular encantado possesses the *pai de santo,* he may leave the ceremony temporarily and give consultations to a long line of clients. During most of this activity the overt manifestations of the trance state are reduced to the minimum. At the beginning of trance the leader may tremble, or perspire heavily, or give other evidence that he is having an unusual experience, but this stage quickly passes. From time to time the demeanor of the leader may change dramatically (at least for a few minutes) as he is thought to receive different encantados. During most of the ceremony, however, the behavior of the leader appears so normal that not only an outside observer, but even the intimates of the leader, may not be sure at any given moment whether the leader is still in trance or has become "pure." The degree of control thus demonstrated by the leader is greatly admired.

One aspect of role-taking that is expected of a leader but is not necessarily expected of all mediums is the ability to give consultations as an encantado. When people approach a possessed medium and make known their desire to speak to the encantado, their intent is almost always to get advice of some kind. The response that the encantado makes, speaking through the medium, may be more or less complex. It is sometimes possible for the spirit to give a "yes" or "no" answer, or to prescribe a standard kind of herbal infusion that might be expected to be useful in the resolution of a number of kinds of problems. In either case, the medium would not have to attend too closely to the problem of the petitioner. Usually, however, the medium must listen carefully to the presentation of a specific, personal problem and make a cogent reply. This is obviously a kind of behavior on a quite different level of complexity than dancing or singing a song. It is not surprising that it usually takes a number of years of experience before a medium can handle consultations with any facility and that relatively few mediums become really expert in this aspect of the role of the possessed. For the *mãe* or *pai de santo,* of course, consultation is one of the most important activities associated with their position as leader.

It is evident during any public ceremony that there is a great range of proficiency with which the roles and subroles associated with possession are enacted. Some participants equal the *mães* and *pais de santo* in the easy way in which they enter trance, behave as the encantado, and even give consultations. Other participants, after entering trance, seem unable to do more than stand around looking foggy. As has been indicated, much of the difference can be attributed to the amount of trance experience that an individual has had. However, there is a great deal of variability in behavior even among those members who have had the same amount of trance experience. One factor that has bearing on this variability is the extent to which the individuals have been involved in the Batuque before their first trance experience.

It might be expected that those Batuque members who learned the religion by interaction from infancy with family members who were mediums would be much more proficient in trance than others. This is generally the case. For those who grow up in the religion, there are frequent opportunities during childhood to observe relatives engaged in trance behavior. The children of Batuque members may observe their mothers in trance in the home several times a week. During public ceremonies the children of the mediums often gather somewhere nearby and carry on their own mock ceremony. They sing and dance and pretend to be possessed. Girls in their early teens often join their mothers in the public ceremony, if they can afford a costume, and become skilled in singing and dancing. The only aspect of the total role then remaining is the trance state. This usually occurs for the first time in the late teens. It is not surprising that teen-age boys and girls who have grown up in the Batuque often show rapid mastery of the role of the encantado. Even during their first trance experience some of them may be able to sing and dance in a quite acceptable fashion. At least, some claimed that they had been able to do so; no actual cases were observed.

It was extremely difficult to ascertain how much exposure to trance behavior the other half of Batuque members had had, those members who had not grown up in the religion. Considering the widespread interest in possession in Belém, and the many opportunities to witness trance behavior, whether in Batuque ceremonies, curing sessions, or spiritualistic séances, it is difficult to imagine that anyone residing in the city for any length of time could be completely ignorant of some of the expectations regarding the behavior of someone possessed by a spirit. All of our informants reported at least some first-hand observation of trance behavior before they themselves had the experience, although in a few cases individuals claimed to have attended only spiritualistic séances before unexpectedly being seized by an encantado at their first visit to a *batuque*. In any case, although our data are not completely satisfactory, they do indicate that converts to the Batuque had significantly less experience with trance behavior, and also had a more difficult time learning the role of the possessed medium, than those members who grew up in the religion.

It is difficult to find out about the career of the developing medium because one cannot accept at face value the accounts that the accomplished mediums provide. Their stories are all very much alike and have clearly been modified to conform to a standard version. According to the standard story, the medium is possessed for the first time at the age of seven, begins to receive encantados on a regular basis during the late teens, and by the early twenties is receiving a number of spirits without difficulty. However, considering the experiences of the many mediums we knew who were still developing, it would appear that very few people find the process this simple. It is possible, for example, that some mediums who had grown up in the religion did sing the first time they were possessed, but this would be exceptional. More commonly the first trance experience, and often many of the succeeding ones, does not include any behavior other than a relatively uncontrolled entry into trance and perhaps some clumsy dancing. The encantado is mute, and there is even a widely held convention that the encantado never speaks for six months (some say a year) after it first possesses its devotee.

In a few cases we were able to observe the beginning phases of a medium's career. The first case was that of a girl in her late teens, whose name we never learned. She was observed first at a ceremony on September 26, 1962, when she went into a trance while standing in the audience. She was led into the ceremonial area, where she stood stiff-legged, her head down, her eyes closed, her arms rigid, and her fists clenched. Periodically she reeled this way and that but seemed quite unable to dance. After she had been in trance for several minutes, the *pai de santo* passed through, saw that she was a stranger and unable to control her movements, seized her by the arm, and led her into the chapel. Once in the chapel, the girl had her head squeezed by one of the mediums and readily came out of trance, in a few minutes looking "normal if somewhat confused," according to our notes.

Since we were never able to interview this girl, it is not known if she had ever been in trance before. Considering her behavior, it would seem likely that she had had very little experience. Three days later, in another ceremony at the same *terreiro,* she went into trance again and behaved in exactly the same way. The next night, during a third ceremony, she went into trance while sitting on a bench in the audience. She was helped to her feet and stood stiffly, as before, but she had learned that she should kick off her sandals when possessed, and she now danced barefoot. On this occasion no one forced her out of trance, although one medium complained that she could neither sing nor dance, and after twenty-five minutes she staggered and came out of trance without apparent stimulus. One of the mediums helped her to a bench where she sat for some time "looking dazed."

A month later the girl's performance was much improved. This time she went into trance when embraced by a possessed medium (she had been standing near the ceremonial area). This was a correct response since possession is often induced in this way. Our notes indicate that we were much impressed by the change in her behavior, particularly the extent to which she now moved about the floor and whirled from time to time, however stiffly. Her arms were still rigid, however, her fists clenched, and her eyes closed. In addition to entering trance on cue, she now also left trance on cue. Several other mediums were about to go out of trance and had gathered in front of the drums. The girl joined them, and as they keeled over backward, she staggered and returned to normal.

The last occasion on which we saw this girl was two months after our first observation of her. She had now joined the *terreiro* as a *filha de santo* and took part in the ceremony from the beginning, wearing a costume and carrying an *espada* (ritual scarf). It was soon obvious that she still had a great deal to learn. She made no attempt to sing the songs but concentrated on dancing. Yet, in spite of carefully watching the feet of the other participants and trying to copy their movements, she could not seem to master the relatively simple dance step. She stayed on the floor most of the night, and finally at 1:40 A.M. she went into trance. Over-all, her performance was not as successful as on the previous occasion. She moved about fairly well, but she kept bumping into people and dropping her *espada*. After ten minutes she reeled stiffly backward and fell flat on the floor. She was helped to her feet, still in trance, and continued to stagger about. When some annoyance was expressed that she kept getting in people's way and could neither dance nor sing, one of the mediums took her part, telling the others, "Let her alone, the poor thing doesn't know how yet." Finally, after the girl had been in trance for fifteen minutes and continued to fall down, the *pai de santo* pressed her head and blew in her ears, and she returned to normal. She sat down on a bench and was fanned by one of the other mediums, looking "somewhat dull but not particularly confused."

There is some reason to believe that the behavior of this girl reflected a rather unusual lack of co-ordination. On another occasion when we observed someone dancing for reportedly the first time, there was much less difficulty, at least with the dancing. This young woman, about twenty-five, entered a trance state within ten minutes of the start of the ceremony, in fact, shortly after the first possession of the evening. She did not dance very gracefully, doing a considerable amount of hopping (very common among inexperienced girls), but she also did some whirling. After about ten minutes she stopped, held her head for a while, sat down, and returned to normal. When she was possessed again twenty minutes later she danced in a more acceptable manner, with one arm raised. This trance also lasted about ten minutes, at the end of which time she sat down with a pained expression. An hour later she went up to greet a newly arrived encantado and, after the embrace from the possessed medium, immediately went into trance. This time she was enough under control that she at least held still while someone came to welcome her encantado (never identified). Assuming that this really was this woman's first experience dancing in a ceremony, she behaved in a much more acceptable manner than the first girl. In part this seemed to be due simply to her better muscular co-ordination, although other factors may have been significant as well (e.g., she had probably had previous trance experiences, even though this was her first appearance in a public ceremony).

We observed many other young girls go into trance while spectators at ceremonies, and most of them behaved much as the two cases just described. Since the other participants treated them as beginners, it seems reasonable to assume that in most cases they had had very little experience in trance, although it was rarely possible to verify this assumption. One difficulty that some of these girls seemed to encounter was an uncertainty as to what sort of expression they should have on their faces when possessed by an encantado. After all, what does an encantado look like? This is an especially difficult question in the beginning when the girl is not certain which encantado she is receiving or even what kind—gay or serious. As an example, the following notes refer to a girl about twenty, who was observed only once:

> At about 1:40 a young girl in the audience was possessed. She was obviously known by some of the *filhas,* but she had also obviously had little experience. She did not know how to dance and did a lot of hopping up and down, almost like skipping in place. She did not know how to look possessed and kept changing her face. She kept her eyes squinched but open, she twisted her mouth, sometimes she stuck out her tongue. All of this was done with great energy and very clumsily. She went around giving embraces to all the other dancers, then made the rounds of the audience. She was largely ignored.

In contrast to the foregoing cases, an older woman whose career we were able to follow over a period of time showed a much greater facility in learning the role of the possessed. This was not surprising, however, since she had been involved in the Batuque since childhood. When we met Sara in 1962 she was forty-four years old. She was much in evidence around Antônio's *terreiro* but seemed never to dance, and when we inquired, both she and her many friends among the mediums assured us that she had never been possessed. Her interest in the Batuque had developed at an early age, although no one in her family was an active medium. Her mother sometimes went into trance states at home but refused to take part in public ceremonies. None of Sara's four siblings became mediums, but Sara became an established hanger-on at Antônio's *terreiro*. She regularly helped in the preparations for ceremonies, and during the ceremony she was usually to be found in the chapel administering to the needs of the mediums in trance. According to her own testimony, during her long experience in *batuques* she had never "felt anything" before 1963.

When we returned to Belém in 1965 we found that Sara had become an accomplished performer, receiving Guapindaia as her *senhor* and Jaguarema as a *caboclo* (and hard-drinking carouser). According to her account, she had become possessed for the first time in June of 1963, but it was not until a year later that her encantado identified himself. In the year that followed, Sara had apparently mastered all aspects of the general role of the possessed, for when we saw her go into trance on two occasions she gave every indication of being a veteran performer. She seemed to have some difficulty entering trance, but once in trance she danced a sedate, arm-pumping dance, led songs in a loud clear voice, manipulated her *espada* expertly when other mediums came up to greet her encantado, and came out of trance smoothly. Her many years of intimate acquaintance with others in trance had apparently provided her with the basis for a rapid learning of the appropriate behavior. Even so, it should be noted that it was a year before her encantado identified himself, i.e., before she was able to sing while in trance.

Once the medium has mastered the major features of the role of the possessed, he or she discovers that there are a number of other activities that are expected of the really accomplished medium. There is, for example, the matter of being possessed on cue, i.e., entering a trance at a given moment. There are many occasions when a medium is expected to enter trance in response to certain stimuli, whether these are songs asking a particular encantado to descend or requests that an encantado appear for consultations. The ability to enter trance on the spot is absolutely necessary for a *mãe* or *pai de santo,* since many of the rituals that they conduct must be performed by particular encantados. For other mediums there is more leeway, and individuals who occasionally fail to enter trance when trance is expected are not unduly criticized. Within fairly wide limits, however, a competent medium is expected to enter trance with regularity in response to the appropriate cues.

Ideally, during ceremonies all mediums enter trance on cue —the cue being the song used to "call" the encantado. However, this ideal is not taken very seriously, and only under certain circumstances is a specific doctrine expected to lead automatically to the arrival of a specific encantado. When a major festival is being held for an encantado and that spirit is called, the medium who regularly receives the spirit is almost always possessed. During the early hours of any ceremony, as the *senhores* are being invoked, the medium who enjoys the status of being considered an expert devotee of one of the *senhores* often becomes possessed as the appropriate doctrines are sung. But not always. Sometimes the medium "feels nothing," and after a few songs are sung without effect, attention is turned to other spirits. Throughout any ceremony, however, mediums frequently become possessed by spirits other than the one being called at that particular moment. Although there may be no close connection between the spirit being called and the one that arrives, at least they should belong to the same category of encantado. Thus if a *senhor* is being invoked, it is quite inappropriate for a medium to receive a gay *caboclo*. It is not quite as bad for mediums to receive *senhores* when the singing is directed to *caboclos,* so that a *senhor* may appear at any time during the ceremony.

There are occasions when certain songs may initiate trance states in a number of mediums at the same time. During these mass possessions, the mediums involved are all believed to be possessed by different encantados. One of the standard occasions when this is expected to occur is when the encantado Japetequara arrives and sings his cycle of songs. It is taken for granted that at least those mediums who regularly receive one of the Curupiras will be possessed during these songs, since the Curupiras (of which there are a large number) are part of Japetequara's "tribe." It usually happens, however, that many other mediums go into trance during the Japetequara songs, and many of the encantados involved have no relationship at all to Japetequara.

The arrival of Japetequara, the singing of his cycle of songs, and the rapid entry into trance of six, eight, or even a dozen mediums is one of the most exciting features of any Batuque ceremony. At the first line of Japetequara's first song, an air of expectancy is clearly evident among the mediums. This first song, however, is long and draggy and is often repeated several times. No one becomes possessed—this first doctrine essentially sets the stage. In dramatic contrast, the second song and the succeeding ones are rapid, rhythmic, and apparently compelling. Mediums begin keeling over on all sides, and members of the audience are often caught up as well. The Curupiras are expected to dance very wildly, with a great deal of head-bobbing, and to bark and yelp like dogs. With eight or ten women going through the initial stages of trance at once, their arms flailing, their heads bobbing and hair flying, the ceremony takes on an atmosphere of frenzy that is rarely present under other circumstances.

Our informant Clara was the most successful Japetequara that we encountered. Her singing of the cycle invariably led to numerous possessions; on one occasion fifteen women went into trance within about sixteen minutes. A man whom we observed only once was almost as effective, inducing six possessions within as many minutes. Two other women who received Japetequara were much less galvanic, and their singing of the same songs produced little response. One thing that these differences illustrate is the complexity of the cues that initiate the trance state. It is not just the Japetequara cycle of songs that prompts mass possessions, but a combination of the songs and the reputation of the medium who sings them. If the medium has a reputation for having a great deal of "force," as Clara did, her singing of the songs will initiate a number of trance states. Otherwise exactly the same songs may have no effect.

In addition to songs, other kinds of activities may serve as the immediate stimulus for the trance state. When a medium who is not in trance goes up to greet an encantado in a possessed medium, contact with the possessed person often leads to a trance state in the unpossessed medium. If the encantado in question is the chief of the medium doing the greeting, it is expected that the medium will show signs of incipient possession, and sometimes the encantado is thought to pass from one medium to the other—the greeter goes into trance and the greeted becomes normal. What kind of signal may pass from one individual to the other in order to effect this change is an intriguing question, but on occasion the signal is missed and both mediums remain in trance. Since it is thought to be impossible for two people to be possessed by the same encantado simultaneously, one of the two mediums involved may be led to the chapel and brought out of trance. If this is not done and two or more mediums appear to be possessed by the same encantado, cult members argue that only the first medium to enter trance really "has" the spirit. The other devotees who are apparently possessed are only *sombriado* (shaded) by the encantado or in a state of halfway possession. According to one informant, each encantado has seven shadows, and thus as many as eight individuals might appear to be possessed by the same spirit at one time.

More commonly, the medium who performs the ritual of salutation is not a devotee of the encantado believed to be present. If he is stimulated to go into trance by contact with the possessed person, he is expected to receive a different encantado, one of those that he usually receives, and no embarrassing questions as to which medium really "has" the encantado arise.

Although a person in trance is usually relatively passive during the greeting, sometimes he takes a more active role. Rather than simply accepting the greeting of the other mediums, he takes the occasion to attempt to induce trance in anyone he can get his hands on. The greeting embrace ordinarily ends with a final clasping of the hands, but a medium attempting to induce trance in another person holds on to the other's hands, raises his arms above his head, and forces him to revolve, first in one direction, then in the other. This is usually done quite forcefully, the person being whirled co-operating because of the pressure on his hands and his desire to placate the encantado. Of the many factors that play a part in determining whether the person who is whirled goes into trance, the most important is again the reputation of the possessed medium. Given a reputation of having force, a medium who is thought to be possessed by a prestigious encantado can sometimes produce a series of trances in rapid-fire order that rival the mass possessions induced by the Japetequara songs. The most impressive display of this kind of force that we witnessed occurred at the *terreiro* of Dona Marina:

> During the singing to Averekete, Marina became possessed. As the *filhas de santo* came up for the greeting, Marina whirled each one, first to the right, then to the left. She did this with considerable force, and the muscles in her arms stood out prominently. This kind of whirling is often awkward, because the arms get tangled up, and in the present case Marina's short stature complicated things further. Some of the *filhas* looked confused or even embarrassed as they tried to whirl as directed. But without exception they ended up in trance. Some were possessed only briefly, others for longer periods. But twelve women went forward, were whirled, and became possessed. After that we lost count.

One point to note in the foregoing description is that some of the trance states induced by whirling do not last very long, only a minute or two in some cases. Some of the trances occurring during the Japetequara songs are equally short, and it is probably a safe generalization that possessions brought on by such special cues have a shorter duration than those that occur under normal circumstances.

In the discussion thus far of some of the stimuli that seem to be the direct antecedents of trance behavior, the situations considered have been those in which a certain leeway is allowed the medium as to whether or not he will enter trance. There are also occasions when the medium has no choice and must enter trance at once. The *mãe* or *pai de santo* must often receive certain encantados before particular ceremonies can be carried out. When baptisms are held, the godparents are usually encantados, and the mediums who receive the appropriate spirits are expected to produce them at the prescribed time. Women who give consultations in their homes have appointed times, usually once a week, when clients can be assured that the encantado will be present. For the accomplished medium, entering trance at a desired time is usually simply a matter of "concentration," as they explain it, and they rarely have any difficulty.

If the less accomplished medium "feels nothing" when trance is expected but the appearance of the encantado is not crucial, he may readily pass off the situation by remarking that the spirit must have been busy elsewhere ("I can't imagine where he could have been," one informant said casually after she had

failed to go into trance at a ceremony in honor of her encantado).
But if the presence of the encantado is thought to be necessary,
various techniques are used to force the medium into trance.
The most common is pressure applied to the base of the neck
in back, or sometimes light blows to this area with the edge
of the hand. Sometimes one of the arms is jerked in time to
the drums while pressure is applied to the back of the neck.
If these measures are not effective, a variety of other techniques
are used, most of which are illustrated in the following incident:

> Carlos, the *pai de santo,* now attempted to induce Madalena to
> receive her encantado Mariana. (He did this deliberately, as he
> explained the next day, because Madalena had not been feeling
> well, and he thought being possessed by Mariana would get rid of
> some of the evil influences around her.) Getting Madalena to enter

A *pai de santo* seeks to induce a medium to enter trance by ringing a bell in
her ear, while she joins in singing the chorus to the song he has led.

trance was not easy. She stood in front of the altar while the drums beat and the mediums sang. Carlos first popped his *espada* close behind her. This had no effect. He then hit her about the neck and shoulders with his bundle of *arara* feathers. She swayed from side to side, her head down, but made no further move until Carlos rang a small bell close beside her head. She then jerked a few times, stepped out of her slippers, and then just stood there. A bottle containing a herb infusion was brought and her head and hands were rubbed with the liquid. Carlos took his *espada*, wrapped it around Madalena's waist, and pulled it as tight as he could. No response. Finally he put his forehead against the back of her head, wrapped his *espada* around both their heads, and pulled it tight. This did the trick. Madalena did a few violent head-bobs, jerked all over, waved one arm, and a few minutes later led a song as Mariana. The whole episode lasted about ten minutes.

Successful, he turns away a few moments later. The medium, now in trance, has kicked off her slippers and unfurled her *espada*. The woman on the right is also in trance.

Less systematic efforts to induce trance are quite common, and mediums very often encourage one another to go into trance during ceremonies. The basic idea is simply that being possessed is a good thing, everyone is at the ceremony to be possessed, and anyone who seems to be having some difficulty entering trance should be helped to do so. The mediums usually watch one another fairly closely, and when a woman is seen to be near trance, the others often gather around and sing loudly in her ear. Sometimes a medium touches another on the back of the neck or, if possessed, may dance with an arm around an unpossessed person until he succumbs. This is all done with good humor, often with broad smiles on all sides. Very rarely is any resentment shown by the person being aided to enter trance, although they sometimes seem to be having a somewhat painful experience. In the following incident, which illustrates several of the points just made, the women were seated because they were at a session of "development" rather than at a public ceremony.

> The next woman to go into trance was Anita. She was sitting on a bench next to Raimunda, and began to look even more unhappy than usual. Raimunda seemed to take this as a sign of imminent possession and began to sing very loudly and clap close to Anita's ear. Anita began to make faces, most of which seemed to indicate that she was having very unpleasant sensations. She might have just drunk a large shot of raw liquor or been dazzled by a very bright light. She looked desperate, as if she might suddenly be sick or burst into tears. So acutely did she seem to be suffering that it seemed quite incongruous that she continued to sit there—one expected her to jump up and run away, or at least to scream at Raimunda to stop the torture. But she made no move, and although she seemed to be struggling against what was about to happen to her, this impression was probably due simply to her rigid arms and the awful faces she was making. Raimunda smiled and continued singing and clapping. Suddenly Anita closed her eyes, heaved up and back, slammed against the wall so violently that she knocked a plank loose, staggered into the dance area, got her balance, and began to dance vigorously. Within a few minutes she was dashing around the room cracking jokes and being extremely extrovertish, the very antithesis of the placid, almost forlorn woman who had come to the session. Her long blond hair, usually worn in a demure bun, now flew wildly about her head . . . Anita later induced possession in a young man by putting her *espada* behind

his head and pulling him toward her. When he became possessed she smiled gaily and seemed quite pleased with herself.

In most of the cases of trance just described, it is possible to pinpoint some specific stimulus that seemed to provide the final impetus for entry into the trance state. This selection of cases may in fact give the impression that the observer can predict when most possessions will occur. This is definitely not the case. During any public ceremony, probably a majority of the mediums go into trance in response to cues that are not at all obvious. The songs being sung may have no particular significance for the medium, there may be no physical contact with others, the drums continue their monotonous beat. Suddenly the person goes into trance. It seems likely that in some cases the immediate cue for trance is not consciously recognized by the medium either, since there is often an element of surprise manifested by a person entering trance.

As far as coming out of trance is concerned, it is even more difficult in most cases to specify the immediate stimulus that leads a medium to return to normal. After a variable period—a minute or two or an hour or two—the medium moves in front of the drums and the encantado "goes away." As in the case of entry into trance, many of the cues leading to coming out of trance seem to be internal.

In some cases, however, the stimuli involved in coming out of trance are fairly obvious. As was noted earlier, the standard leave-taking procedure is for a medium to sing a song indicating that the encantado is about to leave. The songs usually say, in a variety of ways, "I am going away." Moving to the area in front of the drums, a woman usually stands in one spot and rotates her upper torso and arms around and around, the circles becoming gradually larger. Suddenly she keels over backward into the waiting arms of the other mediums. She then immediately opens her eyes, looks around with a more or less startled expression, and is out of trance. Sometimes the revolving from the waist occurs while the medium is kneeling rather than standing, and under certain circumstances the drumming becomes more and more rapid as the leave-taking dance continues, but the result is the same—the medium falls backward and comes out of trance. It is most impressive when two or more mediums, usually women, go through this routine together and keel over at precisely the same instant. Since the women have their eyes closed, do not necessarily touch one another, and may be rotating out of phase, their sudden and perfectly timed lurch backward is quite dramatic. Although the co-ordination of movements must mean that some kinds of signals are exchanged between the women, the nature of these signals is obscure.

As usual, there are many variations on the above themes. Instead of coming out of trance, the medium may simply change encantados after going over backward and continue in trance as soon as he has regained his balance. It sometimes happens that when two or three mediums go through the leave-taking routine together, one will miss the signal, whatever it is, and remain in trance. Often the mediums about to come out of trance together link arms or put their arms around one another's shoulders, which makes their co-ordinated behavior somewhat easier to explain. In all of these cases, it should be noted, some of the mediums are stimulated to come out of trance by the others. There is a cue being provided, and appropriate behavior follows.

A situation in which the stimulus for coming out of trance is even more obvious is when the individual is forced out of trance. In the incidents described earlier, several examples were given of occasions when forcing a medium out of trance is deemed appropriate. Most commonly, mediums are forcibly brought out of trance if they cannot control their movements properly. The techniques used include squeezing the head (one hand on the forehead, the other hand on the back of the head), blowing in the ears, and, in extreme cases, striking the forehead sharply with the heel of the hand. It should be stressed, however, that there is considerable compunction about forcing people out of trance. This seems to arise out of consideration for the person rather than any fear of displeasing the supernatural. A medium who is having trouble maintaining his balance is allowed to stagger about for some time, and often to fall repeatedly, before measures are taken to bring him out of trance. Then it is only the *mãe* or *pai de santo,* or one of the older and respected mediums, who takes it upon themselves to squeeze the person's

Two mediums who were singing a farewell song together both come out of trance at precisely the same moment.

head. The usual justification given for this action is that the medium will harm himself by falling, either because he is not yet developed enough to have control or because the encantado is attempting to throw him on the floor.

The strongly held belief that everyone has the right to be possessed, when and where and as long as he or she likes, is sometimes overridden by ritual considerations. At Antônio's *terreiro* it was common practice to encourage mediums to come out of trance before the Exu ceremony held at midnight. This encouragement was often quite overt. It took the form of herding the possessed mediums up in front of the drums and singing a going-away song. The mediums usually took the cue and began to revolve, and most of them returned to normal. Those who failed to come out of trance were shut up in the chapel during the following ceremony. It might be noted, however, that this somewhat highhanded treatment was afforded only the relatively unsophisticated and inexperienced mediums. The older mediums would have been highly indignant at such interference and usually left the dance floor of their own volition until the Exu ceremony was over.

The only other time that mediums are expected to come out of trance on cue is at the end of the public ceremony. At some *terreiros* there is a standard closing ritual that includes an opportunity for all of those in trance to return to normal. Even where the end of the ceremony is more informal, the possessed mediums are usually given some warning that the ceremony is about to close. In either case, there are almost always some mediums who remain in trance after the drums have become silent. Since the encantados that remain are invariably carousers, the mediums may continue to carry on around the *terreiro*, or, if the night is still relatively young, may set out in search of another *terreiro* where a ceremony is still in progress.

In time, given the proper motivation and sufficient aptitude, most men and women in the Batuque are able to enter and leave trance without difficulty, at least on most occasions. It is very difficult to estimate how many of them go on to become proficient in consultation, the most complicated aspect of trance behavior. During public ceremonies only a few mediums are consulted—the *mãe* or *pai de santo* and a few of the older mediums—and these only when they are thought to be possessed by very important encantados. But many mediums go into trance in the privacy of their homes and are consulted by members of the family, neighbors, and also by strangers who have heard of their prowess at contacting the supernatural.

The activities that occur during consultation will be discussed in detail in Chapter VIII. The behavior involved is extremely complex, and the person in trance must not only take the role of an encantado, but also must interact in very intimate ways with a variety of individuals. Problems of a very specific nature must be dealt with, and reasonable solutions often involve an extensive knowledge of the petitioner's circumstances and background. In short, all of the medium's faculties must be operating, and he must at the same time be impressive as a supernatural being. To the observer, the behavior of the medium appears largely normal, and even the perspiration and flushed appearance can be directly related to the considerable energy that goes into a good performance. Entry into trance may be quite simple—the medium sits and concentrates, his eyes closed, and after a few minutes he breathes deeply a few times, jerks and trembles, and goes into trance. Coming out of trance is equally unspectacular. In terms of stimuli that induce trance, in the case of consultation there are no external stimuli at all. There are no drums, usually no singing, no bodily contact. Consultation, the most complex kind of trance behavior, is in some ways the simplest and the least impressive.

Thus far we have considered possession as a role that individuals enact while in a trance state. It has been suggested that this role is learned and that individuals who have been in the religion the longest show most proficiency in taking the role. There would thus seem to be clear similarities between the role of possessed medium and other roles in the society. However, there are also striking differences. Whereas any normal individual might be expected to learn almost any role in his society, given enough time and motivation, this is not true of the roles in the Batuque. There is a very great range of variation in the extent to which individuals are able to master the role of the possessed medium. Although the performance of most mediums does improve as they have more trance experiences, the degree and rate of improvement varies greatly. In a few cases, the whole role of medium is precluded because individuals cannot enter a trance state. In other cases a person may be able to enter trance, but is unable to dance or sing. Some people can perform the general role of possessed medium but cannot master the subroles. And finally, almost all mediums, even the most experienced and the most skilled, occasionally have some difficulty in behaving appropriately as an encantado. It seems clear that, in taking the role of possessed medium, a great many factors are involved other than the simple learning of the appropriate behavior.

Of the many kinds of difficulties that individuals encounter in taking the role of the possessed, the most extreme is the inability to enter a trance state. A striking case we encountered was that of Lulu, a woman of about forty who had been trying for twenty years to have a trance experience, but without success. Lulu had grown up in the Batuque and as a child had had several experiences that suggested that she was a potential medium. Her mother was an accomplished medium, and from adolescence Lulu participated actively in public ceremonies, wearing a costume and often dancing from beginning to end. At least once during each ceremony, and sometimes several times, Lulu would give every indication that she was about to go into trance. But she somehow never made it. The following excerpt from our notes describes a typical performance:

> At about 11:50 Lulu had one of the seizures that some of the other mediums call *aquela tontura* (that fit of dizziness). She shows all of the proper signs of incipient possession—makes faces, perspires, presses her forehead. Then she closes her eyes and begins to whirl. It is not a controlled whirling but a blind reeling stagger. It appears certain that she will fall at each revolution, but she somehow manages to retain her balance at the last split second. She seems to be almost unconscious, falling into the audience and bumping into other dancers, but there is some control, since she stays within the ceremonial area and never falls on the floor. Just when it seems that she will enter a typical trance state, she suddenly opens her eyes, looks around wildly, makes terrible faces, and returns at once to normal.

Unlike Lulu, most Batuque members are able at least to go into trance, but sometimes only with great effort. An expression often heard is *"Custa muito para êle receber"* (It is very difficult for him to receive). This comment refers most often to men whose infrequent trance experiences are probably directly related to the opprobrium attached to being a male medium. There are also women, however, who find entering trance difficult, and who may dance many hours, with several partial successes, before they have a satisfactory trance experience.

There are a surprising number of mediums who enter trance easily, can dance fairly well, but who never sing or speak as the encantado. Some of these people have been participating in Batuque ceremonies for ten or fifteen years. Often their diffi-

Other participants watch critically to see whether the woman whirling will successfully enter trance.

culty is explained as being due to the fact that, because of insufficient preparation, they are only *sombriado* (shaded) by the encantado rather than fully possessed. In such cases, even though the medium never identifies the possessing encantado, the identification is made by the *mãe* or *pai de santo*. The medium is accepted as a full-fledged member of the religion but is usually regarded with sympathy and treated with some condescension by the more skillful mediums.

Another fairly common difficulty is the inability to enact specific roles, even though the general role is performed quite competently. Mariazinha, in her early twenties, was the daughter of one of the leading *mães de santo* in the city. She was being groomed to take over the *terreiro* when her mother died. Although she had been participating in ceremonies and going into trance since her early teens, Mariazinha was somewhat backward as far as her skill in taking specific roles was concerned. She went into trance easily, danced well, and sang songs that indicated the presence of at least three different encantados. But her behavior was always exactly the same, whichever encantado was supposed to be present. The major characteristic of her performance was its violent nature. She danced wildly, her long hair flying, her rigid arms swinging vigorously up and down, her face contorted, giving inarticulate yells from time to time. On those occasions when the spirit was supposed to be an Exu, her performance was applauded as exactly fitting the demonic character of the supernatural. On other occasions, however, such behavior was clearly not appropriate. When shown a photograph of herself in action, during a ceremony when she was supposed to be possessed by a somewhat sedate and prestigious encantado, Mariazinha was appalled. After exclaiming at how ugly she was, she said at once that from her appearance one would suppose that she were possessed by an Exu. It seems likely that in time Mariazinha will learn to modify her behavior to suit the encantado, but for the present she still falls short of being an accomplished medium, much less a promising *mãe de santo*.

It sometimes happens with older mediums who have had many years of experience in the Batuque that one encantado comes to monopolize all of the trance states that the medium enters. This is considered to be a calamity, since the encantado is usually a carouser *caboclo* (or worse, an Exu), and the medium is thus prevented from receiving his *chefe* or the other high-status encantados who are his major protectors. Isabel was an accomplished medium in her fifties. We observed her enter trance fourteen times, and every time but one the encantado was the same—Manoelzinho. It was easy to recognize the arrival of this encantado because Isabel had a quite unusual way of dancing and singing when receiving him. On a few occasions Isabel had some difficulty getting into the routine, and it seemed possible that some other spirit might be about to appear. But in the end the doctrine beginning *"Sou eu Manoel"* (I am Manoel) made it clear who had arrived. Both Isabel and her friend Clara were much concerned with the disappearance of Isabel's other encantados. Manoelzinho was a gay, outgoing *caboclo* who liked to drink, and Isabel obviously enjoyed taking this role, but it was feared that Isabel's *chefe,* Basilio Bom, and some of her other encantados might resent their long exclusion and punish her in some way.

It is even more serious when a *mãe* or *pai de santo* has this problem, since much of the leader's appeal is based on the ability to receive a variety of encantados. It was said of Antônio that he was becoming more and more dominated by one of his *caboclo* spirits, and it was common gossip that Mãe Mira received only an Exu, who sometimes gave the name of another encantado to create confusion. Although these stories may have been inspired by malice, as such stories often are, they were based on behavior by the two leaders that was clearly considered to be both inappropriate and unfortunate by those who wished to consult more prestigious encantados.

As it turned out, almost every Batuque member had one problem or another in taking the role of the possessed, at least on some occasions. This was one of the most puzzling aspects of trance behavior that we encountered. Why should a woman who ordinarily goes into trance easily and takes the role of many encantados with facility suddenly fall on the floor, or become extremely belligerent, or destroy her ceremonial costumes? The answer in a few cases was simple enough: alcohol. Although relatively large amounts of rum or beer could be drunk during trance without producing perceptible signs of intoxication, really excessive amounts often had clear-cut effects. The individual ceased to behave as an encantado should and acted just like a sore-headed drunk. But most cases of divergent or inappropriate behavior by usually skilled mediums cannot be accounted for in this way, and in fact we have no good explanation to offer.

In one interesting case that we were able to follow over time, there was a major loss of acquired skills. We first observed Mauvina in 1962 and considered her to be a fairly accomplished medium. She was a woman of thirty-five, had grown up in the Batuque, and had had her first trance experience at the age of nineteen. She most frequently received the encantado Rompe Mato, who is one of the few spirits expected to act in a specific manner. Anyone possessed by this spirit is supposed to dance with the eyes open and the unfocused gaze directed upward. During 1962 Mauvina went into trance while we were present on a number of occasions, and each time she performed well as Rompe Mato. After the first seizure she moved around the floor alternately doing a violent head-bobbing, then crossing her arms sedately over her chest and staring upward in proper Rompe Mato fashion. In 1965 something had happened, and Mauvina could no longer dance properly. On three occasions she went into a trance state but could not seem to do more than stagger around. Each time other mediums recognized that she could not gain control and led her into the chapel, where she quickly returned to normal. The accepted explanation among Mauvina's friends for her loss of control was that she had not had certain rituals performed on her behalf by her *pai de santo.* It is also possible that problems not of a religious nature may have had some effect—her husband was out of work and one of her children was ill. At any rate, there had been a clear regression in her mastery of the role of the encantado.

On the second occasion when Mauvina was led into the chapel and brought out of trance, the woman who took charge of her was our informant Clara. When we asked Clara why she had not let Mauvina continue in trance, she replied that she had realized that Rompe Mato was about to "throw Mauvina down." The idea of the *jogada,* when the encantado is said to throw the medium on the floor, probably developed as a way of explaining the fact that individuals in trance sometimes suddenly collapse for no apparent reason. It is not just neophytes who have this experience but also women like Mauvina who have been in the Batuque for years, mediums who have much greater skill than Mauvina, and even on occasion the *mãe* and *pai de santo*. As was indicated in Chapter III, sometimes the sudden collapse is followed by a coma-like condition from which it is difficult to rouse the medium, but ordinarily the *jogada* is less severe. The following example, which occurred during a public ceremony, involved a young man who aspired to become a *pai de santo*.

> Ernesto was dancing sedately, from time to time puffing on a long-stemmed pipe. He was in trance, but the encantado was never identified. Suddenly he looked up wildly, his eyes bulging, threw out his arms (in the process throwing away the pipe and fan he was holding), took a quick step backward, and fell full length on the cement floor. He was helped out. When he returned a few minutes later he was still in trance, but apparently possessed by another encantado.

Another *jogada* we witnessed was during a curing session. The *pai de santo,* Haroldo, had been receiving a long series of encantados, and he now knelt in front of a small altar and weaved back and forth. Suddenly he pitched forward on his face, striking his head violently against several bottles standing in front of the altar, then rolled over on his back and remained inert. His wife and one of the experienced mediums helped him to a sitting position, the medium shaking a *maracá* close to his head. After about thirty seconds Haroldo began to show signs of life, and shortly thereafter he carried on as another encantado. Although we never witnessed a *jogada* in which the medium remained unconscious for a long period, we were told of a number of such cases, usually involving individuals with long experience in trance.

As was pointed out earlier, in terms of Batuque beliefs the *jogada* is thought to represent an expression of anger on the part of the encantado and is often considered to be punishment. Since most mediums expect to be punished at one time or another, the *jogada* is accepted as a normal part of the life of the medium. At the same time, the *jogada* is considered to be dangerous and is greatly feared. Mediums ordinarily avoid entering trance unless there is someone around who knows how to take care of them if something goes wrong. It is largely for this reason that mediums who engage in curing always have an assistant and that mediums do not like to live alone or travel alone. It would seem, then, that from the perspective of the participant the trance state is not a simple and innocuous experience. Regardless of how easily trance may be entered, or how similar trance behavior is to normal behavior, for almost all mediums there seem to be occasions when they lose control and engage in behavior which, if not really dangerous, is at least frightening.

It would be possible to give many other instances of actions by accomplished mediums that are less dramatic than the *jogada* but still demonstrate loss of control. Most often, perhaps, the medium simply seems to lose contact with the external environment, and for brief periods ceases to interact with the other participants in the ceremony. The medium may tremble violently, make terrible faces, and keep his eyes tightly closed. Sometimes there are few signs that anything is amiss, but suddenly the medium begins to do some simple act in an exaggerated manner. The *mãe de santo* Marina once began a ritual in which she was supposed to thrust a dagger into the ground. She uttered an invocation, stabbed the ground, stabbed again, then seemed to be carried away in a frenzy of stabbing and hacking. One of the mediums rushed over, seized her arms, took the dagger away from her, and led her away. Marina recovered at once and carried on with the ceremony in a completely controlled way. Lapses of these types are sprinkled through the performances of most cult leaders, and as far as could be determined were not produced for effect but were genuine losses of control.

Thus far the discussion has dealt with possession from the observer's point of view. But what are the subjective experiences of those who enter trance and carry on as an encantado? What is it like to be possessed? This is a difficult subject to investigate, since there is a strong convention among Batuque members that they have complete amnesia for the trance experience. This attitude may be changing at the present time because of the influence of Umbanda, where a distinction is made between "conscious" and "unconscious" mediums, but there is still almost complete unanimity among older Batuque members that they remem-

Mediums sometimes visibly show signs of dissociation when in trance, as does this woman possessed by the spirit Maria Mineira de Luz . . .

ber nothing. Although all of our informants were willing to accept the idea that some mediums were vaguely aware of what was going on during trance, only five would admit that they themselves had such an awareness. And four of these insisted that it was only at certain times, with certain encantados, that they became foggily conscious, and that most of the time they were completely unconscious.

It became obvious early in our research that a fairly large proportion of those mediums whom we interviewed about their participation in public ceremonies had good recall for their activities while in trance. Almost everyone who participated in the ceremony, and especially the *mãe* or *pai de santo,* was usually quite eager to discuss the rituals that had been performed and to discuss unusual possessions about which we had questions. Since the individuals with whom we discussed these matters had been in trance themselves and supposedly remembered nothing of the proceedings, the fiction was always maintained that they had been told by their friends what had taken place. However, it was often easy to elicit details about which their friends could have known nothing or even to discuss matters to which only we and the medium were privy, e.g., topics dealt with during consultation. Although it was never possible to determine how much a medium remembered, there was no question that most mediums did remember some of their experiences while in trance.

There were other kinds of evidence as well that this was the case. The *mãe* and *pai de santo,* and the more experienced mediums, are often caught in the dilemma of wanting to impress people with their supernatural experiences, and yet not wanting to admit that they remember what happens during trance when most of these experiences occur. Sometimes the problem is simply ignored. "Thank God I am an unconscious medium," Antônio told us. "Otherwise I would never be able to endure what goes on while I am possessed." He then told us story after story of his adventures while possessed by the encantado Joãozinho—how the spirit had thrown him down a well, taken him to the hospital to see a friend, taken him to the barber to have his head shaved. Antônio was such a good storyteller that presumably few among his listeners were much concerned with how he could have learned so much about his exploits while possessed. Our friend

and this medium engaging in a hopping style of dancing while possessed by a dolphin spirit, Bôto Tucuxí.

Clara was more aware of the problem, and she usually included in her stories explicit statements to the effect that from time to time the possessing encantado left her long enough for her to realize what was going on, then possessed her again. But Clara, like most of the others, insisted that when she was possessed her mind was a complete blank.

All mediums talk freely about their sensations just prior to entering trance. There is such close agreement, however, that this may be another case of an accepted convention. Almost everyone listed cold hands and feet, a rapidly beating heart, shortness of breath, and dizziness as the major concomitants of the imminent trance. Two mediums said that they felt blows on the back of the neck, and Clara said she felt weight on her shoulders as though the encantado was settling on her back. There was general agreement that the sensations varied in intensity with the nature of the encantado and that they were much stronger when a prestigious *senhor* was about to arrive.

Of the five mediums who admitted that they remembered some of their trance experiences, three were Batuque members of long standing, one had approximately two years of experience, and one was a novice who had only been possessed a few times. All were influenced to some extent by ideas from Umbanda. The novice, a woman in her thirties, said that she remembered everything that went on, "but I know that it is not me acting." She was undoubtedly influenced by her sister, who was also a *médium consciente* (conscious medium) and who had had a great deal of experience in Umbanda and in spiritualism.

The three mediums who had had many trance experiences, all men, described trance in very similar terms. In the beginning everything was a blank. But after a few minutes in trance they began to be vaguely aware of what they were doing. One man said that he knew when people came up to greet the encantado possessing him, but that since he could not open his eyes, he did not know who it was, nor did he know what was said by either the encantado or the other person. He also stressed that he did not know why he behaved as he did, that there was some "force" moving him about. All three men compared trance to two normal activities—dreaming and being dead drunk. They also all agreed that they only remembered parts of some trance experiences, and on some occasions they did not remember anything. They were unanimous in maintaining that whatever pretense other mediums might engage in, most or all of them also had some recall for their trance experiences.

The subjective experiences of these three men are almost exactly what we would have inferred them to be on the basis of our observations. There seem to be many cases when individuals go into trance, behave briefly as encantados, come out of trance, and have total amnesia for the period involved. More commonly, however, the medium seems largely unaware of outside stimuli during the initial phases of trance, but rapidly becomes aware of much that is occurring. Very likely there is often an ebb and

A medium who has just come out of trance presses her head and looks foggy. It sometimes takes a few minutes to regain complete consciousness.

flow of awareness, with the medium sometimes in contact with the events around him and sometimes aware only of internal sensations. When the medium comes out of trance, he remembers a variable amount of what went on. It is also quite likely that the amount of awareness and the amount of recall varies with the occasion, the encantado supposedly present, and a number of other unknown factors. Considering the incomplete nature of our data, this reconstruction of the subjective aspects of the trance should be considered a series of conjectures that deserve further investigation.

Although our knowledge of the subjective sensations of Batuque mediums is not completely satisfactory, the over-all picture of the medium in trance is relatively complete. Since the behavior in question is not normal behavior, the question may be raised as to whether or not it is in some sense pathological. As was noted at the beginning of the chapter, there is still some tendency to see trance as evidence of mental instability.

If trance behavior as it occurs in the Batuque is compared with behavior considered to be psychologically abnormal in American society, it is apparent that the Batuque medium does not behave in ways that are characteristic of people who are psychotic. For one thing, the behavior of the medium in trance is basically rational in terms of Batuque beliefs, and secondly, the medium usually communicates effectively with other people. A person who is psychotic is not rational and usually cannot communicate. Among the neuroses, some forms of hysteria show some similarities with trance, but the major difference is again the much greater rational interaction with other people that occurs in trance.

Turning to behavior that is considered psychologically unusual, rather than abnormal, there are a number of striking similarities between Batuque trance behavior and behavior that typically occurs during hypnosis. At first glance these similarities may be obscured by what may seem two outstanding differences. In trance there is no hypnotist, and people in trance do not act relaxed or sleepy as hypnotized subjects usually do. Neither of these differences is really as great as it appears. In the first place, in the Batuque there sometimes is an "operator," as the hypnotist is often called. Several cases were described earlier in which leaders or even other mediums assisted a person to enter trance. Even when no operator is involved, there is often a standard set of cues that form a kind of induction procedure. A person who receives a particular encantado knows that when the songs for that encantado are sung, he should go into trance. Being whirled by a medium in trance or hearing the Japetequara song cycle are other occasions that should lead to trance.

It must be admitted, however, that there are an irreducible number of instances when there is obviously no operator of any kind. Many times mediums go into trance during ceremonies when there seem to be no cues except the drums. And in many cases mediums go into trance outside the ceremonial context without observable cues. They simply "concentrate," according to their own reports. What would seem to be involved in these cases is some form of self-hypnosis. This kind of hypnotic induction has not been studied intensively, but the validity of the procedure seems to be generally accepted (London 1967, pp. 49–50; Marcuse 1959, pp. 200–2). Good hypnotic subjects with some experience can apparently enter a hypnotic state at will, and self-hypnosis is taught as a part of some therapeutic programs, especially in the case of allergies (Le Cron 1961).

The idea that people who are hypnotized should act sleepy and lethargic may have arisen simply because hypnosis was originally thought to be a form of sleep (Gill and Brenman 1959, pp. 221–36). In modern studies of hypnotic phenomena, induction is still usually found to be most effective when the subject is comfortable and relaxed. On the other hand, once the subject has entered the hypnotic state, he is able to behave very actively without coming out of trance. The fact that lethargy is not a necessary part of the hypnotic state is perhaps best illustrated by the cases in which hypnotized subjects were told to act as though they were not in a hypnotic state. In some cases their behavior appeared so normal that experienced hypnotists were unable to tell whether they were hypnotized or not (Gill and Brenman 1959, pp. 38–39). In the Batuque, behavior during trance is certainly not relaxed or lethargic. On the contrary, especially when taking the roles of carouser *caboclos,* mediums are hyperactive. On the several occasions when mediums who were leaving trance managed to fall on top of one of us, it was surprising how rigid and tense (rather than limp and relaxed) their bodies were. Entry into trance is also often quite hectic, although in the case of the medium sitting and concentrating, the situation is quite similar to some forms of hypnotic induction. There are clearly considerable differences between the typical hypnotic state and a typical Batuque trance in the degree to which they resemble sleep. But in other respects it would appear that there is a considerable amount of overlap.

From the perspective of the participants, both the hypnotic subject and the Batuque medium have a basic sensation in common. They feel that they are being manipulated. Hypnotic subjects often report that they accept commands and carry them out without the feeling of volition on their part. Batuque members say they feel coerced by an outside force, which of course they identify as the encantado. One of our informants reported a change in body image (one of her feet seemed to increase greatly in size), a type of phenomena very common during hypnotic induction (Hilgard 1965, pp. 25–26).

From the observers point of view, the most striking similarity between hypnosis and trance is that in both cases individuals in altered psychological states enact specifically defined roles. The hypnotic subject takes the role of the hypnotized person, the Batuque member takes the role of a person possessed by a supernatural being. In both cases the individual attempts as best he can to conform to certain conceptions he has of what the role entails. In both cases learning is very important, since the individual must know what behaviors are expected before he can carry them out. In addition, individual capabilities are crucial, since it is clear that some people can learn and perform the roles much more readily than others.

The analysis of hypnosis in terms of role enactment has been developed primarily by Sarbin (1950; 1954; Sarbin and Andersen 1967). In addition to discussing hypnosis in this context, Sarbin (1954, pp. 233–34) has suggested that there is really a continuum in role enactment from simple everyday role playing to dramatic acting, to hypnosis, to hysteria, to "ecstasy." As one moves from casual role playing to ecstasy, there is more and more involvement of the "total organism." In this scheme Sarbin places possession in the category of "ecstasy," but since he defines this category as "usually involving suspension of voluntary action," he clearly was not referring to the type of possession found in the Batuque. We would place Batuque trance behavior in the same category as that of the hypnotic subject, or at the most between hypnotic subject and hysterical fugue.

There are many minor aspects of trance behavior in the Batuque that resemble hypnosis. Amnesia has already been discussed. Some mediums do seem to have partial amnesia for the trance experience, but it would be very difficult to determine how extensive this is. As far as anesthesia is concerned, our data are inconclusive. Mediums claim that when they are in a trance state they can walk on glowing coals or broken glass, put their hands in boiling oil, or burn gunpowder in the palm of the hand without feeling pain. On a number of occasions we observed the burning of gunpowder in the unprotected hands of mediums in trance, but it is not clear how painful this would be under ordinary circumstances. Two men regularly danced with lighted candles, slowly passing the flame under the chin and along the underside of the arms without flinching. On one occasion Antônio, possessed by one of his more flamboyant encantados, cautiously placed his bare heel on a small mound of glowing coals that he had called for. He seemed clearly to feel something and had an assistant immediately wash the foot. On two occasions cult leaders appeared to have doubts about the physical stamina of mediums whom they did not know well and refused to permit them to put their anesthesia to the test. In one incident a young woman, whose possession by José Tupinambá was questioned (another medium was already possessed by the spirit) called loudly for glowing coals to prove the possession. She was simply ignored by the cult leader. In the other incident, a woman possessed by an Exu demanded that gunpowder be burned in her hand. Carlos, the *pai de santo* involved, reluctantly yielded to her request, but placed several thicknesses of paper under the powder.

There was a time when students of hypnosis debated the question as to whether subjects in a hypnotic state would engage in immoral or immodest acts. Although the problem was never resolved, the evidence seemed to indicate that under most circumstances they would not (Marcuse 1959, pp. 107–14). As far as modesty is concerned, this conclusion is borne out by our observations of Batuque mediums in trance. No matter what gyrations the women went through, they almost always managed to avoid exposing more of their legs than was considered proper. Ordinarily this is not much of a problem when a woman is wearing a ceremonial costume, since the long full skirt keeps the legs well covered no matter how vigorously the woman may dance or whirl. But on many occasions young girls were possessed while in the audience and were led out on the floor to dance wearing an ordinary skirt (at the time of our research, skirts were worn about knee length). It was quite striking how careful the girls were about their skirts, no matter what behavior they engaged in. They might dance with their eyes tightly closed, leaping and whirling in a relatively uncontrolled way, but they always seemed to be aware of the position of their skirts. If necessary, they held one or both hands at their sides to keep their skirts from rising.

In these various ways, then, the Batuque trance seems to be quite closely related to hypnosis. If this is the case, then one of the issues raised at the beginning of the chapter is resolved. Since the ability to be hypnotized is not pathological (some 80 per cent of American college students can perform to some degree as a hypnotized subject[3]), there is no reason to suppose that Batuque mediums are necessarily psychologically abnormal. Our impression, freely granting that we are not experts in the matter of mental health, was that many of the mediums that we knew well were relatively well-adjusted individuals.

The other question, whether mediums consciously and deliberately pretend to be possessed, is more difficult. It can safely be assumed that some mediums pretend some of the time. But it seems highly doubtful that any of them pretend all of the time. If a medium did not at some time have subjective sensations that proved to him that he was indeed possessed, there would be no reason for him to undergo the sacrifice and hardship that being a medium entails. Moreover, the *jogada* and other signs of loss of control that the most experienced mediums display on occasion suggest that even those most polished performers still have strong trance experiences. Although there is a clear-cut role of the encantado that is learned in fairly straightforward fashion by most mediums, learning the role alone is not enough. Simply being able to enter trance is also not enough. The essence of possession in the Batuque is enacting a role while in a psychological condition very similar to the hypnotic state.

FOOTNOTES

1. We use the term "possession" to mean any behavior that members of the Batuque interpret as indicating the presence in the human body of a supernatural being. "Trance," as we use the term, refers to an altered psychological state. It probably resembles the hypnotic state, but our data do not allow a more precise description or definition.

2. Ribeiro (1959) has also discussed possession in the Xangô cult of Recife as role enactment, but with a different emphasis.

3. See Hilgard (1965, p. 80) for a summary of recent studies.

Chapter VII

Organization

"The Batuque is a beautiful religion, but it's very disunited," Inês once commented, somewhat wistfully. She went on to caution us that we would find that Batuque leaders not only disagreed about doctrine and ritual, but that there was also sometimes open hostility between them. She was most concerned, however, by the lack of comradeship within the *terreiro* to which she belonged. Not only were the other mediums not very friendly, but her *mãe de santo,* Dona Ana, was clearly exploiting her mediums by charging very high prices for preparing them. Inês confessed that she had become so disillusioned that she had taken several recent problems to the *pai de santo* Antônio, only to find that he was just as willing to take advantage of her as was Dona Ana.

Inês' conception of the Batuque as being permeated by selfishness, deceit, and conflict was probably colored by the fact that she belonged to the *terreiro* of Dona Ana, undoubtedly one of the more impersonal *terreiros* in Belém. However, other informants complained in much the same terms about other *terreiros* and other leaders. Even clients and hangers-on frequently commented on the jealousy and discord that characterized most *terreiros* and on the slipshod way in which most of the cult groups were organized.

Interviews with Batuque leaders, however, always elicited quite a different conception of *terreiro* organization. Each leader saw his own *terreiro* as a tightly knit group of friendly and faithful followers who were organized in a quite formal way. It became clear that there was an ideal of *terreiro* organization that leaders attempted to realize but invariably fell short of, at least in the estimation of their followers. A closer look at the ideal picture will provide a good beginning for a realistic assessment of the complaints of Inês and others.

In the ideal *terreiro,* the leader is truly the *mãe* (mother) or *pai* (father) of the *filhas* (daughters) and *filhos* (sons). Since the leader assumes not only the title but the status of parent, he or she is obeyed and shown respect. The lives of the mediums center around the *terreiro,* where much of their time is devoted to tasks associated with preparations for the next public ceremony. Their loyalty to the leader and to the *terreiro* is founded on the fact that it was here that they were first possessed by an encantado, and it was the *mãe* or *pai de santo* who prepared them to be mediums and performed the rituals initiating them into the religion. To be loyal to the *terreiro* means to appear when summoned for ceremonies, to make any sacrifice necessary to obtain the costumes prescribed by the leader, and not to take part in the ceremonies of any other center without the express permission of one's own leader.

The ideal *terreiro* has three officers in addition to the *mãe* or *pai de santo*. There is a second-in-command, almost always a woman, who is called the *mãe pequena* (literally, little mother). The major responsibility of the *mãe pequena* is to take charge during ceremonies when the leader is occupied with non-ceremonial matters. It is necessary for someone to fill in, since the leader is often busy giving consultations, greeting guests, or sometimes conducting secret rituals. The direction of the singing and dancing then passes to the *mãe pequena.* It is sometimes expected that the *mãe pequena* will become the leader of the *terreiro* in the event of the death of the existing leader, but, as will be pointed out later, this usually happens only under special circumstances and is rarely taken for granted.

Another officer is the *ogan,* who may be either male or female, and who is not necessarily a medium. Usually living at the center, the *ogan* is the general caretaker of the *terreiro*. He or she sees to the upkeep of the dance pavilion and chapel, runs errands of all kinds during ceremonies, and performs other menial chores.[1]

The third position that is of some importance is that of head drummer. This should be a man who knows the proper beat to accompany any of the songs that may be sung during ceremonies and who is able and willing to attend ceremonies whenever they may be held. Ideally, drummers observe the same taboos as the mediums prior to a ceremony, and the head drummer is supposed to see to it that the men who serve as drummers "have clean bodies," i.e., observe dietary and sexual taboos. But, in fact, in most *terreiros* almost anyone who cares to may take a turn at the drums, and it would be quite unreasonable to expect the head drummer to inquire into the ritual condition of each one. Ordinarily this ideal is simply ignored.

One *pai de santo* gave us a longer list of *terreiro* officers and insisted that he had passed through all of the positions he listed in his own progress to the top. However, his experience had been primarily in Maranhão, not in Belém, and no one else in Belém even mentioned an *ogan* who wards off evil or an *ogan* in charge of sacrifices. All of our informants agreed, however, that every *terreiro* should have the three officers described above. All conceived of the ideal *terreiro* as being run with more or less an iron hand by the *mãe* or *pai de santo,* ably assisted by a loyal and conscientious *mãe pequena,* an industrious *ogan,* and a ritually alert head drummer. Under the leadership of these four people, the rank-and-file mediums were expected to be obedient, co-operative, and steadfast.

In the real world, however, this ideal organization is rarely realized. Some *terreiros* do not have a *mãe pequena,* others have no *ogan,* and in only a few is there a clearly designated head drummer. The duties that should be performed by these officers are carried out in a very casual fashion by mediums or hangers-on, under the immediate direction of the leader. There are a variety of reasons why a leader might fail to fill the lower posts. In some cases likely candidates are not interested. Zuzu told us that the *pai de santo* Antônio had asked her to serve as *mãe pequena.* She said she had promptly refused on the grounds that no one would obey her orders. Everyone connected with Antônio's *terreiro,* she said, wanted to be the boss. Zuzu then confided that she would not, in any case, care to work that closely with Antônio, since she considered his ritual erroneous, his direction of the *terreiro* too slipshod, and she did not get along with his carouser encantado. If she only had the funds, Zuzu continued, she would prefer to open her own *terreiro*.

The attitudes underlying Zuzu's remarks are quite typical of developed mediums. Such attitudes go a long way toward explaining the loose organization of most *terreiros* and the problem that most leaders face in trying to control their followers. Far from exhibiting the desired traits of loyalty and docility, most experienced mediums tend to manifest an air of independence and to make a show of their ritual knowledge. They freely criticize their leaders (at least behind their backs) and, in most respects, consider themselves their equals. Zuzu's last remark is especially noteworthy. Many mediums appear to cherish aspirations of someday, somehow, having a *terreiro* of their own. Although for most mediums this remains an unattainable dream, it is one that seems never to be completely abandoned.

As was pointed out in the last chapter, the beginning medium is quite dependent on the cult leader for the identification of the possessing encantado and instruction in the necessary obligations. However, it is not uncommon for even a beginning medium to decide, at an early period in his indoctrination, that the leader under whose direction he is developing is not satisfactory. Some of our informants had tried three or four different leaders before they found one whose personality and religious knowledge were wholly to their liking. Then, as mediums gain more expertise, it is quite common for them to visit other *terreiros,* in spite of the objections of their current *mãe* or *pai de santo,* and if they find a *terreiro* where their talents seem better appreciated, they may readily change allegiance.

A few of the older, experienced mediums deliberately maintain an independent status and do not belong to any *terreiro*. This can be a very satisfactory arrangement, assuming that the medium has the proper reputation. Our friend Clara, whose knowledge, verve, and ability to induce trance in others were well known, was much in demand. She received invitations almost every week to participate in ceremonies in *terreiros* all over Belém. When it came time for her to hold the annual ceremony for her major encantado, Japetequara, it often happened that several *terreiros* would vie for the right to hold the ceremony. Clara was quite proud of both her popularity and her independence, frequently boasting that she had no *pai de santo* and could do as she pleased.

At any given moment, however, most mediums are identified with a particular *terreiro* and a particular *mãe* or *pai de santo*. And in spite of the moving about and the uncertain status of some members, there are always some mediums who are steadfast over long periods, never changing allegiance and devoting themselves to one *terreiro*. There is consequently enough stability of membership in all *terreiros* for the members to have some sense of being part of a congregation. If the membership of the *terreiro* is derived from the immediate neighborhood, many of the women may be neighbors and friends and as such may have regular contacts outside the *terreiro*. Most of the women attached to Antônio's *terreiro,* for example, lived within a few minutes walk of the cult center. Many of them had been together for a number of years, having earlier been members of the *terreiro* of José Ubiratan until the death of that *pai de santo*. Some of the women went by the *terreiro* almost every day to chat with Antônio, to gossip with friends, or to spread the word about available bargains in cloth for costumes. The women frequently served as godmothers for one another's children, visited one another when illness occurred, and always co-operated with one another when it was thought desirable to get messages from one of their encantados. For some of the women involved, the *terreiro* group was the most important social unit to which they belonged, outside of their immediate family.

The membership of such neighborhood groups of believers may remain constant even though the mediums change *terreiro* affiliation. In 1962 we identified twenty mediums (sixteen women, four men) associated with Antônio's *terreiro* who were members of a neighborhood in-group. An additional ten mediums (all women) who lived in the neighborhood were part of the same group, participated in many of the ceremonies at Antônio's *terreiro,* but were members of other *terreiros* or had the status of independent mediums. When we returned to the city three years later, Antônio had moved to Rio de Janeiro, but the neighborhood group was still largely intact. Of the thirty mediums, two had died, one had moved away from Belém, three had moved to other neighborhoods, and two had abandoned the cult or at least had stopped participating in ceremonies. The remaining twenty-two mediums were still in fairly close contact with one another. Half of them continued to identify with Antônio's *terreiro,* hopefully awaiting his return. The other half had become affiliated with a new *terreiro* that opened in the neighborhood in 1964, and it seemed likely that most of the first group would soon follow their example.[2]

Not all mediums become part of the fellowship group, even at a neighborhood *terreiro* such as Antônio's. Some mediums appear only for the major ceremonies, fulfill their obligation to their encantados by being possessed, then disappear until the next ceremony. There is nothing in Batuque theology that requires fellowship with other mediums. There are also *terreiros* where very little in-group feeling develops, even among mediums who participate regularly. Such was the case at the *terreiro* of Dona Ana, where our friend Inês found the atmosphere so cold and unfriendly. A number of factors contributed to the low morale of this *terreiro,* but one of the most important was simply that the mediums were not neighbors. Dona Ana was so famous that she attracted mediums from all over Belém. Most members of the *terreiro* had no contact at all except for relatively infrequent ceremonies, and it was not uncommon for them to be ignorant of one another's names.

Even within the most tightly knit *terreiro* group there is always some hostility between mediums. This hostility is ordinarily quite low-keyed, and it is rarely manifested during public ceremonies, when mediums almost always interact in a warm and friendly way. Only by being present in mediums' homes when they are discussing one another can the outsider acquire some conception of the jealousy and rivalry that permeates their interpersonal relationships. In these surroundings, fellow mediums are often criticized because they "do not know anything," either about ritual or the encantados. It may be suggested that, since the other medium was prepared incorrectly by the cult leader, his ignorance may not be entirely his own fault (a way of criticizing two fellow cult members at once). Perhaps the most cutting allegation, aside from the ultimate accusation that a person pretends to be possessed, is to insist that a medium has been possessed by an encantado other than the one supposedly present. This is a common charge, made especially by experienced mediums who wish to discredit the trance behavior of younger or less experienced colleagues. Since it is generally believed that encantados sometimes give false names when they descend, this is not an unreasonable allegation in terms of Batuque beliefs, and it cannot effectively be refuted. It implies that the person who has been duped is too ignorant to know which encantado has possessed him, while the person making the charge is shown to have as much skill as a *mãe* or *pai de santo* in recognizing encantados.

Although this kind of gossip goes on continuously in the homes of cult members, there is one occasion when antagonism between mediums is also expressed in public. This is when two mediums claim to be possessed by the same encantado at the same time. Since simultaneous possession is thought to be impossible, it is assumed that one of the mediums is either pretending or, more commonly, is really possessed by a different encantado who is giving a false name. If one of the mediums involved in such a confrontation is a beginner, he or she is usually summarily forced out of trance and the problem is solved. But if both of the mediums are experienced, the confrontation is ideally settled by an ordeal. It is said that both mediums handle live coals or put their hands in boiling *dendê* oil, and the one who is really possessed by the encantado in question suffers no ill effects. Our informant Clara claimed that on one occasion she poured boiling *dendé* oil over her head to prove the presence of the encantado Mariana. Having never witnessed an ordeal, we cannot vouch for the accuracy of these accounts. In our experience, however, in most cases of simultaneous possession one medium simply withdrew, or the cult leader might even close the ceremony to avoid an embarrassing showdown.

Much of the controversy over the true identity of possessing spirits arises because experienced mediums often try to maintain their exclusiveness by claiming that they alone receive a particular encantado. Clara insisted that she was the only medium in Belém who received Japetequara. When we reported having seen other mediums possessed by this encantado, Clara looked down her nose and said she would believe it only if she saw it herself. One of her friends supposedly received Japetequara, she said, but she knew very well that it was a Curupira giving Japetequara's name. If an encantado is very popular, a medium does not dare claim that others do not also receive it. However, the medium always watches with jealous interest when others are possessed by the spirit, ever ready to claim a mistaken identification if the behavior of the medium in trance does not conform to the established pattern.

The antagonism illustrated by these kinds of behavior is best understood as the direct result of competition for both prestige and income. As far as prestige is concerned, it was noted in previous chapters that mediums strive for recognition by their peers of their ability to receive important supernatural beings. Once a medium has established this reputation, he can often convert it into income by performing services for clients. Since every medium is a potential seller of services, and since there is a limited number of clients, some of the competition among mediums would seem ultimately to be based on economic factors. On the other hand, it is usually impossible to disentangle economic motives from other kinds, and it would be a mistake to assume that all mediums are equally involved in the quest for clients. A medium begins by performing small services for relatives, friends, and neighbors, and probably a majority of mediums never go beyond this small and usually impoverished circle. Economic return looms large only for those mediums whose reputation brings clients from a wider area.

All mediums compete for prestige, however, regardless of whether or not they ever compete very hard for clients. In every *terreiro* there is a rough but perceptible ranking of the members, and this ranking is manifested fairly clearly during ceremonies. When some mediums go into trance the event may go largely unremarked. Others receive almost as much deference as the *mãe* or *pai de santo,* with the other participants literally standing in line to greet the newly arrived encantado. The status hierarchy also becomes apparent when the leader is absent from the pavilion and disputes arise over who will lead the singing. The drummers and most of the mediums follow the lead of the most

When a medium who enjoys high status enters trance, other participants literally stand in line to greet her encantado.

This salutation has a special significance for the woman kneeling, for she believes she is addressing the spirit Tapinaré, her own *senhor*.

prestigious member present. Direct and obvious competition between mediums during public ceremonies is frowned upon, however, and does not often occur. Only occasionally does a medium in trance grab anyone within reach in an attempt to prove his ability to induce trance in others, and even less often does a high-status medium sharply reprove another for some ritual infraction.

Mediums become involved in competition for status initially because of the satisfactions they derive from their positions as intermediaries with the supernatural. Informants frequently found the opportunity to tell us of incidents during which their performance in trance had prompted the admiring comment of knowledgeable observers. During ceremonies the gestures and facial expressions of those in trance gave clear indication of their pleasure with the deference paid them. For many mediums, taking the role of an encantado makes possible an enhancement of status that bears directly on their self-esteem and self-realization. Individuals who may be minimally successful in their secular lives, perhaps partially dependent on charity or the good will of upper-class patrons, can sometimes not only gain the respect and admiration of their fellow mediums, but may even be in a position to dispense charity themselves by performing supernatural services gratis. It should not be supposed, however, that every medium derives equal satisfaction from being an agent of the supernatural. In every hierarchy there must be someone at the bottom, and on several occasions we saw women in trance burst into tears when they were treated with indifference by the other participants in a ceremony.

Once an individual has acquired a modest reputation as a medium and begins to do services for clients, competition with other mediums may or may not become intense, depending on how ambitious the individual is. Those who compete the hardest are those who have serious aspirations of becoming a *mãe* or *pai de santo*.

As was noted above, many mediums talk vaguely about someday having a *terreiro,* but only a very few make a real effort to turn this dream into a reality. There are two routes by which a medium may attain the status of leader. It is sometimes possible, by being a faithful follower, to gain recognition as the second-in-command of a *terreiro* and more or less to inherit it when the leader dies. We learned the history of eight *terreiros* and discovered one case in which this kind of succession had occurred. That it does not occur more often is due to several circumstances. In the first place, the ownership of the land on which the *terreiro* is built passes to the family of the dead leader, and unless the *mãe pequena* or *contra-guia* (as the infrequent male second-in-command is called) is a close relative, the transfer of ownership often presents insurmountable problems. Consequently, the continuation of the *terreiro* as a physical plant rarely occurs, and there is some scattering of the mediums in the process of moving the *terreiro* to a new location. Ordinarily the mediums who find the new leader congenial stay with him, while those who do not have no compunction about going elsewhere.

The other obstacle standing between a *mãe pequena* and a routine assumption of leadership when her chief dies is the fact that the *mãe pequena* usually does not have the personality of a potential leader. What seems to happen is that the *mãe* or *pai de santo* chooses a woman for *mãe pequena* who is loyal above all else. Such a choice is apparently prompted by a fear on the part of the leader that his second-in-command may try to usurp his position. Needless to say, none of the leaders gave us this explanation. It is based on several beliefs and stories that indicate a good deal of hostility between Batuque leaders and their followers. In some cases the stories are quite explicit. One *mãe de santo,* for example, was said to have killed her daughter and driven her granddaughter crazy to prevent them from threatening her position as leader of the *terreiro.* In other cases, hostility can be inferred from certain beliefs, such as those centering around a practice called the *trocar de cabeças* (exchange of heads).[3] It is believed that if a *mãe* or *pai de santo* is threatened with death and is forewarned, one of the mediums of the *terreiro* can be substituted to die in the leader's place. Those leaders who live to an advanced age are thought to have managed to live so long only by causing the death of a number of their followers. The final set of ideas that fits this theme relates to the manipulation of supernatural power, especially in the practice of sorcery. It is a common complaint, heard in all *terreiros,* that leaders never teach their followers anything, or at least not very much.

The usual explanation is that the leader is afraid to do so. If he taught his followers anything about sorcery, for example, he could expect that they would try out their newly acquired powers on him, with fatal results.

Given this set of ideas, and the attitudes they suggest, it is not surprising that a leader would choose a *mãe pequena* who seemed safe rather than a woman with the dynamic qualities of a potential leader. In any case, only one of the eight *terreiros* that we studied had a prominent *mãe pequena*. Dona Ana, who was well along in years, was grooming her adopted daughter to be her successor. This girl was so placid and pliable, however, that she clearly presented no threat to her mother. In the other *terreiros* that had such an officer, the *mãe pequena* was a competent, industrious, and completely loyal woman who was so lacking in charisma that it is hard to imagine her becoming a successful *mãe de santo*.

A really ambitious medium is not likely to take the *mãe pequena* (or *contra-guia*) route to a leadership position, since it requires a long period of complete subordination, and the results are uncertain. Anyone with the drive and determination necessary to be a successful leader is likely to strike out on his own early in his religious career. According to their own accounts, several Batuque leaders embarked on an independent course even before they could have been considered very accomplished mediums. As in many other religions, potential leaders in the Batuque appear to experience some sort of "call" to enter the competition for a following, and several of our informants explained their decision to attempt to become a leader as a response to explicit orders from their encantados.

No great outlay of capital is needed to make a start. The would-be leader usually begins, like other mediums, by performing services in his home for friends, neighbors, and acquaintances. In the beginning the medium offers the services of his encantados gratis. While he is thus building his reputation, he is likely to be assiduously participating in the ceremonies at various cult centers. A great deal must still be learned, especially about ritual and the characteristics of the encantados. The only way to learn how to conduct ritual is by observing established leaders in action. The books on Umbanda that are available in every bookstore are oriented toward the Umbanda of Rio de Janeiro and have essentially no applicability to the Batuque. The best way of learning about the encantados is thought to be by interacting with them, that is, by interacting with experienced mediums in trance.

The aspiring leader may struggle for years to attract a following. In reminiscing about this time of trial, most leaders like to stress how difficult it was and how only the aid of their encantados made it possible for them to survive. Dona Jorgina maintained that she began with an altar set up on an empty kerosene can and decorated with strips of wrapping paper. Dona Ana insisted that she treated the sick for many years free of charge before her encantados finally gave her permission to accept presents. Her husband abandoned her and their three small children, and her health was poor. During this period she supported herself and the children by doing sewing, a skill she said was taught her by her chief encantado in dreams. The spirit also discovered dressmaking customers for her and sent them to her home.

After the medium has begun to attract a clientele, the next step is to start holding small ceremonies in the home. As the young *mãe de santo* Magda explained the process, some people who came to her with problems became possessed by a spirit while she was treating them. They were obviously potential mediums who had to develop their powers, and they begged Magda to help them. She was thus obliged "to open," that is, she let it be known that ceremonies for the development of mediums would be held in her home once a week. Such ceremonies are usually held in the *varanda,* a large room toward the rear of the house that is used primarily as a dining room. Depending upon the leader's success in helping would-be mediums develop their skills, additional prospects may appear for the *varanda* ceremonies. There seem to be a considerable number of people in Belém who believe that they have mediumistic gifts and are interested in developing them, but who are intimidated by the impersonality of a large *terreiro* or *seara* and the necessity of performing in front of a large audience. The *varanda* sessions of a beginning leader offer a more intimate, friendly atmosphere. The leader is much more solicitous of the new medium than is a well-established *mãe* or *pai de santo,* and there is no audience except other prospective mediums and a client or two. It should be noted in passing that mediums who develop in such circumstances have a relatively low status among other Batuque members. To be recognized as important intermediaries with the supernatural, such mediums must eventually become part of a group where possession occurs in public.

The next step in the career of the typical Batuque leader would be the opening of a *seara*. There is no sharp dividing line between holding ceremonies in the *varanda* and opening a *seara* except that in the latter case the cult leader may register with the police as the operator of an organized religious group. By applying for a license, the leader not only advertises the fact that he now has a following of at least semideveloped mediums, but also that he intends to celebrate some of the more important rituals of the ceremonial calendar. Unless his house has an unusually large *varanda,* the leader is usually forced to do some remodeling to provide more space. Sometimes a separate building is constructed. If the new *seara* survives, Batuque members will begin to call the leader a *mãe* or *pai de santo* instead of *curandeiro* (curer), the term applied to individual practitioners.

As was indicated earlier, a *seara* differs from a *terreiro* in that no drums or other musical instruments are used in a *seara,* and the ceremonial room and chapel are usually more modest in size and appointment. Some cult leaders, those most influenced by the Umbanda ideology from southern Brazil, oppose the conversion of a *seara* into a *terreiro* on doctrinal grounds. For most Batuque members, however, and for most clients, there is no question that the prestige of a cult center is greatly enhanced when the *mãe,* or *pai de santo* adds drums and constructs a *terreiro* proper. The conversion of a *seara* into a *terreiro* usually requires a considerable outlay of cash, and this in itself is a measure of the success of a leader. It proves that he has been able to provide satisfactory services for clients with money, usually to the extent of being able to support himself entirely through his religious activities. Leaders of *searas,* on the other hand, often hold other jobs or are supported by gainfully employed family members.

The foregoing description of the development of a typical cult leader represents the longest, most difficult route to cult leadership. From beginning medium in a *terreiro,* to curer and provider of small supernatural services, to leader of sessions in the

The chapel of this *terreiro* is large enough so that all participants can kneel in prayer before the main altar.

varanda, to head of a *seara,* to *mãe* or *pai de santo* of a *terreiro* may take many years. Most of the people who begin this sequence drop out along the way. Some concentrate on treating illness, some are content to divine or deal with the marital problems of their neighbors, some never get out of the *varanda.* Those who finally succeed, such as Dona Ana, Mãe Décia, or Dona Jorgina, are individuals with strong personalities, supreme self-confidence, and fierce determination. In addition they are the possessors of several talents that a leader must have: a certain

At a less prosperous *terreiro,* the chapel is a small curtained alcove and the mediums and members of the audience participating in the prayers must stand in the pavilion facing the alcove. The *pai de santo,* fanning himself, is not participating.

stage presence, a singing voice that at least is loud and strong, and some ability to communicate an interest in others. Not all aspirants for leadership have these necessary qualities. Milton, for example, occasionally talked of opening his own *terreiro;* cult members who heard him expand on this subject agreed that he had the knowledge and the resources to "open," but they were dubious about his chances for success because he was a notoriously poor singer. In another case, Ernesto, a much younger

At this *seara,* the chapel is an even smaller alcove.

man, was eager to be recognized as a prospective *pai de santo.*
Ernesto was an experienced medium with a good singing voice,
he was an indefatigable dancer, and he had quite a reputation
as a curer. However, Ernesto's abrasive personality, his complete
lack of a sense of humor, and his aggressive, brusque manner
when in trance tended to alienate prospective mediums. He had
other problems as well, mostly financial, but in any case he did
not seem a likely prospect to become a successful *pai de santo.*

It is sometimes possible for individuals to take short cuts to the top. Carlos, for example, took over the direction of the *seara* where he was developing when the man who had organized the *seara* suddenly moved to another city. Although Carlos had only been active as a medium for a few months, such was his charisma that the other mediums in the *seara* accepted him as their new leader. Within three years the *seara* was so successful that Carlos gave up his outside job and devoted himself full time to being a religious leader. Edson had an even easier time. Bolstered by the reputation of being a born healer (his mother had dedicated him to the encantados before birth, as described in Chapter IV) and supported by his parents and relatives, he opened a *seara* at the age of nineteen. He still held a full-time job in 1965, six years later, but he had attracted a respectable number of mediums and could probably have supported himself from his religious activity if he had so desired.

Once a man or woman has achieved the goal of becoming a leader, it is soon evident that there are headaches and problems as well as rewards connected with the position. As far as rewards are concerned, it proved impossible to acquire any kind of accurate information about income. Of the eight leaders whose income we could at least estimate, probably only one, Dona Ana, had the equivalent of a middle-class income. Dona Ana had managed to raise a large family in reasonable comfort, and in her declining years she enjoyed luxuries such as a refrigerator, television, and much better medical care than any of her mediums. She also traveled a great deal, flying to Rio de Janeiro at least once a year. All of the other leaders lived somewhat more comfortable lives than most of their followers, but often the difference was not very striking.

There are other rewards associated with being a leader. For Carlos, it was quite clear that other considerations outweighed the economic. According to his own testimony, it was his independence that pleased him most. In a sense he was now self-employed and, as he said, he could get up in the morning when he felt like it and generally do as he pleased. He reported a peace of mind and a feeling of security never known before. Although Carlos' house and possessions were of the simplest, and his pavilion on the verge of collapse, for a man who had only a third-grade education and who had worked first as street cleaner and then as cook in a house of prostitution, his position as *pai de santo* gave him a higher status than probably any other occupation open to him.

In contrast to Carlos, Antônio tended to stress the drawbacks of being a *pai de santo* rather than its advantages. This difference in perspective was undoubtedly due to Antônio's having formerly been a primary school teacher. He felt that he had come down in the world by becoming a cult leader, not up. For a time, Antônio explained, he had tried to teach school and participate in the Batuque at the same time, but he had often had the experience of arriving at school still possessed by his encantado Joãozinho and had finally been forced to give up teaching. What seemed to disturb Antônio the most was that as a *pai de santo* he was at the beck and call of anyone with a problem—the sick, the insane, the financially destitute. People came to him for help at all hours of the day and night, and he did not feel that he should turn them away. Although in fact he often did turn people away and was extremely callous with others, he seemed to feel guilty if he did not make some effort to help everyone who sought his aid. This obligation he felt as a great burden. The life of a *pai de santo,* he was fond of saying, "is a life of sacrifice."

There are many other problems associated with the role of the Batuque leader. If the complaints of leaders are taken at face value, the most onerous problem they have is simply the control of their followers. At one time or another, all the leaders we knew well complained of how *safado* their mediums were—how inconstant, undependable, frivolous, and undisciplined. In specific cases, mediums were accused of not carrying out their obligations to their encantados, not appearing for ceremonies, not being possessed at the proper time, not knowing ritual, not singing, and often simply not obeying the orders of the *mãe* or *pai de santo*. These complaints, often legitimate enough, acquired an added bitterness because there were few if any sanctions that the leader could apply to keep his followers in line. The leader was required to maintain a very delicate balance between being authoritarian in the interest of the *terreiro* and, at the same time, being permissive enough not to offend the developed mediums.

Some discipline must be maintained in any *terreiro* if it is to develop a good reputation. Mediums must be motivated to come for ceremonies, to purchase new costumes, to patiently wait during long, involved rituals before they go into trance, and, above all, to develop their mediumistic skills rapidly. Where such discipline is maintained, large, relatively orderly audiences can be expected at public ceremonies, and, ultimately, new converts and clients will be attracted. However, a leader must be very chary about putting too much pressure on his followers. The young mediums, who feel dependent on the leader until they develop more expertise, will put up with quite a bit of bullying before they decide to go elsewhere. But, as was noted earlier, the developed mediums have a quite different attitude. Even if they are not in fact looking for an excuse to break with their leader, they are easily offended and will not accept very many reprimands. If they do become fed up and decide to leave the *terreiro,* there is nothing the leader can do about it. Since each individual makes his own contract with the supernatural, there is no such thing as excommunication in the Batuque.

Leaders sometimes lecture their followers about their shortcomings during a public ceremony. The leader first enters trance, thus adding the authority of his encantado to his criticisms. Dona Ana often stopped a ceremony altogether and harangued the mediums at length about the inappropriateness of their behavior. Almost any of her encantados was likely to engage in this kind of instruction. Antônio, on the other hand, was brusquely authoritarian when possessed by some encantados and extremely permissive when possessed by others. On one occasion that we witnessed, Antônio, possessed by Ubiratan, sent instructions that the mediums should leave the ceremony in progress and come to him in the house one by one. As each woman entered the house, she was told to hold out her hand. She was then given a sharp slap with a *palmatória,* a small paddle that is used to punish children, and told by Antônio-Ubiratan that this was punishment for her many acts of disobedience during the year. When possessed by his playful encantado, however, Antônio was always very indulgent with his followers. He often engaged in pranks with them that certainly did not enhance the reputation of the *terreiro* as a place where serious interaction with the supernatural was the rule.

The extent to which a leader must be solicitous of the mediums varies according to the reputation that the leader has already been able to establish. Dona Julia, whose *terreiro* was only a year old in 1965, spent most of each ceremony overseeing the possession experiences of her *filhas*. Rarely possessed herself, she spent the evening helping people in and out of trance, showing great respect for those possessed by important spirits, and smiling fondly at those who had reached the carousing stage. Dona Julia's motives seemed clear enough. She hoped to make her *terreiro* so attractive that a number of developed mediums who were participating on a temporary basis would become permanent members.

Dona Ana, on the other hand, with her reputation, had no need to go out of her way to be nice to her mediums. In fact, she seemed quite indifferent to them, to a degree that was unique among the leaders whom we knew. She completely dominated ceremonies, often being possessed by three or four encantados in rapid succession, carrying out a series of rituals, and then abruptly closing the ceremony because she was tired. If other mediums did manage to enter trance, they were often ignored, or sometimes even led into the chapel and brought out of trance to clear the floor for another ritual. It was a common complaint that Dona Ana never taught her mediums anything and that she charged outrageous prices for preparing them. It is not surprising, under the circumstances, that developed mediums rarely remained at her *terreiro* very long. Of the seven developed mediums attached to her *terreiro,* four were members of her family, and the other three participated only infrequently in ceremonies. Even so, such was Dona Ana's reputation that new mediums still came to be prepared, clients continued to appear, and large crowds packed her pavilion for ceremonies. She could afford to treat her mediums in a highhanded manner.

Another problem that every cult leader faces is how to finance the activities of the *seara* or *terreiro*. It is one thing to hold private ceremonies in a *varanda,* but quite a different undertaking to hold a yearly cycle of public ceremonies. For any major ceremony the pavilion should be refurbished, the altar redecorated, and often a loud-speaker rented, complete with technician. Refreshments must be provided, not only for the mediums, but also for all important guests. In a *terreiro* an important item of expense is liquor for the drummers. Since the drums are beaten for such long periods, six or eight men may each take a turn during the ceremony, and each of them expects a few drinks. The major ceremonies of the *terreiros* last at least two days, and sometimes four or five, so that the over-all expense is considerable.

It proved to be impossible to find out exactly how much was spent by cult leaders on ceremonies. In most cases they did not keep records, and although they would give a figure readily enough if asked, the figure might differ widely on successive days. In the examples that follow, the sums given should be taken as suggestive only.

It was not uncommon for affluent tourists visiting Belém to order and pay for a Batuque ceremony. The tourists, who were usually Americans, might be provided with the name and address of a Batuque leader by employees of one of the hotels or by a tourist or travel agency. Ceremonies arranged for tourists were impromptu affairs, not requiring any special preparation and usually ending early, as soon as the tourists left. The usual payment in 1962 was 5000 cruzeiros (about $7.00). Carlos was usually ready to hold a ceremony of this type, and he seemed well satisfied with the payment. The same amount, 5000 cruzeiros, was charged by some *terreiros* for an "anniversary" ceremony. Ideally, each developed medium should sponsor such a ceremony every year. It is intended to celebrate the occasion on which the medium was first possessed by his major encantado. Not many mediums can afford to hold this ceremony, but those who can in effect hire the *terreiro* for the night, or sometimes two nights, and a regular public ceremony is held at their expense. It was widely rumored that Dona Ana charged 20,000 cruzeiros ($28.00) for such a ceremony, but we were unable to find anyone who had paid such a large sum. At the time of our study very few mediums had a monthly income of 20,000 cruzeiros, and most lived on much less.

Most of the ceremonies on the ritual calendar of a *terreiro* are not paid for by a medium, but are the responsibility of the *mãe* or *pai de santo*. Carlos told us that his major ceremony of the year, for St. Barbara, cost between 15,000 and 40,000 cruzeiros ($21.00–$56.00). This was a three-day ceremony that included a procession through the streets (without a band), the use of a loud-speaker (provided free), and a complete repainting of the inside of the pavilion. According to Carlos, the greatest expense was food and drink. The mediums had several meals at the *terreiro,* and there were several out-of-town visitors who were given hospitality.

The most expensive ceremony that we attended was a five-day affair for St. Expeditus held at Antônio's *terreiro.* There were four days of Batuque ceremonies, a secular dance, a procession complete with band and fireworks, and a loud-speaker. All this cost 78,000 cruzeiros ($109.00) according to Antônio, but this estimate is probably a little high. The procession cost almost 10,000 cruzeiros (over 6000 for the band and 3000 for the fireworks). Decorating the altar was almost as expensive, since flowers cost 6000 cruzeiros and candles almost 3000. The cost of the loud-speaker, which was in operation for at least two days, was not determined. The remainder of the expense, by far the largest proportion, was again for food and liquor. During the five days an entire pig was eaten (it had been fattened at the *terreiro* for some time before being slaughtered for the ceremony), plus a dozen ducks, four chickens, and a huge pot of *maniçoba* (a dish made of manioc leaves and, in this case, thirty pounds of meat). Most of this food was consumed by the mediums, hangers-on, and a few visitors from out of town. In spite of the large amount of food provided, several important guests who had contributed toward the expense of the ceremony were heard to complain that they had received very little in the way of refreshments. This was a complaint often heard around Antônio's *terreiro.*

There are several ways that leaders defray the expense of ceremonies. In the poorer *terreiros,* the mediums are sometimes assessed a modest sum, and Carlos said he asked 500 cruzeiros (less than a dollar) from each of his *filhas* before a ceremony. If a medium's husband has an unusually large income, he often makes a contribution much greater than the usual amount. In some *terreiros,* a number of *juizes* (judges) are named who agree to sponsor the ceremony. This practice is taken directly from folk Catholicism, in which "judges" are appointed to play major roles in festivals held on saints' days. In the Batuque, the service to be provided by each *juiz* is clearly specified. The "judge of the altar" is expected to contribute toward the refurbishing of the altar; the "judge of the fireworks" should provide fireworks for the procession. Being asked to be a *juiz* is an honor, and the greatest honor is accorded the "judge of the festival," who is the principal sponsor. In Carlos' ceremony for St. Barbara mentioned earlier, the judge of the festival had access to a loudspeaker, which he made available to Carlos free of charge. He also contributed 5000 cruzeiros.

In most cases, the contributions by the mediums or the judges do not provide sufficient funds for a big ceremony. Other funds come from clients who are currently being treated by the leader or who have been helped in the past and maintain a continuing interest in the *terreiro*. Contributions may also be made by individuals who hope to gain the future support or good will of the cult leader. In 1962, when local and national elections were being held, politicians were a source of funds. An alderman campaigning for re-election to the city council put in an appearance at Carlos' *terreiro* during one ceremony that we attended. He stayed only a short time, but somewhat ostentatiously presented Carlos with 1000 cruzeiros before he left. During the same campaign, a candidate for a seat in the state legislature cultivated the support of Dona Ana by making what she reported as substantial contributions for *terreiro* expenses and by attending ceremonies regularly.

If none of these sources of funds is sufficient, then the *mãe* or *pai de santo* must make up the difference. It was never possible to determine exactly how much the leader contributed, but it is safe to assume that he usually added a considerable amount, especially for a major ceremony. It was our impression that leaders put every cent they could scrape together into their big annual festival. To do less would be to risk invidious comparisons with other *terreiros*. Much of the reputation of a *terreiro* depends on the size, duration, and spirit of the major ceremonies, and every effort is made to make an impressive showing.

The major income of cult leaders comes from the clients for whom they perform services. These services, for which we have adopted the Batuque term *cura* (curing), will be discussed in detail in the next chapter. Here it need only be pointed out that in return for the activities of their encantados on behalf of the client, the *mãe* or *pai de santo* is given presents. These may be in the form of money, or clothing, or sometimes expensive items of household furniture such as stoves or refrigerators. The higher standard of living of most leaders is due more to these gifts than to any propensity to spend money on themselves. With this income the leader supports himself and his family, pays for the upkeep of the *terreiro,* and contributes to the cost of ceremonies. Most leaders have small families, but there are often other people living at the *terreiro.* There is the *ogan* (the caretaker), and there are usually resident guests as well, such as patients undergoing treatment or visiting friends or relatives from out of town. Some of these family members and guests are gainfully employed, and it is very difficult to estimate how much of their support is derived from the *mãe* or *pai de santo* or how much they contribute toward the expenses of the household.

In any case, a cult leader ordinarily spends most of his income on ceremonies, the upkeep of the *terreiro,* and the support of his dependents, and relatively little on his own comforts. This allocation of income is actually not a matter of choice—it is a necessity, especially for younger leaders. A poor, run-down *terreiro* is obviously one where there are no important supernaturals intervening on man's behalf, while a large, well-maintained *terreiro* provides concrete evidence of supernatural support. Prospective clients know that a prosperous *terreiro* is the result of contributions by satisfied customers. In some cases clients seek out smaller *terreiros* to avoid publicity, but ordinarily the larger the *terreiro,* the more clients it attracts. It is clearly in the best interest of the *mãe* or *pai de santo* to have bigger ceremonies and a more elaborate *terreiro* than anyone else.

The reputation of a *terreiro* does not depend entirely on its size and ornateness, however. Another important factor is the number of developed mediums who participate in ceremonies and receive important encantados. The presence of such mediums and their encantados is what gives the *terreiro* the reputation of being *forte* (strong). For the *mãe* or *pai de santo,* the problem of acquiring developed mediums can be handled in various ways. The simplest procedure, of course, is to inspire the neophytes who come for development to acquire the skills of the experienced medium as quickly as possible. Another possibility is to invite developed mediums who are independent to attend ceremonies. A common way of attracting these mediums is to offer to hold their "anniversary" ceremony at the expense of the *terreiro*. Or, finally, it is sometimes possible to entice mediums away from other *terreiros* simply by making them feel that their talents are more appreciated in the new setting.

In any event, Batuque leaders are in direct competition with one another for developed mediums, just as they compete for clients. As might be expected under such circumstances, leaders are often hostile to one another. We rarely had an interview with a *mãe* or *pai de santo* in which some disparaging remarks about other leaders were not made, although such remarks were never very heated. Rival leaders were most commonly criticized for not having gone through the complete initiation ritual, and this was given as the reason for their lack of knowledge and their failure to have a command of proper ritual. There was frequent reference to the excessive drinking that occurred in other *terreiros,* as well as the number of fights that broke out in the audience. Certain *terreiros* might be referred to as being *fraco* (weak), which meant that few of the mediums became possessed during ceremonies and those that did received unimportant encantados. Derogatory comments might also be made about a rival's personal morality, his sex life, his ineffectual attempts at sorcery, or his exploitation of clients.

In spite of these incessant criticisms, Batuque leaders invite one another to ceremonies, and when together they usually interact in a reasonably friendly way. When a new *terreiro* is opened by a stranger, a local *pai de santo* is invited to inaugurate the dance pavilion. Younger leaders regularly visit the ceremonies held by the more established leaders, sometimes by invitation, sometimes of their own accord. It is commonly supposed that the main purpose of these visits is to learn the secrets of the veteran leader, but the visitor is usually invited to take part in the ceremony and may in fact dominate the proceedings for long periods. At the time of his major annual ceremony, a leader is likely to invite several other leaders to attend with all of their followers. In the cases that we observed, the *mãe* or *pai de santo* showed up with only a few of his experienced mediums, and sometimes the visiting group joined the spectators instead of participating in the dancing.

We also encountered one case where two leaders had entered into a long-term co-operative arrangement. Antônio and Dona Ana at one time agreed that they would not hold ceremonies on the same dates, the idea being to avoid competition for crowds and attention. This deal lasted only as long as the two leaders maintained a friendly relationship. A quarrel over a client soon led to a collapse of the agreement.

On only one occasion during our research did we witness a public display of naked antipathy between Batuque leaders. In this instance one *pai de santo* threatened to kill another by means of sorcery. The universal condemnation of this action made it clear that the *pai de santo* making the threat had gone far beyond the bounds of propriety. Whatever leaders may say about one another in private, they are expected to maintain some show of friendliness in public. Ordinarily each leader has one or two fellow leaders with whom he interacts more or less regularly and at least one implacable enemy whom he avoids at all costs.

Whether the leaders are friendly or not, all *terreiros* are completely independent of one another. This was the case at least until 1964, when a Federation of Afro-Brazilian Cults was established in Belém. As it was constituted a year later, when we visited the city in 1965, the federation was more of a mutual-aid society than it was an ecclesiastical body. The founders of the federation, Manoel Colaço and João Cardoso, had modeled it after federations in existence in Recife and Rio de Janeiro. In return for monthly dues, the member was entitled to the services of a lawyer retained by the federation and a burial payment. The organizers of the federation hoped to build a small hospital and emergency clinic to which members would have access. Bonds were being sold to provide funds for the construction of these facilities, and a concerted attempt was made to induce every medium in Belém to obtain a membership card. By August of 1965 over 500 mediums had signed up and paid an initiation fee. Included in this figure were more than 150 cult leaders, who had no recourse but to join. The organizers had arranged with the civil authorities to handle the registration and licensing of all Afro-Brazilian religious groups. Whereas formerly the leader of a *terreiro* was required to obtain a permit from the police before holding a ceremony (the permit exempted him from a city ordinance prohibiting noise after 10 P.M.), the permit now had to be obtained from the federation.[4]

The founders of the federation seem to have intended that the organization would make some attempt to reduce the dissension within the Batuque. A Ritual Council was set up, composed of several prominent leaders and independent mediums, whose charge was to resolve conflicts and produce some standardization of ritual. While we were in Belém in 1965 the council was considering a case of simultaneous possession, but the half-hearted way in which the council went about its work did not augur well for the resolution of similar conflicts in the future. There was also some talk among federation officials about giving leaders tests of ritual competence before issuing licenses, but no such tests had been given and, in view of the bitter disagreements over ritual detail, none seemed likely.

A year after its founding, the federation was being run by a small group of people whose motivation was probably not wholly religious. By gaining control of the licensing function they were able to force Batuque leaders to join the federation, but many leaders regarded the federation with suspicion or even disdain. It seems likely that the majority will continue to come for their licenses and permits, but otherwise will have little to do with the federation.

Much of this chapter has dealt with conflict and competition, yet, as was indicated in an earlier chapter, Batuque beliefs are relatively homogeneous. In part, at least, this homogeneity is due to the fact that there is so much competition.[5] An individual who wishes to be a leader must prove that he knows Batuque theology better than anyone else. He does this, of course, by being more orthodox than anyone else. In this religion of rampant individualism, there are relatively few individualists, or at least few innovators. All leaders do innovate to some extent, but only after they have established a reputation for knowing the traditional way of doing things. There is interminable discussion of orthodoxy by Batuque leaders, each claiming to have the true beliefs and the proper rituals. As was noted earlier, a common criticism of rival *terreiros* is that the ritual followed there is all wrong. It should be noted, however, that in order to make such criticisms a fairly precise knowledge of what goes on in other *terreiros* is necessary. In fact, all leaders keep a sharp eye on their rivals, and while some practices are condemned, others are copied. The result is that beliefs and rituals tend to be quite similar everywhere. Even newcomers from Maranhão, who supposedly come from the land of the true faith, quickly modify their ceremonies to conform to local practice.

Another force for conservatism are the independent mediums. These men and women, who regularly attend ceremonies at several *terreiros,* are usually highly critical of innovations. Not only do they tend to participate in those *terreiros* where they feel the ritual is conservative, but they also openly express their displeasure if events during a ceremony do not conform to their notions of orthodoxy. In an earlier chapter, an incident was described in which a medium claiming to receive Oxalá was effectively challenged by the other mediums who refused to sing the choral responses. Our friend Clara, who was present on this occasion, led the rebuff simply by standing mute and staring disdainfully at the unfortunate girl who claimed to receive Oxalá. On another occasion, at Antônio's *terreiro,* a visiting *pai de santo* departed from the established pattern of the midnight Exu ritual to run out into the street and there kill two sacrificial chickens by biting their throats. The gory incident appeared to titillate spectators, but several experienced mediums abruptly left the pavilion, changed clothes, and went home, denouncing Antônio for permitting such "buffoonery" in his *terreiro.*

The most innovative of the Batuque leaders was Dona Maria de Aguiar. In earlier chapters it was pointed out how this *mãe de santo* "crossed" Umbanda with Mina-Nagô and how she introduced King Louis XVI into the Batuque pantheon. In one instance, however, Dona Maria's attempt to innovate was a complete failure. She announced, for reasons that remain obscure, that the encantado Mariana had withdrawn from mankind and would no longer possess people. Since Mariana is one of the most popular encantados in Belém, this pronouncement could not fail to be of interest to a large number of mediums. The reaction was some indignation, some puzzlement, and then almost universal indifference. Most mediums did avoid possession by Mariana when participating in ceremonies at Dona Maria's *terreiro,* but this was simply to avoid an embarrassing situation. At one ceremony that we attended, a devotee of Mariana received the spirit as soon as Dona Maria had left the pavilion. Mariana loudly called attention to her presence, but discreetly went away before Dona Maria rejoined the ceremony. It seems clear that this particular kind of innovation—banishing a popular encantado —would be doomed from the start, and that only Dona Maria would have attempted it. Her reputation was so secure, however, that she could afford to be relatively indifferent to what other leaders or the independent mediums thought of her.

The major sanction against innovation is ridicule. Older mediums sneer at younger mediums, established leaders scoff at newcomers. It might be supposed that such attitudes would have little effect, since each individual has his own contract with a spirit and might behave quite autonomously. But it seems to be quite impossible for anyone to carry on as a medium without the support and approbation of other mediums. Individuals do not seem to find their trance experiences compelling enough to sustain them in aberrant behavior. When an encantado speaks, it could presumably say anything, and it might set up an entirely different code of behavior for its medium. But the fact is that when an encantado speaks, it says pretty much what all other encantados say. If it does not, apparently the medium is never so far in trance that he is not aware of the disapproval of his fellow mediums. And in most cases the next supernatural utterance is more in keeping with accepted beliefs.

It might be well, in closing this chapter, to admit that the interpretation presented may be a slight distortion of reality. We may have overstressed the conflict in the Batuque and not given enough space to comradeship and solidarity. If our account is distorted, it is because most of our informants were upward-striving people. Had we spent more time with the more humble, the less ambitious, and the less articulate mediums, our account might very well be somewhat different.

However, there can be no question about the basic ambivalence that characterizes most of the interpersonal relationships in this religion. Mediums do love one another, or at least some do, even as they compete for prestige. Mediums are often devoted to their leader, and at the same time they resent his lack of interest in them and fear his exploitation. Some leaders do honestly want to help their followers attain success with the supernatural, but the leader is in an exceedingly difficult position, attempting to control an often rebellious following with no real sanctions at his disposal, and his frustration is bound to spill over periodically. In a religion where supernatural power is available to everyone, where every individual makes his own contract with the spirits, and where prestige and solvent clients are in short supply, some conflict among the members is inevitable.

FOOTNOTES

1. There is thus a marked difference between the *ogan* of the Batuque and the *ogan* of the Candomblé of Bahia. In the Candomblé the *ogan* is a patron or sponsor of the *terreiro,* usually a person of prestige or wealth, who is always given a seat of honor and treated with great respect (Ramos 1951, pp. 62–64).

2. We found similar continuity in the case of Carlos' *terreiro,* which attracted mediums from the surrounding streets in the Guamá district. In 1962 we identified fifteen mediums (thirteen women, two men) as members of the *terreiro* and of a neighborhood in-group. Three years later one of the fifteen had died. Two had switched to other *terreiros* in the same neighborhood, but all fourteen survivors were still friends.

3. The same expression is used in Bahia to refer to a curing technique in which disease is transferred from the patient to an animal (Bastide 1961, p. 67; cf. Ramos 1951, p. 180).

4. The founding of the federation seems to be related to the reorganization of the Belém city government that followed the military coup of March 1964. The mayor of Belém was removed from office on grounds of corruption and replaced by a career military man. We were told that the new government had been unsympathetic to the Batuque until Manoel Colaço persuaded the chief of police that a federation would maintain greater harmony and order within the religion. We did not discuss the matter with city officials and do not know how accurate this account is.

5. Ribeiro (1952, pp. 115–20) made the same point with respect to the Afro-Brazilian cults in Recife: competition and rivalry among cult members actually served as "elements of integration" and reinforced orthodoxy. The idea has been further developed by Bastide (1960, pp. 326–33).

Chapter VIII

Curing

The Batuque is oriented toward manipulating the supernatural for the attainment of human ends. For Batuque members these ends are not salvation, immortality, or nirvana, but the resolution of the difficulties that mortal man is heir to on this earth. Since the members of the Batuque are poor, unskilled, and minimally educated, many of the problems they face are related to income and employment. Since they live in crowded housing with rudimentary sanitation in a tropical environment, they are vulnerable to a great variety of diseases. Since there are few social welfare agencies in Belém, individuals are extremely dependent on their families in time of crisis, and family dissolution is seen as a catastrophe. Batuque members believe that it is possible to handle any of these problems by appealing to an encantado, and attempts to resolve any of these problems in this way are referred to by the same term, *cura* (curing). Because the connotation of the English translation of this term is misleading, it should be stressed that an attempt to obtain employment or to regain the affections of a wandering spouse are just as much a part of *cura* as the treatment of disease. It is in this broad sense that the title of this chapter is to be taken.

A number of the problems treated by Batuque curers derive from the quality of life of the urban poor in contemporary Brazil, but *cura* itself dates back long before the appearance of modern cities. Batuque curing is in all essential respects identical with *pajelança,* the shamanistic tradition that has thrived in the Amazon Basin since the arrival of the first Europeans. *Pajelança* developed when curers among the European colonists borrowed a number of ideas and procedures from the indigenous Indian shamans, especially those of the Tupí-speaking tribes.[1] Today the Batuque curer shakes a rattle and blows smoke on his patient just as the Tupí *pajé* has done from time immemorial. In absorbing *pajelança* into the Batuque, the only major change necessary has been the substitution of the encantados for the animal spirit helpers of the Amazonian shaman.

Whereas most Batuque mediums engage in *cura* to some extent, not all mediums are considered to be equally prepared in what is considered to be a highly specialized activity. As a matter of fact, it is commonly asserted that there are actually two basic kinds of mediums in the Batuque—those prepared in the *linha de tambores* (line of the public ceremonies), and those prepared in the *linha de cura* (line of curing). In the former case, the medium maintains his contract with the encantados by participating in ceremonies and carrying out other obligations, but he does not necessarily help other people. Only a medium prepared specifically in the *linha de cura* should carry out curing rituals. This distinction is carried over into conceptions about the supernatural. As was noted in an earlier chapter, encantados often give different names in curing rituals. Moreover, the attitude of the spirits toward the two activities is thought to be different. "The encantados descend in *tambores* to have fun," one woman observed, "but they come in *cura* to work."

In actual practice almost all mediums, at least those with some experience, consider themselves to be competent to some extent in both lines. Certainly most mediums give consultations of some type in which they deal with problems presented by clients. But working in the line of curing is a matter of degree, and several types of curing rituals are recognized and given separate names. The simplest form is the *chamada* (call or summons). Many developed mediums make a regular practice of preparing for a *chamada* on a given day once a week. In a sense the day is considered sacred to the medium's chief encantado, and the medium may fast, fumigate the house, and place new offerings on the altar. If a client appears, or if a member of the family has a problem, or if the medium himself wants the answer to a question, the encantado is "called," the medium goes into a trance, and a regular consultation is held. Once in trance, the medium may receive several encantados in addition to his chief, especially his carouser encantado, but the number is limited. Often, if no client comes or if no problem seems pressing, the day passes without the medium going into trance. Or sometimes on this day the encantado suddenly appears without being called, seizes the medium with unusual violence, and leaves a message —usually a decision about some project the medium has been contemplating. In any case, the *chamada* occurs in the intimacy of the home, with at most a dozen friends, relatives, and clients in attendance. It is the typical performance of the developed medium attempting to establish a reputation as an especially successful intervener with the supernatural.

At one *chamada* that we attended, we took the roles of clients with problems rather than simply observing. We were invited to attend the *chamada* by one of our informants after we had mentioned to her that one of our relatives was seriously ill. She said she would call her encantado and we could ask the spirit how our relative was (we had received no mail in over a week) and what the outcome of the illness was likely to be.

When we arrived at the medium's house on the evening of the appointed day, we found five other clients already there. Three were relatively well dressed and clearly a notch above most Batuque members in income and education. One was a sergeant in the Brazilian Air Force who, having been injured in a recent plane crash, now sought both to recover his health and to be granted a medical discharge and pension. His wife, who in general seemed more interested in the proceedings than he did, had no particular complaint, but she was a novice medium and seemed fascinated by trance and all it entailed. The third well-dressed client was a young woman, recently widowed, who had various problems connected with debts owed to her deceased husband. Her seven-year-old son was with her. The other two clients were from the immediate neighborhood and had more prosaic problems. One was a middle-aged woman whose husband was ill and the other a man whose wife had been taken to the hospital that afternoon.

The medium was already in trance when we arrived, and from her serious and deliberate manner it was clear that she was possessed by her *senhor*. She led all of the clients into the living room, where we were seated more or less in a circle. Also present during the consultation were a friend of the medium and various members of the medium's family. Speaking as the encantado, the medium opened the session by telling us that our relative was very ill but would not die. He was in the hospital and was being treated well, receiving "baths of light," which were promoting his recovery. Various of the other clients agreed with the encantado's prognosis, remarking that in the United States medical science was very advanced.

After this brief but general discussion of our problem, the woman whose husband was ill went forward and knelt in front of the medium in order to consult with the encantado in private. She whispered to the medium, who whispered back. Meanwhile the widow, who was sitting nearby, leaned over to listen, then asked the woman a question. In a short time the three were discussing the woman's problems in a normal tone, and it was not long before all of the clients joined in the conversation. When the encantado told the woman to have her husband avoid certain foods and drink a prescribed herb tea, several people commented on the appropriateness of these suggestions. The remainder of the consultations followed this same pattern. Beginning as a more or less private discussion between the client and the medium, it quickly turned into a general conversation in which anyone who was interested felt free to make comments. At times the conversation among the clients was so lively that the medium had to make an effort to regain the attention of her audience. This type of free exchange between medium and audience, and between members of the audience even to the exclusion of the medium, is characteristic not only of the *chamada* but also of the other curing rituals. The encantado is always shown respect, but its pronouncements are usually liable to discussion and are rarely accepted as dictums from on high. However, a great deal depends on the medium, and some attempt to be more authoritarian when in trance than others.

The problems of the sergeant were not discussed during the early part of the *chamada,* since the sergeant had indicated that he wished to consult another of the medium's encantados. After about an hour the medium sang a song indicating that her *senhor* was ready to leave. Everyone said good-by to the spirit, the medium covered her face briefly, her body jerked a few times, and everyone greeted the new encantado. This was Mariana, received as a carouser *caboclo*. In keeping with the character of a carouser spirit, the medium now made every effort to be not only amusing, but shocking, and she seemed deliberately to try to embarrass everyone present. She began by accusing her son of having lost his virginity and her unwed daughter of being pregnant again. She then urged the widow to control herself, no matter how much she longed to have a man to sleep with, because men would now be after her money. When the sergeant suggested that Mariana tone down her remarks so as not to embarrass the American lady present, the medium cheerfully accused the lady in question of always wanting to talk about the homosexuals in the cult. She then asked her American clients to explain the meaning of an English four-letter word that she had often heard used by American sailors. Dealing more specifically with the widow's problems, the medium urged her to dress shabbily and not make up her face—this would make it easier for her to play on the sympathy of her debtors. To illustrate the effectiveness of this technique, the medium described several of her own experiences, speaking of herself in the third person. In each of the incidents described, the medium's behavior turned out to have been somewhat immoral, but since these stories were being told by the encantado about the medium, they were accepted as amusing rather than as real indictments of the medium's character.

After carrying on in a somewhat manic way for some time, the medium finally turned to the sergeant and asked him what luck he had had on a recent trip to Rio de Janeiro to see the Air Force doctors. When told that the trip had been in vain, Mariana promised the sergeant that she would help him, but that he must be patient. When the sergeant asked, with considerable entreaty in his voice, if he would ever recover from his injuries, Mariana assured him emphatically that he would. She warned him, however, that he must be resigned to some further suffering before all of his problems were solved. He should realize too that the encantados suffered with him even as they struggled on his behalf.

The medium next considered the problems of the last client, the man whose wife was ill, then began to tell a long series of stories. Apparently intended to entertain, the stories dealt with the experiences of the medium while possessed by Mariana on previous occasions. Told with an unflagging excitement and verve, most of the stories were amusing or somewhat ribald. However, her clients quickly became satiated with this part of the performance, in part undoubtedly because they could no longer participate, and by the time the encantado finally announced that it was leaving, most of the audience seemed to be half asleep. After coming out of trance, the medium bid her clients good night in a very subdued way, looking pale and very tired. She had been performing as an encantado for almost three hours and had every right to be exhausted.

At this particular *chamada* no presents were given to the medium in return for the aid of her encantados, but the subject came up several times. At one point the widow promised to sew a blouse for Mariana. The encantado then asked the sergeant why she had not received a skirt he had promised her. In a perfectly complacent tone he replied that at the moment he was short of cash. At a later *chamada,* however, the sergeant promised to buy a butane stove for the medium's kitchen if he received his discharge. Two of the other clients had already made contributions to the medium's welfare. We had paid for several of her ceremonial costumes, and the other man present was in the process of remodeling her house in return for past favors he accredited to Mariana.

The *sessão* (session) is a larger gathering than a *chamada,* involving a cult leader and several mediums, and it is held in an established center rather than in a private home. It might be considered the *chamada* of a leader, since it is held on a set day each week and the leader receives only one or two encantados. In this setting, however, not only the leader but most of the mediums go into trance. The clients who attend the session usually present their problems to the encantado of the leader, but the presence of encantados in the other mediums is said to "give force" to the leader's curing activities. It is recognized by all involved that the *sessão* has another purpose in addition to the treatment of clients. It provides mediums with the opportunity to gain trance experience, and as was noted in an earlier chapter, in some *terreiros* this function is considered to be at least as important as curing.

Some Batuque leaders spend considerable time during these weekly sessions giving *passes* to their mediums, neighbors, and clients. The *passe* is a laying on of hands that is undoubtedly the most common therapeutic technique used in the Batuque. Obviously derived from the idea of giving a blessing, the *passe* is also prominent in spiritualism and *pajelança*. The basic act involves touching the patient, usually with the hands, and reciting a prayer. In the Batuque, *passes* may be given whether the medium is possessed or not, but most commonly the medium is in trance and it is thought to be the encantado that performs the act. The medium may place his hands on the client's shoulders or squeeze his head while reciting the prayer, or he may brush the client with a bundle of *arara* feathers or an *espada*. Wiping motions are often involved, clearly symbolizing the withdrawal of evil influences. *Passes* are thought to be good for any malady, and they may also be sought as a precaution against future misfortune or to ensure good luck in some undertaking.

The *passes* given by Carlos (usually when possessed by the encantado Jarina) at his weekly *sessão* were extremely popular in the neighborhood. At every *sessão* that we attended, a long line of candidates, including a number of children, appeared. Carlos had worked out a kind of assembly-line method of giving *passes*. He had the people line up across the *terreiro,* then went down the line behind the recipients, whisking the back of each one with his bundle of *arara* feathers while muttering a prayer. This completed, he went down the line a second time with an *espada,* first touching the scarf to the back of the neck of each person, then snapping it in the air several times. This mass treatment method seemed to be used only for those wanting a *passe* as preventive medicine. Clients with special problems received more individual attention.

The other forms of curing ritual are considered to be quite different from the *chamada* or *sessão*. They are thought to be more dangerous, for one thing, because the curer may be harmed by his contact with exceptionally powerful supernatural beings. In addition, these rituals are prohibited by law. Any treatment of disease by Batuque curers in which medicines are prescribed is punishable by law as the practice of medicine without a license. Although this law is not often enforced, newspapers do fairly often carry stories of "sorcerers" who have been arrested.[2] There are two kinds of curing rituals that may be raided, the *passagem* and *cura* proper.

The *passagem* (literally, passage), from the point of view of those who participate in it, is really quite innocuous, but since the police are not likely to recognize the difference between this rite and *cura* proper, it is usually held behind closed doors. In the *passagem,* as in *cura,* a medium may receive between ten and one hundred encantados (usually about thirty), one right after the other. Each encantado identifies itself by singing a song, then is replaced by another. It is believed that if a medium who specializes in curing does not allow his many spirits to possess his body periodically (some say every two weeks) he will become ill. The primary purpose of the *passagem* is to allow the encantados to "pass through," so to speak. Sometimes there are not even any clients present when the *passagem* is held, but ordinarily there are a few members of the audience who present minor problems for the consideration of some of the encantados. No one else becomes possessed, all attention being focused on the curer.

A *passagem* may be held in the late afternoon or early evening, but *cura* proper is always held at night and some effort is made to keep the proceedings secret. Some curers prefer not to take a chance on being raided by the police, holding all of their sessions in secluded locations outside the city limits. Others seem much less concerned, and we attended one ceremony held by a well known *pai de santo* where no one even bothered to close the door. In none of the curing sessions that we were able to attend, however, was there a seriously ill client. It is when the client is in danger of dying or when sorcery is being performed or counteracted that the most intense security measures are taken. One Batuque leader, who frequently undertook such cases, maintained a house outside the city where she could work in private, and this seems to have been more common in the past when the Batuque was more intensely persecuted.

It should be noted that there are a number of curers in Belém who are said to be prepared only in the *linha de cura.* Some of these *curandeiros* never take part in Batuque ceremonies and are not associated with any *terreiro*. They are often referred to condescendingly by Batuque leaders as practitioners of *pajelança*, but if the two *curandeiros* that we observed were typical, their curing ritual is indistinguishable from that of a *mãe* or *pai de santo*. They received essentially the same spirits, sang the same songs, and used the same techniques of treatment.

In terms of role-taking, the performance of a *curandeiro* or Batuque curer is extremely demanding. For one thing, he always has a highly critical audience. An assistant is always present, since, as was noted earlier, curers do not operate alone for fear their encantados may leave them in a coma. The independent *curandeiro* has a regular assistant, who is sometimes an understudy learning the craft. If a *mãe* or *pai de santo* is holding a curing session, one or more of the mediums of the *terreiro* stands by to assist. In addition, there are almost always other mediums present who have some problem to be resolved. The clients, usually half a dozen or so, have often had prior experience with other curers, since their problems tend to be chronic and they try one curer after another. The audience at a curing session thus tends to be well versed in curing lore, will recognize many of the encantados that put in an appearance, and may join in singing some of the songs. Far from being a ceremony designed to mystify the uninitiated, a curing ritual is a performance before a knowledgeable and critical audience.

The second challenge faced by the curer is how to clearly differentiate the thirty or forty different encantados that are expected to possess him in rapid succession. It is not enough simply to sing a different song for each; some change in behavior is also expected. Each curer develops his own repertoire of encantados, each of which may dance in a particular way, demand a different beverage, or have some unusual speech or behavioral characteristic. There are always some serious encantados and some carefree ones, some that speak properly and others that use crude expressions, some that ignore the audience and some that insist on greeting everyone present, some that are warm and friendly and others that act withdrawn and imperious. Some encantados stutter, some use baby talk, some speak in unrecognizable languages, and some do not speak at all. On two occasions we encountered encantados that spoke in verse, at least for brief periods. Of the motley assortment of spirits that puts in an appearance, only a few are expected to engage in the work of solving problems, and it is only to these that requests are made. Most of the spirits in the procession make no apparent contribution to the purposes of the ceremony, although their very number suggests the great supernatural resources available to the curer.

Before a *cura* ceremony begins, a number of preparations are necessary. Special offerings are made to some of the encantados, the ones expected to take an active part in the ritual, and offerings are also made to the Exus to induce them to keep away from the proceedings, just as in a public ceremony. A table, covered with a white cloth, is placed next to the chair from which the curer will operate. On the table the curer's paraphernalia are laid out—a gourd rattle, a bundle of *arara* feathers, several *espadas* (scarves), cigars, and one or two large cigarettes made with a wrapping of *tauari* bark. Refreshments for the expected encantados are also placed on the table: bottles of rum, beer, perhaps a bottle of *guaraná* (a soft drink) for the child spirits that may appear. The premises are thoroughly fumigated by burning certain dried herbs and incense; some curers then ask everyone attending the ceremony to walk over the purifying smoke by straddling the small brazier that is placed in the center of the room. One curer blew smoke from a *tauari* cigarette into a glass of rum and then went around the room dipping his finger in the rum and marking crosses on the foreheads, hands, and feet of everyone present. *Cura* is very "delicate," informants assured us, and spectators must co-operate in taking certain precautions.

Most of the paraphernalia as well as the preliminary rituals of Batuque curing have been taken over unchanged from traditional *pajelança*. The white-covered table, the gourd rattle, the bundle of *arara* feathers, the *tauari* cigarette, the provision of rum, the preliminary fumigation of the premises—all are found in *pajelança*. All that is new in the preparations undertaken by the Batuque curer is the provision of several *espadas* and of beverages other than rum for the spirits, plus the preliminary offerings that are made, especially the offering made to placate and send away the Exus. The *pajé* did not have to contend with Exus, and his familiar spirits were apparently less finicky in their drinking tastes.

The curer, dressed in a Batuque costume, usually goes into trance seated by the table, singing a series of introductory songs and shaking the rattle close by his ear. The first seizure may be somewhat violent, but the beginning of subsequent possessions would often pass unnoticed except that each new encantado sings an identifying song. Essentially, the curer remains in trance for several hours, while a procession of spirits is thought to enter his body in rapid succession. Many encantados only pause long enough to sing one song, then each gives way to the next. Others ask for a drink of rum or a cigar. None stays very long, but those who are known to be the most adept at curing may return several times during the session.

As the seemingly endless procession of spirits continues, the curer may attempt in various ways to enhance the dramatic effect of the performance. Some curers dance, adopting a heavy-footed, arm-revolving kind of whirling that is rarely seen in public ceremonies. One *pai de santo* engaged in such bravado activities as removing the cap from an unopened bottle of rum with his teeth and stepping on live coals with his bare foot. Another curer put out his cigar by rubbing the lighted end on his tongue. All curers are expected to drink liquor; the consumption of rum or beer after the curer enters trance is thought to give more "force" to his activities. The amount of drinking would seem to vary considerably. Of the five curers that we observed in action, one drank most of a bottle of rum in an hour, one drank several bottles of beer, one drank a large pitcher of what appeared to be an evil-tasting herb infusion, and two drank very little of anything. A *mãe de santo* did not drink the rum that was offered to her from time to time, but rubbed it on her wrists and ankles. It seems likely that more drinking occurs during curing sessions held outside of town, since a number of our informants assured us that the sessions we attended were not typical as far as drinking was concerned.

Another technique that is sometimes used to maintain the interest of the audience, as well as to increase the faith of clients, is an assertion by the curer, speaking as a specific encantado, that the spirit remembers an earlier meeting with one of the clients. At one curing session that we attended, the *pai de santo,* speaking as the encantado Antonio Luiz Corre-Beirado, said to a client, "I saw you in Recife." The client became very excited, shouting to all present that in fact he had consulted the same encantado recently in Recife, but of course incorporated in a different medium. The *pai de santo,* who obviously had some inside source of information, then asked several questions about the business deal that the client had been concerned with in the Recife consultation. The client was clearly very much impressed, exclaiming several times that his faith in the encantados had been confirmed. However, as might be expected, this technique is not often used, since the curer ordinarily does not have any knowledge of prior consultations and references to such consultations by clients may be highly embarrassing. Later in the same curing session, another client reminded the encantado Mariana that she had not kept a promise made to him at another *terreiro.* In this instance the *pai de santo* brazened out the situation by maintaining that the man must be mistaken—perhaps he thought he had spoken to Mariana, but it must have been a different encantado. More commonly, in these circumstances, the curer makes a noncommittal remark and changes the subject as quickly as possible.

When one of the encantados arrives that is expected to do work for the clients, the pace of the ritual slows and a regular consultation is held. The encantado listens to problems and prescribes remedies. In addition, certain kinds of treatments are given on the spot, such as the *passe* described earlier. The *passe* is often followed by a smoke treatment. Soon after entering trance, the curer lights either a cigar or a *tauari* cigarette and smokes off and on throughout the ritual. To treat a client with smoke, the curer puts the lighted end of his cigar or cigarette in his mouth and blows. The thick stream of smoke thus produced is directed first down the front of the patient's body, then down the back. The belief that tobacco smoke has sacred and therapeutic properties was of course widespread among American Indians, both in North and South America, and the use of tobacco in *pajelança* and in the Batuque is derived from this source. Unlike the Indian shaman, however, the Batuque curer does not smoke very much during his performance, nor does he ordinarily rely on tobacco narcosis to enhance his trance state. On only one occasion did we observe a curer swallow tobacco smoke (in contrast to inhaling it) in typical shamanistic fashion.[3] Smoking is used as a prop, in the sense that different encantados are identifiable by whether they prefer a cigar, a puff of the *tauari* cigarette, or a pipe, and as a kind of treatment. Blowing smoke on clients is also quite common during public ceremonies, when the *caboclos* often smoke cigars and may treat members of the audience in the middle of the ceremonial area.

Curers may also use more flamboyant means of treatment. One such is the momentary suspension of the patient on the back of the medium—brought about by the two standing back to back, arms locked at the elbow, and the medium then levering the client off the floor. On one occasion we witnessed a rather slight, middle-aged woman in trance quite easily lift and hold on her back a husky young man who was considerably taller than she was. What seemed to be a unique form of contact had been devised by a young girl medium. She positioned her client carefully, having him stand with legs apart and head lowered. After several trial runs, she bounded forward and butted his head with hers with considerable force. This was apparently intended to be a kind of *passe,* but we never learned what had inspired this unusual technique.

In addition to *passes* and these other kinds of treatment, the client is usually given a prescription for either a *banho* (bath) to be applied externally or a *remedio* (medicine) to be taken internally. Both are derived from infusing herbs in water, and in most cases the herbs are common plants that can be collected locally or readily purchased in the markets.[4] Since each prescription usually has three or four ingredients, clients are often provided with pencil and paper to note them down. *Banhos* are usually indicated in cases of unemployment, desertion, or any kind of bad luck, while the *remedios* are prescribed for illness. Any prescription of medicine is always accompanied by a list of *resguardos,* or dietary restrictions, and often the foods proscribed are the most common foods eaten. At one curing session a woman was told to give her ailing husband a herb tea, and at the same time she was warned that manioc flour, beans, and

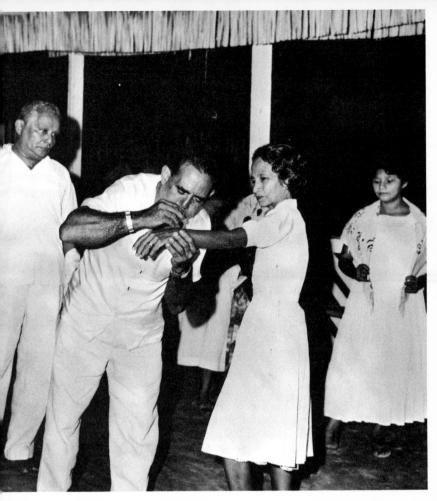

A medium possessed by a *caboclo* spirit blows smoke from his cigar on the ailing wrist of a spectator.

coffee were poison to him while he was taking the medicine.

If the problems of a client are diagnosed as due to harassment by the Exus, a quite different resolution is suggested. The client is given instructions for the preparation of a present for these evil spirits. The present may be simple, consisting of several yards of black ribbon, or a box of matches, or three black candles; or it may be very complex, including plates and silverware, bowls of food, and bottles of wine and beer. Whatever its contents, the present must be left at a crossroads at midnight to ensure that the Exus will find it. The spirits are expected to respond by ceasing whatever trouble they have been causing.

If it is suspected that the client's problems are due to his resisting becoming a medium, then he is urged to begin his "development." He may be given a *passe,* but no treatment is expected to have any lasting effect. As was noted earlier, it is sometimes possible to persuade the encantado to withdraw or to stop trying to possess the person's body, but this is believed to be easier in the case of a child than an adult.

As a curing ceremony continues, there is usually an alternation of working encantados with more playful ones that provide comic relief. The latter encantados joke with members of the audience, often chiding them for various shortcomings, tell amusing anecdotes about the curer, slander other *terreiros* or curers, or sing lively songs. In some cases the carouser encantado of the curer is considered to be adept at curing, but most serious problems are treated by serious encantados.

When all clients have been taken care of, the curer begins to sing going-away songs and comes out of trance. This is usually a simple procedure, but on occasion there may be complications. At the end of one curing session, during which he had received thirty-eight different encantados, a curer sang several closing songs and then seemed to go to sleep sitting up. His assistant began to shout his name, blew in his ears, patted his forehead, and shook him vigorously. The curer stirred, opened his eyes, and looked about with a puzzled expression. Everyone assumed that the session was over, when suddenly the curer closed his eyes again and began to sing another song. The encantado identified herself as Princesa Flora and complained that she had been left out of the earlier proceedings. The medium then gave a jerk and came out of trance for good. Since we never saw this curer again, we do not know if this added fillip at the end was a standard feature of his routine or whether he had gone on so long being encantados that he found it difficult to stop. As was noted in an earlier chapter, curers sometimes become unconscious and are difficult to rouse after a long performance. In any case, the unexpected arrival of Princesa Flora was a very effective piece of dramatics. It served to demonstrate quite clearly that the medium was only the passive instrument of this myriad of spirits who came and went as they pleased.

Some curers charge a flat fee for a curing ceremony, whereas others expect presents from their clients. It is not uncommon for the medium in trance to remind individuals of earlier promises of assistance, as occurred in the *chamada* described above, or to suggest the kind of present that would be appreciated in the future. In all cases, presents are considered to be given to the encantado that provides the service rather than to the medium. If the medium is a woman, her encantados are most commonly promised cloth for ceremonial costumes, especially the expensive material needed for skirts. The sex of the encantado involved makes no difference. A male encantado is thought to be gratified by a gift of skirt material if the medium who receives him is a woman. A *pai de santo* also welcomes fancy cloth, which he can have made into shirts. Items of household furniture, such as stoves and refrigerators, are also given in the name of an encantado. When money is given as a present, it is usually understood that it will be spent in some specific way, either to take care of some need of the medium, or of the *terreiro* if the medium is a *mãe* or *pai de santo*. Once the medium has the money, he of course spends it as he sees fit, but he usually makes some effort to indicate to the donor that the encantado named as recipient will be pleased by the way the money is used.

The idea that gifts are always given to specific encantados sometimes leads to the conception that there is competition between a medium's encantados. It somehow always worked out that our gifts to our friend Clara were defined as being given to her *senhor,* Japetequara. This was the source of some acrimony when Clara's carouser, Mariana, put in an appearance. Mariana never complained directly to us about being neglected, but we were frequently given reports that she expressed her displeasure in no uncertain terms when we were not present.

Several characteristics of the clients who bring problems to Batuque curers should have emerged from the preceding descriptions of actual rituals. For one thing, clients take their problems to specific encantados, either because they have been helped by the spirit on previous occasions or because they have heard of the prowess of the spirit from others. But clients are equally choosy about the medium who receives the spirit; everyone tacitly acknowledges that a given encantado is more effective in some mediums than in others. There are a number of situations in which a client may seek a consultation, ranging from the public ceremony to a full-fledged *cura* ritual. As a general rule, clients with minor problems or few resources attend the *chamadas* of developed mediums or the *sessões* of the beginning leader, whereas those who have more serious problems and can afford it take their problems to famous curers.

Some of the problems that clients bring to the encantados have already been noted. A large proportion of these are related in one way or another to marriage and family relationships. Young girls in search of a husband or even simply pining over the indifference of a boy friend may seek supernatural assistance from a neighborhood medium. Older women, especially those with young children, often have much more serious concerns. Because of the prevalence of common-law marriage, the impossibility of divorce, and the lack of legal sanctions against desertion, women often find themselves in desperate circumstances if the men with whom they are living begin to wander. In most cases, the women want their husbands or lovers back, and some mediums specialize in preserving domestic unions. At one curing session that we attended a woman whose husband had deserted her and taken the children was determined to have the children returned but was quite indifferent about their father. Men do not always do the deserting and on one occasion a man who did not want to leave his "companion" (and their eight children), even though the woman was boasting of her infidelity, petitioned for help in regaining her affections. Another common domestic problem taken to Batuque curers is excessive drinking by some family member, usually the husband.

Another set of problems prominent in any type of curing session is basically economic. People who are unemployed are frequent petitioners, but there are many other situations that are thought to be amenable to supernatural intervention. We encountered one man who wanted to be awarded a family allotment, another who desired a promotion, as well as the sergeant who sought a discharge from the Air Force (with pension). We did not often meet the businessmen who consulted the leaders in private about the probable outcome of risky business ventures, but a number of our informants assured us that such consultations were commonplace.

In most cases the businessmen who consult Batuque mediums are in legitimate businesses, but several cult leaders had smugglers among their clients. Like other businessmen, smugglers sometimes turned to the encantados for advice on the advisability of pursuing certain business contacts. More often, the smuggler wanted help in recovering contraband that had been seized by customs. Since the mediums had no knowledge of legal technicalities, their encantados could not really give smugglers legal advice. What usually happened was that the smuggler proposed a course of action, which the leader, in trance, either approved or disapproved. In one case described to us by the leader involved, the smuggler was advised to retain legal counsel and contest the seizure of his goods. This he did, successfully. He was so grateful that he contributed a sum large enough to construct a new *terreiro* for the *pai de santo* handling the case. In another instance a man was advised not to get involved in a court case. He decided not to take this advice, hired a lawyer, lost the case, and ended up a pauper. The *mãe de santo* whose encantado had warned him to beware told this story with considerable smugness.

Smugglers are not the only people in risky occupations who look to the Batuque leaders for assistance. Prostitutes and owners of brothels are also often clients. Prostitutes do not have to worry very much about the authorities, since they are rarely prosecuted, but they are concerned about the other uncertainties of their profession. A woman is always in danger of losing her looks, becoming thin and unattractive, or sometimes simply losing her steady customers for no apparent reason. In addition, there is the belief that prostitution is subject to more malignant influences of an unspecified nature than most other occupations. To protect themselves from any or all of these calamities many prostitutes obtain *banhos* from a *terreiro* or from a medium who practices privately. These *banhos,* which the woman pours over her body when bathing, are expected to both ensure good luck in acquiring customers and to provide protection against evil influences.

Owners of brothels sometimes engage the services of a *mãe* or *pai de santo* to carry out periodic cleansing rituals for the entire establishment. One thing that is especially dreaded by brothel owners is fighting among customers since this attracts the unwelcome attention of the police, and one effect of the cleansing ritual is expected to be a reduction of violence. We were unable to determine what remuneration a cult leader might receive for this service, but that it was probably substantial is indicated by the competition that sometimes occurs for his source of income. The friendship of Dona Ana and Antônio came to an abrupt end, for example, when Antônio secured the patronage of a brothel owner who had been Dona Ana's customer for years. When the owner of a brothel is the regular customer of a leader, all of her girls are likely to purchase their *banhos* from the same *terreiro*. Even though the price of a *banho* in 1962 was only 100 cruzeiros (14 cents), the total income from a large brothel was probably considerable.

Since obtaining money from smugglers and prostitutes may seem rather sordid, it should be pointed out again that for the people in the Batuque neither of these activities is considered to be particularly reprehensible. For most cult leaders, brothel owners and smugglers are not considered to be much different from other successful businessmen. Their money is certainly not "dirty." The only tainted money in the Batuque comes from sorcery, as will be pointed out below.

In addition to the clients seeking supernatural help for marital or economic problems, there are always individuals at curing rituals whose major complaint is ill health. All kinds of ailments may be treated, from headache to cancer, but in most cases the condition is chronic. Ordinary aches and pains, minor digestive upsets, and respiratory infections are rarely brought to the attention of a Batuque curer. Such run-of-the-mill ailments are treated at home with patent or herb medicines in accordance with the dictates of local folk medicine, which stresses purgatives and *resguardos* (the avoidance of certain foods and activities during illness or convalescence).[5] It is only when an ailment fails to respond to standard home remedies that the ill person or his family considers seeking outside medical aid. The patient may then go to a doctor, he may go to a Batuque curer, or he may very well do both. It should not be supposed that Batuque curing is regarded as being in competition with, or serving as a substitute for, doctors and hospitals. On the contrary, a medium in trance may very well recommend that a patient be taken to a doctor, just as a medium may recommend that a smuggler consult a lawyer. Batuque curing is seen as supplementary to other medical techniques, except that it is thought to be necessary in cases where diseases have supernatural rather than natural causes.

Since we were never able to attend a curing session held outside the city, we never saw a seriously ill patient being treated. The people with physical ills who came to the curing sessions we attended complained of such things as persistent headaches, liver trouble, fainting fits, pains in the joints, insomnia, difficulty in breathing, or skin infections. In the many stories of successful cures that we were told, there was great variation in the kinds of claims made. One *pai de santo* insisted that he did not treat physical ailments at all, but only diseases of the mind. Others claimed that they had cured people of cancer, advanced gangrene, and paralysis. Several patients described as *louco* (insane) were being treated during our stay, and all curers considered insanity to be within their competence. Several of our informants who seemed to have had severe neurotic or even psychotic symptoms before becoming mediums told us that they had been advised by their doctors to seek "other means" of treatment, which they had interpreted as meaning a Batuque curer. In any case, insanity is a condition often treated, and curers boast about their successes.

Insanity is considered to be especially amenable to treatment by Batuque curers because it is thought to be due to the intrusion of evil spirits into the body of the patient. A number of examples have been given in earlier chapters of other kinds of problems that are attributed to supernatural causes, and it should be clear that almost anything may be blamed on the encantados or other spirits. Clients are often told that their misfortunes arise from the persecution of a spirit that wishes to possess them. When it is a medium who is in trouble, some infraction of ritual law is immediately suspected. Encantados that cause people to suffer are usually thought to have good reason to do so—few of them are conceived of as simply sadistic.

But there are other basically evil spirits, such as the Exus, and other vaguely conceptualized evil influences that may cause problems for even the most virtuous. Souls of the dead may also harass the living, again without any provocation, and anyone is liable to the threat of sorcery. In sorcery, supernatural agents do not act against man of their own volition, but are directed by human beings.

It should be stressed, however, that Batuque members do not attribute all misfortunes to the supernatural. They believe that disease may equally well be due to germs, dust, amoebas, bad food, or excesses of all kinds. Unemployment may be due to laziness or too much drinking. Desertion may reflect the shrewish nature of the wife or her unfaithfulness. If an individual's problems arise from such causes, then there is no reason to seek supernatural relief. The alcoholic must simply give up rum, the deserted woman reform, the ill person obtain medical attention. Of course it does not do any harm to ask the encantados to lend a helping hand. The spirits are capable of reinforcing one's will power or giving special efficacy to drugs or injections. But if a misfortune is believed to be due to natural causes, then the Batuque member seeks natural remedies first. A person who becomes ill goes to a doctor if he has no reason to suspect supernatural intervention. If doctors do not help him, he is likely to decide that he made a mistake in his self-diagnosis and that a Batuque curer was needed all along.

Since it is ordinarily impossible to determine from the symptoms of the patient whether his problems are of natural or supernatural origin, some form of divination is considered necessary to decide the issue. Most commonly a patient simply describes his problem to an encantado, that is, to a medium in trance, and the omniscient spirit is believed to know at once what the cause of the trouble is. Curers sometimes use cowrie shells or playing cards as aids in diagnosing illness, but this is not common. Both of these techniques are frequently used, however, as a means of learning about future events.

If a curer determines, through some process of divination, that the source of his client's misfortune is sorcery, the treatment he will prescribe may be somewhat different than any of the techniques thus far described. Sorcery is considered to be in a special category, quite distinct from other supernatural causes of trouble. In the case of sorcery, it is believed, the forces acting on the individual and producing his problems are supernatural forces, but they are being marshaled and directed by a human being. Since a human agent is involved, the treatment of sorcery must begin with the identification of the person practicing the sorcery or, more commonly, paying to have it done. Once the sorcerer is known, it may be possible to counteract the supernatural attack. According to most accounts, the best way to treat sorcery cases is to send the sorcery back to its instigator or, in other words, to turn it around so that the initiator himself, rather than the intended victim, feels the effects of his nefarious work.

Batuque members know that sorcery is prohibited by law and that sorcerers are liable to criminal prosecution by civil authorities. In addition, as a deliberate attempt to harm another human being by allying oneself with demonic forces, sorcery is clearly a sin that may be punished by the Christian supernaturals. Consequently, although most of our informants were obviously fascinated by the subject, they always preferred to describe the activities of others, usually in a disapproving way, rather than discuss their own experiences. We were thus able to obtain a number of stories, mostly of an overtly slanderous nature, but we were never invited to attend a ritual in which sorcery was actually practiced. That such rituals occur there can be no doubt. Every leader that we interviewed remarked that he was often sought out by clients who wanted him to work sorcery against someone. Every leader denied that he ever gave in and "did evil," as they all expressed it, but each accused all of the others. "Sorcery is in great demand," said one leader in an unguarded moment, "and every *pai de santo* has his *trabalhos* [works of black magic]." This was the same leader who once mentioned with an embarrassed air that it was best not to have all of the saints' images belonging to the *terreiro* blessed, since some were needed for *trabalhos*.

According to the stories we were told, all of the renowned Batuque leaders were willing to perform sorcery for a price, and most of them had reputedly used sorcery for their own benefit. A prominent *pai de santo,* for example, was said to have killed his wife through sorcery when he became interested in another woman. One *mãe de santo,* described by several of our informants as the leading sorcerer of Belém, was said to have "put many people below ground," including some of her own flesh and blood. After causing the death of her daughter, this *mãe de santo* then decided that her granddaughter was learning too much, whereupon she somehow managed to "tie up" all of the girl's encantados. Unable to receive her spirits, the granddaughter went crazy. As was noted in the last chapter, this story was cited by informants to illustrate how leaders sometimes attack those of their followers who seem predisposed to usurp their position.

Considering these and similar stories, one might get the impression that rank-and-file members lived in constant fear of the occult powers of Batuque leaders. This is far from being the case. A reputation of being a successful sorcerer seems to have no obvious bearing on the way a leader is treated by either outsiders or his followers. Most leaders never flaunt their knowledge of sorcery techniques, and even though it may be generally assumed that they practice sorcery from time to time, they are not seen by their followers as being particularly threatening.

Moreover, it is assumed that most mediums are quite able to take care of themselves. In one instance, the *pai de santo* Antônio seemed to be reluctant to complete the preparation of Célia, a young woman who was said to have "many spirits." The two frequently quarreled, and one day Antônio became enraged by what he considered her impertinence and threw some slop water on her. According to the story that spread rapidly among the mediums of the *terreiro,* Célia then threatened that as soon as she learned one more thing, she would "swallow" Antônio, a common way of threatening sorcery. It is not surprising that Antônio thereafter lost all interest in Célia's further development.

Since sorcery is not only illegal but also considered sinful, it is ordinarily practiced in secret. Sometimes sorcery cases are treated in regular curing ceremonies, but ordinarily both the instigation and treatment of sorcery occur during special rituals. Not only do leaders ordinarily deny having anything to do with sorcery, but they profess contempt for those few who boast about their prowess in public. In one unusual case, a priest who was touring

Brazil preaching against Umbanda issued a challenge to the cult leaders of Belém to try their utmost to attack him through sorcery (Kloppenburg 1961, pp. 144–46). His challenge was promptly accepted by several Batuque leaders, who published a letter in a newspaper threatening the priest in the name of a host of Exus with unspecified disaster "within a short time." A few days later, however, another *pai de santo,* one of the most respected Batuque leaders in Belém, also wrote to the newspaper to repudiate and ridicule the letter of his younger colleagues. Priests were respected by Batuque members as ministers of God, the older leader's letter asserted, and therefore were not likely targets for a *trabalho.* Besides, the proposed sorcery of the other leaders was nonsense since the others had, in their ignorance, invoked the aid of nonexistent Exus instead of the real ones.

During our study we encountered only one cult leader who boasted in public of his prowess as a sorcerer. This was also a rather unusual situation, since the man no longer lived in Belém and may have felt somewhat less inhibited as a visitor. On the other hand, this leader was the only *pai de santo* who deliberately set out to present as frightening an image as possible. One of his standard routines was to dance with both hands filled with burning candles, passing the flames so close to his face that his hair sometimes caught fire. Since on these occasions he was thought to be possessed by an Exu, it was only appropriate that he should make grotesque faces, and his large staring eyes and snarling mouth gave him quite a demonic look, especially when seen through the candle flames. Another act clearly intended to produce cold chills in his audience was the manner in which he sacrificed chickens to the Exu possessing him, as described in the last chapter. After killing the chicken by biting its throat, the *pai de santo* then ran about with the body dangling from his bloody mouth. His behavior was thought to be quite bizarre by other leaders and by many mediums, but it did of course attract large crowds. It also undoubtedly enhanced the *pai de santo*'s reputation as a potential sorcerer.

Other behavior of this *pai de santo* detracted considerably from this image, however. When he became possessed by female encantados, his behavior was at times so effeminate that he was derided by members of the audience.[6] At one ceremony that we attended, the *pai de santo* took exception to some of the insults being shouted at him, stopped the ceremony, and made a long speech. Among other things, he boasted that he had caused the death of five recently deceased Batuque leaders and that he was about to do away with a sixth, whom he named. Although this speech had little effect on his immediate audience, it was taken seriously by the *pai de santo* whose life was threatened. The next day he held a special ceremony to invoke the protection of his encantados and, according to rumors, filed a complaint with the police. His son-in-law appeared at the house where the self-proclaimed sorcerer was staying, meaning to fight him, but the sorcerer stayed out of sight until things calmed down.

The varied interpretations of this event show how flexible beliefs about sorcery tend to be. No one with whom we discussed the matter took the boasts seriously. We raised the question as to who had claimed credit for the five deaths—was it the spirit possessing the *pai de santo* or was it the man himself? At the time of the speech, the *pai de santo* was supposedly possessed by his carouser encantado, Jarina. While it was conceivable that Jarina might be involved in sorcery, it was not considered likely that she would practice it on such a grand scale. Was the *pai de santo* really possessed by the Exu that he frequently received? This was considered a likely possibility. Antônio, however, said flatly that the man was not possessed at all. After throwing his cowrie shells, he divined that the man had been merely drunk and that he had made the threats and boasts in his own right. Therefore, in Antônio's opinion, it was all simply alcoholic bravado. With this latitude of interpretation possible, boasting in public is hardly the best way of enhancing one's reputation as a sorcerer. As in so much of the Batuque, what counts are results, not empty claims.

One factor that is always important in the diagnosis of sorcery is the motive. In the case just described, there was no obvious reason why the *pai de santo* should have killed the five leaders he named as his victims, but it seemed reasonable that he might attack the sixth as he threatened, since they were old enemies. In the incident reported by Kloppenburg, the Batuque leader who repudiated the sorcery threat felt that no cult member had an adequate motive for attacking a priest. Sorcery is believed to arise out of conflict, usually overt, and often the instigator is thought to be attempting to get even for a previous injury. The sorcery that is often ordered against a wandering spouse, for example, or the spouse's lover, is seen as retaliation. In some cases sorcery may be attributed to envy, but this is less common.

Considering the amount of competition that was described in the last chapter, accusations of sorcery by one medium against another are remarkably rare. Those mediums who practice sorcery almost always do so on behalf of a client, and since most clients come from outside the Batuque, most sorcery is directed outward. When sorcery does occur between Batuque members, it most commonly reflects the conflict between leader and follower described earlier. But on occasion two mediums may quarrel, and the upshot may be an accusation of sorcery by one or both. Our friend Zuzu, for example, was being treated for sorcery during our first visit to Belém. She had come from her home in São Luís specifically to be treated. As she explained her case, it all began with a quarrel between herself and a close friend with whom she had been living. Shortly after the quarrel, Zuzu's health began to deteriorate. She lost her voice for a time and developed a terrible pain in one shoulder. Recognizing the danger she was in, Zuzu abandoned her house and possessions and went to Belém (her home town) to be treated. Her ten-year-old son elected not to accompany her but remained in São Luís with the friend, who was the boy's godmother. As far as Zuzu was concerned, her friend had ruined her health, alienated the affections of her son, and dispossessed her of her property, all through sorcery.

In Belém, Zuzu was treated by at least four curers. The only treatment of which we learned the details was that of Antônio. His diagnosis was that through sorcery, Zuzu's friend had broken the *conta* in Zuzu's shoulder. A *conta* is a small beadlike object that some mediums are given during the course of their development. It is swallowed by the initiate and is believed to remain permanently in some part of the medium's body. The indicated treatment in Zuzu's case, the removal of the broken *conta,* was accomplished through suction, according to witnesses. After sucking out the pieces, Antônio presented them to Zuzu in a glass of water. Zuzu, who was herself a curer, complained that to complete the cure Antônio should have replaced the broken *conta* with a new one, but she eventually admitted that the treatment was efficacious. Her health improved, and she brought her son to live with her in Belém.

Zuzu did not know what type of sorcery her ex-friend had employed. There are three basic kinds. The simplest involves various herbs or other substances used as poisons. Informants insisted that these substances are innocuous without the appropriate spell. They may be given to the victim in his food, in a cup of coffee, or even added to his (or her) perfume. In the second type of sorcery, stress is on imitative magic. After writing the name of the victim on a piece of paper, the sorcerer then puts the paper in an unpleasant environment with the expectation that the victim will be affected. If the paper is put under the drums during a ceremony, the victim will suffer from an excruciating headache. If the paper is put in the mouth of a frog, and the frog's mouth sewed up, the victim will die when the frog does.[7]

In either of the foregoing types of sorcery, the encantado of the sorcerer is thought to be intimately involved. The encantado must prescribe the ingredients for poison and give instructions about the proper incantations. In addition, the encantado can be expected to use its supernatural power to ensure that the desired result will occur. But in the third type of sorcery, the most feared, a spirit is called upon to attack the victim directly. Most often the spirit appealed to is an Exu, whose demonic nature and pagan status make it singularly suited to carry out nefarious acts. The Exu is given an offering, called a *despacho,* as an inducement. Batuque leaders make a sharp distinction between a present for the Exus and a *despacho.* Both are offerings left at crossroads or in cemeteries, but the present is left to placate the Exus, while a *despacho* is designed to incite the demons to attack someone. A present for an Exu consists of new, unused things—black ribbon, a box of matches, or prepared food served on new dishes. In a *despacho* the utensils are old or broken and food offerings are uncooked. For example, a *despacho* might include the body of a black rooster, unplucked and undrawn, with the rooster's severed head and its blood in an old *cuia* (gourd bowl). If there is any prepared food in a *despacho,* it is probably a portion of the intended victim's lunch and is offered to direct the malevolence of the Exu toward the victim. A photograph of the victim, a lock of his hair, or an article of his clothing might serve the same purpose. In addition, the *despacho* might be left at the intersection nearest to the victim's house, or even on his doorstep. The crucial factor in this type of sorcery is knowing the right combination of items that are to be left in a *despacho* and the correct formula to recite as the *despacho* is set up. Only a cult leader or curer, inspired by his own spirits, is likely to come up with a "recipe" that will work.

There was some disagreement among our informants as to whether encantados other than the Exus might be willing to carry out sorcery. Most agreed that many encantados, especially the *senhores,* were too "elevated" to harm anyone intentionally, except as punishment for infractions of the law of the sect. Some of our more cynical informants, however, felt that almost any encantado, irrespective of rank, might be induced to attack an innocent victim, since encantados, like men, are vain and open to bribery. There was general agreement that many of the lower-echelon encantados, especially the wild sons of Legua Bogi and some of the hard-drinking, unbaptized *caboclos,* were just as adept at sorcery as the Exus.

It is because of the involvement of the spirits in sorcery that it is so difficult to treat. When a curer undertakes to send sorcery back to the instigator, he sees himself as bucking a complex system of forces and beings. The initiator of the sorcery has engaged the services of a *mãe* or *pai de santo,* or a *curandeiro,* to attack the victim. The cult leader setting up the sorcery is personally always shielded by his own spirits and has enlisted the aid of an Exu or of one of his unregenerate *caboclos* to carry out the attack. When the curer attempts to send the sorcery back to the initiator, he must not only discover who has performed the *trabalho,* but he must also overcome the determined efforts of the spirits involved to complete their work. If these spirits happen to be especially powerful ones, it is thought that the curer may be in danger of being overcome himself. One curer told us how ill she had become, nearly dying, after neutralizing a *despacho* that had been left on a client's doorstep. In spite of the danger, most curers are quite willing to handle sorcery cases, and a number of special techniques are available. One *pai de santo* explained how his chief encantado sometimes seized the soul of the *pai de santo* who had set up the *trabalho* and forced the man's soul to undo the sorcery. However, this was only possible when the offender was asleep, and since most *pais de santo* deliberately stayed up until after midnight to avoid having their souls spirited away, this technique could not always be used.

Ideally, sorcery is sent back to its origin, and this is said to result in the death of its initiator. However, it is the person who paid for the sorcery who is expected to die, not the medium who invoked the spirits. In one typical story of sorcery successfully returned, a woman came to a *pai de santo* with a variety of complaints. Her health was poor, she was exceedingly nervous, and she could not control her children. The *pai de santo,* possessed by the encantado Rompe Mato, diagnosed her problem as sorcery and identified her husband's mother as the culprit. The *pai de santo* then undertook a series of treatments, including a culminating public ceremony in honor of Rompe Mato, paid for by the patient. The ceremony ended at 2 A.M., and as the last drumbeat sounded, the patient's mother-in-law died. According to the *pai de santo,* his encantado Rompe Mato, assisted by a host of slave Exus, had managed to return the sorcery.

In most cases, however, there are no such fatal results. As in the story of Zuzu given earlier, the curer ordinarily treats the sorcery victim in relatively routine ways, and neither the victim nor the instigator of sorcery dies. In another case, a woman sought to regain the attentions of her husband, who was spending more and more time with his mistress. Although the diagnosis was that the mistress was paying someone to use sorcery to attract the man, the proposed cure was a series of *banhos* designed simply to break the mistress' hold on the woman's husband.

All in all, sorcery does not seem to be as prevalent as it might be expected to be, and in ongoing cases the results are not nearly as baleful as might be gathered from listening to mediums talk about cases in the past. From the viewpoint of the Batuque curer, there is no question that sorcery beliefs are good for business. But in our experience, curers tend not to exploit this potential source of diagnosis and treatment. They are much more likely to diagnose the problems of their clients as being due to harassment by spirits or even to accident than to sorcery.

It is possible that the incidence of sorcery accusations in the Batuque may increase; this would be a likely consequence of the greater importance given the Exus in recent years. As was pointed out in Chapter V, until relatively recently the basic attitude of cult members toward the Exu demons was emphatically negative. The Exus were recognized as important supernaturals who might be manipulated by certain encantados, but their evil nature required that human beings avoid them at all costs. Offerings to the Exus were designed to keep them away from ceremonies, and no one would consider seeking possession by one of them. Not only is it now common for the Exus to be called at midnight during public ceremonies, but there is a growing interest in a set of beliefs distinguishing those Exus that are implacably evil from another group that can be induced to do good. Considering the intimate role that Exus have in sorcery, it seems possible that as they increase in popularity, it will be assumed that they are increasingly being invoked to attack people.

Throughout this discussion of misfortune, its causes and treatment, and especially when disease was the topic, it may have seemed that the description must relate to some isolated community far from modern hospitals and medical technology. In actual fact, of course, the citizens of Belém are quite familiar with modern medicine. Everyone has had some experience with doctors and hospitals, directly or indirectly, and many have some conception of the germ theory of disease, at least in broad outline. Under these circumstances, the appeal of Batuque curing is more difficult to explain than would be the case if the people involved were members of a society where scientific medicine was unknown and only supernatural explanations of disease existed. Where this is the case, the efficiency of the curer is measured in terms of how many patients recover after treatment. Since the curer usually treats all ailments—colds, stomach-ache, and sprains as well as serious conditions—most of his patients recover regardless of what he does for them, and since he gets credit for the apparent cures, his rate of success is quite high.[8]

The Batuque curer, however, ordinarily does not treat simple ailments. The complaints that he must struggle with are often chronic and may have already proved refractory to home remedies, patent medicines, and perhaps even expert medical diagnosis and treatment. With the exception of psychosomatic conditions, it seems unlikely that the Batuque curer effects very many dramatic cures. If we assume that the patients who go to the Batuque curer make a rational comparison between his effectiveness and the effectiveness of doctors, then it would seem obvious that they could not fail to choose the doctor. Yet *cura* flourishes.

There are a number of considerations that have bearing on this apparent paradox. In the first place, as Erasmus (1961, pp. 33–56) and others have effectively argued, one crucial factor in such situations is the opportunity the individual has of benefiting fully from scientific medicine. In Belém the poor man rarely has the opportunity to accurately assess the effectiveness of scientific medicine because he does not have complete access to all of its facets. Even if Batuque members are able to afford a visit to a doctor, they may be unable to buy the medicines that the doctor prescribes, and they are quite unable to provide themselves with special diets or undertake long-term therapy. Secondly, even under the best of circumstances the effect of scientific medicine may be merely palliative, since many of the diseases from which the people of Belém suffer—filariasis, malaria, leprosy, the salmonella infections, amoebiasis, tuberculosis, fungus infections of all kinds—are very difficult to treat or cannot be completely cured. Consequently, even when a Batuque member goes to a doctor the result may not be completely satisfactory.

A patient who goes to a Batuque curer also may not obtain any very striking results. But from the perspective of the patient, there are compensations attached to seeing a curer, even if the patient's health does not immediately improve. For one thing, the curer can tell the patient at once if his problem is caused by supernatural agents. If this is the case, there is no point in spending money on doctors until the supernatural has been placated. In cases where the patient is in fact suffering from a chronic or incurable disease, a visit to a Batuque curer revives hope for a miraculous exception to the prognosis offered by scientific medicine. Miracles are a curer's stock in trade, and the patient has heard that the curer has not only cured other people of similar diseases, but has also "cured" them of unemployment and marital problems. And finally, sometimes repeated visits to a curer or several curers does seem to result in improved health. This may be the result of the spontaneous remission of the patient's symptoms, or it may be the outcome of the shotgun approach that most patients take to their health problems. In addition to visiting a *pai de santo,* a patient is likely to try home remedies, take patent medicines, pray to a saint, go to the nearest pharmacy for a penicillin injection, and visit a doctor. Regardless of the actual curative effect of any of these actions, if he has a firm belief in the encantados, he is likely to assume that the *pai de santo* was the effective cause of his cure.[9]

Curers increase their chances of success by carefully avoiding promises of immediate cures. In all of the curing ceremonies that we attended, the curer promised to help the patient, but only at some indefinite time in the future. The patient was urged not to expect too much, and patience and perseverance were emphasized, as well as faith. Although the patient was assured that he would attain his ultimate desires, he was warned that he must be prepared for a further period of suffering and trial. Time is always on the curer's side, and if there is an improvement in the patient's health even after a relatively long period of time, it is always possible to credit the encantados, given a predisposition to expect help from the supernatural.

Essentially, then, the successful cures of a Batuque curer depend upon a predisposition on the part of his patients to interpret any good thing that happens to them as being caused by the encantados. For mediums, whose awareness of the supernatural is constantly reinforced by their trance experiences, such interpretations become second nature. For non-mediums the initial approach to a Batuque curer may be prompted by desperation, but the number of clients who repeatedly take their problems to the encantados indicates that non-mediums often come to have the same expectations as mediums. The ease with which these predispositions develop is related to the traditional conception of man and his world that is shared by most of the inhabitants of Belém.

As we noted earlier, Batuque *cura* is essentially *pajelança,* the curing tradition of the Amazonian shaman. From the beginning, Europeans in the Amazon Basin accepted the Indian conceptions of the unending forest as being inhabited by a myriad of spirits, mostly evil, ever ready to attack the few pitiful humans who dared enter their domain. Although the Church and the saints might give some protection, man's best hope was the *pajé,* the man who, by being possessed by some of the forest spirits, was able to counteract the mischief of the others. Although the *pajé* might treat·such maladies as sterility or *panema* (persistent bad luck), his major role was as a curer of disease.

In the process of absorbing *pajelança,* Batuque curers have made several significant modifications, some of which have made it better adapted to the conditions of the present day. For one thing, modern curers no longer treat many minor ailments that doctors can clearly handle more efficiently, but concentrate instead on those cases where medical science is still effectively helpless. More significantly, the Batuque curer is now no longer primarily a healer. Curers probably treat more cases of desertion and unemployment than of disease, and Batuque leaders have expanded their clientele to include businessmen and smugglers. Much more versatile than the *pajé,* the Batuque curer has little to fear from modern medicine since he is rarely in direct competition with it.

In spite of these modifications, however, Batuque curing is still based on the idea that man is beset by spirits, many of them evil. Whether these are animal spirits of the forests and rivers or whether they are the Exus and the wild sons of Legua Bogi makes no difference. As long as misfortune is explained in supernatural terms, there will always be a demand for an expert in manipulating supernatural forces, and the Batuque curer will thrive, as the *pajé* did before him.

FOOTNOTES

1. See Wagley (1953, pp. 224–33) and Galvão (1955, pp. 118–47) for accounts of *pajelança* as practiced in the interior of Pará.
2. E.g., *Folha do Norte,* July 20, 1962; December 5, 1962. *Jornal do Dia,* August 29, 1962; December 5, 1962. Kloppenburg (1961, pp. 180–85) complains bitterly that the "crime of *curandeirismo*" takes place throughout Brazil without police interference.

3. See Wagley (1943) for a graphic description of the use of tobacco by the Tapirapé shaman.

4. The largest market in the city, Ver-o-pêso, is famous for its stocks of all the herbs, plants, roots, bark, and preserved animal tissues that might conceivably be used in *pajelança*. Cf. Tocantins (1963, pp. 291–93).

5. The folk medicine of Amazonia is discussed by Wagley (1953, pp. 241–52).

6. Duarte (1960–61) describes a similar incident involving apparently the same *pai de santo*.

7. Cf. Ribeiro (1956, pp. 111–12).

8. During a nine-month study of the Maué Indians, who live near the Amazon River about 600 miles above Belém, we found that the curers had a remarkably high percentage of apparent cures. During the nine months only one person died, out of several hundred patients treated.

9. Lieban (1967, pp. 86–96) suggests that many of the same factors are significant in the success of the folk curer in the Philippines.

Chapter IX

Ritual

As the Afro-Brazilian sects have become less African and more Brazilian, they have become less group-oriented and more individualistic. The Batuque represents one extreme of this development, and in previous chapters we have stressed some of the ways in which this individualism is manifested. As far as ritual is concerned, the relative freedom of the individual medium to make a direct contract with an encantado and to become independent of his *mãe* or *pai de santo* has had less effect than might be expected. Batuque rituals are less elaborate than rituals in the more conservative sects, and there are fewer of them. But the public ceremony is still a central feature of the religion, and a number of lesser rituals are observed as well.

The ritual system of the Batuque, as well as the degree of individualism that it reflects, can best be appreciated by contrasting the Batuque with the more conservative Afro-Brazilian sects, those that have remained the most African. All students would agree that the most conservative sects remaining in Brazil are some of the Candomblé groups in Bahia (especially in the city of Salvador), some of the Xangô groups in Recife, and the Casa das Minas in São Luís. Although there are some striking differences in ritual and belief in these sects, in all of them there remains a strong sense of an ultimate African derivation, and the members try to maintain African traditions. The deities have African names and are thought to have permanent residences in Africa, and all of the songs the faithful sing are in what are supposedly African languages. Another characteristic shared by these three sects is a stress on ritual. Not only are many ritual acts observed, but great attention is paid to the correct performance of each act, with a resultant need for long periods of training for both leaders and rank-and-file members. Many of the rituals center around elaborate initiation rites, including the isolation of the neophyte and the sacrifice of animals. Another striking feature of these groups, especially when seen from the perspective of the Batuque, is the authority of the leaders and the hierarchy into which the members are organized.

The overwhelming effect of formalized ritual prescription is seen even in possession. The trance states of participants in public ceremonies are rarely if ever spontaneous; rather, mediums[1] always go into trance on cue, they dance together as the deities, then they come out of trance together. In the Candomblé and the Casa das Minas, the deities are called in a prescribed order. After all of the mediums have gone into trance, the ceremony is stopped temporarily while the mediums are taken into adjoining rooms and dressed in elaborate costumes appropriate to the possessing spirit. Returning to the ceremonial area, the possessed mediums dance as the deity for long periods—in the Casa das Minas for two or three hours. Coming out of trance is somewhat different in the two cases, but again it occurs on cue. In the Casa das Minas, the medium lies down and is covered with a cloth; as soon as she is uncovered the trance ends. In the Candomblé the mediums come out of trance one by one as songs of farewell are sung in the reverse order of the songs calling the spirits[2] (Eduardo 1948, pp. 86–95; Bastide 1961, pp. 21–31).

The pattern of possession in the Xangô is equally formalized, although in these groups all of the mediums are not possessed at once, nor are they dressed in special costumes after entering trance. The deities are called one at a time, in a prescribed order, and those mediums who are dedicated to a particular deity go into trance when their spirit is called. These mediums then perform as the spirits, while those dedicated to other spirits look on. Then, at a signal from the leader, the mediums in trance are led out and forced out of trance by having their ears blown into or being given water to drink. After all have been brought out of trance, the next deity in the sequence is called, its devotees are possessed, dance, and return to normal, and so on through the relatively limited pantheon (Ribeiro 1952, pp. 74–84).

It should be clear, even from these brief sketches, that public ceremonies in the conservative cults are much more group-oriented than are Batuque ceremonies. Although the individuals who make their bodies available to the spirits expect many of the same rewards as a Batuque member does, their behavior while possessed is much more restricted by the requirements of a quite inflexible choreography. According to all reports, with the exception of a few mediums who may not be able to enter trance on cue, the ceremonies always follow the expected pattern. The individual must subordinate himself to the demands of the group rite, one of the major purposes of which is to honor all of the spirits on behalf of the whole *terreiro*.

The self-discipline necessary to participate properly in the public ceremony is instilled in the medium during a long and involved initiation. In the Candomblé this may last between three months and a year. During this time the initiate lives in the *terreiro* and undergoes a long succession of rituals involving the shaving of the head, taking baths in sacred springs, being anointed repeatedly with the blood of sacrificed animals, eating sacred foods, and having the head painted and washed with special *banhos*. Finally, clad in an elaborate costume, the newly initiated *filha* or *filho* is presented at a public ceremony with great pomp and celebration. In the case of female initiates, there may be yet another major ritual in which the *filha* is "sold" to her parents or to her husband if she is married, and her initiation is complete. She is now said to be *feito* (literally, made) and becomes a full-fledged member of the *terreiro* (Bastide 1961, pp. 41–58; Herskovits 1953).

After seven years a *filho* or *filha de santo* in the Candomblé assumes a higher status within the groups. The medium is now allowed to set up a shrine in the home where offerings to the spirit are made on a given day each week. Although the medium theoretically is now a free agent, participation in all the ceremonies of the *terreiro* continues, and the medium is expected to remain obedient to the *mãe* or *pai de santo*. The *filho* or *filha* usually becomes responsible for some important *terreiro* function, such as caring for the stones that represent the deities, cooking the foods used in offerings, or leading the singing during ceremonies (Bastide 1961, pp. 58–59; Herskovits 1955).

In the Xangô of Recife, initiation is similar, although it usually does not last as long. Some of the stages found in Bahia do not occur, such as the "sale" of the initiate, but the seclusion, the sacrifices, the anointing with blood all occur. In various ways the initiate is more closely tied to the *terreiro* than in Bahia, since in the Xangô the stone representing the medium's spirit is kept permanently in the *terreiro,* and the medium must go there to make the weekly offering. Even so, the Xangô leader seems to have problems in controlling his followers, as he is said to sometimes beat them and may attack them with sorcery if they attempt to leave his *terreiro,* either to join another or to establish a *terreiro* of their own (Ribeiro 1952, pp. 67–74, 114–18).

Initiation has effectively ceased in the Casa das Minas; when Eduardo studied it in 1943–44 there had been no initiations in thirty years. However, as described, the initiation was apparently relatively complex. What set the Casa das Minas off from the other conservative cults was its exclusiveness. Since it was the only Dahomean *terreiro* in São Luís, the members had developed the idea that their deities would only possess members of the group, and only children of members were candidates for initiation (Eduardo 1948, pp. 71–73).

Divination plays a very important role in the conservative groups, and representing as it does one of the more obvious carry-overs of an African tradition, it has been studied intensively. In these groups, although the deities are thought to speak at times when possessing a medium, the primary way of obtaining messages from the supernatural is by means of mechanical forms of divination. The most common and widespread is the use of cowrie shells, usually sixteen in number. In Recife and Bahia the shell is altered so that there is an artificial opening opposite the natural opening. When the shells are thrown on a flat surface, either the artificial opening or the natural opening remains uppermost, and it is the different proportions of "open" (artificial opening uppermost) or "closed" (natural opening uppermost) that are interpreted. For example, according to one set of interpretations given to Ribeiro in Recife, if the shells turn up with twelve open and four closed, the deity Xangô promises a favorable outcome if given certain sacrifices. Six shells open and ten closed indicates a warning of serious illness from the deity Orishala. Apparently at an earlier period in Bahia the role of diviner was separate from that of cult leader, and the former specialist used other techniques of divination in addition to cowries. Today, however, these specialists seem to have disappeared (Ribeiro 1952, pp. 84–97; Bastide 1961, pp. 139–53; Carneiro 1961, pp. 147–50).

In the Xangô, divination occurs on all ritual occasions, and the cowrie shells are thrown repeatedly during a ceremony to make sure that the deities approve of each step of the proceedings. The deity to whom one should become dedicated (if there is some sign that one is destined to become a medium) is determined in the same way. Moreover, if any of the mediums of the *terreiro* have problems, they go at once to the *mãe* or *pai de santo* to discover through divination whether their spirit is punishing them, and if so, what offering they should make to regain its favor. It is not clear to what extent the spirits are believed to deliver messages through the spoken word. Often, at least, the spirit in a possessed medium speaks in a supposedly African language that is translated by the *mãe* or *pai de santo,* or the spirit may communicate through gestures (Ribeiro 1952, pp. 63, 78).

The fact that most communication with the supernatural is through divination means that a member of one of the conservative groups is greatly dependent upon his *mãe* or *pai de santo,* who alone has the ability to learn the wishes of the deities. Another source of dependence is the necessity of offering sacrifices to the spirits, since sacrifice is a privileged act. In all of the conservative groups sacrifices are offered on a regular basis as well as in time of crisis. Birds, especially chickens, ducks, and pigeons, are offered most frequently, but sheep, goats, and, rarely, pigs are also sacrificed. To the accompaniment of drumming and singing, the animal is killed, some of its blood is poured on the stone representing the deity to whom the offering is being made, and sometimes parts of the animal's body are placed in bowls before the altar. The remainder of the body is cut up, cooked, and, after being handled in various ritual ways, is eaten by the assembled members of the *terreiro*. In the Casa das Minas, the head drummer carries out the *matança* (act of killing), whereas in the Xangô and the Candomblé only the cult leader or an appointed official can carry out the act (Eduardo 1948, pp. 69, 98–99; Ribeiro 1952, pp. 66–67; Bastide 1961, pp. 20–22). Since under normal circumstances a member of any of these groups must offer sacrifices to his deity at least once a year on the anniversary of his initiation and in time of difficulty can only obtain the help of the deity or regain its favor by offering additional sacrifices, it behooves any member to maintain a good relationship with his *terreiro* and his *mãe* or *pai de santo*.

As the foregoing description makes clear, the conservative cults are organized in such a way that the individual must toe the line, at least for many years after entering the religion. The long, expensive initiation, the stress on divination, the need for sacrifices all combine to produce a *filho* or *filha de santo* with characteristics that a Batuque leader would consider ideal. The subordination of the individual is neatly reflected in some beliefs about the expected relationship between a medium and the single deity to which he is dedicated in the conservative sects. A member of the Xangô, for example, is expected to have the same personality traits as his deity. The *filho* of Ogun is expected to be industrious, the *filho* of Xangô brash and adventuresome, the *filho* of Oxun vain and inconstant. Ideally, marriages are arranged so that the deities of the spouses are congenial. A *filha* of Xangô should marry a *filho* of Inhaçan, since in mythology these two deities are married. Although few marriages follow the ideal pattern, some attempt is made through divination to gain the approval of the spirits to any proposed union (Ribeiro 1952, pp. 125–27). These beliefs can be contrasted with the Batuque notion that some mediums receive an encantado as a dignified *senhor* while others receive the same encantado as a carousing *caboclo*. In the Xangô the individual is expected to conform to the personality and assigned characteristics of the deity he receives, while in the Batuque the encantados are so loosely conceptualized that the individual can decide for himself which characteristics of the spirit to emphasize.

In almost every ritual act that occurs in the Batuque there is some vague echo of the ritual systems we have just described. In Batuque ceremonies there is at least some attempt to call the encantados in a prescribed order, if only in the sense that the *senhores* are called first and the *caboclos* are called later. Some leaders divine, some sacrifice chickens, and some devise relatively elaborate initiation rituals on occasion.

But Batuque rituals are not just imperfect copies of those held in the conservative sects. Many of their characteristics arise not from a failure to continue a tradition, but from an orientation toward a membership that is no longer very dependent on the cult leader and that is little concerned with group ends. Moreover, although it might seem obvious that similarities should exist between the Batuque and the conservative sects, since the Batuque probably developed out of a sect much like the Xangô,[3] the situation is actually more complicated than this. Some Batuque leaders have read the very books that we have been citing, and there have been several recent attempts to introduce ideas from the more conservative cults, especially the Candomblé. A new *terreiro* that opened in 1964, for example, had a number of exterior shrines and an internal arrangement that supposedly resembled a Candomblé *terreiro*. The *mãe de santo* attempted to teach her *filhas* to sing songs in "African" languages, and the drummers were urged to use sticks to beat the drums rather than their hands. At some of the ceremonies, one or two of the mediums were led out and dressed in elaborate costumes after entering trance. None of these innovations were an immediate success, but it is conceivable that some of them might catch on. Under the circumstances, it would be very risky indeed to try to distinguish those features in the Batuque that represent "survivals" of traditional forms from those that are of relatively recent introduction.

Most of the ritual acts in the Batuque take place. in connection with the public ceremony, and many of them have already been described in Chapter I. One ritual that was not mentioned occurs during the afternoon of the day on which the public ceremony is held. This is an offering to the Exus, made by

On rare occasions, mediums are dressed in elaborate costumes after entering trance. This *pai de santo* has provided his chief spirit, Juremeia, with red velvet pantaloons and a matching cap.

the *mãe* or *pai de santo,* consisting usually of rum, certain foods, and lighted candles, intended to induce the demons to keep away from the ceremony. In those *terreiros* in which the Exus are called at midnight, they are still urged to stay away both before and after their brief appearance. If this preliminary *despacho*[4] of the Exus does not take place, it is feared that these spirits will disrupt the proceedings by causing fights.

In the *batuque* described in Chapter I, the ceremony was preceded by a *defumação,* a smoke purification of the *terreiro* and environs. As was noted earlier, the use of smoke as a purifying agent is common in *pajelança,* but since burning incense with the same intent is such an ancient European practice, it would be pointless to attempt to pinpoint the origin of the *defumação* (Cascudo 1962, pp. 271–72). It does not appear to be common in the conservative cults.

The ceremony described opened with a short prayer in the chapel led by the *pai de santo.* Each leader designs his own version of the "correct" opening ritual, but most begin with some sort of prayer to the saints. Before important ceremonies, a *ladainha* is held in the *terreiro*'s chapel. An important feature of folk Catholicism, a *ladainha* is a series of prayers, some chanted and some sung, which lasts at least half an hour and often much longer. Each *ladainha* is intended to honor a particular saint, although the prayers may address the Virgin and various other saints. Mediums sometimes hold *ladainhas* in their homes as part of their annual obligation to their encantados.

Once the Christian supernaturals have been honored, attention turns to calling the encantados. Before doing so, however, a number of leaders sing several songs directed to the Exus, asking them to leave the ceremony in peace.[5] This is apparently an old tradition in Belém (see Appendix A). Following the songs to the Exus, most leaders sing to Averekete, although on special occasions Badé, Ogun, or some other spirit may be called first. After Averekete, it is customary to call Rainha Barba. The only other spirit certain to be called early in the ceremony is the one in whose honor the *batuque* is being held. Otherwise the spirits are called in no particular order, except that the *senhores* tend to be called first and the *caboclos* later. As was noted in Chapter VI, although almost any encantado may be expected to arrive at any time, regardless of the song being sung at that moment, the great majority of spirits arriving during the early part of the evening are *senhores* or the more serious *caboclos,* and only rarely does a carousing *caboclo* put in an early appearance.

During public ceremonies the proceedings are often halted temporarily while special rituals of one kind or another are carried out. Many of these rituals are sponsored by individuals and are considered to be the fulfillment of an *obrigação* (obligation) to a particular encantado. It was noted in Chapter III that every Batuque medium has a number of obligations to his encantado, the most common being the provision of offerings, usually ordinary foods or beverages, which are placed in the shrine at the medium's home. But mediums have other obligations as well, and one of the most common is to provide a special food or beverage, not for the encantado, but for the other members of the *terreiro.* The beverage provided most frequently under these circumstances is *ajurá,* a mildly fermented drink made of coconut milk, rice flour, and sugar. This is served from a large earthenware jar and drunk from a *cuia,* the gourd bowl that is used to dispense ritual beverages of all kinds. In some respects the drinking of *afurá* resembles a form of communion, and everyone maintains a very serious demeanor. There is usually some special dancing about by the two mediums carrying the earthenware jug. A large lighted candle stands beside the person delegated to serve, who is sometimes in trance, sometimes not. To the accompaniment of drumming and singing, those who partake always kneel, often in a line, and pass the *cuia* from one person to the next, each drinking in turn. On some occasions only the mediums may be served, but, more commonly, important guests are invited to take part, and in some *terreiros* large numbers of children are served first.

There are several other drinks that are offered less frequently as an *obrigação,* as well as several foods. At Carlos' *terreiro* we once observed the ritual sharing of a food called *maijá.* As Carlos led the singing and an overenthusiastic *filha* kept swinging the incense burner until the *terreiro* was thick with smoke, the other twelve mediums present knelt around a white cloth placed on the floor. As the singing continued, Carlos began to

Mediums maintain a solemn demeanor while partaking of *afurá,* a sacred beverage.

tremble and was possessed by his *senhora,* Mariana. He was then given a large bowl of *maijá,* a thick, gelatinous porridge, and began to ladle out portions into the cupped hands of the mediums. Before she had finished eating, one of the women sagged slowly forward onto the floor in trance; she was quickly helped to her feet. Another woman began trembling violently, but she remained on her knees. A third woman became possessed and stood up abruptly. When everyone had eaten, all stood up and began to dance around the cloth. At a signal from Carlos, a large *espada* (scarf) was brought out and held extended over the bowl of *maijá* and over the large candle that had been placed beside it. Ducking under the *espada,* Carlos picked up the bowl, a medium joined him to take the candle, and still under cover of the *espada* they carried the bowl and candle into the chapel. The ceremony had lasted almost an hour.

Although the *maijá* ceremony just described was clearly a complex group activity, it was defined as an *obrigação* offered by one of the mediums for her encantado, Dona Rosalina. It was assumed that Dona Rosalina would be pleased with this ritual because everyone knew that it was in the encantado's honor. An *obrigação* such as the provision of *afurá* or *maijá* may be a standing obligation, to be carried out every year, or it may be imposed on a medium by the encantado at short notice for some special occasion.

The leaders have obligations just like everyone else, and the rituals they sponsor tend to be the most elaborate of those held. At the *terreiro* of Antônio there were sometimes as many as eight or ten different food offerings placed in dishes in front of the altar at important ceremonies. Some of these foods were of the everyday variety; others were sweets or foods usually prepared for holidays. In all cases, each food was thought to be especially appreciated by a particular encantado. At the five-day *festa* held for St. Expeditus in 1962, which Antônio held as the major event of the year, the food offerings were especially numerous. In addition, Antônio offered *afurá* as an *obrigação* to Oxalá, and a drink made of wine and bread, called *bela de pão,* to Inhaçan. He killed five roosters for Badé in return for past favors. Another ritual was planned to honor Legua Bogi, but due to unexpected developments this was postponed. If the *mãe* or *pai de santo* has fewer resources, then of course the offerings he can afford are considerably less impressive. Carlos, for example, at his big ceremony for the encantado Zezinho, had only glasses filled with beverages before the altar. He had a very elaborate *afurá* ceremony, but no animal sacrifices.

As in the conservative sects, animal sacrifices are not public acts in the Batuque. They usually occur prior to the public

The communal sharing of another sacred food. Mediums kneel while waiting their turns.

ceremony or in the chapel with the door closed while a ceremony is in progress. We were able to witness only two *matanças,* and it is possible that they occur more commonly than we are aware of. From all reports, however, and all of our informants talked freely about such matters, animal sacrifice is very infrequent. Some leaders are noted for their refusal ever to practice it, whereas others who insisted they were well versed in the techniques seemed rarely to actually carry out the rite. There is a widespread feeling that too much blood is bad, and

The sacrifice of a rooster in the chapel of a *terreiro*. The rooster's blood is dripping on the sacred stone that serves as the "seat" of the spirit being honored.

there is a general consensus that blood should never be offered to the Exus. The murder of a *pai de santo* a few years ago was attributed to the fact that he had accustomed the Exus to receiving blood, and when the sacrifices stopped they took his blood as a substitute.

The usual sacrifice is a rooster. It is offered to a specific encantado, its throat is cut, and its blood is allowed to run on the stone that serves as the "seat" of the encantado. The head, wings, and feet are put in a bowl and placed before the altar, while the body of the rooster is cut up and cooked. The cooked pieces are also placed before the altar for a brief period, then are eaten by the members of the *terreiro*.

In the last chapter an incident was mentioned in which a *pai de santo* sacrificed chickens by biting their throats. This man, who was atypical in so many ways, stressed sacrifice to an unusual degree. At one initiation ceremony we attended, he killed nine chickens, two ducks, one guinea hen, and two doves. No other *pai de santo* of our acquaintance mentioned sacrificing more than five chickens at one time. Several leaders stated with some pride that they also knew how to sacrifice sheep, but no instance of such a sacrifice came to our attention.

Another ritual of a different kind that may occur during a public ceremony is the baptism of infants. This rite is a fairly close replica of baptism in the Catholic Church, with the *mãe* or *pai de santo* officiating. The major difference is that encantados serve as godparents but, as pointed out in Chapter III, sometimes encantados are godparents in Church baptisms as well. The ritual in a *terreiro* is also considerably less formal. There is often exuberant dancing and singing as the infant is passed from the *pai de santo* to the godparents and back again. The *pai de santo* recites the Christian formula: "I baptize you in the name of the Father, and of the Son, and of the Holy Spirit" and everyone present shouts, "Baptized, baptized!" Infants are only baptized in the *terreiro* if it is felt that because of illness or some other problem they are especially in need of the protection of encantado godparents.

Infants may become the center of attention on other occasions, when mediums in trance dance with them as a way of giving them what amounts to a *passe*. During one *batuque,* a woman possessed by a carousing encantado seized an infant from the lap of its mother and danced away with it. The mother watched placidly as the baby was taken to the front of the *terreiro,* held upside down, and had its face rubbed lightly on each of the drums. Screaming lustily, the infant was brought back to its mother and half thrown in her lap, whereupon it calmed down immediately. Sometimes the baby is simply turned upside down or kissed, but the basic idea is that being handled by the encantado is beneficial.

A *pai de santo* begins a new song as he prepares to baptize the baby he holds in his arms.

When a *festa* lasts several days, the important rituals that are planned are usually scheduled to take place on the first few days. The *festa* for St. Expeditus mentioned earlier began on Saturday night with a typical public ceremony. Dancing began at 9 P.M. and lasted until dawn, with half an hour out for the *afurá* ceremony. On the second day the major event was a procession in honor of the saint. In this instance the procession left the *terreiro* about 4:30 P.M. and made a circuit through the neighborhood, returning to the *terreiro* at 6:15. It was composed of most of the mediums of the *terreiro*, in some cases with their families, a number of hangers-on, and a five-piece band. A large image of the saint, two and a half feet high, mounted on a carrying frame with poles projecting front and rear, was carried on the shoulders of four women. Following immediately behind the saint was the band, which played popular melodies when not accompanying the hymns that were sung from time to time. Several hundred yards in front, a man fired rockets into the air in a steady series of explosions. The large

A small procession through neighborhood streets in honor of St. Expeditus was organized by one medium as part of his anniversary celebration for his chief *encantado*, Guapindaia.

numbers of children that were thus attracted were arranged in two lines, boys on one side, girls on the other, to form long advance columns. As the procession moved through the residential streets, a few householders came out to watch it go by, and a few passers-by asked what saint was being honored, but no one showed more than casual interest. Processions of this type are not unusual in the streets of Belém, sponsored either by *terreiros* or, more commonly, by lay Catholic organizations.

Most *terreiros* hold at least one procession a year, usually during the major *festa*. In some cases the image of the saint is taken first to a church where a mass is ordered in the saint's honor, then the image is carried back to the *terreiro*. Often the band is omitted because of the expense, but fireworks of some sort are considered a necessity, since fireworks always figure in any saints' day celebration.

As the saint's image is brought to his house, the medium, dressed in a Batuque costume and holding up a *toalha,* prepares to receive it. The young man in the foreground is swinging a small charcoal brazier on which incense and herbs are being burned to purify the premises.

Antônio did not accompany the procession, but was waiting in the street when it returned. As expected, when the image of the saint was carried into the *terreiro,* Antônio was possessed by his chief encantado, Legua Bogi, who adores St. Expeditus and was the co-recipient of the *festa.* After receiving the greeting of many of those present, Antônio went into the chapel and held consultations for half an hour. Not until the consultations ended did Antônio, still possessed by Legua Bogi, assemble the mediums and start a regular *batuque.* At 9 P.M. the dancing was interrupted for a *ladainha* in honor of St. Expeditus. This was followed by the *obrigação* featuring the drink called *bela de pão*. Then a man and woman had their heads washed (a purifying ritual, not a baptism), after which dancing resumed and the *batuque* continued until 2 A.M.

The third day a secular dance was held, again to honor the saint. A loud speaker was set up, and when the dance music began teen-agers came from all over the neighborhood. Dancing occurred only in Antônio's house, not in the pavilion. Most of the mediums, as well as Antônio, took advantage of the occasion to catch up on their sleep.

We did not attend the fourth day of the ceremony. On the fifth and final day only a few mediums showed up, and those who did appear were obviously very tired. As frequently happens on the last day of a long *festa,* visitors—mediums from other *terreiros* who came by to watch and then joined the dancing— took an active part in the ceremony and at times completely dominated the proceedings. On this night no special rituals were held. Antônio, looking haggard and bleary-eyed, brought the marathon to a halt at 2:20 A.M.

The ritual calendar of each *terreiro* is somewhat different from all others, and within any given *terreiro* vagaries of finance and other circumstances make the list of dates celebrated highly variable from year to year. In most *terreiros* in Belém, however, the following saints' days are considered the most important, and at least several *terreiros* can be expected to hold a public ceremony on or near the date given[6]:

Date	*Saint*	*Encantado*
January 20	St. Sebastian	Rei Sebastião, Oxossi
February 8	St. John of Matha	João da Mata
March 19	St. Joseph	Dom José
April 23	St. George	Rompe Mato, Ogun
June 24	St. John the Baptist	Dom João
June 29	St. Peter	Dom Pedro Angaço
July 26	St. Ann	Rainha Eowa, Nana Burocô
August 23	St. Benedict	Averekete
September 27	St. Cosmas and St. Damian	Cosme and Damião
September 30	St. Jerome	Xangô (Badé)
December 4	St. Barbara	Rainha Barba (Inhaçan)
December 8	Our Lady of Conception	Imanjá, Navéroaim

Some of these saints' days are also observed by other religious or secular groups in Belém. However, the days of John of Matha, George, Cosmas and Damian, Jerome, and Barbara are unlikely to be celebrated by any group other than an Afro-Brazilian cult center. The celebration of St. Cosmas and St. Damian's day at *terreiros* is well known by the general public. The day of the twin saints is dedicated to children, and any *terreiro*

The feast day of St. Cosmas and St. Damian is dedicated to children. At this *terreiro,* a crowd of children wait for the *mãe de santo* to begin distribution of the candy, cakes, and balloons that have been prepared for them.

holding a *batuque* on this day distributes candy, cake, and balloons to the hordes of children who appear and wait patiently for the windfall.

In addition to commemorating several of the foregoing dates, every leader holds a major ceremony each year for two or three of the more important encantados that he receives. These ceremonies are usually considered to be obligations, and they are held not on a saint's day but on the anniversary of the day on which the leader was first possessed by the encantado involved. The feast day of St. Expeditus comes in April, but Antônio held the *festa* just described in November, since it was on November 17 that he was first possessed by Legua Bogi. The *terreiro* is also made available to any of the mediums who wish to hold an "anniversary" ceremony for their chief encantados, assuming of course that they are able to pay for one. Occasionally the *mãe* or *pai de santo* helps with the expense of such a ceremony, and sometimes a ceremony is provided for an independent medium of some renown whose presence at the major *festas* of the year is thus compensated. Another ceremony that must be held periodically is a *tambor de chôro* (ceremony of mourning), which is held at the death of a member of the *terreiro*.

A number of religious holidays during the year may serve as the occasion for a *batuque*. In many *terreiros,* for example, *batuques* are held on Christmas Eve, New Year's Eve, and on Holy Saturday (the eve of Easter). A number of *terreiros* hold a ceremony in October on the occasion of the Círio, the major local religious festival honoring Our Lady of Nazareth. In addition, as was noted in Chapter VII, in some *terreiros* ceremonies may be held on request for tourists, if the price is right. *Terreiros* where ceremonies occur too frequently are criticized as being frivolous, but leaders are aware that their mediums become restive if no ceremony occurs for three or four weeks, and it is usually possible to find some legitimate reason to bring out the drums at least that often.

The other rituals that occur in the Batuque take place outside the public ceremony, and most of them occur in private sessions with only other Batuque members or clients present. These rituals are related either to curing or to the spiritual development of the individual. The rituals connected with *cura* were described in detail in the last chapter and need not be considered further. The rites associated with the "development" of the individual correspond to the initiation carried out in the conservative sects. As was pointed out earlier, in the latter groups there is considerable stress on passing through the initiation ritual before being accepted as a full member of the religion. Our investigation of initiation in the Batuque was considerably complicated by our knowledge of the Candomblé and the Casa das Minas and our expectation that initiation would have the same importance in the Batuque. The Batuque leaders with whom we first discussed the topic all agreed that only someone who had been initiated could properly initiate others, and they were often openly scornful of other leaders who were not *feito*. Our confusion can be imagined, then, when we later learned that several of these same leaders had never been "made" themselves. When we asked Dona Ana about her initiation, she calmly said that God had "made" her and that she had been taught everything she needed to know by her encantados. Carlos was somewhat more defensive, but readily admitted that he had never been "prepared" properly. We never questioned Dona Jorgina about these matters, but one of her *filhos* told us that he had been warned by one of Jorgina's encantados, while it was possessing Jorgina, that she was not *feito* and could not perform the necessary rituals for him.

For a few leaders, and aspiring leaders, initiation did seem to be of considerable significance, at least to judge from the stories they told us. Of the four leaders who claimed to have passed through the full initiation ritual, one said she had been "made" by a local *mãe de santo,* two claimed to have been initiated in São Luís, and one told an elaborate story of having gone through a typical Candomblé initiation in Bahia. One *curandeira* told us a quite similar story about having once visited Bahia and having been initiated there. Three other mediums indicated that their initiation had taken place in Belém, but that the ritual had been carried out by a *pai de santo* from São Luís or Bahia, who had remained only briefly in Belém and then returned to his native city. In two of these latter cases, the mediums later changed their stories, and there were other indications that most of these accounts were fabrications intended to enhance the reputation of the medium involved.

For most rank-and-file members of the Batuque, however, as for the leaders mentioned earlier, elaborate initiation rites are not considered to be particularly significant or desirable. Everyone is aware that being *feito* involves a period of isolation, ideally a week but at least several days, and considerable expense, and few mediums are willing to spend either the time or money. In the four *terreiros* where we knew the membership fairly well, none had more than two or three mediums who had been through the complete initiation ritual. Rather than talk about being "made," mediums usually spoke of the *serviços* (services) that had been done for them in the course of their development. As it turned out, although given different names, these *serviços* were everywhere essentially the same.

The basic *serviço* involves washing the medium's head with a special herb infusion. As was noted earlier, this is a prominent feature of initiation in the conservative cults, where the infusion is called *amasí* or *amasin* (Eduardo 1948, p. 72; Bastide 1961, p. 353). Some Batuque leaders use the same term. The act of washing the medium's head, however, may mean different things under different circumstances, and before carrying out the act the *mãe* or *pai de santo* is expected to specify what the rite is intended to do. Sometimes the intent of the leader is not made clear, and some of our informants were not at all sure how far their development had progressed.

For the beginning medium who has had a trance experience and whose encantado has been identified, washing the head is intended to confirm an already existing situation. It strengthens the relationship between the medium and the encantado in the sense that the spirit is now said to be established more securely in the medium's head.[7] If a person has had incipient possession experiences, but the encantado has not been identified, the *mãe* or *pai de santo* must first determine which spirit is involved. This is done either through divination with cowrie shells or, more commonly, simply by asking the encantado of the leader. Once the encantado is identified, the leader is then said to "put the spirit in the head" of the individual, and if all goes well, the person becomes the medium of that encantado.

In most cases, but not all, at the same time that the encantado is "put in the medium's head," it is also baptized. Most of the mediums considered to be relatively developed had at least one of their encantados baptized, usually their *senhor*. It is sometimes necessary to baptize carousing *caboclos*, but only if they are so wild that they continually cause trouble. The Exus should also be baptized, since they are considered to be pagan. The baptismal ceremony is again copied from the Catholic rite, with the godparents being encantados rather than people. Holding a candle, the medium (either man or woman) possessed by the encantado who is the godfather stands on one side of the neophyte, while the medium whose encantado is godmother stands on the other. The *mãe* or *pai de santo* officiates, reciting the same Catholic formula that is used to baptize infants. Although the baptism is very explicitly of the encantado in the medium's head, the medium is not necessarily in trance during the proceedings. Moreover, the godparents are construed as being the godparents of the initiate, not of the encantado. To a large extent this baptism of the encantado has taken the place of the more elaborate initiation ritual that occurs in the conservative cults; it is often the only rite observed in the Batuque.[8]

Once a medium has been through the initial head-washing, subsequent rituals of the same kind may have somewhat different meanings attached to them. In some *terreiros* all of the mediums have their heads washed at least once a year, usually on the occasion of the major ceremony. The basic idea, according to Antônio, was to ritually cleanse his mediums. On one occasion Antônio washed the head of a *filha* in order to improve her health, but we did not observe this use of the ritual elsewhere.

There is some resistance to the idea that all encantados can or should be baptized. Clara, who had had her head washed but had never been through the baptism ritual, argued that her chief encantado, Dom João, was a dignified *senhor* and it would be absurd to baptize him. Carlos was indignant that Dona Marina would hold a ceremony in which she attempted to baptize Oxalá, since, as the most prestigious of all *orixás*, Oxalá could not properly be baptized by mortal man. There is also opposition to the idea of baptizing Exus, since it is maintained that this act "breaks the power" of the demon.

It is generally agreed, however, that a *mãe* or *pai de santo* can "put an encantado in the head" of someone or can withdraw an encantado already present. Ordinarily, of course, a leader would not attempt to put an encantado in anyone's head unless the person showed signs of being an incipient medium. But some leaders have chosen to broaden the conception of possible recipients, and they are willing to "put an encantado in the head" of anyone, for a fee. Dona Ana sometimes explained to her clients that their bad luck would surely change if they had an encantado looking out for them. If they are willing, she would hold a complete baptismal ritual on their behalf, telling them who their encantado was, what obligations they should observe, and who their baptismal godparents were. Some of the people who went through this ritual then began to participate in the ceremonies of the *terreiro,* hoping to be possessed, but most did not. It was apparently enough that they now had an encantado serving as a kind of guardian angel. Dona Ana was quite open about holding these baptisms of non-mediums, and although we did not encounter this type of baptism in any other *terreiro,* the practice was remunerative and other leaders probably engaged in it. We cannot say with any certainty, however, how widespread this practice was.

On one occasion, we witnessed Dona Ana baptizing a bus that belonged to one of her clients. Perhaps this particular ceremony could have been construed more in the nature of a blessing than a true baptism, although Dona Ana, possessed by João da Mata, did pronounce the baptismal formula and splash a bucket of water on the vehicle's hood. The implication was that the bus would henceforth have João da Mata as its guardian spirit. One could not help feeling that, in view of the vehicle's advanced age and the condition of the city streets, it was very wise not to rely exclusively on St. Christopher.

Since Batuque leaders are believed to have the power of putting encantados in the heads of mediums as well as withdrawing them, the leader is often blamed when a medium fails to develop normally. If a *mãe* or *pai de santo* performs a *serviço* for a medium and there is no obvious improvement in the medium's ability to receive the spirits, it is assumed that the leader has botched the job. In Chapter VI the sad story of Lulu was related—she was the woman who tried for many years to enter trance but never succeeded. Her basic difficulty, according to Clara, was that the *pai de santo* who had prepared Lulu had identified her encantado incorrectly. To compound his error, he had then performed a service to withdraw the original encantado and replace it with another—this attempt had also failed. In the meantime, the encantado Tapinaré had possessed a relative of Lulu and stated unequivocally that he was Lulu's encantado. Lulu's problems would be solved, Clara contended, if she would allow the *mãe de santo* Julia to baptize Tapinaré "in her head." Both Lulu and Julia were agreeable, and the rite would soon be performed. When we returned to Belém, Clara promised, Lulu would be "receiving" as well as anyone.

Carlos claimed that he had yet another kind of control over the encantados of his *filhos*. If one put rum in the *banho* with which the head of a medium was washed, he said, the encantado being baptized would demand rum when it possessed the medium. If the *pai de santo* used wine instead, the encantado would refuse hard liquor. Carlos claimed that he had "cut the drink" of all of his mediums by using this technique and that none of them drank rum when possessed. We were unable to check this somewhat astonishing claim, since we did not learn of it until very late in our study. Although it was impossible to miss the smell of rum when being embraced by some of the mediums at Carlos' *terreiro,* it is at least conceivable that all those who drank had not yet been baptized. If the claim were true, it would mean that Carlos' *terreiro* was unique among the *terreiros* we knew.

In all of the cases just described, the *mãe* or *pai de santo* is seen as having some control over the encantados of their mediums. But only, it will be noted, during the early stages of the medium's development. In many cases, especially if an individual has grown up in the religion, there is never any question as to which encantado the individual is receiving, and the only role of the leader is to wash the medium's head to validate the relationship. Even if the encantado does not identify itself right away and the leader determines its identity, once the encantado has been baptized, the leader has no further role to play. It is only in exceptional cases, when the medium is unable to be possessed properly, that the various attempts at manipulation occur.

We were unable to obtain very many details about the rituals that may occur during the isolation period observed by those few mediums who are *feito*. Our assumption is that this means that not much goes on, but possibly we were not told about rituals considered to be secret. According to the accounts we were given, the medium spends from three days to a week lying down in the *camarinha* (a small room at the *terreiro*). At the end of this period the encantado is baptized as described earlier. The expense connected with initiation comes primarily at the end of the isolation period when the initated medium is expected to sponsor and pay for a public ceremony celebrating his new status.

In the conservative Afro-Brazilian sects, the date that is commemorated by every medium is the date of initiation. In the Batuque, however, a much more important date is the date when the medium was first possessed by a particular encantado. It is on this date every year that the medium makes special offerings to the spirit or, if possible, pays for a *batuque*. Sometimes it is possible, with the encantado's permission, to change the date to correspond with the day of the saint whom the spirit adores, and this is sometimes done by the leaders. This makes it possible to incorporate their anniversary into the *terreiro*'s ritual calendar. But for most mediums, the date of first possession, not the date of any *serviço* performed on their behalf, is the date from which they count the years that a spirit has been "in their head."

This contrast between the Batuque and the conservative sects can serve as the final example of the reorientation that has taken place in the Batuque. As we have seen, in every instance the change has been toward greater freedom of the individual. Unlike the situation in the Candomblé or the Xangô, where the medium must seek help even to obtain a message from the supernatural, the Batuque medium need only enter trance to make the encantado available for consultation. Sacrifices are not considered necessary in the Batuque, and each medium is quite capable of providing the necessary offerings for his spirit. Consequently a developed medium is not dependent on his *mãe* or *pai de santo*. Initiation is theoretically necessary only for those who have aspirations of becoming a leader, but in practice being

Mediums prepare for the closing of a *batuque* by tying scarves around their heads. Fatigue shows in the faces of the participants and the few remaining spectators. The *pai de santo* sings the solo of the closing song.

feito is of little importance to anyone. Those aspiring leaders who feel compelled to impress their clients need only make up a story about having taken a trip to São Luís or to Bahia and being initiated there. That so few leaders bother to tell such stories shows how little importance is attached to initiation. With divination, sacrifice, and initiation of little significance in the Batuque, many of the occasions for ritual no longer occur.

The drummers switch to the proper rapid, muffled, closing beat and continue until . . .

It should not be supposed, however, that this increased individualism means that all group rituals will soon disappear or that the Batuque is likely to become just another form of *pajelança,* with each medium performing separately. In spite of their independence, mediums accept the basic obligation of their contract with the encantado to receive the spirit in a public setting, they believe that their spiritual development depends on being regularly possessed in public, and they recognize the responsibility of sponsoring rituals or entire *batuques* to honor their

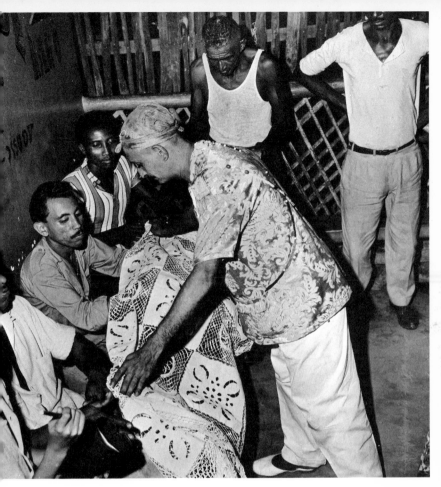

the leader places a shawl over the drums.

encantados whenever they can afford it. Moreover, they give every indication of appreciating well-organized and elaborate rites, and they often speak approvingly of *terreiros* in which decorum and self-discipline are displayed. Needless to say, once the important rituals of the evening have been carried out, everyone enjoys the partylike atmosphere that characterizes the closing phases of the public ceremony. There are some mediums who show impatience during long rituals, and some who will not wait but go into trance when this is quite inappropriate, and of course there are no effective sanctions against such behavior. But the great majority of mediums seem committed to an orderly public ceremony as the central ritual act of the Batuque, in spite of the lack of controls of the type found in the conservative sects.

Batuque leaders and aspirants for leadership positions usually show the greatest interest in ritual detail. As was pointed out in Chapter VII, the prospective leader must demonstrate his knowledge and his orthodoxy in ceremonial matters in order to attract a following and a clientele. A leader continues to compete after he is established, and the more elaborate and well-ordered the ceremonies he is able to hold, the greater his reputation among his colleagues and among prospective clients.

The rituals of the Batuque thus continue to serve a number of important functions. Although they are now defined largely in individual terms—they are held ostensibly to allow mediums to be possessed, or be baptized, or carry out obligations, or have a good time—it is clear that they are the major occasions for group interaction and sources of whatever group solidarity may exist. They also certify to the larger society that the Batuque is in fact a religion and not simply a group of individuals who go into trance and carry on. When Batuque rituals are contrasted with those of the more conservative Afro-Brazilian sects, they seem few and simple, but they still constitute a vital part of the Batuque religion.[9]

FOOTNOTES

1. The term "medium" is not used in the conservative groups. In the Casa das Minas the Dahomean word *vodunsi* is used for women mediums (men do not receive the spirits) (Eduardo 1948, p. 69). In the Candomblé and Xangô *filha* and *filho de santo* are general terms. Special terms are used to indicate individuals who have reached different stages of initiation (Ramos 1951, pp. 58–61; Ribeiro 1952, pp. 42–43).

2. The best sources in English on the conservative cults are Eduardo (1948) on the Casa das Minas and Pierson (1967) and Herskovits (1953, 1955, 1958) on the Candomblé. There is no material in English on the Xangô.

3. As was noted in Chapter II, the Batuque as a distinct Afro-Brazilian sect began in São Luís. The immediate source of the Batuque was not the Casa das Minas, however, but several modified Yoruban groups similar to the Xangô.

4. For the various meanings of *despacho* see the Glossary.

5. Exu is called first in both the Candomblé (Bastide 1961, pp. 23–25) and the Xangô (Ribeiro 1952, pp. 76–77), but in these sects he is asked to assume his role as intermediary with the deities and bring them to dance.

6. The Batuque's date for St. Benedict is probably an "anniversary" date of a prominent cult leader that has come to be generally accepted in the cult as the proper time to honor the saint and Averekete. In folk Catholicism in Amazonia, several days in December are celebrated as St. Benedict's feast days.

7. The conception that the head is the part of the body where the deity is localized is found in all of the conservative cults, as well as in the Batuque.

8. The baptism of the encantado is also an important rite in the Yoruban-derived sects in São Luís, although there it occurs as the culmination of a somewhat more complex initiation (Eduardo 1948, p. 75).

9. In anthropology there is currently an interest in discovering what rituals "mean." To do this on an overt level requires many painstaking hours of interviewing to determine what connotations informants attach to specific ritual acts. To uncover "unconscious" meanings requires primarily a lively imagination. We did not have enough interest in ritual to adopt the first approach, and we are not sure that the second is worthwhile.

Chapter X

Conclusions

We went to Belém to study the Batuque handicapped by a set of false assumptions. We supposed that the Afro-Brazilian religion we would encounter there would be much like the Candomblé of Bahia. We were prepared for some minor changes in the pantheon, to be ascribed to "syncretism," and since we had seen three ceremonies on an earlier trip we knew that the ritual was somewhat different. But essentially we expected that in Belém we would find people of primarily African ancestry, organized into tightly knit *terreiro* groups, still worshipping African gods.

It happened that the first Batuque members we met were the best read and the most inclined to admire the Candomblé and the other conservative cults. Although they never deliberately misled us, they were perfectly willing to let us continue supposing that the Batuque was not all that different. We went to our first *batuque* at Antônio's expecting to see Yoruban *orixás,* and when a woman carrying a red *espada* went into trance, we supposed it must be Xangô (Xangô's colors are red and white). It was several days later, when discussing the ceremony with Antônio, that we had our first glimpse behind the façade. Antônio was quite puzzled by our reference to a possession by Xangô, and, after inquiring of several of the other mediums who had been present, he finally suggested that the spirit in question was probably the dolphin Bôto Tucuxí. In the days that followed, as we continued to collect names of spirits completely foreign to any African pantheon, as we were confronted with *orixás* who acted silly and drank rum, and especially as we came to know some of the rank-and-file members and began to understand their conceptions of the religion, we came to realize that most of our preconceptions were quite wrong. The Batuque was not the Candomblé, and it was not a watered-down version of the Candomblé; it seemed instead to be quite a different religion. We began again, from the beginning, to try and find out what it was all about.

Our initial assumption that the Batuque would be similar to the Candomblé was based on our knowledge of the literature, which seemed to suggest that all Afro-Brazilian religions were in many ways alike. The reason for this apparent homogeneity, however, was simply that only certain kinds of Afro-Brazilian religions had been studied intensively. Practically all of the students of these religions had been primarily interested in studying the "Negro" in the New World, and they had consequently chosen those religions for study that seemed most African. The Candomblé, the Casa das Minas, the Xangô were all well known because they all had retained many African features. With a few notable exceptions,[1] no one had paid much attention to those religions, like the Batuque, that had diverged most from their origins, and even when these religions were investigated, they were found to be so "syncretized" and "disorganized" or such pale imitations of the conservative sects that they were not considered of much interest.

As we became familiar with the Batuque, it seemed clear that far from being some kind of imperfect copy of the Candomblé, it was in fact an independent, coherent religious system that deserved recognition in its own right. Its ultimate African origin was obvious, but the extent to which it had become "Brazilianized" attracted more and more of our attention. Not only had the membership been broadened to include people of all physical types, but the pantheon was composed mostly of spirits with Brazilian names, the hierarchy in the pantheon reflected the Brazilian class system, most of the songs were in Portuguese, many Catholic rituals had been incorporated—the list seemed endless. Whatever questions we might ask about the Batuque, they would clearly be different questions from those asked by most earlier students.

It did not seem particularly useful, for example, to emphasize, as Herskovits[2] and his students[3] had done, what came to be called "Africanisms." Since Herskovits was interested in the acculturation of the Negro in the New World, his approach was to trace not only traits that had been preserved intact by the descendants of African slaves, but also those traits that had been "reinterpreted." The concept of "reinterpretation," as applied to New World Negroes, referred either to those traits of African origin that had been modified to fit new circumstances (e.g., polygyny became serial monogamy) or to those borrowed traits of foreign origin that had been modified to fit the traditional belief system (e.g., the Catholic saints were "identified with" African deities). Ultimately Herskovits hoped to explain why some groups of Negroes had preserved much more of their traditional culture than others. The first step was to determine how much each group had actually preserved, and it was for this reason that he and his students were oriented toward finding "retentions" and "Africanisms" in the Afro-Brazilian religions that they studied.

From our perspective, a major difficulty with this approach was that the members of the Batuque could not in any meaningful way be considered "Negroes." Even if they were racially homogeneous, however, the drawback of concentrating on the process of reinterpretation was that there was an inevitable stress on the past, on the "old forms" that have been given new meanings.[4] It would have been possible in our account of the Batuque to have stressed the odds and ends of "Africanisms" that remained— Averekete, *amasin*, animal sacrifice—but the result would have been a quite distorted picture of what the modern Batuque was like. Our approach to the history of the Batuque reflected our interest in understanding the varied sources that had contributed to its modern form, of which the African was only one, and also an interest in the remarkable creativity that had gone into their amalgamation into a single religious system.

There seems to be little record of the early history of the Batuque, but a rough outline of its development is readily discernible. The religion was brought to Belém from São Luís around the turn of the century. At the time it was exported, the religion had probably already incorporated a number of ideas and practices of folk Catholicism and certain themes from Brazilian and Iberian folklore and history, as well as certain ideas from the Catimbó cult of northeastern Brazil and the *pajelança* of Pará. The move of Dona Doca (or some other *mãe de santo* like her) to Belém occurred during the height of the rubber boom, a time when there was a sizeable migration of people from the northeastern states into Pará. Many of the migrants were undoubtedly familiar with Catimbó. The first major change that occurred in the Batuque, once it was transplanted to Belém, was the deepening and strengthening of both the Catimbó and *pajelança* elements already present in it. This meant not only the addition of new spirits and new songs to the ones brought from São Luís, but a greater emphasis on curing (prominent in Catimbó as well as in *pajelança*) and perhaps increased individualism; with every medium becoming an incipient *pajé,* the cohesion of the *terreiro* would naturally be reduced.

Within the last generation the most obvious change in the Batuque has been the incorporation of spirits and rituals of the Umbanda cult of southern Brazil, and, to a much lesser extent (and partially through Umbanda), of some ideas of the Brazilian spiritualist movement. The borrowing of religious themes from Rio de Janeiro and São Paulo reflects the increasing mobility of the Brazilian population and the great improvement in national communication that has occurred since World War II. It is highly probable that the relative weight of Umbanda elements within the Batuque will increase in the future.

As to how any of these changes came about, we can of course only speculate. But on the basis of our knowledge of a few recent changes, we can assume that in every case some individual *mãe* or *pai de santo* decided, in or out of trance, that a new ritual or a new belief would enhance his position vis-à-vis his followers or his competitors. As was indicated in Chapter VII, changes in the Batuque tend to be resisted by the developed mediums, so that in every case this conservatism would have to be overcome. Once adopted by the members of one *terreiro,* the change would probably be at first scorned by all others, then eventually adopted by most. It would presumably be this relatively slow process of adoption that would allow the new belief or ritual to be modified sufficiently to be incorporated into the existing system. Even so, there are still many only partially assimilated items, and it should be admitted that, in discussing the behavior and beliefs of Batuque members, we have sometimes ignored ambiguities and inconsistencies in order to help the exposition. The Batuque today is far from being a completely systematized body of beliefs, and, at the rate it is still changing, this condition seems likely to continue. Batuque members seem rarely to be troubled by the lack of a highly rationalized theology, since their interest is usually pragmatic rather than philosophical. The lack of philosophical coherence may limit the Batuque's appeal to individuals with intellectual pretensions, but of course the very looseness and lack of rigid systematization of its theology provides one explanation for the ease with which new themes are absorbed.

The origin of one of the Batuque's most distinctive features, the carousing *caboclo,* remains obscure. The conception that certain spirits not only enjoy drinking and having fun but that they also demand that their mediums engage in these activities as part of their religious obligation has not been described for any other Afro-Brazilian religion. However, although it is hard to imagine that such an unusual and striking set of ideas could be overlooked, it would be unwise to suppose that the fun-loving spirits were invented by members of the Batuque. There are hints in the literature that spirits with similar characteristics are found in the so-called Candomblés de caboclo of Bahia,[5] and we know from some of our informants that they are prominent in São Luís. Although it is impossible to guess when these ideas developed, we have suggested elsewhere[6] that the prototype of the *farrista* was probably the *tabosa,* child spirits found in the Casa das Minas, or perhaps the *éré* spirits of the Candomblé.

There have thus been many creative modifications of the items old and new that have been brought into the Batuque from so many varied sources. The term "syncretism," usually employed to describe the development of religions like the Batuque, fails to do justice to the creative process involved, since it suggests a rather mechanical bringing together of disparate ideas. The creativitity of Batuque mediums, their ingenuity in adapting new themes to fit a given ideological framework, and their skill in devising new songs and rituals are all the more remarkable if one considers the underprivileged status of most cult members, and the grinding struggle for basic necessities that absorbs most of their time and attention. The culture of poverty may indelibly mark the personality of those caught in it but, in Brazil at any rate, it does not extinguish creativity.

Besides asking historical questions about the Batuque, we also asked a number of questions that were essentially sociological in that they sought to establish the place of the Batuque in the larger Brazilian society. In part our interest in the social specifications of Batuque members was inspired by Herskovits (1955), who, in addition to dealing with historical problems, also suggested that most early accounts of Afro-Brazilian religions had dealt almost exclusively with the beliefs and rituals and had ignored the membership. We found, as he had for the Candomblé, that most Batuque mediums were poor, minimally educated,[7] and female. There were some indications, however, that the number of male participants and of middle-class converts may be increasing.

Race seemed to have no significance as far as membership was concerned. Most participants were aware that the Batuque was once a religion of dark-skinned descendants of slaves, but today, as in the recent past, it is clear that *"a mediunidade não escolha a côr* [mediums are not chosen by their color]," as one informant put it. In fact, considering the modern pantheon, the members of which are practically all conceptualized as *brancos,* Amerindians, or racially mixed *caboclos,* it would seem that the African origin of the Batuque has been all but forgotten. It might be pointed out that the Pretos Velhos, the spirits conceptualized as former black slaves, are most popular in those centers that are most influenced by Umbanda, where the membership tends to be the most well-to-do and the lightest in skin color.

Two of our findings were unanticipated. We were surprised that there were so few migrants from rural areas in the Batuque, in view of Camargo's (1961) finding that in São Paulo migrants made up a large part of the membership of the Umbanda centers he studied. His contention, later supported by

Willems (1966), that sects like Umbanda served as important means of integrating rural migrants into urban environments, seemed to have little relevance for the Batuque.

We also had not expected to find that half of Batuque mediums were converts, or that so few children of mediums followed their mothers into the sect. On the basis of the literature, we had supposed that most mediums would be recruited from within the religion, and especially that daughters would follow their mothers in receiving the spirits.[8] However, in the Batuque no one took mediumship for granted, and it was generally accepted that only a few of a medium's children were likely to become mediums. Young girls often resisted because they thought they looked ugly when possessed or because "boys don't like mediums." Sons of mediums were inhibited by the stigma of effeminacy attached to the role of male medium, although they often served as drummers when young. It seemed clear that, in the Batuque, trance was not perceived as a simple, normal act that anyone might experience as a matter of course. Being a medium was regarded as requiring not only divine selection, but also commitment and natural aptitude on the part of the individual. Only a few of a medium's children were expected to meet all three requirements; the rest were expected to remain essentially passive members of the religion, attending and perhaps participating to a limited extent in ceremonies, but never receiving the encantados.

In examining the relationship between the Batuque and the other institutions of Brazilian society, we found it difficult to accept Bastide's interpretation (1960, pp. 522–26) that religions like Umbanda and the Batuque represent a protest by "Negroes" or a "colored class" against their lower-class status. According to Bastide's analysis, after the Brazilian slaves were freed they found security by isolating themselves and maintaining mostly African values and practicing African religions. As the isolation of these communities has broken down in recent years, and as the descendants of the slaves have adopted more and more Brazilian values, their religions have changed dramatically. Rather than the group-oriented religions such as the Candomblé and the Casa das Minas, the "colored class" has developed "sects of imitation" such as Umbanda, in which the individual has free rein to express his desires, his frustrations, and his hostility to the domination of the upper classes.

We have already objected to this analysis once, in Chapter IV, on the grounds that Bastide overstresses the racial aspect of the newer religions. But even if there is no "colored class" in Belém, it is worth considering the possibility that the Batuque does in fact serve the function of allowing the expression of protest, in this case not of a racial group but of an impoverished lower class. Conceivably the poor and downtrodden might find in a non-comformist sect such as the Batuque an outlet or a vehicle for the expression of feelings of resentment toward the Establishment. We found no evidence, however, that the Batuque is a protest movement of any kind. In the ideology of the religion there seem to be very few overt or covert expressions of hostility toward any racial or social elite, nor is there the "symbolic subversion of the traditional power structure" that Willems (1966, pp. 226–30) seemed to find among Pentecostalists. One exception was noted in the discussion of the Batuque pantheon, when it was suggested that perhaps the high esteem in which the *turcos* are held may represent an identification of the slaves with the Moors, antagonists of their European masters. On the other hand, one of the more striking features of the Batuque pantheon is the identification of the major encantados with the upper classes. Not only are these spirits called *senhores, brancos,* and *gente fina,* all terms used for members of the upper class, but they are always treated with respect and deference. In some respects, the attitude of the mediums toward the upper-class spirits seems to be modeled on the patron-client relationship that is still prominent in rural Amazonia. One of our informants, who was rather dark and sometimes referred to herself as a *preta* (black woman), always called her chief encantado *"minha branca"* (my white, upper-class lady). The context of her remarks when speaking about her *branca* often gave the impression that she was speaking of a revered upper-class patron from whom she might expect favors.

The lower-class spirits, the *caboclos,* are conceived of as both inferior to, and subservient to, the *senhores.* They come later at ceremonies, they quickly retire if confronted by a *senhor,* they are expected to defer to the chief *encantado* of their medium. Sometimes a *caboclo* complains of its secondary role, but this is always treated as a good joke—and the laughter that we heard seemed genuine. In short, Batuque ideology seems to reflect not only a society divided into two strata, but a society in which the lower class knows its place and keeps to it.

This is not to imply, of course, that Batuque members are not often bitterly discontented with their living conditions, nor that they do not resent those members of the upper classes who could be considered responsible. In 1962, when the rate of inflation exceeded 50 per cent, when there were frequent shortages of the basic foods that were supposedly price-controlled, when the city government failed to clean or repair the streets, and when both the city and the state governments were from four to eight months in arrears in meeting the salary schedules of their employees, a number of Batuque members expressed acute dissatisfaction with the politicians who, it was felt, were robbing and ruining the country. In 1965 the new military government was considered an improvement, since the streets were much better kept, the markets were better supplied, and government salaries were usually paid on time. Nevertheless, the new government did not provoke much enthusiasm. *"Olha, a vida do pobre não muda"* (Well, the life of the poor man never changes), shrugged one informant, when asked to give an opinion about the change in government.

As far as we could determine, the vast majority of Batuque members are normally quite uninterested in politics. There was very little interest shown in the general elections held in 1962. A candidate for the state legislature gained the support of Dona Ana, who put his campaign sign up in front of her *terreiro* and made several speeches on his behalf during public ceremonies. During the campaign he made repeated appearances at the *terreiro,* sometimes to receive *passes* from Dona Ana, sometimes to make large contributions toward the upkeep of the *terreiro*. Dona Ana did have some sympathy for his party, which she identified in her speeches as the party of the poor man, but she treated him primarily as just another client. No one else who frequented the *terreiro* showed any interest at all in his candidacy, and after the election it was difficult to find anyone who was even aware that he had lost.

Bastide (1960, p. 326) suggests that in the more conservative Afro-Brazilian sects, members support whatever political party is in power, in exchange for freedom from persecution. This certainly seemed to be the case in Belém. Being in the good graces of the government was especially important in the 1920s, when the Batuque was actively persecuted, but even today, although the present Brazilian constitution ensures freedom of worship, it would be relatively easy for a hostile administration legally to curtail Batuque activities. All-night ceremonies could be banned as a public nuisance—both because of the noise and the fights that sometimes occur among drunken spectators—or the police could enforce the law against curing rituals, with a drastic effect on *terreiro* income. If the new Federation of Afro-Brazilian Cults becomes a viable institution, it may help to insulate the *terreiros* from direct interference from local authorities, but as long as the *terreiros* remain as vulnerable as they are today, the leaders are likely to support whatever party controls the police.

In the past only a few politicians made a favorable impression on Batuque members. A number of the older mediums speak with reverence of Getúlio Vargas, President-dictator of Brazil from 1930 to 1945 and again from 1951 to 1954. Magalhães Barata, who entered state politics as Vargas' *interventor* in 1930 and who later served as senator and as governor of Pará, is remembered as a patron and friend of the Batuque, who ended the pattern of official harassment of the cult. In recent years the only politician to arouse much enthusiasm was Jânio Quadros, who resigned the presidency in 1961. We did not inquire into how widespread this enthusiasm was; it was brought to our attention because one of our informants proudly recited to us a song for Quadros that her encantado had composed during a *batuque*. This song, most notable perhaps for its complete lack of any real political content, was composed by the carousing encantado Mariana:

Jânio Quadros é meu homem;	*Jânio Quadros is my man;*
Jânio Quadros é que se quer.	*Jânio Quadros is what is wanted.*
Eu vou me embora pra Brasília;	*I'm going off to Brasília;*
Lá eu bebo o que quiser.	*There I'll drink whatever I wish.*

E a cabocla Mariana não avoa,	*And* cabocla *Mariana won't fly,*
Vai a pé.	*She'll go on foot.*
Vai chegar até Brasília,	*She'll get as far as Brasília,*
Bebe tudo o que dé.	*She'll drink everything offered.*

Since we never heard this *doutrina* sung during any of the ceremonies that we attended, it was obviously forgotten as rapidly as was the President it was meant to immortalize.

From the perspective of the members, the appeal of the Batuque is not that it promises to change the world in which the members live, but that it will help them to survive in that world. Every medium knows that there are manifest inequities in life, that he is desperately poor, and that many other people are incredibly rich. Ordinarily, however, this situation is taken as being in the nature of things. There is no recognized political procedure for changing the way things are, and there is no conception that any of the supernatural beings man can contact have any control over the nature of the world. The awful problems that the poor must face are part of that world, and the only hope man has is to gain supernatural support in coping with them.

In addition to considering the history and sociology of the Batuque, we also attempted to deal with a series of fundamental (and very difficult) psychological problems. Many of these problems centered around the trance experience that Batuque members interpreted as possession. The first crucial question we asked about the trance state was whether or not it was a pathological condition and whether only individuals who were psychologically abnormal could have the experience. Every student who has studied the Afro-Brazilian religions for any length of time has asked the same question, and each has concluded that trance is not necessarily a sign of pathology. Rodrigues (1935, pp. 109–16), who studied the Candomblé before the turn of the century, concluded that in most cases possession was much like "somnambulism" or hypnosis. Ramos (1951, pp. 214–45) argued that trance was actually a very complex phenomenon and that in certain cases at least he saw many similarities with forms of hysteria. But even Ramos did not suggest that trance was limited to abnormal individuals. The most unusual position on this point was taken by Herskovits (1948, p. 67), who went to the opposite extreme and considered trance to be simply a cultural phenomenon. He argued that since trance was defined as "normal" by the members of the Candomblé, it was those individuals who were unable to enter trance who were the least "adjusted."

In most cases students of Afro-Brazilian sects who have offered an opinion about the "normality" of those who frequently enter the trance state have had very little systematic information about the individuals involved. Very few students have used psychological tests to obtain data on the personality characteristics of cult members. One outstanding exception was Ribeiro (1959), who used the Rorschach test in an attempt to gain more data on some of his informants in the Xangô. After showing the Rorschach inkblots to a number of mediums, both in and out of trance, and interpreting the responses, Ribeiro concluded that the individuals involved were able to resolve a number of their personality problems through the trance experience. One of the women, for example, had problems with aggression, which she could keep under control by being aggressive while in trance. Another used the occasion of trance to indulge in regressive behavior. But whatever their problems, these tended to be within the normal range, and Ribeiro concluded that all of the women he tested were reasonably well adjusted.

In light of these conclusions, and the impressions of the other students of Afro-Brazilian religions, we began our study of Batuque mediums with the assumption that they were reasonably normal people. Since we did not do any psychological testing, our basis for assessing the mental health of our informants was similar to that of most other students—day-to-day interaction. This produced a firm conviction that most of our informants were as well adjusted as the non-mediums we knew. When a few mediums described what seemed to be psychotic episodes in their pasts and when others claimed to have been in mental hospitals, we accepted the apparent fact that some mediums were not "normal" by any definition. However, we concluded that for most mediums, at least, the trance experience was not dependent on any psychological abnormality.

The second problem related to trance was how to explain the great variability in trance behavior that was apparent during any public ceremony. Clearly some mediums were far superior to others in their enactment of the roles of supernatural beings. The simplest explanation seemed to be that there was a strong learning component involved and that those mediums who took the role of the encantado best were those with the most experience. This hypothesis was attractive in part because it was acceptable to the Batuque members themselves. However, although learning was obviously important, there was no simple relationship between experience and proficiency; in many cases, mediums with the same amount of experience showed quite different proficiency in behaving as supernatural beings. There seemed to be an irreducible psychological factor that would not go away, no matter how hard we tried to circumvent it. The simple fact was that some individuals found the trance state more congenial than others and were able to learn to perform as an encantado much more rapidly. Some individuals, on the other hand, either could not enter trance at all or were unable to behave properly while in trance even after years of trying. If trance as it occurs in the Batuque is as closely related to hypnosis as we suppose it to be, then we could expect that some of the same personality traits would characterize a good hypnotic subject and a skillful medium. Our data are much too incomplete, however, to carry this argument any further.

In considering why the Batuque is now thriving and why religions like it are growing in popularity throughout Brazil, it is obvious that these religions have a great deal to offer their members. As we have repeatedly stressed, the Batuque is an extremely instrumental religion, and in many respects it seems almost perfectly designed to serve the needs of the people who participate in it. Living in a very difficult environment, confronted with all the problems described earlier, a medium finds in the Batuque a religion that promises direct, immediate, day-to-day support. For those individuals who have the requisite skills and adequate motivation, participation in the Batuque may provide not only the promise of a resolution of financial, health, and family problems, but also an enhancement of status both within the religious group and with neighbors and friends. For some mediums, a reputation as an expert intermediary with the supernatural can be converted into economic reward, a position as head of a *terreiro,* or both. This leaves to one side the hedonistic elements of the religion, which are too obvious to need much elaboration. For those mediums who become proficient in taking the role of a carousing *caboclo,* the dancing, smoking, drinking, and horseplay provide major sources of recreation and enjoyment. Even for those individuals who are unable to take this role, the color and excitement of the public ceremony are enough in themselves to encourage participation.

It is quite possible that participation as a medium enables some individuals to resolve personality problems of various kinds, although on the basis of our data we cannot really say much about such matters.[9] Some of our informants who had presumably been mentally ill did insist that their symptoms were much improved after they became mediums.

In addition, the Batuque offers its members at least some of the fellowship and sense of group communion with the supernatural that most religions provide. Throughout this study we have emphasized the rampant individualism found in the Batuque, but we have also tried to show that social controls are obvious and pervasive, and that there are definite limits beyond which individualism may not be carried. Even the trance experience, presumably completely private, must conform to a standard pattern if it is to be accepted as possession by the spirits. Consequently, even though there are few group goals in the Batuque, there are still congregations of mediums that under the right circumstances may be quite cohesive groups.

Beginning as a religion that gave hope and comfort to the slaves, the Batuque has become a religion that appeals most to the poor and disadvantaged. Our interpretation has stressed the continuing instrumental nature of the Batuque as the reason for its popularity. The test of our interpretation will come when the poor of Belém come to have a more secure existence—when they have more income, better health services, some sort of welfare program. For the forseeable future, however, no such test is likely to occur, since the standard of living of the poor people of Belém is improving at an agonizingly slow rate. It seems perfectly safe to predict that the drums will sound, the medium dance and sing, and clients seek out their favorite encantados for many years to come.

FOOTNOTES

1. Eduardo (1948) studied the less traditional sects in Maranhão as well as the Casa das Minas. Ramos (1951, pp. 88–161) described the *macumba* found in Rio de Janeiro and other cities of the south. Carneiro (1937; 1961, pp. 57–60, 86–88, 99–102, 128–31) devoted some attention to the less traditional sects in Bahia, but never studied them very systematically. The best summary is by Bastide (1960, pp. 241–65, 298–305, 422–75).

2. The most important of Herskovits' works on the Afro-Brazilian religions are listed in the bibliography. His theoretical position is spelled out in *Man and His Works* (1948, pp. 542–60, 612–16).

3. Ribeiro, who studied the Xangô of Recife, and Eduardo, who studied the sects of Maranhão, were both students of Herskovits.

4. See Ribeiro (1955) for a good example of the result of this approach.

5. For example, the Bahian spirit Martim-Pescador, described by Carneiro (1961, pp. 88–89), sounds like a Batuque *farrista*.

6. See Leacock (1964b).

7. Our data on formal education are very poor; most mediums had less than five years of schooling.

8. For example, see Eduardo (1948, p. 71). The same conclusion is at least implied by Bastide's (1960, p. 520) contention that trance is "cultural, normal, and obligatory" in "Negro societies."

9. An interpretation that would equate the medium's chief encantado with his superego and his *farrista* with his id will surely appeal to any reader with Freudian persuasions. Support for such an interpretation will be found in the life history given in Appendix B.

Songs of the Batuque

The songs given below represent a small sample of the *doutrinas* of the Batuque; mediums and drummers memorize an astonishing number of songs. The folklore research team headed by Alvarenga (1948; 1950a) recorded some of the songs of the Batuque in Belém and São Luís in 1938, and a few songs from Belém, recorded in 1931, are included in Andrade's *Música da feitiçaria no Brasil* (1963, pp. 105, 233–34, 264). Many of these *doutrinas,* in substantially the same form, are still being sung in Belém more than a generation later.

We heard all of the songs recorded below on more than one occasion and in more than one cult center. In a ceremonial setting, with the drums and *ganzá* going full blast, it is difficult to distinguish all of the words in a song. In most cases, informants repeated the words for us later on. The songs are primarily in Portuguese, but include a sprinkling of non-Portuguese words that are said to be Nagô (Yoruban). These non-Portuguese words are meaningless to most Batuque mediums, and, although some Batuque leaders would, if asked, reel off a Portuguese translation of Nagô phrases, one had the strong impression that they were improvising. Most mediums do not think of Nagô as an African language but rather conceive of it as a sacred language that is used by all of the spirits, including the American Indians, the dolphins, and the Turks. In the songs given below, Nagô words or phrases are spelled as they would be spelled by a Portuguese speaker and no attempt is made to translate them.

All of the *doutrinas* sung during a public ceremony follow a solo-chorus pattern; during curing rituals the curer sings a number of songs that do not require a *resposta* (response). The chorus usually repeats the words sung by the solo at the end of each stanza. In cases where the chorus sings a substantially different response, we have indented the words sung by the chorus. Each song is sung through at least twice, but may be repeated over and over again for much longer periods, depending on the lead of the solo. After the song is sung through once, a certain flexibility is often allowed the solo, who may choose to repeat certain lines more often than others and may even improvise new lines.

A. Opening songs.

The initial songs sung during a *batuque* are considered extremely important by cult members. Unless the ceremony is "opened" correctly, few encantados will descend. Each leader tends to develop his own repertoire of correct opening songs. It seems likely that the five *doutrinas* given here were formerly used in most *terreiros* to open a ceremony, but at present only a few leaders continue to open with these songs. All five are designed to salute the Exus and to send them away from the premises.

1. Baraba-ô oji, Baraba-a i aná,
   Baraba-ô i an.
   Quem mandou colicô coria-na
   Ô bogiba gori ana
   Fara ai-no-glê, ojan di nai, ai-
       no-glê,
       Ai-no-glê, ai-no-glê.
   Fara loçun,
       Ai-ma.
   Todo fé,
       Ai-ma.
   Fara loçun.
       Ai-ma.
   Todo fé,
       Ai-ma.

2. Ó Barabô-Tiriri, Nana,
     Barabô-ti.
   Ó Barabô-Tiriri, Nana,
     Barabô-ti.

3. Oh, Legba não é vodun,
     Kerê, kerê-ê,
   Oh, Legba não é vodun,
     Kerê, kerê.
   Ogun mandou levar Exu
     Para um kerê, kerê.
   Oh, Legba não é vodun,
     Kerê, kerê.

   Oh, Legba is no vodun,
     Kerê, kerê-ê,
   Oh, Legba is no vodun,
     Kerê, kerê.
   Ogun ordered Exu removed
     For a kerê, kerê.
   Oh, Legba is no vodun,
     Kerê, kerê.

4. Exu-Malê, Exu-Malê,
     Ô la ê la.
   Exu-Malê, Exu-Malê,
     Ô la ê la.

5. Com licenç-ai-ê, com licença
     ê-a,
   Com licença de dono da casa,

   Com licença de ogan-ai-a.
     (Chorus repeats)
   Com licenç-ai-ê, com licença
     ê-a,
   Com licença de todos voduns,

   Com licença de ogan-ai-a.
     (Chorus repeats first stanza)
   Com licenç-ai-ê, com licença
     ê-a,
   Com licença de caboclo da rua,

   Com licença de ogan-ai-a.
     (Chorus repeats first stanza)

   With the permission ai-ê, with the
     permission ê-a,
   With the permission of the owner of
     the house,
   With the permission of the ogan-ai-a.

   With the permission ai-ê, with the
     permission ê-a,
   With the permission of all the
     voduns,
   With the permission of the ogan-
     ai-a.
   With the permission ai-ê, with the
     permission ê-a,
   With the permission of the caboclo
     of the street [Exu],
   With the permission of the ogan-
     ai-a.

B. Songs for specific encantados.

The songs in this section are used both to call the spirit named and to identify a spirit that has possessed a medium. The songs are given more or less in the order in which they might be sung during a *batuque*. There are no rigid rules about the sequence in which spirits are to be called, however, and in any actual ceremony songs will be sung as·they occur to the leader or as mediums enter trance. The spirit featured in each song is indicated in parenthesis.

1. (Averekete)
   Ó Dom, Dom Ja, ó Dom, Dom Ja,
   Verekete, Verekete,
      Ó Dom, Dom Ja!
   Averekete puxa guia,
      Ó Dom, Dom Ja!
   Averekete é mina d'ouro,
      Ó Dom, Dom Ja!
   Averekete é nossa guia,
      Ó Dom, Dom Ja!

   O Dom, Dom Ja, O Dom, Dom Ja,
   Verekete, Verekete,
      O Dom, Dom Ja!
   Averekete brings spirits,
      O Dom, Dom Ja!
   Averekete is a gold mine,
      O Dom, Dom Ja!
   Averekete is our guide,
      O Dom, Dom Ja!

2. (Averekete)
   O que sá, que sá, o que sá lá,
   Verekete é da Mina, que sá lá.
      (Chorus repeats)
   O que sá, que sá, O que sá lá,
   Rei Turquia é da Mina, que sá lá.

   He who is, who is, he who is there,
   Verekete, who is there, is of Mina.

   He who is, who is, he who is there,
   King Turquia, who is there, is of Mina.

   (Any other encantado may be named in additional stanzas.)
   O que sá, que sá, o que sá lá,
   Todo mundo é da Mina, que sá lá.

   He who is, who is, he who is there,
   Everyone who is there is of Mina.

3. (Averekete)
   Chama Averekete!
      Averé!
   Chama Averekete!
      Averé!
   Hum, hum, hum!
      Averé!
   Hum, hum, hum!
      Averé!

   Call Averekete!
      Averé!
   Call Averekete!
      Averé!
   Hum, hum, hum!
      Averé!
   Hum, hum, hum!
      Averé!

4. (Rainha Barba-Inhaçan)
   Lá vem Barba nas ondas do mar;
   Barba vem rolando no rôlo do mar.

   There comes Barba on the sea waves;
   Barba comes rolling on the rolling sea.

5. (Rainha Barba-Inhaçan)
Barba Sueira, Barba Sueira,
Barba Sueira, Maria-a.

6. (Rainha Barba-Inhaçan)

Maria Barba junta pedras no mar.	*Maria Barba gathers stones by the sea.*
Hoje é dia de folga, senhor.	*Today is a day off, sir.*

7. (Rainha Barba-Inhaçan)

Eram duas ventarolas, duas ventarolas	*There were two fans, two fans*
Que vieram lá do mar.	*That came from the sea there.*
Eram duas ventarolas, duas ventarolas	*There were two fans, two fans*
Que vieram lá do mar.	*That came from the sea there.*
Uma era d'Inhaçan, o a lê lê,	*One was Inhaçan's, o a lê lê,*
E a outra era d'Imanjá.	*And the other was Imanjá's.*
Uma era d'Inhaçan, o a lê lê,	*One was Inhaçan's, o a lê lê,*
E a outra era d'Imanjá.	*And the other was Imanjá's.*

8. (Rainha Barba-Inhaçan)

Inhaçan, orixá na Umbanda,	*Inhaçan, orixá in Umbanda,*
Rainha de nossa gongá,	*Queen of our sanctuary,*
Saravá Inhaçan	*Hail Inhaçan*
Lá na Ruanda e parê, parê!	*There in Ruanda and parê, parê!*
Inhaçan vence demanda.	*Inhaçan wins the battle.*
Inhaçan, saravá com Xangô;	*Inhaçan, salute her and Xangô;*
No céu trovão roncou,	*In the sky thunder rumbled,*
E lá na mata o leão badou.	*And in the forest the lion [roared?].*
Saravá Inhaçan! Saravá Xangô!	*Hail Inhaçan! Hail Xangô!*

9. (Badé-Xangô)
Cravê oço, Badé sorou.

10. (Badé-Xangô)
Ô Badé sorou gama, gama-ô.

11. (Badé-Xangô)

Tu não vais, Badé? Eu vou.	*Aren't you going, Badé? I'm going.*
Tambor te chama. Eu vou.	*The drum is calling you. I'm going.*

12. (Badé-Xangô)

Badé chama povo do céu.	*Badé is calling spirits from the sky.*
É o dia de folga, senhor.	*It's our day off, sir.*

13. (Badé-Xangô)
    A—ê, a—ê,
    Xangô é uma beleza,
    A—ê.

    A—ê, a—ê,
    Xangô is a beauty,
    A—ê.

14. (Badé-Xangô)
    Xangô bami o pema Ogun,
    Xangô bami o pema Ogun-ô,
    Ogun-ô.

15. (Badé-Xangô)
    Ai o lê o li o lê,
    Ai o lê o lê o lá,
    Ai o lê o li Xangô,
    Ai o lê o lê o lá.

16. (Dom João Sueira)
    Ô lé lé Dom João,
    Para vodun e dou,
    Aguas bela.

17. (Dom João Sueira)
    A di mi, a di mina,
    Aguas bela.

18. (Dom João Sueira)
    Dom João Sueira, cavalheiro do
        mar e céu,
    Dom João Sueira, cavalheiro do
        mar e céu,
    Desce nalguma, somente para
        bailar.
    Ó Sueira, beirão do mar,
    Ó Sueira, beirão do mar.

    Dom João Sueira, horseman of sea
    and sky,
    Dom João Sueira, horseman of sea
    and sky,
    Possess someone, if only to dance.

    O Sueira, dweller by the sea,
    O Sueira, dweller by the sea.

19. (Dom João Sueira)
    Ó Sueira, beirão do mar,
    Ó Sueira, beirão do mar,
    Ó Sueira, beirão do mar,
    Dom João Sueira, beirão do
        mar.

    O Sueira, dweller by the sea,
    O Sueira, dweller by the sea,
    O Sueira, dweller by the sea,
    Dom João Sueira, dweller by the
    sea.

20. (Imanjá)

Veio do céu, Imanjá, veio do céu;
Veio do céu—u.
Veio do céu, Imanjá de Deus,

Veio do céu.
Veio do céu—u.

She came from heaven, Imanjá, came from heaven;
Came from heaven—u.
She came from heaven, Imanjá of God,
She came from heaven.
Came from heaven—u.

21. (Imanjá)

Samba colê, missa ô la ô,
  É Manjá, é Manjá.
Ô ô ló dê,
Samba colê, missa ô la ô,
  É Manjá, é Manjá.

22. (Imanjá)

É de lá, é d'Imanjá;
Olha um que kerê flori fofi
  ô lou ô dou,
  É de lá, é d'Imanjá.
Olha um que kerê flori fofi
  ô lou ô dou,
  É de lá, é d'Imanjá.

23. (Jamaina)

Ela é sereia, serei-i-ar,
Ela é sereia, rainha do mar.
  (Chorus repeats)
Oh, Jamaina é princesa real;
Ela é encantada na cobra-coral.

She is a mermaid, mermaid-ing,
She is a mermaid, queen of the sea.

Oh, Jamaina is a royal princess;
She is enchanted in the coral snake.

24. (Jamaina)

E agô, Badé;
E agô, sereia do mar.

25. (Oxossi)

Oxossi beliquê, beli-ou,
Beli, beli-uá.

26. (Oxossi)

Oxossi é, Oxossi é,
Oxossi é a luz que alumeia.
  (Chorus repeats)
Oxossi é, Oxossi é,
Oxossi é a estrêla que alumeia.

Oxossi is, Oxossi is,
Oxossi is the light that is shining.

Oxossi is, Oxossi is,
Oxossi is the star that is shining.

27. (Oxossi)

Eu vi chover e relampear,
Mas assim mesmo o céu estava azul.
Firma seu ponto na folha da jurema.
Oxossi é bom lá na Aracajú.

I saw rain and lightning,
But at the same time the sky was blue.
Base your ponto *on the jurema leaf.*
Oxossi is good there in Aracajú.

28. (Jurema)

Aruandê, Aruandá,
Os caboclos de Pema
Vem da Jurema
Para trabalhar.

Aruandê, Aruandá,
The Indians of Pema
Come from Jurema
In order to work.

29. (Jurema)

Filho da Jurema,
Eu vou para Jurema,
Juremê, Juremá.

A son of Jurema,
I'm going to Jurema,
Juremê, Juremá.

30. (Jurema)

Na sua aldeia tem seus caboclos,
Na sua mata cachoeirinha,
No seu saiote tem rendas douradas,
Seu capacete brilha na alvorada.

In your village are your Indians,
In your forest there is a waterfall,
On your petticoat there is gold lace,
Your helmet gleams in the dawn.

31. (Jurema)

A-ê, ela é filha da Jurema.
Pernambuco é meu;
Eu passei por Alagoas,
Quem me viu, correu.

A-ê, she is Jurema's daughter.
Pernambuco is mine;
I passed through Alagoas,
Whoever saw me, ran.

32. (Zezinho)

Salve Deus! Salve a patria! Salve os homens!
Salve todos que estão aqui!
Salve Deus! Salve a patria! Salve os homens!
Salve os caboclos do Brasil!

Hail God! Hail the fatherland! Hail mankind!
A salute to everyone here!
Hail God! Hail the fatherland! Hail mankind!
A salute to the caboclos *of Brazil!*

33. (Ogun)

Ogun, vai arrear seu cavalo
Para terreiro girar.
Ogun vai, Ogun vem, Ogun vai,
Êle torna a voltar.

Ogun, go harness your horse
To make the terreiro *spin.*
Ogun goes, Ogun comes, Ogun goes,
He returns again.

34. (Ogun)

Olha, Ogun está lá afora!	*Look, Ogun is outside there!*
Stá, stá!	*He is, he is!*
Olha, Ogun está lá afora!	*Look, Ogun is outside there!*
Stá, stá!	*He is, he is!*
Olha, Ogun vem de Umbanda!	*Look, Ogun comes from Umbanda!*
Vem, vem!	*He comes, comes!*
Olha, Ogun vem de Umbanda!	*Look, Ogun comes from Umbanda!*
Vem, vem!	*He comes, comes!*

35. (Oxun)

Ai—ê—ê, ai—ê—ê, Mamãe
    Oxun,
Ai—ê—ê, ai—ê—ê, Mamãe
    Oxun,
Ai—ê—ê, Mamãe Oxun, ai—ê
    —ê, Oxun-marê,
Ai—ê—ê, Mamãe Oxun, ai—ê
    —ê, Oxun-marê.

36. (Japetequara)

Grande tremor deu na aldeia,	*A great tremor struck the village,*
Aldeia balanceou.	*The village rocked.*
Foi o nosso rei dos indios	*It was our Indian king*
Quando na Jurema entrou.	*When he entered Jurema.*
Foi o nosso rei dos indios	*It was our Indian king*
Quando na Jurema entrou.	*When he entered Jurema.*

37. (Japetequara)

Ê—i—i, ê—i—a,	*Ê—i—i, ê—i—a,*
Japetequara é indio velho brasileiro.	*Japetequara is Brazil's Old Man Indian.*
Desceu nalgum arreador do Seu Tranqueiro.	*He possessed one of Seu Tranqueiro's mediums.*
Desceu nalgum arreador do Seu Tranqueiro.	*He possessed one of Seu Tranqueiro's mediums.*

38. (Japetequara)

Imba fora, Surupira!	*Get out, Surupira!*
Imba fora, Guerreiro!	* Get out, Guerreiro!*
Imba fora, Surupira!	*Get out, Surupira!*
Imba fora, Guerreiro!	* Get out, Guerreiro!*
Ó Caboclo Velho	*O Old Man Indian*
Da Barra do Carirí.	* From the Barra do Carirí.*

Lagoa grande secou,
   Todos morreram e eu
      não morri.
Por aqui passou caboclo,
   Caboclo de Canindé.
Trago meu arco e trago flecha,
   Minha candeia no pé.

The large lake dried up,
   All died and I did not.

An Indian went by here,
   Indian of Canindé.
I bring my bow and I bring arrows,
   My candle on my foot.

39. (Japetequara)
   Olha, caboclo é nagô e canga,
      E—ê—a,

   Caboclo Velho é nagô e canga,
      E—ê—a.
   Olha, vodun é nagô e canga,
      E—ê—a,

   Japetequara é nagô e canga,
      E—ê—a.
   Todo vodun é nagô e canga,
      E—ê—a,
   Olha, caboclo é nagô e canga,
      E—ê—a.

Look, the caboclo *is Nagô and*
   Canga,
      E—ê—a,
Old Man Indian is Nagô and Canga,
      E—ê—a.
Look, the vodun *is Nagô and*
   Canga,
      E—ê—a,
Japetequara is Nagô and Canga,
      E—ê—a.
Every vodun *is Nagô and Canga,*
      E—ê—a,
Look, the caboclo *is Nagô and*
   Canga,
      E—ê—a.

40. (Japetequara)
   Ô pai a pema, Chico Pema, pai
      a pema,
   Ô pai a pema, Chico Pema, pai
      a pema.
      Pai a pema, Guerreiro,
         pai a pema,
      Pai a pema, Guerreiro,
         pai a pema.
   Olha pema, Chico Pema, olha
      pema,
   Olha pema, Chico Pema, olha
      pema.
      Olha pema, Guerreiro,
         olha pema,
      Olha pema, Guerreiro,
         olha pema.

41. (Rompe Mato)

Seu Rompe Mato tem a côr morena;	*Mr. Rompe Mato has a brunette complexion;*
Êle é caçador da nossa Jurema.	*He is hunter for our Jurema.*
Êle jurou, tornou a jurar	*He swore and swore again*
Seguir os conselhos que Jurema lhe dar.	*To follow the advice Jurema gives him.*
Na sua aldeia, onde êle é caboclo,	*In his village, where he is caboclo,*
Êle é Rompe Mato, Seu Arrancatoco.	*He is Rompe Mato, Mr. Bully.*
Na sua aldeia, lá na Jurema,	*In his village, there in Jurema,*
Não se faz nada sem ordem suprema.	*Nothing is done without orders from above.*

42. (Exu Tranca Rua)

Exu Tranca Rua é homem,	*Exu Tranca Rua is a man,*
Exu Tranca Rua é homem	*Exu Tranca Rua is a man*
Na linha de Umbanda.	*In the Umbanda line.*
Exu Tranca Rue é homem.	*Exu Tranca Rua is a man.*

43. (Exu Tranca Rua)

Seu Tranca Rua é homem	*Mr. Tranca Rua is a man*
De nome.	*Of fame.*
Na encruzilhada	*At crossroads*
É êle que manda.	*He gives the orders.*
Com seu chicote	*With his whip*
Ninguem se meta.	*No one meddles.*
Seu Tranca Rua	*Mr. Tranca Rua*
Vence demanda.	*Wins the battle.*

44. (Exu Pomba Gira)

É de Pomba Gira, de Pomba Gira, meu pai.	*It is Pomba Gira, Pomba Gira, Father.*
É de Pomba Gira, de Pomba Gira, meu pai.	*It is Pomba Gira, Pomba Gira, Father.*

45. (Exu Pomba Gira)

Ó Gira, Gira, Gira!
Ó Gira, Gira, Gê!
Ó Gira, Gira, Gira!
Ó Gira, Gira, Gê!

46. (Jandira)

Sou Jandira, sou rainha do mar.	*I am Jandira, I am queen of the sea.*
Quem quer me, vê no céu;	*Whoever wants me, look in the sky;*
Quem quer me, vê no mar.	*Whoever wants me, look in the sea.*
Eu sou a india Jandira,	*I am the Indian Jandira,*
Sou rainha do mar.	*I am queen of the sea.*

47. (Ita)

Ita, companheira Ita,	*Ita, comrade Ita,*
Ó Ita, vamos pelejar.	*O Ita, let's go to battle.*

48. (Guerreiro)

Guerreiro de Alexandria	*Guerreiro of Alexandria*
É um caboclo bonito.	*Is a handsome* caboclo.
Filho do Rei da Turquia	Caboclo *Guerreiro is*
É caboclo Guerreiro.	*Son of the King of Turkey.*
Vem de aguardente,	*He comes with rum,*
É um caboclo bonito,	*He's a handsome* caboclo,
Filho do Rei da Turquia.	*Son of the King of Turkey.*

49. (Mariana)

Lá fora tem dois navios	*Out there are two ships,*
No meio tem um farol.	*In between there is a beacon.*
É uma esquadra da marinha	*It's a squadron of the Brazilian*
Brasileira. Mariana	*Navy. Mariana*
Lá na praia do Lençol.	*There on Lençol Beach.*

50. (Mariana)

Eu sou cabocla,	*I am a* cabocla,
Vem da ilha, meu pai.	*Who comes from the island, Father.*
Eu me chama Mariana,	*My name is Mariana,*
Moro nas ondas do mar.	*I live on the waves of the sea.*
Eu me chama Mariana,	*My name is Mariana,*
Moro nas ondas do mar.	*I live on the waves of the sea.*

51. (Mariana)

Ela é Dona Mariana;	*She is Dona Mariana;*
É sim a dona	*She is really the lady*
Da vila da Canindé.	*Of the town of Canindé.*
Meu vestido se molhou	*My dress got wet*
No passar igarapé.	*In crossing the creek.*
Escorreguei mas não caí;	*I slipped but didn't fall;*
Isso é queda da mulher.	*That's the way of a woman.*

52. (Tapinaré)

Onde tu vais, Madalena,	*Wherever you are going, Madalena,*
Na cidade de com que,	*In whatever city,*
Se passar lá na Turquia,	*If you pass through Turkey,*
Lembranças para Tapinaré.	*Give my regards to Tapinaré.*
Tapinaré é uma flor	*Tapinaré is a flower*
Que brilha no rompé do dia.	*That blooms at the break of day.*
Viva o caboclo guerreiro,	*Long live the warrior caboclo,*
Filho do Rei da Turquia.	*Son of the King of Turkey.*

53. (Tabajara)

Meu navio está no porto,	*My ship is in port,*
Tranqueiro.	*Tranqueiro.*
Oh, mar e céu, mar e céu,	*Oh, sea and sky, sea and sky,*
Eu só vejo mar e céu.	*I see only sea and sky.*

54. (Tabajara)

Alumiou e alumiou;	*It shone and shone;*
Seu Tabajara está no porto,	*Mr. Tabajara is in port,*
Alumiou—ô.	*It shone—ô.*

55. (Pedro Angaço)

Ó Senhor Angaço,	*O Mr. Angaço,*
Ó Angaçozinho,	*O Angaçozinho,*
Da licença	*Give your permission*
Dançar um bocadinho.	*For a little dancing.*

56. (Pedro Angaço)

Olha a familia do Pedro Angaço!	*Look at the family of Pedro Angaço!*
O mundo inteiro é seu,	*The entire world is yours,*
Vem chegando, vem arriando,	*Come right now, come on down,*
Vem da luz, aqui não tem.	*Come from the light, which is lacking here.*
A—i—céu, no mundo de Tentarem.	*A—i—heaven, in the world of Tentarem.*

57. (Bombeiro)

Lá na minha terra	*In my country*
Tem colinas e montanhas.	*There are hills and mountains.*
Eu sou Bombeirino,	*I am Bombeirino,*
Filho de Dom Pedro Angaço.	*Son of Dom Pedro Angaço.*

Eu perdi, perdi,
Perdi meu canal.
Se tem bebida, me dei,
Eu não posso demorar.

I've lost, lost,
Lost my way.
If you have a drink, give me some,
I can't stay.

58. (Manoelzinho)
Eu venho de longe,
Cheguei da beira do mar.
Sou eu Manoel,
    Boa.
Filho de Legua,
    Boa.
Sou perverso,
    Boa.
Sou feiticeiro,
    Boa.
Sou malvado,
    Boa.
Sou atrevido,
    Boa.
Meu pai é Legua,
    Boa.

I come from far away,
From the seashore.
I am Manoel,
    Boa.
Son of Legua,
    Boa.
I'm wicked,
    Boa.
I'm a sorcerer,
    Boa.
I'm cruel,
    Boa.
I'm a bold one,
    Boa.
My father is Legua,
    Boa.

59. (Manoelzinho)
Cheguei na minha barquinha;
Nela mesma vou virar.
Sou filho de Legua Bogi,
Eu sou Manoelzinho Boa.

I came in my little boat;
I'll turn around in it.
I'm the son of Legua Bogi,
I am Manoelzinho Boa.

60. (Manoelzinho)
Codó é minha terra
Aonde eu nasci.
Eu me chama Manoel,
Filho de Legua Bogi.

Codó is my country
Where I was born.
My name is Manoel,
Son of Legua Bogi.

61. (Barão de Goré)
Tu não me chama pajé.
Tu não me chama pajé.
Meu pai é Rei de Mina,
Eu sou Barão de Goré.

Don't you call me shaman.
Don't you call me shaman.
My father is King of Mina,
I am Barão de Goré.

62. (Barão de Goré)
O tubarão, peixe baleia,
O tubarão, peixe baleia,
Virou navio do mar.
Virou, virou,
Virou navio do mar.

Oh shark, whale fish,
Oh shark, whale fish,
He capsized an ocean liner.
Capsized, capsized,
He capsized an ocean liner.

C. Closing songs.

Just as each cult leader develops his own set of opening songs, so all devise their own closings. The following songs are used in some of the more conservative *terreiros*.

1. Oh, Deus mandou orixá virar,   *Oh, God ordered the* orixá *to turn around,*

    É de signo Salomão.   *It's Solomon's seal.*

    Oh, Deus mandou orixá virar,   *Oh, God ordered the* orixá *to turn around,*

    É de signo Salomão.   *It's Solomon's seal.*

    Oh, Deus mandou orixá virar,   *Oh, God ordered the* orixá *to turn around,*

    É de signo Salomão.   *It's Solomon's seal.*

    Deus mandou virar para Roma,   *God ordered a turn towards Rome,*

    É de signo Salomão.   *It's Solomon's seal.*

2. Eu vim mandar, eu vim mandar,   *I came to order, I came to order,*

    (Chorus repeats each line after solo)

    Eu vim mandar, eu vim mandar,   *I came to order, I came to order,*

    Eu vim mandar fechar na Guma;   *I came to order the closing of Guma;*

    Eu vim mandar fechar terreiro.   *I came to order the closing of the terreiro.*

3. O i la i la,

    A la má—a!

    O i la i la,

    A la má—a!

4. Eu vou levar meus voduns,   *I'm going to take my* voduns *away,*

    Já nô kerê kerê—ê,   Já nô kerê kerê—ê,

    Vou levar meus voduns,   *I'm going to take away my* voduns,

    Já nô kerê kerê.   Já nô kerê kerê.

D. "Have mercy" songs.

Some leaders include a *misericórdia* song in their series of closing songs. These *doutrinas* are also used in a crisis situation, such as when a medium falls into a coma, and to mark especially "holy" occasions, such as during Holy Week. The following two *misericórdia doutrinas* seem to be the most frequently sung.

1. Agô ê lei, mamãe, agô ê la.
   Agô ê lei, Nana-Burucô, agô
      ê la.
   Ô ô, Nana, agô ê lei; ô ô, Nana,
      agô ê la.

   Dom José, agô ê lei; Dom José,
      agô ê la.
   Averekete, agô ê lei; Averekete,
      agô ê la.
   Toi Aduçu, agô ê lei; Toi
      Aduçu, agô ê la.
   (Any other spirit can be added. Chorus repeats first stanza after each
   three named.)

2. Oh, misericórdia, nosso pai,	*Oh, have mercy, our Father,*
Socorro do céu!	*Heaven help us!*
Misericórdia, nossa mãe,	*Have mercy, our Mother,*
Socorro do céu!	*Heaven help us!*
Pelo amor de Deus, eu peço	*For the love of God, I beg*
Socorro do céu!	*Heaven help us!*
Ai, seus filhos estão arrependido,	*Aye, your children are repentant,*
Socorro do céu!	*Heaven help us!*
E afastar de nós a peste,	*And deliver us from disease,*
Socorro do céu!	*Heaven help us!*
E afastar de nós a pena,	*And deliver us from sorrow,*
Socorro do céu!	*Heaven help us!*
E afaster de nós a fome,	*And deliver us from hunger,*
Socorro do céu!	*Heaven help us!*
Ai, pelo amor de Deus, eu peço	*Aye, for the love of God, I beg*
Socorro do céu!	*Heaven help us!*
Ai, todos nós estão arrependido,	*Aye, all of us are repentant,*
Socorro do céu!	*Heaven help us!*
Oh, misericórdia, nosso pai,	*Oh, have mercy, our Father,*
Socorro do céu!	*Heaven help us!*
Oh, misericórdia, nossa mãe,	*Oh, have mercy, our Mother,*
Socorro do céu!	*Heaven help us!*

E. Farewell songs.

During the course of a *batuque* a number of encantados will
signal their intentions of leaving the mediums they are possessing
by singing one of the farewell songs. There are some farewell
songs that are considered appropriate only for specific encantados,

such as those for Japetequara, Ogun, and Rompe Mato. Others, however, are more general and are used for any encantado.

1. Eu vou embora, Maria,
   Eu vou embora para Bahia.
   Vai embora, Maria,
   Vai embora para Bahia.

   I'm going away, Maria,
   I'm going away to Bahia.
   Go away, Maria,
   Go away to Bahia.

2. Meu pai me chama
   Lá no alto mar;
   Eu vou me embora
   No som dêste abatá.

   My father is calling me
   Out there on the high seas;
   I am leaving
   With the sound of this drum.

3. Vou embora, aleluia!
   A—ê, a—ê, aleluiê!

   I'm leaving, hallelujah!
   A—ê, a—ê, hallelujay!

4. Tambor me chama lá dentro;
   Tambor me chama lá.
   Eu vou lá dentro do pegí;
   Tambor me chama lá.

   The drum is calling me inside there;
   The drum is calling me there.
   I'm going there inside the altar;
   The drum is calling me there.

5. Adê—vô, adê—vá,
   Adeus, terreiro,
   Já vou pro mar.

   Adê—vô, adê—vá,
   Good-by terreiro,
   I'm leaving for the sea.

6. (Rompe Mato, also used for
      Exu Tranca Rua)
   Rompe Mato, vai embora,
   Stá chegando sua hora.
   Rompe Mato, vai embora,
   Stá chegando sua hora.
   Vai à mata virgem
   Com Deus e Nossa Senhora.
   Vai à mata virgem
   Com Deus e Nossa Senhora.

   Rompe Mato, go away,
   Your time is about up.
   Rompe Mato, go away,
   Your time is about up.
   Go to the virgin forest
   With God and Our Lady.
   Go to the virgin forest
   With God and Our Lady.

7. (Japetequara)
   Olha, olha, três com que,
   Olha, olha, três com ca.
   Olha, olha, três com que,
   Olha, olha, três com ca.
      Olha, olha, verde mar,
      Olha, olha, verde mar,
      Olha, olha, verde mar.

   Look, look, three with que,
   Look, look, three with ca.
   Look, look, three with que,
   Look, look, three with ca.
      Look, look, green sea,
      Look, look, green sea,
      Look, look, green sea.

Eu vou me embora para verde mar.	*I'm going away to the green sea.*
Olha, olha, verde mar.	*Look, look, green sea.*
Eu vou me embora para verde mar.	*I'm going away to the green sea.*
Olha, olha, verde mar,	*Look, look, green sea,*
Olha, olha, verde mar,	*Look, look, green sea,*
Olha, olha, verde mar.	*Look, look, green sea.*

8. (Ogun)

Ogun já vai,	*Ogun is leaving already,*
Já vai pra Ruanda.	*Leaving for Ruanda.*
Ogun já vai,	*Ogun is leaving already,*
Já vai pra Ruanda.	*Leaving for Ruanda.*
Adeus, meus companheiros,	*Good-by, comrades,*
Ogun vai a outra banda.	*Ogun is going to another band.*

F. Fillers.

There are moments, after a *batuque* has been in progress for several hours, when none of the mediums in trance have any songs they want to lead, and when the *pai de santo* or *mãe pequena* have temporarily no inspiration about what encantado to call. The leader then resorts to a "filler" song, which is usually short, simple, and not directed toward any specific spirit.

1.
Meu pai é flor,	*My father is a flower,*
Flor do mar.	*Flower of the sea.*
João da Mata é flor,	*João da Mata is a flower,*
Flor do mar.	*Flower of the sea.*
Jarina é flor,	*Jarina is a flower,*
Flor do mar.	*Flower of the sea.*
Curupira é flor,	*Curupira is a flower,*
Flor do mar.	*Flower of the sea.*
Assistência é flor,	*The audience is a flower,*
Flor do mar.	*Flower of the sea.*
Terreiro é flor.	*The terreiro is a flower,*
Flor do mar.	*Flower of the sea.*

(Any additional encantado or thing can be added)

2. Bolí, bolê, ganga,
   Bolí, bolê, ganga.

3. Oxalá mandou,
   Oxalá mandou,
   Mandou buscar
   Os caboclos da Ruanda.

   Oxalá ordered,
   Oxalá ordered,
   Ordered the bringing of
   The caboclos of Ruanda.

4. Caboclo é brabo e zangado.   *The caboclo is wild and angry.*

5. Meu pai é brasileiro,
   Eu também sou brasileiro.
   Meu caboclo é brasileiro,
   Eu também sou brasileiro.

   My father is Brazilian,
   I'm Brazilian too.
   My caboclo is Brazilian,
   I'm Brazilian too.

6. Porque eu cheguei,
   Guamaré, guamaré.

   Because I've come,
   Guamaré, guamaré.

(This song is not strictly a "filler" since it signals the arrival of a *farrista*. It is non-specific, however, and might be sung by any encantado who is possessing a medium in order to drink and have fun.)

G. Songs sung during curing rituals.

Most of the songs sung by curers are identical, or nearly identical, with those sung during a *batuque,* except that the chorus is often omitted. It is possible that the songs given below are also sung during public ceremonies, and that we simply did not happen to hear them at the *batuques* we attended. The first four songs were used by two curers to "open" their sessions.

1. Nossa Senhora da Conceição,
   Venha abrir a minha mesa,
   A Mãe de Deus,
   Nesta ocasião.

   Our Lady of Conception,
   Come open my session,
   Mother of God,
   This time.

2. Vale me Deus
   E viva Jesus.
   É a flor da noite;
   É da vera cruz.

   Help me, God,
   And long live Jesus.
   He is the flower of the night;
   He is of the true cross.

3. Dona Pequaquara
   É a senhora do mundo;
   Vem abrir a minha mesa
   Com povo do fundo.

   Dona Pequaquara
   Is the lady of the world;
   Come open my session
   With spirits of the deep.

4. Juruparí,
   Chega agora,
   Bota inimigo
   A porta pra fora.

   Juruparí,
   Come now,
   Throw our enemies
   Out the door.

5. (Pena Verde)
   Sou vindo, sou vindo,
   Caboclo de Pena Real,
   Aqui chegou Pena Verde, seu
     dono,
   Pena de arara-real.

   I'm coming, I'm coming,
   Caboclo of Pena Real,
   Pena Verde, your master, has
     arrived,
   Feather of the arara-real.

   Ó indio, ó indio,
   Tu fazes o que eu te mandar.
   Vai buscar minha conta verde,
   Vai botar na minha maracá.

   O Indian, O Indian,
   You do whatever I tell you to do.
   Go get my green bead,
   Go put it in my rattle.

6. (Açulão)
   Sou passarinho,
   Sou Açulão.
   De baixo de agua
   Sou mergulhão.

   I'm a little bird,
   I am Açulão.
   Under the water
   I'm a diving bird.

7. Eu quero meu nome,
   Eu não posso lhe dizer.
   Eu mora em Santa Rita,
   E muito gente quer me ver.

   I want to keep my name,
   I can't tell it to you.
   I live in Santa Rita,
   And a lot of people want to see me.

8. (Tartaruga da Amazonas)
   Ó pena, ó pena!
   É pena arara.
   Sou cabocla, sou cabocla,
   Tartaruga da Amazonas.

   O feather, O feather!
   It's an arara feather.
   I am a cabocla, a cabocla,
   Tartaruga da Amazonas.

   Cobra Grande do meio do rio,

   Quem vem beirando do mar,
   Ela é bela princesa,
   Foi quem me ensinar curar.

   Giant Snake from the middle of the
     river,
   Who comes skirting the sea,
   She is a beautiful princess,
   She was the one who taught me how
     to cure.

9. (Tango do Pará)
   Graças a Deus, já cheguei
       Olha, Tango do Pará!
   Da Borbaleta, onde eu moro.
       Olha, Tango do Pará!
   Alguma coisa nêste mundo,

   Thanks to God, I've come here
       Look, Tango do Pará!
   From Borbaleta, where I live.
       Look, Tango do Pará!
   There is one thing in this world,

Alguma coisa eu vou contar.   *One thing I am going to tell.*
Olha, Tango do Pará!   *Look, Tango do Pará!*

(At one curing session the curer then made comments in verse to most of the clients present. To the American observer, he sang the next stanza to rhyme with the couplet above.)

Meu branco, nêste mundo   *The gentleman is going to*
Pouco tempo vai viajar.   *Travel abroad very soon.*
Olha, Tango do Pará!   *Look, Tango do Pará!*

Life History
of a Batuque Medium

Although Clara did not become our informant for several months, we noticed her at the first *batuque* we attended. According to our notes of the ceremony, relatively few participants entered trance until a "heavy-set, middle-aged woman" did; then followed "a feverish flurry of possessions." We noticed Clara again the next week when we attended a ceremony inaugurating a *mãe de santo*'s new pavilion. A number of other cult leaders and mediums had been invited. We were struck by the deference shown to Clara; she received more attention than most of the other mediums and was asked to take charge of the *afurá* ceremony. She did so with a dignified composure and a firm dispatch that suggested incontrovertible knowledge of correct procedure and considerable experience in leading ceremonies.

As we discovered later, Clara's self-assurance and authoritative manner extended beyond the ceremonial setting. She ran her household and dispensed advice to her neighbors and friends with the same alert decisiveness. These imposing traits were tempered by a lively sense of humor and a warm sympathy for others. Clara was obviously intelligent, naturally gregarious, interested in many things, with an ear for gossip and a natural flair for story telling. She was, in short, not only an excellent informant, but a remarkable and very likeable person.

When we first got to know Clara in 1962, she was fifty years old, physically a stout, dark-complexioned (number 5 on our color scale, see page 110 above) woman with European facial features and with kinky hair, which she always wore combed tightly back in a neat bun. Clara was a native-born inhabitant of Belém and, in fact, had lived most of her life in the same Pedreira neighborhood. She was born on April 19, 1912, in a house that stood only six blocks from the location of her home in 1962. Clara's mother, Florina, had also grown up in that neighborhood, having been brought to Belém from the state of Piauí by her parents when she was a small child. Clara never learned to know her father, who came from Maranhão, since he died when she was three months old. She does not remember any of her grandparents nor any relatives on her father's side.

The size of her mother's family compensated for the lack of paternal kin, and Clara grew up, as many Brazilians do, as a member of a large family in which kinship is not exclusively based on blood or marriage ties. Florina and her three brothers and one sister had grown up very close to the children of a neighboring family that had two boys and two girls. A marriage, as well as the childhood association, eventually linked the two families: Florina's oldest brother, Bento, married Clotilde, one of the neighbor's two girls. Clara grew up making no distinction between her mother's siblings and the siblings of Clotilde—all were uncles or aunts to her and she considered all of their offspring her cousins. In addition to this troop of aunts, uncles, and cousins, Clara had a brother, Rudolfo, four years older than herself, and three half-brothers and a half-sister younger than herself. Florina had remarried a year or so after her first husband died.

When Clara was born, her mother and a number of her uncles and aunts were deeply involved in the Batuque. Both Florina and Clotilde, as well as their respective sisters, were active mediums. Clotilde's two brothers, Danico and Caetano, had both become *pais de santo,* with *terreiros* located only about a block apart. None of Florina's own three brothers became actively involved, however, and one of them, Bento, was bitterly hostile to the cult and everything about it.

After first "developing" in another *terreiro,* Florina switched to that of her "brother" Danico. She continued to attend public ceremonies at Danico's even after she had her *varanda* enlarged and began holding curing sessions every Wednesday and Saturday. This occurred when Clara was four or five years old. Clara remembers that there were often patients living with the family for short periods. In addition, the mediums that her mother was preparing in the *linha de cura* were frequent visitors.

In those days (1915–1930) the Batuque was a much more persecuted sect than it is today. Clara recalls that in 1923, for example, all *terreiros* in the city were closed by order of the governor of Pará, and all ceremonies had to be held secretly outside the city until official vigilance relaxed. Curing was always prohibited, as it still is today, and when the official heat was on, it was the cult leaders caught treating patients who were most likely to be arrested. The curing activities of Clara's mother escaped detection, but Caetano was once arrested. Actually, on this occasion, Clara's uncle Bento had acted as informer. After a quarrel with Caetano, Bento had gone to the police and told them that his brother-in-law was holding a curing session. The police raided the *terreiro,* arrested Caetano, and confiscated bottles of *banhos* and the drums. However, the officer carrying the bottles to the station was sympathetic to the Batuque; he managed to drop and break the bottles en route. Caetano was soon released for lack of evidence.

Bento never acted as informer again, but he made no secret of his hostility to the cult. When in the right mood, he composed songs ridiculing the encantados that his relatives received and then went to their houses to sing his compositions at the top of his lungs to a Batuque beat. Clara can still remember some of Bento's take-offs on the sacred songs of the Batuque.

The relatives who were cult believers and mediums did not always get along in peace and harmony either. The Batuque was apparently as marked by personal rivalry, competition, and conflict a generation ago as today, and ordinary family friction was exacerbated by doctrinal disputes. Clara remembers her uncles Danico and Caetano as always ready to "swallow" each other, i.e., to attack one another with sorcery. Quarrels over clients precipitated some of their more spectacular fights. One of them might treat a patient for months without any visible results; the client, discouraged, might then go to the other brother and be cured overnight, to the chagrin and rage of the first. Florina was also involved in family-cult squabbles and, in fact, was even arrested once in consequence. She had developed a deep antipathy for the encantado Barão de Goré, especially when the spirit possessed Caetano. On one occasion when Barão de Goré, possessing Caetano, quarreled with Florina, she picked up a machete and attacked him. She was restrained, arrested, and detained long enough to cool off.

Danico, Caetano, and Florina were not always so antagonistic, however, and Clara can remember them all in trance, sitting and conversing amicably as encantados. On one occasion, for example, Guapindaia, possessing Caetano, reminded Tapinaré, the encantado possessing Danico, of the time Tapinaré had visited hell, fallen in love with an Exu, and stayed for three years. Tapinaré's father, Seu Turquia, had finally sent Guapindaia down to hell to bring back his brother.

Clara thus grew up in an atmosphere steeped with Batuque lore. She learned the laws of the sect by listening to the encantados themselves, she is fond of pointing out, not having to rely on books or phonograph records as some leaders today seem to do. Clara feels that the encantado Japetequara, one of her mother's principal spirits, practically brought her up. Clara's birthday was the same as her mother's and, as a result, a little more of a special day in the family than were the other children's birthdays. Japetequara often possessed her mother as soon as she got up in the morning on that day. He then would call Clara over, review her conduct for the past year, lecture her, and administer needed discipline by swatting her hand with the *palmatório*. When Clara was about nine years old, Japetequara-Florina gave her older brother and herself each three *contas* (beads) to swallow. Clara could not believe that the *contas* would remain in her body and watched to see if they would be eliminated. Much later she discovered that they had found a resting place on her kneecaps. Sometimes she can feel them there between the skin and bone. One of the *contas* swallowed by Rudolfo came to rest in one of his ear lobes, and for a while the lobe was inflamed and swollen. Clara's have never given her any trouble.

In retrospect, the cult activities of her mother, uncles, and aunts provided the most interest and color to Clara's childhood.

In other respects her life was very ordinary. Like other girls she had to help with the housework, take care of her younger siblings, run errands, and go out and gather firewood. Clara remembers the Pedreira district of her childhood as "mostly woods with just a house here and there." What is now Cururu (a street built on fill and lined with houses on stilts) "was all swamp with enormous trees." Life was a little easier in those days. "There were various creeks that had good fishing, and you could gather firewood in the forest, burn it to make charcoal, and then sell the charcoal. Now there is no forest left. There are some empty lots, but they all have owners, and they are putting people in the water to live. You have to go as far as Bem Fica [a small town about twenty miles from Belém] to find any forest and even then it is all owned."

It was all quite different in Clara's childhood when the forest was all around and seemed to belong to no one but the forest spirits. Clara recalls several childhood encounters with these supernaturals. On one occasion she and one of her younger half-brothers were on an errand in the Guamá district of the city, which was then, like Pedreira, largely wooded. The children lost their bearings and were looking for someone to direct them when they saw a very small girl on the path in front of them. They called to her, asking where her mother was. The little girl said nothing, but turned off the path into the woods. They followed, thinking her house must be nearby. After they had gone deeper in the woods and become more completely lost, the little girl suddenly vanished. Then, of course, the children realized they had seen and followed a Curupira—the mischievous forest spirit that likes to trick people into losing their way.

Clara had an encounter with a more frightening forest spirit when she was about sixteen years old. She and a friend, Maria, went down to the creek that is now a street named 9 de Janeiro to take a bath. Clara has a habit of blessing herself in the water before bathing, but Maria plunged right in as soon as she had undressed. Clara waited for her friend to come up before jumping in herself, but Maria did not emerge. Finally Clara saw her head bob up a long way off, then Maria dived under again. Clara screamed for help, and neighbors came running. Caetano's *terreiro* was located nearby, and someone called him. They mannaged to pull Maria out even though she fought to stay under water. She had been possessed by the *mãe d'agua* (water mother) that owned that stretch of the creek, and Caetano had to baptize the spirit before Maria could be calmed down.

As a girl Clara attended school rather briefly and learned the rudiments of reading and writing. It was a school run by nuns, not the public school. She did not begin until she was ten years old. She remembers this because one day the teacher asked how old each child was, in order to find out who was ready for first communion. Clara did not know her own age and was sent home to ask her mother. She never completed the second year, for her mother died that year, and Clara's childhood come to an abrupt end.

In recounting the story of her mother's death, Clara still gets cold chills. Like so many other events in her life, this personal tragedy was shrouded in supernatural mystery and prefaced by ambiguous omens that no one interpreted correctly. Clara remembers it all very clearly. She was twelve years old and she, her older brother, her half-sister, and a younger half-brother were sitting in the *varanda* at two o'clock in the afternoon of the Wednesday before Easter, watching their mother "close" for Holy Week. Clara's stepfather was asleep in his hammock in the next room. Japetequara descended as Florina was performing her closing rituals and possessed her. When Clara went up to greet the spirit he told her to tell her mother that this body (her mother's) would be on the obituary list within a week. "I didn't believe it," said Clara, "and so I said nothing to my mother. This is the one regret I have, that I said nothing. But I did say to Rudolfo that we must be careful not to annoy Mama since she only had a week left."

Clara's skepticism appeared justified when the week passed without incident. The next Wednesday Florina reopened her *varanda* for a curing session, but not a single encantado descended. Puzzled and upset, Florina spent the night in front of her altar. On Saturday, the day of her next scheduled ceremony, she woke up with a terrible headache and never got out of her hammock. As the pain appeared to get worse, she sent Clara to get her uncle Caetano to come over and "bless" her head. Still later in the day, Clara asked her mother's permission to go out in the woods to collect firewood. Florina moaned something that Clara took to be dismissal. Out in the woods Clara saw a goat wandering around (possibly a spirit, since Exus take this form) and began to chase it. Then she heard her brother calling her to come back. Her mother had had an "attack" and was being taken to the hospital.

That night Dom João (one of the encantados her mother received) possessed Danico and announced that he wanted Florina buried in the Batuque costume designated as his. Early the next morning, Caetano came over and told the children their mother had died. She was thirty-five. Clara then tearfully told her uncle what Japetequara had said the week before. Caetano said it was a pity she had not mentioned it sooner, since a *trocar de cabeças* (exchange of heads) might have been arranged—either one of the *filhas* Florina was preparing in *cura* or one of her own children might have died in her place.

The sudden death of their mother left Rudolfo and Clara orphans. Until this time, Clara's stepfather had played a minor role in her life, since her mother had dominated and run the family. The stepfather now decided that both Rudolfo and Clara should leave home and go to work. Clara was sent to live with a family in another section of the city, earning her keep and a very small salary by serving as nursemaid to the family's small children. It was her first separation from her family as well as her first job.

Clara found the adjustment to the changed circumstances of her life very difficult. Her adolescence was a joyless period of hard work and harsh discipline. She stayed on the nursemaid job for over a year, then quit when the man of the house made advances to her. By this time Clara's stepfather had sold their old house, remarried, and moved to the house of his new wife. Clara moved in with them and almost at once was embroiled in quarrels with her new stepmother. One day when the stepmother was whipping one of Clara's younger half-brothers, Clara intervened to stop her. The stepmother barred the door and began to beat Clara. Neighbors heard Clara's screams, broke down the door, and took Clara to the court that dealt with the problems of juveniles. The judge officially removed her from the custody of her stepfather and made her a ward of the court. Orphans of her age were always sent out to work, and Clara was placed with another family to work as a maid. Rebellious and unhappy, she soon ran away from that job and took refuge in the woods near her childhood home. For three days she hid out while the police looked for her, then, hungry and tired of hiding, turned herself in. This time the judge turned her over to her uncle Bento, her mother's brother, making him her legal guardian.

Clara remained in the custody of her uncle for over four years, from age fifteen to nineteen. He assumed responsibility for her conduct, but he had his own family to support, and Clara was still expected to earn her own way. She found a new job as servant, but this time instead of serving in the house, she worked most of the time in the stable, taking care of the cows the family kept, going out to cut grass for them, and cleaning the stable. She received no salary, only food, lodging, and clothing, and remembers these employers as being particularly brutal; they seized on the slightest pretext to thrash her. She was so miserably unhappy at this time that she frequently went off by herself, knelt down in the grass, and prayed to Japetequara to take her away. "How I called on him to take me away from there. I called and I called. After all, he had always helped my mother, and he had raised me." But Japetequara did not answer and she continued to work as a stable girl for two years.

When Clara was seventeen one of her cousins got her a job in a button factory, and her life at once improved. A factory job meant a private life apart from her employers and much greater opportunities for socializing. She worked with many other girls during the day and had the company of her cousins at her uncle Bento's house at night. Once again she managed to attend Batuque ceremonies. Her uncle, who still disliked the cult, forbade her to go, but Clara occasionally sneaked out, leaving a log in her hammock. She danced in Caetano's ceremonies and enjoyed them very much, but at this time never felt any approximation of trance.

The button factory closed down, and Clara worked in a Brazil nut-packaging plant for a while. When laid off there, she had to return to domestic employment, finding a job as a live-in washerwoman. Since her duties were specific and limited and her employer kindhearted, Clara did not mind this job, though she still thinks of her factory employment as work of much higher status.

While at the button factory, Clara met her future husband. Nonato did not work there, but his brother was one of the foremen of the factory, and Nonato came every day to lunch with his brother. All of the factory personnel ate in the same lunchroom, and here Nonato met Clara and began courting her. Until this time Clara had never had a boy friend. Nonato continued to see Clara even after the button factory closed and even though his family objected to the liaison. "His family objected because I was black, and he was your color," Clara told us. They also felt that she was beneath them because she worked in the factory and because they suspected that she danced in *batuques;* Nonato's brother had heard her leading her co-workers in singing *doutrinas.* When Nonato told her he was very annoyed to hear that she was involved "with that *batuque* business," Clara blithely denied that she ever went near *terreiros* and suggested he ask her uncle Bento if he did not believe her. Bento, unaware that she sneaked off to *batuques,* assured Nonato that though most of the rest of the family were involved in the cult, Clara was not. The marriage—a civil, not a church ceremony—took place in December 1931.

When we became acquainted with Clara and her family in 1962, Clara was clearly the head of the household, making the decisions for the family. Her husband, then still alive, played a somewhat vaguely defined role in the background. Clara described him as "good-looking but not worth much" and complained that he was undependable and lazy and would not exert himself even to the extent of doing necessary repairs around the house. She also complained that she had to "be the man of the house" and make all of the purchases and handle all business matters. On the other hand, it seemed obvious that a role as silent and submissive wife would never have suited Clara.

Her evaluation of her husband at that time was made from the vantage point of thirty years of married life, and it is unlikely that she began married life with so low an opinion of her spouse. Nonato had become a house painter and in the beginning earned enough to support them. Clara did not have to resume working for four years after her marriage. Then she began taking in washing to supplement Nonato's earnings. By this time she already had given birth to three children and buried one of them; it died at two months of "that children's disease that they now call gastroenteritis." Also, by this time Clara had become a medium, and she and Nonato had had their first big fight.

Apparently in deference to Nonato's dislike of the Batuque, Clara did not participate in any cult activities the first year and a half of their marriage. Although she had always enjoyed Batuque ceremonies, she felt no obligation to participate; no spirit had ever claimed her, and even though many mediums in trance had whirled her in an effort to induce trance, she had never felt a thing. When Japetequara possessed Clara for the first time on July 24, 1933, another decisive turning point in her life had been reached.

Japetequara descended without being called, not in a *terreiro* but in Clara's house, a short time after she had "saved a life." On the evening of that day Clara had gone to get some *açaí* (juice of a palm tree fruit). She had to cross the 9 de Janeiro creek. A narrow boardwalk provided passage. She was returning with the *açaí* when she met a woman, carrying a baby, lingering at the creek. It was a dark night, just beginning to rain, and since the woman was unfamiliar with the crosswalk, she was waiting for someone to lead the way. Following Clara, the woman was nearly across when she lost her footing, fell into the creek, and dropped her baby. Clara threw down her jug of *açaí* and jumped into the creek to help find the infant. When she found it she held it up by the ankles to empty it of water, then hurried the woman and child to her own house to dry off and warm up before continuing on their way. Clara was ministering to the rescued child when Japetequara possessed her. Even though she had never been in trance before, she behaved correctly as a medium— i.e., the encantado sang a song identifying himself. He also asked for a cigar.

When Japetequara descended a second time, two months later at a *tambor* for Cosme and Damião at Caetano's *terreiro,* he made it clear that he intended to possess her regularly and demanded that she assume the obligations of a medium. Lacking a Batuque costume, Clara had attended wearing a street dress. "Japetequara sang," Clara recalls. "Then he said he wanted proper clothes, a skirt, and he ripped off my dress, leaving me in my slip."

When Nonato learned of what had happened he was furious. He did not want his wife to be a medium at all, much less to expose herself in public. They had an inconclusive fight. Several days later Japetequara possessed Clara at six o'clock in the evening, shortly after Nonato had come home from work. He gave Nonato a long lecture in which he warned that if Clara were not allowed to continue her "mission" he (Japetequara) would take her away, since he had brought her up and she belonged to him. The next week the encantado Guapindaia possessed Clara's uncle Caetano and came over to lecture Nonato further on the subject. Guapindaia-Caetano explained that Clara must develop as a medium and must receive her spirits in public ceremonies, not only in the privacy of the home.

After protracted quarreling, Clara and Nonato finally made a bargain. He would allow her to dance in *batuques,* and she would allow him to go out to parties and social dances. "For years whenever there was a *batuque* we both left the house—I for a *terreiro* and he for some *festa.* He refused to stay home and take care of the children—he didn't want to be on the losing end of our contract. He always went dancing; he died dancing."

The bargain did not solve all of their difficulties, however, and Clara's participation in the cult remained a source of friction between them. Clara's *batuques* always lasted longer than Nonato's *festas;* he got home first and became very irritated waiting for her, or he went to the *terreiro* to look for her and became jealous when he saw male mediums embracing his wife. He was always angry when she refused to have sexual relations with him for three days before a *batuque.* "No matter how often I explained the law of the cult to him, he always insisted that I wouldn't because I didn't want to." Although he appeared to respect Japetequara and to enjoy conversing with him when he possessed Clara in their home, Nonato always remained *meio discrente* (only half convinced) about the encantados. When Clara would light a candle for one of her spirits, he would ask brusquely what that was supposed to be for. "He had no respect for the light," complained Clara.

Once she became a medium, cult activities highlighted her life, but in other respects her life was quite routine. In an eighteen-year period, from 1932 to 1950, she gave birth to twelve children, including one pair of twins. One child, born prematurely, was stillborn. Four others did not survive the hazards of infancy. The others, four girls and three boys, had reached adulthood or adolescence when we became acquainted in 1962.

One of the children, the youngest boy (the tenth child) had been given an encantado as a godparent. This was arranged somewhat accidentally before the baby was born. At the time Clara was concerned about her ninth child, then an infant of less than a year, who was ill. Seeing a neighbor, Rita, passing by and knowing that the woman "worked" in the line of *cura,* Clara asked her to come in and give the baby a *passe.* Clara did not know that Rita was in trance at the time, possessed by the encantado Mariana. Mariana-Rita told Clara that she was pregnant again, that the baby was a boy, and that she (Mariana) would like to have it. Clara did not believe that she was pregnant again, but to humor the woman agreed to give her the baby if it were a boy. To Clara, "giving" the baby meant asking the woman to serve as godmother. At the time of the baby's baptism Rita went to the church "pure" but while there was possessed by Mariana, who took her place as godmother. Since that time Mariana, when possessing various mediums (including Clara), has shown great interest in the boy. We observed him being lectured by the encantado on a number of occasions.

In raising her children, Clara had some help from other women. During the early years of her marriage her half-sister, Clorinda, lived with them. By the time Clorinda married and left, Clara's oldest child, a daughter, was able to help with the younger children. In 1954 Isabel, a medium from São Luís, came to Clara's home as a visitor and is still there as an adopted member of the family. Isabel is not related to Clara and did not know her before coming to Belém, but she found life with Clara's family so congenial that she gave up any thought of returning to her own relatives in São Luís. For her part, Clara stated that Isabel had been a great help to her. She not only contributed to household expenses from her salary as cleaning woman in a school, but also helped with the housework and the care of the younger children. As Clara's own children grew up and were able to care for themselves, new children had been added to the household. In 1965 Clara was rearing two small boys who had been given to her by their mother and had also assumed responsibility for the four illegitimate children of her second oldest daughter. Although Clara spoke occasionally (not very convincingly) of throwing out her promiscuous daughter, she had no intention of parting with her grandchildren.

While all of her own children were young, Clara had little time for Batuque activities, since most of the time not spent in running the household was taken up with washing and ironing clothes for others. As the size of their family increased, Clara's earnings as washerwoman were absolutely essential. Nonato was no hustler and, although he was never out of work for any extended period, employment as a painter did fluctuate and generally halted completely during rainy periods.

Clara's meager earnings had to be stretched to meet her obligations to her encantados. She attended ceremonies at her uncle Caetano's *terreiro* whenever she could manage to get away. She never underwent any type of initiation beyond having her head "washed" by Caetano, or rather by Dom José possessing Caetano. Clara feels that she needed no other preparation to be a medium since her mother had already given her *contas,* and Japetequara himself left prescriptions for appropriate baths of purification.

A few years after receiving Japetequara, Clara was possessed by another of her mother's encantados, Dom João. On that occasion she was sitting in the audience at a ceremony. Caetano had prescribed pink costumes for that particular *batuque,* and she had not been able to afford one. Suddenly she heard a noise as though the roof of the pavilion were falling. She leaned forward and put her hands over her head to shield herself from falling timbers. She felt a great weight press down on the nape of her neck and lost consciousness. When she came to, she was seated in the *terreiro*'s chapel and was told the Dom João had descended and sung at once. Her shoulders ached for some time afterward. They still do after she is possessed by Dom João, who is obviously a very large and heavy encantado. Since Dom João was a noble, Caetano decided that he, not Japetequara, must be Clara's *senhor.* Japetequara was very serious and dignified, but he was an Indian and of lower rank than Dom João.

Clara concurred with this reasoning; Dom João had been her mother's *chefe* also. Nevertheless she continued to receive Japetequara much more frequently than Dom João, who only came once or twice a year, and it was Japetequara who maintained a constant surveillance of her conduct and well-being.

Both Dom João and Japetequara were very serious spirits; neither drank nor engaged in the horseplay that seemed to delight many other encantados. Clara had no carouser spirit until she received Mariana in 1943, ten years after she had begun her career as medium. With the arrival of Mariana, who was very insistent about attending ceremonies, Clara became more active in the cult.

Her uncle Caetano died in 1946. Her other *pai de santo* uncle, Danico, had died some years previously. Caetano's *terreiro* was closed for the traditional year of mourning; then it was reopened by Rudolfo, Clara's older brother. Rudolfo was an unusual figure in the Batuque—a man who assumed a leadership role without ever experiencing trance. But he, like his sister, had been fascinated with the cult ever since childhood. When he was a teen-ager, Rudolfo began to serve as drummer and, as such, learned all of the *doutrinas* of the Batuque. Just by hanging around the *terreiros* of his uncles, he acquired as thorough a knowledge of cult lore and ritual as any medium. He knew how to send away the Exus, what offerings to place before the *terreiro*'s altar, how to open and close ceremonies, how to direct *obrigações* such as the *afurá* ceremony. After he reopened Caetano's *terreiro,* Rudolfo even dabbled in curing, prescribing remedies by "intuition." He did not rely on curing for financial support, however. He was married, had a family to support, and kept his full time job as dock worker. Nevertheless he found the time, with Clara's assistance and the support of many of his deceased uncle's mediums, to fete some of the more important Batuque spirits. Clara was always ready to lead the singing and dancing or direct any ritual that required a medium in trance. She in effect became her brother's *mãe pequena.*

Clara's experience of running a *terreiro* did not last long. Five years after he had assumed the role of cult leader, Rudolfo died. He was ill for some time before his death, and the family was given supernatural warning of the probable outcome of his illness. At a spiritualist séance held in the neighborhood, the spirit of their uncle Caetano came back to earth and took possession of a medium. Caetano warned that Rudolfo would soon die, and he asked that when this occurred, Caetano's stone for Oxalá, which was still in the chapel of the *terreiro,* be thrown into the Bay of Guajará. This was done. Since Clara could not afford to run the *terreiro* by herself, it was closed and the lot and buildings sold.

The year before the death of Rudolfo, Clara's younger half-brother Laurinho had died under circumstances suggesting supernatural intervention. Laurinho, like Rudolfo, had begun serving as drummer when still a teen-ager. At the age of eighteen, while beating the drum at a ceremony, he was possessed by the encantado Mariana. Still later Dom João also claimed him as a *filho.* Unlike Clara, Laurinho never received Japetequara, the other major encantado of their mother.

Laurinho was apparently an insouciant, happy-go-lucky individual, a philanderer who "left me many nephews and nieces." He was careless about obeying ritual law and consequently attracted the displeasure of his encantados. "Laurinho received many thrashings from the encantados," Clara recalled. "There are many kinds of punishment; there is unemployment, sickness. He passed through all of that." He did not mend his ways, however, and finally, Clara believes, the encantado Mariana killed him. The offense that provoked Mariana to such drastic action was Laurinho's meddling in curing. Laurinho was interested in being prepared in this line and became the regular assistant of the *pai de santo* Martins. While Laurinho was still learning the skills of curer, Martins went off on an extended visit to Manaus. In his absence Laurinho borrowed his curing paraphernalia and took off on his own tour of the interior, "deceiving the backwoodsmen and making money." In doing this, he committed offenses that Mariana would not tolerate: he drank rum before entering trance, he pretended to be possessed, and he prescribed remedies that he had made up himself in the name of Mariana and other encantados. Laurinho was returning home one morning after "working" in *cura* the entire night, when his canoe tipped over and he drowned. It seemed clear that Mariana was responsible.

Clara also began working in the line of curing shortly after she began receiving Mariana, but in a much more limited way than that attempted by Laurinho. She began holding *chamadas* once every two weeks, in response, she says, to the direct in structions of Japetequara, "who descended and ordered that I prepare my altar, light a candle, and receive the spirits as mother did." At these *chamadas* in her home a number of new spirits began to put in an appearance: José Tupinambá, Goiabeira, Princesa Flora, Guapindaia, and an unidentified child spirit.

As a result of her experience in running her brother's *terreiro,* Clara's reputation for knowledge of ritual and ability to lead ceremonies was securely established. Not only was she personally invited to attend ceremonies in *terreiros* throughout the city, but clients from various parts of the city began to seek her out. Clara insists that Japetequara has thus far refused to give her permission to charge for the *passes* and advice that she dispenses during *chamadas.* "One must practice charity," Clara remarked, without much enthusiasm. "One just has to bear it until the encantados give permission to charge a fee. I myself have no luck at all." She told a story to illustrate the personal costs of practicing charity. At one of her *chamadas* a man appeared who was unemployed and very depressed. Mariana advised him to take a series of nine *banhos,* starting the next Tuesday. He was to come to Clara's house each day to get the infusion for that day. Clara assumed that the man would purchase the necessary herbs and bring them to her house to prepare or would give her the money to buy what was needed. But, as the day approached and he did not appear with either the herbs or the money, she was inclined to forget the whole thing. On Monday Clara was paid for a washing and went down to the Ver-o-pêso market to buy fish. While she was standing in line to get her fish, Mariana possessed her, left the fish stall, took her to another part of the market and purchased all of the herbs she had prescribed for the client's *banhos.* Mariana then put Clara back in the fish line and left her. As Clara returned to her senses, the fish vendor was asking how many kilos she wanted. She stood there with her arms full of herbs and not enough money left to buy fish. When the client arrived the next day, his *banho* was ready, as it was on the succeeding eight days. The man never gave Clara a cent or even said thank you.

Most clients are not that ungrateful, however, and voluntarily make donations to Clara or to her encantados. In addition, although Japetequara has refused to let Clara charge for *passes* and consultations, Mariana shamelessly asks clients for presents. Thus, in spite of her refusal to charge, Clara's *chamadas* have often brought welcome additions to her income.

In one way or another, ever since he first possessed her, Clara credits Japetequara with looking after her. She has often been at wit's end to meet expenses and obtain essentials, but Japetequara has always turned up something, and no one in the house has ever had to go hungry for long. In addition, he takes charge of her in other ways. When she is nervous and upset he sometimes possesses her to calm her down, as he did the time her altar caught on fire. When she wanted to accompany her friend Isabel on a trip to São Luís, Japetequara motivated one prosperous client to give her money for the passage to Maranhão, and after she was stranded there with no money, moved another cult member to send her money for a return passage.

Whenever Clara disobeys or disregards ritual law, Japetequara is quick to discipline her. If she fails to place the offerings under the altar at the required times, for example, or refuses to go to a *batuque* that Japetequara has indicated he wants to attend, or if she eats alligator meat (taboo to her because Japetequara is an alligator) or any bird of the parrot family (taboo because Mariana is a macaw) Japetequara is likely to punish her either by possessing her and throwing her down violently or by refusing to come at all until she makes amends. He usually sends another encantado, José Tupinambá, to administer discipline in the traditional form of possessing her and forcing her to kneel and beat the floor with her hands and arms. After it is over and she is bruised and aching, Japetequara possesses her and consoles her.

José Tupinambá, with Japetequara's approval, administers such punishment for various sins and personal shortcomings as well as for infractions of ritual law. Clara admits that she has many faults. She used to like to drink too much, for example, and sometimes she associates with "bad" companions, gossips too much, or uses "bad" language. She deserves chastisement for such faults and Japetequara and José Tupinambá see to it that she gets it. Sometimes even her *farrista,* Mariana, takes a hand in keeping Clara in line, by possessing her and then confessing to the family whatever misdeeds Clara is trying to conceal from them. For example, one of Clara's former weaknesses was squandering money playing *jôgo do bicho*—a type of numbers game. One day Clara wanted to bet because she had a strong hunch about some animal-number combination, but she had no money. Her husband had a large and beautiful rooster that he had raised from a chick and was very proud of. Determined to bet on her hunch, Clara sold her husband's rooster, meaning to buy it back after she won. Unfortunately, *o bicho não deu* (the animal-number combination she bet on did not win). When it was time for her husband to come home, Clara picked up a machete and went out into the street and began hacking here and there in the tall grass. Nonato appeared and asked what in the world she was up to now. She said she couldn't imagine what had happened to his rooster, she hadn't seen it for hours, perhaps it was sick or had died; she was looking for its body. Nonato joined in the futile search, then sat around for a long time brooding over the loss of his rooster, hypothesizing that some thief had taken it. Years later, Mariana, possessing Clara at one of her *chamadas,* turned to Nonato and said, "Remember that beautiful rooster you used to have?" She then told him exactly what Clara had done with it. "I can never keep anything secret," Clara said. "She [Mariana] always finds out and sooner or later tells everyone."

The encantado Mariana herself, however, is far from being a very moral or proper being. On the contrary, she is impulsive, self-indulgent, completely hedonistic, and the encantado's improper speech, rudeness, and generally immoderate conduct repeatedly cause Clara embarrassment. For example, Mariana not only continually demands new clothes from clients, but also selfishly resists sharing them with other spirits; on occasion she unfastens Clara's skirts at ceremonies so that they fall off her as Mariana takes her leave. As far as Clara is concerned, Mariana's worst fault is her fondness for drink. Formerly she began looking for something to drink as soon as she possessed Clara and, though she preferred *cachaça,* would drink anything she could find. On one occasion when she possessed Clara at home, demanded something to drink, and Nonato refused to provide anything, Mariana drank some gasoline. Such excesses of course left Clara quite sick and, in addition, increased family discord, since Nonato hated Mariana especially for her drinking.

Clara felt that she was at an impasse. Japetequara and José Tupinambá might discipline her when she drank, but neither had any authority over Mariana and could not intervene to stop Mariana's use of Clara's body for excessive tippling. Clara finally consulted her chief encantado, Dom João, when he possessed a friend of hers. She told Dom João that she did not want to receive Mariana any more. Mariana not only drank too much and had a bad reputation, but she had killed Clara's brother. Dom João told Clara to take a bottle of *guaraná*, pour out one half of it into a glass and set the glass under her altar. The half-empty bottle should be filled with *dendê* oil and honey and the cap replaced. She should then send her husband at night to throw the bottle into the Bay of Guajará, after first calling Mariana's name three times.

Clara prepared the bottle as instructed, but, with his usual non-co-operation, Nonato refused to take it down to the bay. Clara lit a large candle that would burn before her altar until she was able to return, wrapped up her bottle, and took a bus downtown. "There was a strong wind blowing as I came near the shore," she recalls. "I called her. I asked in the name of Dom João, Oxalá, and all the other encantados that she come as a young lady. Then I threw the bottle. Just as it hit the water, Mariana seized me, took me back home, and promised never to drink anything stronger than Gancia [a sweet vermouth] when possessing me." Except for occasional backsliding, Mariana has kept her promise and is in general much less wild when possessing Clara today than she used to be.

Clara believes that Mariana killed her brother; she believes that Japetequara killed her husband. Again there were mysterious signs and portents preceding his death in May 1963. Both Japetequara and Mariana issued warnings, but since Nonato was not in the least sick, no one in the family got the message. Clara and Isabel went to a ceremony at the *terreiro* of Dona Marina two days before Nonato died. Japetequara descended, possessed

Clara, wept, and acted so out of character that Isabel says she did not recognize him. He sang a new song that no one had heard before:

Eu atirei minha flecha	*I shot my arrow*
E não errei a pontaria.	*And did not miss my target.*
Eu sou aquêle môço	*I am that young man*
Lá da Barra de Ararí.	*From the Barra de Ararí.*
Lagoa grande secou,	*The large lake dried up,*
Todos morreram e não eu.	*All died and I did not.*

Then he abruptly left. Not a single Curupira descended, and usually a number of them come when Japetequara does. Mariana possessed Clara later on and remarked that she had heard that the "Old Man" was weeping. She added that Clara would have a surprise the next day. Since the next day was Mother's Day, Clara assumed that this meant that her oldest son, who lives in Amapá, was sending her some money.

In spite of these supernatural messages, nothing much happened the next day. The ceremony was a two-day affair and Isabel stayed over at the *terreiro*. Clara, however, went home early in the morning of May 12 to prepare dinner for her husband. Nonato, as usual, grumbled over the fact that she was going back to the *terreiro* that evening. He had no party to go to himself, but was planning on going to one the next night. The rest of the day passed without incident.

The last time Clara saw her husband alive was when he left for his *festa* the next evening. He dropped dead while dancing at the party. Clara is convinced that Japetequara killed him because he had refused to help Clara meet her obligations to the encantados. Just the year before one wall of the house was falling down when the time came for Clara to hold her annual *ladainha* for Japetequara's saint, to mark the anniversary of Japetequara's first possession of her. Nonato refused to undertake the necessary repairs, saying he saw no sense in fixing up the house and painting everything just so she could pray. For over thirty years Japetequara had been patient and tried to educate Nonato but had finally decided that he was a hopeless case.

The sudden death of Nonato removed the principal family breadwinner, but in 1965 Clara reported that the family had not suffered particularly. In fact, she gave the impression that her life had become easier since her husband's death. She was doing only two washings a week, whereas before Nonato died she had always done four or five. Her improved financial situation was due to increased help from her children.

In reviewing her life for our benefit, Clara neither indulged in much self-pity nor in self-recrimination over lost opportunities. On the contrary, she seemed to find satisfaction in the story of her life, to feel that, on the whole, she had not done so badly. Of course, it had all been and still was an uphill and difficult struggle, but so was life for most of the women that she knew. And she had achieved certain things that many others never achieved. She owned her own home. She had traveled, once to São Luís via steamship and once by plane to Amapá to visit her son and his family. She had achieved a position of some eminence in Batuque circles; throughout the city she was known and respected for her knowledge of ritual and her skill as a medium. Of course, there were certain costs that went with the deference generally shown her—costs in terms of the jealousy and envy of less successful mediums. Clara appears to accept such hostility as proof of her own superiority. In the conflict-ridden world of the Batuque, envy and antagonism are taken for granted. Clara is fully prepared to give as good as she gets. If one of her favorite expressions is "There are many eyes watching me," another is "He (or she) doesn't know a thing." She is also fond of characterizing most cult leaders as creatures "of yesterday" in contrast to her own "fifty years of Mina."

In most matters Clara gives the impression of definitely knowing her own mind, but there are two things that she is ambivalent about. For one, she is not sure whether or not she would like a *terreiro* of her own. Sometimes she is so exasperated by the incorrect way things are done in the *terreiros* she frequents that she dreams of opening her own center, but at other times she recognizes that the problems and costs of even holding sessions in her *varanda* would probably be too much for her.

Another thing Clara is uncertain about is whether or not she wants her children to become mediums. None of her seven children has thus far shown any mediumistic ability, although her oldest daughter is married to a curer, and all of the children regularly attend ceremonies. At present, Clara is the only member of the entire family who is a medium. None of her nieces, nephews, or cousins became actively involved in the cult. Once a neighbor came running to get Clara with a report that one of Clara's cousins was in trance. Clara hurried over to talk to the spirit possessing her cousin. The spirit claimed to be Guapindaia, but Clara saw at once that it was really the soul of her uncle Bento, come back to earth and pretending to be one of the encantados that he had never believed in. This cousin never entered trance again, nor did her uncle's spirit ever return.

Clara thinks that one or two of her four daughters will sooner or later become a medium and perhaps receive the same encantados that she receives. "If I am the daughter of Dom João, they are his granddaughters and he will decide when they will receive." She thinks the next to the youngest daughter was on the verge of entering trance several years ago when she was only twelve. On that occasion, Clara intervened to stop a medium in trance from whirling her daughter, since she felt the girl was too young to begin with the Batuque. Sometimes Clara says that she would not care if none of her children become active in the cult, "because it is a heavy cross to bear." On the other hand, she insists that only the aid of the encantados has kept her going and enabled her to rear her family.

Clara does not give much thought to the afterlife. She believes that her soul will be taken to the *encantaria* of Japetequara or perhaps to that of Dom João. She does not look forward to this prospect, however. "When I am tired and have trouble with the family," Clara said, "Japetequara comes and wants to take me away. But I don't want to go. It's ugly there, there is no food, it's like a prison." Clara knows what an *encantaria* is like because she once paid a brief visit to the *encantaria* of Rompe Mato. She was attending a curing session when Rompe Mato, possessing the curer, offered to take anyone who wanted to go for a brief visit to his *encantaria*. She volunteered. He put his hand on her head and her body fell asleep. Her spirit flew away and entered Rompe Mato's virgin forest. At first she thought it was just like entering her own back yard, but then she saw that it was a forest with enormous trees, all of which had brightly colored leaves. The colors may have been pretty, but the forest was absolutely empty, still, devoid of life, and Clara was frightened. Suddenly she spotted an enormous alligator staring at her, and she woke up from fright. Later she realized that the alligator was really Japetequara, who had come to take her soul back to the curing session.

To the outsider, Clara's world may seem dreary and drab, and it is obviously short on food, health, and comfort. But for Clara it is a world that has an unseen supernatural dimension of extraordinary richness and dramatic interest to offset the visible bleakness of poverty. It is a difficult world, but with the help of her encantados, she is determined to make the best of it. Her religion is vague on life after death, but it is very clear on how to continue living here and now.

Glossary

abatá: The drum used in Batuque ceremonies.

abatazeiro: Batuque drummer.

afurá: A slightly fermented drink made of coconut milk, rice flour, and sugar. It is regarded as a sacred food and, on occasion, is served with great solemnity to all participants in a *batuque.*

amasí or *amasin:* A herbal infusion that is poured over the head of a medium by a cult leader in rites of purification or of development.

arara: The macaw, a bird of the parrot family. The tail feathers of the scarlet macaw are used in Batuque curing.

atuado: adj. Possessed by a spirit.

atuar-se: v. To become possessed.

banho: Any infusion of herbs or other plant material, designed to be poured over the body. The intent is to heal, purify, or bring success in some undertaking.

barraca: A small house, usually with earthen walls and thatched roof.

batuque: The principal public ceremony of the Batuque religion. *Syn.: tambor.*

branco: 1. An encantado with high status. *Syn.: orixá, senhor, vodun.* 2. Any person who is considered to be upper class. 3. Any "white," a person who appears to be primarily of European ancestry.

caboclo: 1. An Indian spirit. 2. Any lower-status encantado. 3. An Indian or an uneducated backwoodsman of mixed ancestry.

cachaça: Brazilian rum, the preferred beverage of most carouser spirits. Also used extensively as an offering.

camarinha: A small room at a cult center in which novices are isolated as part of the initiation rites.

Candomblé: The Afro-Brazilian sect of Bahia, especially the more conservative Yoruban *terreiros* of Salvador. The less conservative Bahian sects are usually termed "Candomblé de caboclo."

carnaval: Brazil's major holiday period—the festivities (usually three or four days) prior to Ash Wednesday, the beginning of Lent.

Casa das Minas: An exclusive and conservative sect in São Luís, the most Dahomean of any of the Afro-Brazilian sects.

Catimbó: A religious sect of the northeastern states—Piauí, Ceará, Rio Grande do Norte, Paraíba. Primarily of European and Amerindian origin, the sect emphasizes curing rituals.

chamada: A curing ceremony in which a medium's principal encantado is called to grant consultations to clients.

chefe: The chief or principal spirit received by a medium. *Syn.: dono* (owner), *senhor* (lord).

cheque-cheque: An elongated metal cylinder, partially filled with lead shot; one of the musical instruments of the Batuque. *Syn.: ganzá.*

conta: A small bead given by some Batuque leaders to their mediums. The bead is swallowed and is believed to remain permanently somewhere in the body.

contra-guia: A male medium who holds the position of second-in-command at a cult center.

cuia: A bowl made from a half-gourd. A common kitchen utensil in the Amazon area, but also believed to be the drinking bowl preferred by the encantados.

cura: "Curing," rituals directed toward the resolution of various types of problems, including illness, through an appeal to the encantados. Specifically, the lengthiest and most involved of the curing rituals.

curandeiro: The independent curer who works alone or with an assistant. Also, any leader with a very limited following.

defumação: A fumigation produced by placing a mixture of dried herbs, leaves, and incense over burning charcoal. The smoke is believed to purify the premises. Such fumigations are regularly carried out before a ceremony or curing ritual begins and are often repeated at intervals while the ceremony is in progress.

dendê: The African oil palm (*Elaeis guineensis*), which is also grown in Brazil. The oil extracted from the fruit is regarded as one of the favorite foods of the encantados.

despacho: 1. An offering placed before the Exu shrine at a cult center before ceremonies begin, intended to induce the Exus to stay away from the ceremony. 2. An offering to the Exus designed to incite the demons to attack someone; left at street intersections, in cemeteries, or on the doorstep of the intended victim.

Dona: Mrs. or Miss, a term of address.

doutrina: A song designed to call or to salute an encantado or to identify a possessing spirit.

encantado: The most important supernaturals in the Batuque; any of a special category of spirits who are believed to possess human beings. *Syn.: guia, invisivel, santo.*

encantaria: The dwelling place of an encantado family or tribe, located under the earth or sea or in the depths of virgin forest.

espada: A ritual scarf, the color of which is believed to be pleasing to a specific encantado; it is thrown over a medium's shoulders when he is in trance.

farrista: A carouser spirit, an encantado who likes to drink and be merry.

feiticeiro: Sorcerer.

feitiço: Sorcery.

feito: adj. "Made," i.e., a medium who has gone through the full initiation ritual.

festa: 1. A major ceremony in honor of an encantado, usually including at least two public ceremonies on successive nights. 2. Any religious or secular celebration; a festival.

figa: A good luck amulet, usually made of wood or metal, shaped as a clenched human fist with the thumb protruding between the index and the middle fingers. As a charm to ward off evil, the *figa* is popular throughout Brazil—it is not limited to the Afro-Brazilian cults.

filha de santo: A female medium. *Syn.: média.*

filho de santo: A male medium. *Syn.: médium.*

ganzá: An elongated metal cylinder, partially filled with lead shot; one of the musical instruments of the Batuque. *Syn.: cheque-cheque.*

guaraná: A soft drink flavored with an extract of the *guaraná* fruit, the preferred drink of child spirits.

guia: Literally, "guide." *Syn.:* encantado, *invisivel, santo.*

invisivel: Literally, "invisible." Syn.: encantado, *guia, santo.*

jogada: 1. The throwing down of a medium by his encantado when the spirit is possessing or taking leave of the medium; a form of corporal punishment administered by encantados. 2. The state of coma that mediums occasionally enter after a trance experience; interpreted as another form of punishment administered by encantados.

jurema: 1. Two trees of the mimosa family that are regarded as sacred trees for a group of encantados. The bark and leaves of the *jurema branca* (*Pithecolobium diversifolium Bent.*) and, less frequently, the *jurema preta* (*Mimosa nigra Hub.*) are used in ritual baths and teas. 2. The name of an *encantaria* inhabited by a group of encantados called the "Linha de Jurema."

Kardecismo: A Brazilian spiritualist movement based on the writings of Allan Kardec.

ladainha: A prayer service to the saints, often held before a *batuque* begins.

macumba: The popular term for any Afro-Brazilian religion anywhere in Brazil; originally, the Afro-Brazilian sect found in Rio de Janeiro.

macumbeiro: The term used by outsiders for a member of any Afro-Brazilian sect.

mãe de santo: Female Batuque leader.

mãe pequena: A female medium who holds the position of second-in-command at a cult center.

maracá: A rattle made from a gourd. A large *maracá* is used as a musical instrument during public ceremonies and a much smaller version is used in curing rituals.

matança: The sacrifice of an animal to one of the encantados.

mesa de espiritismo: A spiritualist séance.

Mina-Nagô: The Afro-Brazilian sect that was brought to Belém from São Luís; also called simply "Mina" or simply "Nagô."

moreno: 1. Any person with moderately dark skin color. 2. A brunette.

obrigação: An "obligation," i.e., any food, drink, or ritual act that a medium owes to his encantado.

ogan: The general caretaker of a cult center.

orixá: 1. An encantado with high status. *Syn.: branco, senhor, vodun.* 2. The Yoruban term for deity.

pai de santo: Male Batuque leader.

pajé: Amazonian shaman, primarily a curer.

pajelança: Amazonian shamanism.

passagem: A curing ritual during which the curer invites his spirits to "pass through" or possess him, even though there may be no patients present.

passe: The laying-on of hands by a medium, accompanied by a prayer, with the intention of driving away disease or evil influences from the body of the recipient.

pegí: Altar.

ponto: 1. Any design drawn on the wall or floor of a cult center or any arrangement of sacred objects that has ritual significance. 2. Infrequently, a synonym for *doutrina*.

preto: Any "black," a person who appears to be primarily of African ancestry.

puro: Not in trance, in a "pure" or unpossessed state.

santo: 1. A Christian saint. 2. A synonym for encantado, *guia, invisivel*.

seara: A cult center in which no musical instruments are used during ceremonies. *Syn.: tenda*.

senhor: 1. The chief spirit received by a Batuque medium. *Syn.: chefe, dono*. 2. Any encantado that has high status. *Syn.: branco, orixá, vodun*. 3. Mr., a term of address.

sessão: One type of Batuque curing ceremony, during which a cult leader and a number of his mediums each receive their principal encantados in order to treat patients.

sombriado: The condition of being "shaded" by an encantado; a state of superficial or partial trance.

tambor: 1. The principal public ceremony of the Batuque. *Syn.: batuque*. 2. A drum.

tambor de chôro: A mourning ceremony held in a cult center after the death of one of its members.

tauari: The bark of the Amazonian tree of the same name, used as a wrapper for the cigarettes that curers smoke while treating patients.

tenda: A cult center in which no musical instruments are used during ceremonies. *Syn.: seara*.

terreiro: A cult center; specifically, the pavilion in which the ceremonies are held.

toalha: A large, white, embroidered shawl that is placed around the shoulders or waist of a medium possessed by a high-ranking encantado.

trabalho: A work of black magic, sorcery.

trocar de cabeças: An "exchange of heads"; the death of a follower in place of the leader, a substitution believed to be carried out by leaders who have been forewarned of their own imminent death.

Umbanda: An Afro-Brazilian sect that originated in Rio de Janeiro in the 1920s, representing a fusion of *macumba* with spiritualism. Today found in urban areas throughout Brazil.

varanda: A large room toward the rear of the house, ordinarily used as a dining-family room and often converted into a ceremonial room by the beginning leader.

vodun: 1. An encantado with high status. *Syn.: branco, orixá, senhor.* 2. The Dahomean term for deity.

Xangô: 1. A high-ranking spirit (also called Badé) who is believed to have control over thunderstorms and is credited with sending the sacred stones that are used by encantados as "seats" in *terreiros* and the homes of mediums. 2. The Afro-Brazilian sect of Pernambuco and Alagoas.

Bibliography

Alvarenga, Oneyda.
  1948. *Tambor de Mina e de Crioulo*. Registros sonoros de folclore musical brasileiro, vol. 2. São Paulo: Discoteca Publica Municipal.
  1950a. *Babassuê*. Registros sonoros de folclore musical brasileiro, vol. 4. São Paulo: Discoteca Publica Municipal.
  1950b. *Música popular brasileira*. Rio de Janeiro: Globo.
Andrade, Mario de.
  1963. *Música de feitiçaria no Brasil*. São Paulo: Martins.
Araújo, Alceu Maynard.
  1959. "A congada nasceu em Roncesvales." *Revista do Arquivo,* no. 163, Divisão do Arquivo Histórico, Prefeitura do Municipio de São Paulo.
Bastide, Roger.
  1952. "Le Batuque de Porto Alegre." In *Acculturation in the Americas, Proceedings and Selected Papers of the 29th International Congress of Americanists,* ed. by Sol Tax, vol. 2, pp. 195–206. Chicago: University of Chicago Press.
  1960. *Les religions africaines au Brésil: vers une sociologie des interpénétrations de civilisations.* Paris: Presses Universitaires de France.
  1961. *O Candomblé da Bahia.* Trans. by Maria Isaura Pereira de Queiroz. São Paulo: Companhïa Editora Nacional.
Bettencourt, Gastão de.
  1947. *Os três santos de junho no folclore brasílico.* Rio de Janeiro: Agir.

382   BIBLIOGRAPHY

Biblioteca Nacional.
   1948. *Livro Grosso do Maranhão*. Vols. 66–67 of *Anais da Biblioteca Nacional*. Rio de Janeiro.
Bibliotheca e Archivo Publico do Pará.
   1902–26. "Correspondência dos governadores do Pará com a metrópole." In vols. 2–10 of *Annaes da Bibliotheca e Archivo Publico do Pará*. Belém.
Bourguignon, Erika.
   1965. "The Self, the Behavioral Environment, and the Theory of Spirit Possession." In *Context and Meaning in Cultural Anthropology*, ed. by Melford E. Spiro, pp. 39–60. New York: Free Press.
   1968. "World Distribution and Patterns of Possession States." In *Trance and Possession States*, ed. by Raymond Prince, pp. 3–34. *Proceedings, Second Annual Conference of R. M. Bucke Memorial Society* (1966). Montreal.
Boxer, Charles Ralph.
   1962. *The Golden Age of Brazil, 1695–1750*. Berkeley and Los Angeles: University of California Press.
Calmon, Pedro.
   1959–61. *História do Brasil*. 7 vols. Rio de Janeiro: Olimpio.
Camargo, Candido Procopio Ferreira de.
   1961. *Kardecismo e Umbanda: uma interpretação sociológica*. São Paulo: Pioneira.
Carneiro, Edison.
   1937. *Negros Bantús*. Rio de Janeiro: Civilização Brasileira.
   1940. "The Structure of African Cults in Bahia." *Journal of American Folklore*, 53:271–78.
   1961. *Candomblés da Bahia*. 3rd ed. Rio de Janeiro: Conquista.
Cascudo, Luís da Câmara.
   1951. *Meleagro: depoimento e pesquisa sôbre a magia branca no Brasil*. Rio de Janeiro: Agir.
   1956. *Antologia do folclore brasileiro*. 2nd ed. São Paulo: Martins.
   1962. *Dicionário do folclore brasileiro*. 2nd ed. Rio de Janeiro: Instituto Nacional do Livro.
Duarte, Ophir Martins.
   1960–61. "O desenvolvimento das religiões afro-brasileiras em Belém." In *Boletim da Associação Atlética Banco do Brasil*, vol. 1, no. 3. Belém.
Eduardo, Octavio da Costa.
   1948. *The Negro in Northern Brazil: A Study in Acculturation*. Monographs of the American Ethnological Society, no. 15. Reprint. Seattle: University of Washington Press, 1966.

Erasmus, Charles J.
1961. *Man Takes Control: Cultural Development and American Aid.* Minneapolis: University of Minnesota Press.
Figueiredo, Napoleão and Anaíza Vergolina e Silva.
1967. "Alguns elementos novos para o estudo dos batuques de Belém." In *Atas do simpósio sôbre a biota amazônica,* vol. 2, pp. 101–22. Belém.
Fontenelle, Aluizio.
1953. *A Umbanda através dos séculos.* Rio de Janeiro: Organização Simões.
Foster, George M.
1961. "The Dyadic Contract: A Model of the Social Structure of a Mexican Peasant Village." *American Anthropologist,* 63:1173–92.
1963. "The Dyadic Contract in Tzintzuntzan, II: Patron-Client Relationship." *American Anthropologist,* 65:1280–94.
Furtado, Celso.
1963. *The Economic Growth of Brazil.* Trans. by Ricardo W. de Aguiar and Eric Charles Drysdale. Berkeley and Los Angeles: University of California Press.
Galvão, Eduardo.
1955. *Santos e visagens.* São Paulo: Companhia Editora Nacional.
Gill, Merton M., and Margaret Brenman.
1959. *Hypnosis and Related States: Psychoanalytic Studies in Regression.* New York: International Universities Press.
Herskovits, Melville J.
1937. "African Gods and Catholic Saints in New World Religious Belief." *American Anthropologist,* 39:635–43.
1943a. "The Southernmost Outposts of New World Africanisms." *American Anthropologist,* 45:495–510.
1943b. "The Negro in Bahia, Brazil: A Problem in Method." *American Sociological Review,* 8:394–404.
1944. "Drums and Drummers in Afrobrazilian Cult Life." *Musical Quarterly,* 30:477–92.
1945. "Problem, Method and Theory in Afroamerican Studies." *Afroamerica,* 1:5–24. Mexico City.
1948. *Man and His Works.* New York: Knopf.
1952. "Some Psychological Implications of Afroamerican Studies." In *Acculturation in the Americas, Proceedings and Selected Papers of the 29th International Congress of Americanists,* ed. by Sol Tax, vol. 2, pp. 152–60. Chicago: University of Chicago Press.
1953. "The Panan, an Afrobahian Rite of Transition." *Memoires,*

Institut Français d'Afrique Noire, no. 27, pp. 133–40. Dakar, Senegal.

1955. "The Social Organization of the Candomblé." In *Proceedings of the 31st International Congress of Americanists (1954)*, vol. 1, pp. 505–32. São Paulo.

1958. "Some Economic Aspects of the Afrobahian Candomblé." In *Miscellanea Paul Rivet, Octogenario Dicata,* vol. 2, pp. 227–47. International Congress of Americanists. Mexico City: Universidad Nacional Autónoma de México.

Herskovits, Melville J., and Frances S.

1933. *An Outline of Dahomean Religious Belief.* Memoirs of the American Anthropological Association, no. 41. Menasha, Wisconsin.

1943. "The Negroes in Brazil." *Yale Review,* 32:263–79.

Hilgard, Ernest L.

1965. *Hypnotic Susceptibility.* New York: Harcourt, Brace & World.

Instituto Brasileiro de Geografia e Estatística.

1957. *Enciclopédia dos municípios brasileiros,* vol. 14: *Amazonas, Pará.* Rio de Janeiro.

1969. *Anuário estatístico do Brasil.* Rio de Janeiro.

Kloppenburg, Boaventura.

1961. *A Umbanda no Brasil: orientação para os católicos.* Petrópolis: Editora Vozes Limitada.

Landes, Ruth.

1947. *The City of Women.* New York: Macmillan.

Leacock, Seth.

1964a. "Ceremonial Drinking in an Afro-Brazilian Cult." *American Anthropologist,* 66:344–54.

1964b. "Fun-Loving Deities in an Afro-Brazilian Cult." *Anthropological Quarterly,* 37:94–109.

Le Cron, Leslie M.

1961. *Techniques of Hypnotherapy.* New York: Julian Press.

Lieban, Richard W.

1967. *Cebuano Sorcery: Malign Magic in the Philippines.* Berkeley and Los Angeles: University of California Press.

London, Perry.

1967. "The Induction of Hypnosis." In *Handbook of Clinical and Experimental Hypnosis,* ed. by Jesse E. Gordon, pp. 44–79. New York: Macmillan.

Marcuse, F. L.

1959. *Hypnosis: Fact and Fiction.* Baltimore: Penguin Books.

Monteiro, Duglas Teixeira.
1955. "A Macumba de Vitória." In *Proceedings of the 31st International Congress of Americanists (1954)*, vol. 1, pp. 464–72. São Paulo.
Monteiro, Mario Ypiranga.
1961. "Festa dos cachorros." *Revista Brasileira de Folclore,* 1:29–43. Rio de Janeiro.
Moraes, Raymundo.
1960. *Na planície amazônica.* 6th ed. Rio de Janeiro: Conquista.
Oliveira, José Coutinho de.
1951. *Folclore amazônico.* Belém: Editora São José.
Pereira, Manoel Nunes.
1947. *A Casa das Minas: contribuição ao estudo das sobrevivências daomeianas no Brasil.* Publicações da Sociedade Brasileira de Antropologia e Etnologia, no. 1. Rio de Janeiro.
Pierson, Donald.
1967. *Negroes in Brazil.* New ed. Carbondale: Southern Illinois University Press.
Ramos, Arthur.
1939. *The Negro in Brazil.* Trans. by Richard Pattee. Washington, D.C.: Associated Publishers.
1951. *O negro brasileiro.* 3rd ed. São Paulo: Companhia Editora Nacional.
Reis, Artur Cesar Ferreira.
1942. *Síntese da história do Pará.* Belém: Oficina Gráfica da Revista de Veterinária.
Ribeiro, René.
1952. *Cultos afrobrasileiros do Recife: um estudo de ajustamento social.* Recife: Instituto Joaquim Nabuco.
1955. "Novos aspectos do processo de reinterpretação nos cultos afrobrasileiros do Recife." In *Proceedings of the 31st International Congress of Americanists (1954)*, vol. 1, pp. 473–91. São Paulo.
1956. *Religião e relacões raciais.* Rio de Janeiro: Ministério da Educação e Cultura.
1959. "Análises socio-psicológico de la posesión en los cultos afrobrasileños." *Acta Neuropsiquiatrica Argentina,* 5:249–62. Buenos Aires.
Rodrigues, Raymundo Nina.
1932. *Os africanos no Brasil.* 2nd ed. São Paulo: Companhia Editora Nacional.

1935. *O animismo fetichista dos negros bahianos.* Rio de Janeiro: Civilização Brasileira.

Sarbin, Theodore R.
1950. "Contributions to Role-taking Theory: I. Hypnotic Behavior." *Psychological Review,* 57:255–70.
1954. "Role Theory." In *Handbook of Social Psychology,* ed. by Gardner Lindzey, vol. 1, pp. 223–58. Cambridge, Mass.: Addison-Wesley.

Sarbin, Theodore R., and Milton L. Andersen.
1967. "Role-Theoretical Analysis of Hypnotic Behavior." In *Handbook of Clinical and Experimental Hypnosis,* ed. by Jesse E. Gordon, pp. 319–44. New York: Macmillan.

Silva, Anaíza Vergolina e.
1968. *Alguns elementos para o estudo do negro na Amazônia.* Belém: Museu Paraense Emílio Goeldi, Publicacões avulsas, no. 8.

Smith, Herbert H.
1879. *Brazil: The Amazons and the Coast.* New York: Scribner.

Stainbrook, Edward.
1952. "Some Characteristics of the Psychopathology of Schizophrenic Behavior in Bahian Society." *American Journal of Psychiatry,* 109:330–35.

Tocantins, Leandro.
1963. *Santa Maria do Belém do Grão Pará.* Rio de Janeiro: Civilização Brasileira.

Varnhagen, Francisco Adolfo de.
1948. *História geral do Brasil.* 4th ed. 5 vols. São Paulo: Melhoramentos.

Wagley, Charles.
1943. *Tapirapé Shamanism. Boletim do Museu Nacional,* nova série, Antropologia, no. 3. Rio de Janeiro.
1953. *Amazon Town: A Study of Man in the Tropics.* New York: Macmillan.
1965. "On the Concept of Social Race in the Americas." In *Contemporary Cultures and Societies of Latin America,* ed. by Dwight B. Heath and Richard N. Adams, pp. 531–45. New York: Random House.

Wagley, Charles, and Eduardo Galvão.
1949. *The Tenetehara Indians of Brazil: A Culture in Transition.* New York: Columbia University Press.

Willems, Emilio.
1952. "Caboclo Cultures of Southern Brazil." In *Acculturation in*

the Americas. *Proceedings and Selected Papers of the 29th International Congress of Americanists,* ed. by Sol Tax, vol. 2, pp. 231–43. Chicago: University of Chicago Press.

1966. "Religious Mass Movements and Social Change in Brazil." In *New Perspectives of Brazil,* ed. by Eric N. Baklanoff, pp. 205–32. Nashville: Vanderbilt University Press.